ANATOMY OF SOUND

The publisher gratefully acknowledges the generous support of
the Chairman's Circle of the University of California Press
Foundation, whose members are:

Stephen A. & Melva Arditti
Elizabeth & David Birka-White
Michelle Lee Flores
James & Carlin Naify
Ralph & Shirley Shapiro
Peter J. & Chinami Stern
Lynne Withey

ANATOMY OF SOUND

Norman Corwin and Media Authorship

Edited by
Jacob Smith and Neil Verma

UNIVERSITY OF CALIFORNIA PRESS

University of California Press, one of the most distinguished university presses in the United States, enriches lives around the world by advancing scholarship in the humanities, social sciences, and natural sciences. Its activities are supported by the UC Press Foundation and by philanthropic contributions from individuals and institutions. For more information, visit www.ucpress.edu.

University of California Press
Oakland, California

© 2016 by The Regents of the University of California

Library of Congress Cataloging-in-Publication Data

Names: Smith, Jacob, editor, contributor. | Verma, Neil, editor, contributor.
Title: Anatomy of sound : Norman Corwin and media authorship / edited by Jacob Smith and Neil Verma.
Description: Oakland, California : University of California Press, [2016]
Identifiers: LCCN 2016015750 (print) | LCCN 2016016943 (ebook) | ISBN 9780520285309 (cloth : alk. paper) | ISBN 9780520285323 (pbk. : alk. paper) | ISBN 9780520960855 (ebook)
Subjects: LCSH: Corwin, Norman, 1910–2011. | Radio producers and directors—United States. | Radio broadcasting—United States.
Classification: LCC PN1991.4.C64 A83 2016 (print) | LCC PN1991.4.C64 (ebook) | DDC 818/.5209—dc23
LC record available at https://lccn.loc.gov/2016015750

25   24   23   22   21   20   19   18   17   16
10   9   8   7   6   5   4   3   2   1

CONTENTS

Foreword   *vii*
Michele Hilmes
Acknowledgments   *xi*

    Introduction: Anatomy of *Anatomy of Sound*   1
    Jacob Smith and Neil Verma

    A Corwinography   13
    Jeanette Berard

PART ONE. VOICE: NORMAN CORWIN AS SOUND AUTEUR

1. Radio's "Oblong Blur": On the Corwinesque in the Critical Ear   37
   Neil Verma

2. Norman Corwin and the Blacklist   53
   Thomas Doherty

3. Norman Corwin and the Big Screen: Artistic Differences   74
   Mary Ann Watson

PART TWO. SOUND: CORWIN AND TRANSMEDIA AUTHORSHIP

4. Norman Corwin's Radio Realism   101
   Jacob Smith

5. Corwin on Television: A Transmedia Approach to
   Style Historiography *127*
   Shawn Vancour

6. Media Primer: Norman Corwin's Radio Juvenilia *151*
   Troy Cummings

7. Fix Your Eyes on the Horizon and Swing Your Ears About:
   Corwin's Theatre of Sound *171*
   Ross Brown

PART THREE. EAR: ON CORWIN'S INFLUENCE

8. Transatlantic or Anglo-American Corwin? *195*
   Tim Crook

9. The Odyssey of Me and Norman Corwin *211*
   David Ossman

10. Wondering about *Radiolab:* The Contradictory Legacy of Corwin
    in Contemporary "Screen Radio" *233*
    Alexander Russo

Contributors *253*

FOREWORD

Of all the established arts, radio broadcasting alone has no adequate corps of professional critics.[1]
ROBERT J. LANDRY, 1940

Radio receives little critical attention. Of the various methods for communicating ideas and emotions—books, newspapers, visual art, music, film, television, the Web—radio may be the least discussed, debated, understood.[2]
BILL MCKIBBEN, 2010

To say that an edited collection on the work of Norman Corwin is overdue is to understate the matter: there has *never* been an edited collection focusing on Corwin's work, despite his globe-spanning reputation, as Jake Smith and Neil Verma point out in their introduction. But to understand the full import of this neglect—and how this volume so crucially addresses it—we may need to invoke not only the "anatomy of sound," Corwin's term and the title astutely chosen for this book, but perhaps some form of the "anatomy of criticism"—not in the strictly Northrop Frye sense of the phrase, but addressing some of the task Frye took on in 1957 when he embarked on his influential study of how literature creates meaning across time and cultures.[3]

Frye had a great advantage in that his category, "literature," has not only an immensely long, rich history with a well-established canon but also an enormous infrastructure of production, circulation, preservation, publicity, critical reflection, and scholarship on many different levels, baked into very bones of Western civilization. As the two quotes above—sixty years apart—suggest, we might compare that to poor radio, whose many unique qualities had barely begun to establish themselves, to assert a serious cultural status for soundwork, when, in America at least, it lost its central role. When U.S. radio became largely an adjunct to the music recording industry in the 1960s, it did a lot for popular music but not much for radio as a creative cultural form.

And the fact that radio's transmogrification happened just as a serious body of sound criticism was beginning to develop, with Corwin arguably at its center, had the effect of pulling down the blinds and turning out the lights. The small but promising journalistic critical tradition that had built up in the late 1940s and '50s switched almost immediately to television. As one study showed, "By 1950—just a few years after the 'birth' of television—critics were already devoting 76% of their space to TV." By 1960, that number was 98 percent[4] Despite television having its roots in radio, the older medium lost its critical presence while important, groundbreaking work was still being created, with an impact on the televisual medium that has rarely been explored. This volume is also unique in its attention to Corwin's post-radio work in television and in film, drawing parallels with his soundwork, which not only reveals his authorial signature but documents the creative tension between sound and visual aesthetics, and reveals those important radio roots as well.

Today, despite the fact that we are living in a period of more creative work in sound than at any time since the 1950s, the anatomy of sound criticism has yet to be established. Frye had no need to take into account the whole critical infrastructure that supported his loftier endeavor; in fact, in some ways he was writing against it. But the long tradition of commentary, criticism, review, and analysis that he rejected is what made his task possible. What would it take to bring radio-based soundwork into the same kind of everyday familiarity, centrality, and critical respect that literature, music, film, and yes, even television and video games currently enjoy?

First, it requires the regular circulation of information regarding what is available, what is recommended, and how it can be accessed—the traditional work of press criticism, whether online or in print.[5] For soundwork, this is still sadly lacking in the mainstream press, though certainly public radio, in particular, has benefited from its new online "materiality." A strong body of creativity also requires the kind of deeper popular discussion of meaning and import that takes place, for literature, through publications such as the *New York Review of Books* and *Times Literary Supplement,* as well as (ironically) radio and television discussion programs. For soundwork this kind of informed discussion is rare and widely scattered, though a certain amount of highlighting and criticism has begun to spring up around podcasting, where so much sound innovation is now taking place.[6]

Finally, it is imperative that scholarship and academic analysis lead the way in setting the terms of the critical debate, nominating important works and producers and asking the questions that keep an art form culturally relevant and lively. The last fifteen years have seen an enormous expansion of interest in sound media—after a very long drought. This volume adds handsomely to it and marks a new productive phase. Not only does Corwin get his due, its chapters open doors into spheres of creative activity that have been obscured behind the primacy of visual media for more than sixty years. And we get to hear from a whole new generation of soundwork scholars as well as established ones. Radio's critical anatomy stands immensely invigorated; indeed, it is alive! Corwin himself only narrowly missed seeing this tribute that would surely have delighted him, but he must have sensed that radio's revival was in the air.

Michele Hilmes

NOTES

1. Robert J. Landry, "Wanted: Radio Critics." *Public Opinion Quarterly* (December 1940), 620–29.
2. Bill McKibben, "All Programs Considered." *The New York Review of Books* (11 November 2010), 15.
3. Northrop Frye, *The Anatomy of Criticism: Four Essays*. Princeton University Press, 1957.
4. Maurice E. Shelby, "Patterns in Thirty Years of Broadcast Criticism." *Journal of Broadcasting* 11:1 (1966–67), 27–40.
5. For an illuminating study of the development of radio criticism in Britain, see Paul Rixon, "Radio and Popular Journalism in Britain: Early Radio Critics and Criticism," *The Radio Journal: International Studies in Radio and Audio Media* 13 (December 2015).
6. In the absence of press criticism the blogosphere has compensated, most with weekly newsletters and some with expanded websites and even SoundCloud links. For instance, see *The Timbre* (http://thetimbre.com/), *Hot Pod* (http://tinyletter.com/hotpod), and *The Audio Signal* (http://tinyletter.com/theaudiosignal). Thanks to my colleague Jeremy Morris for pointing these, and more, out to me.

ACKNOWLEDGMENTS

This project began when the two editors realized that they had each interviewed Norman Corwin during the last year of his life. For each of us, those conversations were at once riveting, humbling, moving, and a little surreal. As media historians, we were accustomed to encountering Corwin through the intermediary of musty archival documents or crackly sound recordings from a different era, so there was something vaguely hallucinatory about finding ourselves in dialogue with a historical figure who was still very much alive. Our thanks then go first and foremost to Corwin himself, for his generosity and willingness to talk about his work.

Chapters 1, 5, and 10 began as a part of a series on *Sounding Out!: The Sound Studies Blog* in 2012. We thank Jennifer Stoever, Aaron Trammell, and Liana Silva for their interest, excitement, and input. Thanks are also owed to Jeanette Berard at the Thousand Oaks Library archive where much of the research was done that made the chapters in this collection possible. Special thanks to Diane Corwin, for her support of this project. Mary Francis at the University of California Press showed early enthusiasm and gave wise counsel throughout the process. Rachel Berchten and Zuha Khan helped bring it to completion. Thanks to Barbara Armentrout for her careful work on the copy.

Numerous friends and colleagues have provided advice and encouragement. We would especially like to thank Karin Bijsterveld, Patrick Feaster, Richard Fish, Michele Hilmes, Michael C. Keith, Barbara Klinger, Kate Lacey, Jason Loviglio, James Naremore, Barbara O'Keefe, Philip Proctor, Matthew Solomon, and David Tolchinsky. Finally, we thank our families for their incredible support: Freda Love Smith, Jonah Smith, and Henry Smith; and Maureen Verma, Margaret Verma, and Eloise Verma.

Introduction

ANATOMY OF *ANATOMY OF SOUND*

Jacob Smith and Neil Verma

I am a Dead Sea Scroll.
—NORMAN CORWIN, 1996

When Norman Lewis Corwin passed away in October of 2011, international news headlines referred to him as a "Giant," "King of Radio Theater," and a "Monument to Artistry" who "Gave Voice to the Nation's Big Moments."[1] As these headlines indicate, Corwin was a celebrated author who embodied notions of public creativity in the mass media during the twentieth century, particularly as a radio writer, producer, and director during World War II for the Columbia Broadcasting System. During his heyday Corwin received special recognition from the American Academy of Arts and Letters and a Wendell Willkie One World Award that sent him around the globe as a documentarian and ambassador. Passing away at the incredible age of 101, Corwin outlived an enviable litany of likely eulogists (some by decades), including friends like Edward R. Murrow, Charles Laughton, Carl Sandburg, and Ray Bradbury, as well as admirers such as Robert Altman, Walter Cronkite, James Thurber, Charles Kuralt, Norman Cousins, and Studs Terkel. To these listeners and many others in their generation, Corwin was the greatest author of radio's biggest decade, when more than eight out of ten American families listened for hours each day. But by the time of his passing, this legacy had been forgotten to all but a few historians, fans, and a dwindling cadre of colleagues. "Radio, as Corwin practiced it," NPR producer and collaborator Mary Beth Kirchner wrote succinctly on his one hundredth birthday, "exists no more."[2]

But in the mid-twentieth century, Corwin had as high a profile in the public mind as directors Alfred Hitchcock, Frank Capra, and Orson Welles; broadcasters Walter Winchell, Jack Benny, and H. V. Kaltenborn; and writers Eugene O'Neill, Dylan Thomas, and John Steinbeck. And yet, although these figures have been the subject of productive academic scrutiny for decades, few scholars have investigated Corwin's career in depth—the last fifty years have produced just one major biography—or used his body of work as a framework to approach analytical and historical problems in the way that we routinely do for his peers. *Anatomy of Sound* begins to rectify that omission, while at the same time approaching Corwin as a "new" kind of auteur, one whose association with the domain of narrative sound art, rather than with visual mass media or literature, can prompt a fresh look at authorship in the modern era, an area of thought badly in need of revitalization.

Born in East Boston in 1910 and raised in Winthrop, Massachusetts, Corwin was the third son of a Jewish family with roots in England, Russia, and Hungary. He began his career right out of high school as a reporter for the *Daily Recorder* in Greenfield and later the *Springfield Republican,* rising in the ranks quickly and soon giving reports on the airwaves in Springfield and Boston.

In 1937, he moved to New York, where WQXR gave him a platform for poetry readings and short dramas called *Poetic License,* a show that caught the ear of talent recruiter William B. Lewis of CBS. Soon Corwin was writing and directing programs that gave him a free hand and aired nationwide during radio's most experimental period. His credits from this era include *The Columbia Workshop, 26 by Corwin, An American in England, Columbia Presents Corwin,* and *Transatlantic Call,* along with several specials to mark national events, from "We Hold These Truths" about the anniversary of the Bill of Rights in 1941 to "On a Note of Triumph" to celebrate the defeat of Germany in World War II in 1945 and "Document A/777" marking the United Nation's declaration of human rights.

In these years he worked with Paul Robeson, Archibald MacLeish, Orson Welles, James Stewart, Groucho Marx, Edward R. Murrow, President Roosevelt, and a wide array of composers, directors, opinion leaders, and actors, becoming perhaps the most famous radio auteur in the English-speaking world. His broadcasts regularly reached tens of millions of pairs of ears with everything from fairy tales to bible stories, histories to mysteries, war tales to farces. (We are delighted that archivist Jeanette Berard, who oversees Corwin's main archive in Thousand Oaks, California, has compiled a definitive list of this work—a "Corwinography"—for *Anatomy of Sound*).

After marrying Broadway actress Katherine Locke (with whom he had two children, Anthony and Diane), Corwin was pushed out of radio during the blacklist period—a matter that more than one of the authors in *Anatomy of Sound* explores—and went on to a long-neglected but energetic and experimental career that encompassed the recording arts, television and Hollywood screenwriting, stage plays, and radio revivals, as well as writing social satire and poetry. Corwin served on the boards of the Writer's Guild of America and the Academy of Motion Picture Arts and Sciences, while teaching generations of media writers over three decades at the University of Southern California's Annenberg School.

For more than seventy years he was called the "poet laureate" of American radio. It is likely that he will have no successor in that title. Corwin's works inspired Ray Bradbury and Philip Roth to become writers; they taught Robert Altman about drama and Norman Lear about broadcasting; and few would dispute that he occupies a prominent place in any history of the mass media. "He gave the Golden Age of Radio a greatness, a grasp of aesthetic principles, a promise of intellectual substance," wrote biographer R. Leroy Bannerman.[3]

Yet there has never been a scholarly volume of essays devoted to Corwin's work at the textual, sonic, and medium-based levels, and the few critical works that do exist focus only on his role in WWII programs and subsequent blacklisting as part of longer narratives about entertainment history.[4] Works typically dig into just a few of his recordings, gloss over whole decades of his career, and reduce him to a footnote within longer entertainment histories centered on filmmakers and TV stars. Today such an approach is unfit for expanding intellectual investment in Corwin's work. Indeed, in an era in which radio studies is in renaissance, and as audio narratives and podcasts like *This American Life, Radiolab,* and *Serial* are fostering talk of radio's "new wave" or "second golden age," more and more scholars are rediscovering Corwin and are eager to push beyond previous accounts. *Anatomy of Sound* is an attempt to make that possible, to rethink Corwin at a moment when, as scholars including Kate Lacey, Jason Loviglio, and Michele Hilmes have provocatively proposed, radio is ready to be "made strange" once more.[5]

And that is just one way in which this book is more than a memorial to a poorly remembered figure. The essays in this book also employ Corwin's supple corpus to foster a dialogue between sound studies and theories of the author in media studies.[6] Accounts of media authorship typically begin with French film culture of the 1950s and the idea of the auteur associated with Alexandre Astruc and *Cahiers du Cinema* authors. For decades, partly as a result of an influential 1962 essay by Andrew Sarris, auteur theory was disseminated to a wide array of international critics who seldom looked very closely at sound-based authors—there has not been a "microphone-stylo" concept to match the concept of the *caméra-stylo* on which auteur theory depends.[7]

Moreover, since the 1970s there has been a slow decline in enthusiasm around the term due to a skepticism about authorship inherited from poststructuralist thought, which tended to see the author as a tired patriarchal figure upholding bourgeois notions of agency that modern texts no longer plausibly sustain. At the same time, scholars were increasingly emphasizing a host of other topics: fans and publics, media industries, evolving genres, and mediality itself.[8] Recent accounts move from film across media forms and present authorship as "contested terrain rather than a stable designation . . . an identity that is produced by media industries and creative imagination as much as it is contained by the legal discourses that regulate authorship."⁹ This volume asserts that sound industries and sonic imaginations are a significant part of the contested terrain of media authorship, both past and present.

Sound studies is in a moment of astounding growth today, with publications on everything from sound art to architectural acoustics and listening publics to digital sound technologies, but analyses of the careers of individual creative workers and what Hilmes calls their "soundworks" have been notably absent. In part because of its debts to cultural studies, social history, and more recently to media archaeology—powerful waves that continue to carry it forward—the field tends to foreground cultural forms and discourses over specific texts, sounds, styles, and authors.¹⁰ As a result, we have excellent writing about devices, institutions, and perceptual regimes concerning sound as they evolve over time (along with the politics that they both manifest and obscure) yet few case studies of similar intensity about agile creators whose soundworks have moved both fluidly and frictively through these media and the social forms that they concretize, shaping the notions of value inside these systems. Corwin's distinctive sonic aesthetics across multiple aspects of media production can help fill that void.

In some ways, then, this book represents a prototype for a new strain of sound studies that could embrace "sound auteurs" whose careers pass through several media fields and prompt a rethinking of both sound and authorship as categories: Lou Reed and Yasunao Tone, Sun Ra and Laurie Anderson, Emile Berliner and Dylan Thomas, Alan Lomax and Nina Simone, Janet Cardiff and Miles Davis, Christian Marclay and Bjork, Brian Eno and George Clinton, Paul Robeson and Pauline Oliveros, David Byrne and David Lynch, Walter Murch and Hildegard Westerkamp, to name just a few. It is among these names (and others who think media through sound, and vice versa) that Corwin's life and work can and ought to be reimagined and resituated.

Because "writing in sound" requires working in two mediums at the same time, the "radio author" has been a productively unclear professional category from the get-go, one that always implies an irreducible transdisciplinary existence that comports well with Roland Barthes's notion of the text as a "tissue of quotations drawn from the innumerable centers of culture."¹¹ Many of Corwin's broadcasts are just like that, drawing together places, voices, famous quotations, statistics, peoples, and histories into shared sonic worlds. Historian Bruce Lenthall uses the term *radio-wrights* to refer to creatives like Corwin who were "not simply writers, poets, or dramatists in a straightforward sense" but were crafting "a new form of artistic expression, one that required a new form of creativity."¹² Just as film directors differed from novelists and "wrote with the camera" as their stylus, radio-wrights were "not purely writers, but directors and technical experts as well."¹³

Writing in 1936, just as Corwin's radio career was getting under way, theorist Rudolf Arnheim argued that radio challenged traditional notions of authorship, asserting that the union of writer, producer, and director was more feasible in radio than in film.[14] While "a real poet" would not be likely to "subordinate the word to material considerations in the manner necessary to the film," Arnheim wrote, it was much more conceivable that such a poet might work in radio: "The film demands the visual artist who has also a feeling for words, the wireless on the other hand needs a master of words who has also a feeling for modes of expression appropriate to the sensuous world."[15]

Corwin had just such a feeling, and press coverage testifies to public uncertainty about how to categorize his creativity. In 1942, the *New York Times* called Corwin a combination of poet, dramatist, and producer.[16] Two years later the same paper explained that he was "a number of writers in one," including a satirist, poet, and preacher, as well as a "sure touch as a producer-director."[17] In Carl Van Doren's assessment, Corwin was not only a writer, director, and producer but also a musician since "he hears his play as he composes it."[18] Clifton Fadiman, book review editor of the *New Yorker* magazine, wrote that Corwin was a "technician" before he was a writer, just as Rembrandt had been "a calculating expert in the chemistry of pigments and the mixture of tones before he could be the brooding and tragic visionary of the self-portraits."[19] When Corwin's V-E Day play *On a Note of Triumph* was published in book form by Simon & Schuster in 1945—the first edition reportedly selling out in only five days—the publisher took a full-page ad on the back cover of the *Saturday Review of Literature* describing the script this way: "It is easier to describe by telling what it isn't than what it is. It isn't an essay, an epic poem, a photo-drama, a play, or a series of vignettes. Yet it has some elements of each." The ad goes on grasping for categorical language, calling it a "celebrational" piece, even a "super-questionnaire."

Considering all this undecidability at the heart of public understanding about his craft, it is clear that Corwin (like Orson Welles, his contemporary at CBS) was helping to establish and to shift criteria for what counted as authorship in the era of modern media. We believe that foregrounding the uncertainty about Corwin's creative labor intensifies our awareness of the internal multiplicity of authorship more generally, which is perhaps the best way to update our approach to the term and retain it as a useful analytical category for media studies.

With all this in mind, we propose that a fitting appreciation of the full scope Corwin's remarkable body of work should start from the premise that as a result of being a uniquely radiophonic artist, he was, oddly, also a pioneer of a form of transmedia authorship that is increasingly relevant to our own era of multiplatform content. Over his seventy-five-year career, Corwin was a poet who wrote journalism, a screenwriter and a librettist, a teleplay writer who wrote like a stage dramatist, and a pioneer of live radio who learned to use recording media. He was an author of media *in the plural* during a time in which those media were undergoing profound transformations.

That status suggests that it is time to reengage with the transmedia level of Corwin's career and the discourses that surrounded it because they can help us to understand how media authors both define media forms and navigate the boundaries between them. Therefore, in this book we both revisit Corwin's radio works of the "golden age" and focus on what Corwin was up to decades before that and long afterward, showing how his work refracted many different forms and resonated throughout American culture across several historical eras. If Corwin is a little like a Dead Sea scroll—ciphered, otherworldly, miraculously present, even (why not?) a little heretical—then he is one that is still slowly unfurling, to be learned and studied in fresh ways. As he once wrote, one task of the sound artist is, after all, to "set up new vibrations in the deepest chambers of the imagination."

That quote comes from the radio piece from which this book borrows its title, "Anatomy of Sound," written, produced and directed by Corwin in 1941. "Anatomy" bills itself as a "treatise for solo voice" and was performed by Gale Sondergaard as part of the landmark CBS series *26 By Corwin*. The broadcast is full surprises for newcomers to Corwin's work. In a section on the various sorts of whistle sounds and the spiritual and psychic associations of night trains and ocean liners, Corwin anticipates the reflections of R. Murray Schafer and others in the acoustic ecology movement, an active area of sound studies scholarship since the 1970s.[20] In a section on the various "timbres" of silence, Corwin provides a demonstration of four kinds of "electrifying silence" in a tongue-in-cheek radio thriller skit and notes the powerful poetic and philosophical implications of radio silence, the only kind of silence that can "be in so many places at the same time," with the quiet of one studio producing "whirlpools and eddies" of silence emanating out of a million sets at once. He even prefigures by a decade John Cage's famous epiphany that in a soundless room a listener still hears his or her own body at work, one factor that led to the creation of Cage's landmark *4'33"* silent piece.

"Anatomy" also contains experiments with manipulating effects that would not be out of place in a contemporary digital-era sound art exhibit. Corwin slows down the sound of crowds to produce hurricane winds and booming surf and amplifies the crunch of celery to become thunder, in passages that resemble Foley techniques still in use in Hollywood films as well as some of the experiments of musique concrète composer Pierre Schaeffer. Students of urban sonic history will appreciate Corwin's depiction of an average sonic day (from alarm clock and shuffling newspaper to punch clocks, lunchtime whistle, and cash register) as a miniature sonic archaeology of the texture of a certain working-class life soon to go extinct. Scholars tracing the origins of the sound walk will find an antecedent in what Corwin calls his "poor man's vacation," an experiment in using sound to depict travel that includes the automatic windows of a taxi, the Chicago stockyards, a California swimming pool, and an Australian kookaburra. The play is not without fault, of course, and passages about the sound of "native" ceremonies and

African drums as well as the troubling exclusion of women's sonic experience (and in a piece performed by a woman, too) strike the modern ear as manifestations of what was worryingly excluded from Corwin's sensibilities.

Yet the broadcast still amazes. At the time, gathering all these pieces together may have sounded like the self-indulgent whim of an experimental writer. Today it sounds more like a point of convergence for any number of trajectories of contemporary sonic arts and expressions.

This book not only takes inspiration from this broadcast, but also takes its structure from the concept of "anatomy" that Corwin deploys. According to the OED, one definition of *anatomy* refers to the process and products of the dissection of the body, something grounded in individual material being reduced to components. Such an understanding resonates with the first part of this volume, "Voice: Norman Corwin as Sound Auteur," which contains essays that explore Corwin's style in the context of the media industries. How can we pull apart the role of the auteur—aesthetically, socially, politically—in the domain of sound in the twentieth century? How was the Corwinesque parsed and sometimes damned in popular culture, and what might it tell us about the emergence of discourses of media? How does Corwin's radio style shed new light upon film, a medium onto which Corwin's sensibilities were grafted from outside?

With these questions in mind, Neil Verma's "Radio's 'Oblong Blur': On the Corwinesque in the Critical Ear" investigates how confronting the intricacies and ontologies of radio writing can prompt us to reconsider how we "do" stylistic history. The Corwinesque comes into focus in three historical moments: in the era of live broadcasting; in the contemporary moment when we can pause, rewind, categorize, and remix vast amounts of golden age audio; and in a future when Corwin's work disperses not through air and space but through time and data. Thomas Doherty's "Norman Corwin and the Blacklist" connects Corwin's voice to his sociopolitical context by tracking the rise and fall of the Committee for the First Amendment in the context of Hollywood and the early years of the Cold War. The Red Scare has figured prominently in accounts of Corwin's career, but Doherty's careful analysis is set to become a definitive account, relying on new evidence and detailed study of testimony. The blacklist and Corwin's departure from network radio have often been the end of the story, but Mary Ann Watson's "Norman Corwin and the Big Screen: Artistic Differences" is one of several essays that examines Corwin's career beyond that period, focusing on his film scripts. Corwin's celebrated *Lust for Life* (1956) stands as a fascinating nexus for considerations of authorship, featuring a narrative about the quintessential heroic artist Vincent Van Gogh and involving collaboration with the canonical auteur Vincente Minnelli. Watson's chapter charts the movement of Corwin's voice into new modes of collaboration and regimes of authorship, thereby providing a transition from part 1—which explores the establishment of his distinctive authorial voice—to part 2, which concerns the "sound" of Corwin's voice, particularly as it inhabited interstitial spaces and crossed the technological categories that set one form of mass media off from another.

"Sound: Corwin and Transmedia Authorship," the second part of this book, switches to a second sense of *anatomy,* one focused on bodies of knowledge and artistic sensibilities. Our authors look at how Corwin used his body of experience to move across fields (much like other creative personnel) while engaging with new and other technological forms and protocols of use.[21] Essays locate Corwin at the intersections of music and radio, live radio and tape recording technology, radio and television, and radio and theater. Each case study treats Corwin as a joint between the social, epistemological, and aesthetic systems that made up the texture of modern media, with lessons for how such transmedia authorship is evolving today.

Jacob Smith's "Norman Corwin's Radio Realism" tracks a neglected trajectory of Corwin's career after network radio: his work as Chief of Special Projects for United Nations Radio between 1948 and 1952. Corwin's broadcasts for the UN explored the possibilities of sound recording and challenged him to transform a distinctly national voice for a global listenership. Smith listens to Corwin's authorial voice through the filter of M. M. Bakhtin's theory of style and stylization and brings questions of Corwin's audio authorship into dialogue with canonical works of postwar film theory, including the discourse on realism. If Corwin's foray into recording arts is a surprising turn for this radio author, an even greater one came later with Corwin's television productions, including the 1965 ABC series *FDR* and the 1971-72 Westinghouse-CBC feature *Norman Corwin Presents.* Shawn VanCour's "Corwin on Television" chapter breaks new ground on these programs, exploring Corwin's efforts to adapt radio techniques for the comparatively new and evolving field of visual broadcasting. Routing his analysis through Arnheim's gestalt approach to style historiography, VanCour argues that adapting the Corwinesque from radio to television entailed both the adoption of new sets of stylistic techniques and the strategic negotiation of new sets of institutional pressures and constraints. The third chapter of this section returns us to poetry, a word often linked with Corwin (he was radio's "poet laureate," after all), despite the absence of analysis of Corwin's work *as* poetry. Troy Cummings's "Media Primer" takes us back to Corwin's earliest radio series, *Rhymes and Cadences* (1934-35), *Poetic License* (1936-38), and *Words without Music* (1938-39). Using rare early materials, Cummings tracks the development of Corwin's signature techniques and formats. Ross Brown brings another much-needed perspective to the volume, that of theater history and aesthetics. Brown's study of the Corwin "Picturesque" takes seriously the moniker "theater of the mind" so as to explore Corwin's manipulation of sonic scenography in order to play on the imagination of his listeners. Drawing upon a phenomenological approach to listening, Brown describes the scenic space of Corwin's radio drama and situates it for the first time in a history of experimental theatrical sound stretching back centuries.

To complete the circuit of Corwin's work, the final part of this book, "Ear: On Corwin's Influence," focuses on Corwin as a figure of the past that is still somehow with us, preserved. A third definition of the noun *anatomy*, after all, is as a synonym for a skeleton or preserved mummy. This meaning perhaps has special purchase for an anatomy of radio authorship, since the authors of one of the first studies of the medium—Hadley Cantril and Gordon Allport's *The Psychology of Radio*—argued that, because of the lack of visual cues, radio "skeletonizes the personality of the speaker or performer."[22] If Corwin is a Dead Sea scroll, as our epigraph suggests, the remainder of a lost way of mass communication, how should his interpreters think about their relationship to him? To answer that question, this section focuses on an ever-widening sphere of Corwin's influence beyond the borders of the United States, beyond the decades of classic radio, and even beyond his own lifetime. Tim Crook's "Transatlantic or Anglo-American Corwin?" begins by examining Corwin's reception in the United Kingdom, arguing that the BBC's programming elite saw him as an ally of the BBC post-Marxist school of radio makers as well as the British documentary film movement of the early to middle twentieth century. In Crook's account, Corwin was thus part of a transnational movement in radio aesthetics and politics, and in many ways its avatar. The second essay resituates Corwin's listeners in the mid to late part of the century, when his sonic experiments might have seemed destined for the museum. Yet this was not the case at all. In "The Odyssey of Me and Norman Corwin," David Ossman, a founding member of the legendary comedy group The Firesign Theater, describes Corwin's influence on Firesign's seminal comedy recordings as well as his experiences collaborating with Corwin on several radio projects. Ossman's essay helps us to hear how the Corwinesque was "re-accentuated" in the 1960s.[23] Corwin's wartime broadcasts began to "sound in a different way" during the Vietnam era, and Firesign put a self-conscious twist on Corwin's voice-of-the-people style of radio writing. In the final essay, the first and second golden ages of radio are brought into earshot of one another. Alex Russo's "Wondering about *Radiolab*" considers Corwin's legacy and its impact on contemporary radio production by exploring the sonic style of the popular radio program at the forefront of podcast culture. Russo explores parallels between Corwin's public identity as a radio star and contemporary discourses of public radio stardom that have been applied to *Radiolab*'s producers Jad Abumrad and Robert Krulwich, as well as contemporaries like Ira Glass. Russo also considers the continued life of the Corwinesque in radio stylistics and the aesthetic possibilities and limits of noncommercial radio in Corwin's era and National Public Radio. As the radio industry begins to splinter into many new forms, often turning to narrative-driven audio as a format, it is time to wake up the sleeping mummy.

Indeed, it is surprising how well Corwin's presence and ideas fit in our era of shifting media participation and authorship across platforms, genres, and contexts. The development of new radio forms would surely have given him pleasure. A feeling of reaching toward the future was always a powerful force in the author's sensibilities. In a letter written around the same time as "Anatomy of Sound," Corwin wrote, "I shall die a happy man if I have written ten lines that can move a stranger living a century hence to feel the world more closely."[24] In anticipation of that outcome, *Anatomy of Sound* does its part to reconnect us with Corwin's words—and with their resounding. To quote from Corwin's 1943 play "A Program to Be Opened in a Hundred Years": "Let us continue to remember, and, remembering, continue."[25]

NOTES

1. See, for example, William Grimes, "Norman Corwin, 101, Rendered Radio into Poetry," *New York Times* (October 20, 2011), 18; David Hinckley, "Corwin Gave Voice to Nation's Big Moments," *New York Daily News* (Oct. 21, 2011), 112; T. Rees Shapiro, "Norman Corwin, American Radio's 'Poet Laureate,'" *Washington Post* (October 20, 2011).

2. Mary Beth Kirchner, "Norman Corwin's Splendid Century," npr.org (May 3, 2010), accessed May 6, 2015 (http://www.npr.org/templates/story/story.php?storyId = 126414628).

3. R. LeRoy Bannerman, *On a Note of Triumph: Norman Corwin and the Golden Years of Radio* (New York: University of Alabama Press, 1986), 11.

4. See, for example, Erik Barnouw, *The Golden Web: A History of Broadcasting in the United States, 1933–1953* (New York: Oxford University Press, 1968); Howard Blue, *Words at War: World War II Era Radio Drama and the Postwar Broadcasting Industry Blacklist* (Lanham, MD: Scarecrow, 2002); Matthew Ehrlich, *Radio Utopia: Postwar Audio Documentary in the Public Interest* (Chicago: University of Illinois Press, 2011); Bruce Lenthall, *Radio's America* (Chicago: University of Chicago Press, 2007); Judith E. Smith, "Radio's Cultural Front," in *The Radio Reader: Essays in the Cultural History of Radio*, ed. Michele Hilmes and Jason Loviglio (New York: Routledge, 2002), 209–30; Martin Spinelli, "'Masters of Sacred Ceremonies': Welles, Corwin and a Radiogenic Modernist Literature," in *Broadcasting Modernism*, ed. Debra Rae Cohen, Michael Coyle, and Jane Lewty (Gainesville: University Press of Florida, 2009); and Neil Verma, *Theater of the Mind: Imagination, Aesthetics and American Radio Drama* (Chicago: University of Chicago Press, 2012).

5. See Kate Lacey, "Ten Years of Radio Studies: The Very Idea," *The Radio Journal: International Studies in Broadcast Audio & Media* 6.1 (2008), 21–32; and Jason Loviglio and Michele Hilmes (eds.), *Radio's New Wave: Global Sound in a Digital Era* (New York: Routledge, 2013).

6. On contemporary theories of authorship, see, for example, Virginia Wright Wexman (ed.), *Film and Authorship* (New Brunswick, NJ: Rutgers University Press, 2003); and David A. Gerstner and Janet Staiger (eds.), *Authorship and Film* (New York: Routledge, 2003).

7. Andrew Sarris, "Notes on the Auteur Theory in 1962," *Film Culture* 27 (Winter, 1962), 1–8.

8. For two key texts challenging authorship, see Roland Barthes, "The Death of the Author," in *Image-Music-Text*, trans. Stephen Heath (New York: Hill and Wang, 1978), 142–48; Michel Foucault, "What Is an Author?" trans. Donald F. Bouchard and Sherry Simon, *Language, Counter-Memory, Practice*, ed. Donald F. Bouchard (Ithaca, NY: Cornell University Press, 1977), 124–27.

9. Cynthia Chris and David A. Gerstner, "Introduction" in *Media Authorship*, ed. Cynthia Chris and David Gerstner (New York: Routledge, 2013), 11.

10. The current strengths of sound studies can be traced back to four influential publications from a decade ago by Gitelman, Lastra, Sterne, and Thompson, as well as the Stanford translation of Friedrich Kittler's work: Lisa Gitelman, *Scripts, Grooves and Writing Machines: Representing Technology in the Edison Era* (Stanford, CA: Stanford University Press, 1999); Friedrich Kittler, *Gramophone, Film, Typewriter,* trans. Geoffrey Winthrop-Young and Michael Wutz (Stanford, CA: Stanford University Press, 1999); James Lastra, *Sound Technology and the American Cinema: Perception, Representation, Modernity* (New York: Columbia University Press, 2000); Jonathan Sterne, *The Audible Past: Cultural Origins of Sound Reproduction* (Durham, NC: Duke University Press, 2003); Emily Thompson, *The Soundscape of Modernity: Architectural Acoustics and the Culture of Listening in America, 1900–1933* (Cambridge, MA: MIT Press, 2002). See also key recent compendia and readers that have been shaping the field, including Michael Bull and Les Back (eds.), *The Auditory Culture Reader* (New York: Berg, 2003); Viet Erlmann (ed.), *Hearing Cultures: Essays on Sound, Listening and Modernity* (New York: Bert, 2004); Trevor Pinch and Karen Bijsterveld (eds.), *Oxford Handbook of Sound Studies* (New York: Oxford University Press, 2011); Mark Smith (ed.), *Hearing History: A Reader* (Athens, GA: University of Georgia Press, 2004); and Jonathan Sterne (ed.), *Sound Studies Reader* (New York: Routledge, 2012).

11. Barthes, 146.
12. Lenthall, 204.
13. Ibid., 177.
14. Rudolf Arnheim, *Radio: An Art of Sound* (New York: Da Capo Press, 1972), 205–6.
15. Ibid., 208.
16. S. J. Woolf, "Corwin Presents—Britain at War," *New York Times* (August 2, 1942), SM13.
17. Hutchens, John K. "Mr. Corwin Starts Another," *New York Times* (March 12, 1944), X7.
18. Quoted in Norman Corwin, *Thirteen by Corwin* (New York: Henry Holt, 1942), vii–viii.
19. Ibid., ix.
20. See R. Murray Schafer, *The Soundscape: Our Sonic Environment and the Tuning of the World* (Rochester, VT: Destiny Books, 1992).
21. Lisa Gitelman defines media as "socially realized structures of communication, where structures include both technological forms and their associated protocols, and where communication is a cultural practice, a ritualized collocation of different people on the same mental map, sharing or engaged with popular ontologies of representation." Lisa Gitelman, *Always Already New* (Cambridge, MA: MIT Press, 2006), 7.
22. Hadley Cantril and Gordon W. Allport, *The Psychology of Radio* (New York: Harper & Brothers, 1935), 10.
23. Bakhtin referred to the process of re-accentuation, when texts begin to "sound in a different way" when social languages change. M. M. Bakhtin, *The Dialogic Imagination* (Austin: University of Texas Press, 1981), 420.
24. Quoted in Lenthall, 191.
25. Norman Corwin, *More by Corwin* (New York: Henry Holt, 1944), 395.

A CORWINOGRAPHY

Jeanette Berard

RADIO BROADCASTS WITH NORMAN CORWIN AS WRITER/DIRECTOR

This list is as complete as we can establish, to date. It may not include all rebroadcasts of popular radio shows.

Broadcast Date	Series/Special Title	Episode Title
1934–1935	Rhymes and Cadences	(15-minute series on WBZ in Boston of Corwin reading poetry. Episodes were not titled. Broadcasts were Tuesdays at 2:30, 03-27-1934 to 04-23-1935. No known recordings exist.)
1937–1938	Poetic License	(weekly broadcast on WQXR in Long Island, NY, from 06-14-1937 to 04-20-1939. The format was basically the same as *Rhymes and Cadences*.)
10-07-1938	Americans at Work	(Corwin produced a few, but episodes continued until 02-06-1940.)

Broadcast Date	Series/Special Title	Episode Title
1938–1939	Words without Music	(The first radio series Corwin wrote, directed, and produced for CBS under the proprietary title *Norman Corwin's Words without Music*. Includes 25 programs, 11–03–1938 to 06–02–1939.)
12–04–1938	Words without Music	First episode
12–25–1938	Words without Music	Plot to Overthrow Christmas
01–29–1939	Words without Music	They Fly through the Air with the Greatest of Ease
03–19–1939	Words without Music	The People, Yes
06–02–1939	Words without Music	Final episode
11–29–1938	County Seat	
07–09–1938	Columbia Workshop	The Red Badge of Courage
09–29–1938	Columbia Workshop	The Lighthouse Keepers
12–29–1939	Columbia Workshop	Crosstown Manhattan
04–19–1939	Columbia Workshop	Seems Radio Is Here to Stay
07–24–1939	So This Is Radio	Putting Programs on the Air
07–31–1939	So This Is Radio	Twenty Years, the Career of Broadcasting
08–14–1939	So This Is Radio	Radio Special Events Department
08–21–1939	So This Is Radio	Education via Radio
08–28–1939	So This Is Radio	Arrangement and production of musical programs
09–07–1939	So This Is Radio	National Association of Broadcasters (rebroadcast on 09–29–1939)
02–19–1939	Columbia Workshop	They Fly through the Air with the Greatest of Ease

Broadcast Date	Series/Special Title	Episode Title
06–19–1939	Columbia Workshop	Salesmanship / Journalism in Tennessee
05–15–1939	Columbia Workshop	The Law Beaters
07–20–1939	Columbia Workshop	John Brown's Body
09–29–1939	Columbia Workshop	The Lighthouse Keepers
10–12–1939	Columbia Workshop	Wake Up and Die
10–31–1939	Columbia Workshop	Blennerhassett
11–05–1939	Pursuit of Happiness	Ballad for Americans
12–10–1939	Pursuit of Happiness	Impressions by Thomas Wolfe
02–29–1940	Columbia Workshop	The Great Microphone Mystery: The Case of the Mysterious Leap Year / Leaping Out of Character
03–07–1940	Columbia Workshop	My Client Curley
12–22–1940	Columbia Workshop	The Plot to Overthrow Christmas
06–07–1942	Columbia Workshop	The Little One
08–02–1940	Forecast	To Tim at Twenty
05–12–1940	We Take Your Word	
10–23–1940	Cavalcade of America	Ann Rutledge
01–30–1941	America Salutes the President on His Birthday	
03–16–1941	The Free Company	One More Free Man
04–13–1941	The Free Company	A Start in Life
05–04–1941	26 by Corwin	Radio Primer
05–11–1941	26 by Corwin	Log of the R-77
05–18–1941	26 by Corwin	The People, Yes
05–25–1941	26 by Corwin	Lip Service
06–01–1941	26 by Corwin	Appointment
06–08–1941	26 by Corwin	The Odyssey of Runyon Jones

Broadcast Date	Series/Special Title	Episode Title
06–15–1941	*26 by Corwin*	A Soliloquy to Balance the Budget
06–22–1941	*26 by Corwin*	Daybreak
06–29–1941	*26 by Corwin*	Old Salt
07–06–1941	*26 by Corwin*	Between Americans
07–13–1941	*26 by Corwin*	Ann Was an Ordinary Girl [aka "Ann Rutledge"]
07–20–1941	*26 by Corwin*	Double Concerto
08–03–1941	*26 by Corwin*	Descent of the Gods
08–10–1941	*26 by Corwin*	Samson
08–17–1941	*26 by Corwin*	Esther
08–24–1941	*26 by Corwin*	Job
08–31–1941	*26 by Corwin*	Mary and the Fairy
09–07–1941	*26 by Corwin*	The Anatomy of Sound
09–14–1941	*26 by Corwin*	Fragments from a Lost Cause
09–21–1941	*26 by Corwin*	The Human Angle
09–28–1941	*26 by Corwin*	Good Heavens
10–05–1941	*26 by Corwin*	Wolfeiana
10–12–1941	*26 by Corwin*	Murder in Studio One
10–19–1941	*26 by Corwin*	Descent of the Gods [repeat]
10–26–1941	*26 by Corwin*	The Odyssey of Runyon Jones [repeat]
11–02–1941	*26 by Corwin*	A Man with a Platform
11–09–1941	*26 by Corwin*	Psalm for a Dark Year
12–15–1941	Bill of Rights special	We Hold These Truths
12–07–1941	*Gulf Screen Guild Theatre*	Between Americans
02–14–1942	*This Is War!*	Introduction—America at War
02–21–1942	*This Is War!*	The White House and the War
02–28–1942	*This Is War!*	Your Navy

Broadcast Date	Series/Special Title	Episode Title
03-07-1942	*This Is War!*	Your Army
03-14-1942	*This Is War!*	The United Nations
03-21-1942	*This Is War!*	You're on Your Own
03-28-1942	*This Is War!*	It's in the Works
04-04-1942	*This Is War!*	Your Air Force
04-11-1942	*This Is War!*	The Enemy
04-18-1942	*This Is War!*	Concerning Axis Propaganda
04-21-1942	*This Is War!*	Smith against the Axis
05-02-1942	*This Is War!*	To the Young
05-09-1942	*This Is War!*	Yours Received and Contents Noted
08-03-1942	*An American in England*	London by Clipper
08-10-1942	*An American in England*	London to Dover
08-17-1942	*An American in England*	Ration Island
08-24-1942	*An American in England*	The Women of Britain
08-31-1942	*An American in England*	The Yanks Are Here
09-07-1942	*An American in England*	An Anglo-American Angle
12-01-1942	*An American in England*	Cromer
12-08-1942	*An American in England*	Home Is Where You Hang Your Helmet
12-15-1942	*An American in England*	An Anglo-American Angle
12-22-1942	*An American in England*	Clipper Home
01-13-1943	*Cresta Blanca Carnival*	A Program to be Opened in a Hundred Years (aka "100 Years Hence")
01-30-1943	*America Salutes the President's Birthday Party*	A Moment of the Nation's Time
04-24-1943	*Studio One*	
02-14-1943	*Transatlantic Call*	New England

Broadcast Date	Series/Special Title	Episode Title
02-18-1943	*Transatlantic Call*	Washington, D.C.
03-14-1943	*Transatlantic Call*	Midwest: Breadbasket and Arsenal (Marvin Miller substituted for Corwin, who was very ill.)
08-17-1943	*Passport for Adams*	Introduction
08-24-1943	*Passport for Adams*	Brazil
08-31-1943	*Passport for Adams*	Liberia
09-07-1943	*Passport for Adams*	Marrakech
09-14-1943	*Passport for Adams*	Cairo
09-21-1943	*Passport for Adams*	Tel Aviv
09-28-1943	*Passport for Adams*	Moscow
10-12-1943	*Passport for Adams*	Stalingrad
03-07-1944	*Columbia Presents Corwin*	Movie Primer
03-14-1944	*Columbia Presents Corwin*	The Long Name None Could Spell
03-21-1944	*Columbia Presents Corwin*	The Lonesome Train
03-28-1944	*Columbia Presents Corwin*	Savage Encounter
04-04-1944	*Columbia Presents Corwin*	The Odyssey of Runyon Jones
04-11-1944	*Columbia Presents Corwin*	You Can Dream, Inc.
04-18-1944	*Columbia Presents Corwin*	Untitled
04-25-1944	*Columbia Presents Corwin*	Dorie Got a Medal
05-02-1944	*Columbia Presents Corwin*	Cliché Expert
05-09-1944	*Columbia Presents Corwin*	Cromer
05-16-1944	*Columbia Presents Corwin*	New York: A Tapestry for Radio
05-23-1944	*Columbia Presents Corwin*	Tel Aviv
05-30-1944	*Columbia Presents Corwin*	Untitled
06-06-1944	*Columbia Presents Corwin*	Sandburg
06-13-1944	*Columbia Presents Corwin*	Thomas Wolfe
06-20-1944	*Columbia Presents Corwin*	Whitman

Broadcast Date	Series/Special Title	Episode Title
07-04-1944	*Columbia Presents Corwin*	Home for the 4th
07-18-1944	*Columbia Presents Corwin*	The Moat Farm Murder
07-25-1944	*Columbia Presents Corwin*	El Capitan and the Corporal
08-08-1944	*Columbia Presents Corwin*	A Very Fine Type Girl
08-15-1944	*Columbia Presents Corwin*	There Will Be Time Later
07-03-1945	*Columbia Presents Corwin*	Unity Fair
07-10-1945	*Columbia Presents Corwin*	Daybreak
07-17-1945	*Columbia Presents Corwin*	The Undecided Molecule
07-24-1945	*Columbia Presents Corwin*	New York: A Tapestry for Radio [repeat]
07-31-1945	*Columbia Presents Corwin*	A Walk with Nick
08-07-1945	*Columbia Presents Corwin*	Savage Encounter
08-14-1945	*Columbia Presents Corwin*	L'Affaire Gumpert
11-03-1944	Election Eve special	Roosevelt Special
04-25-1945	UN San Francisco Conference	Word from the People
05-08-1945	V-E Day special	On a Note of Triumph
08-14-1945	V-J Day special	14 August
08-19-1945	Day of Prayer special	God and Uranium
09-16-1945	Stars in the Afternoon	
11-05-1945	Radio's 25th Anniversary	Seems Radio Is Here to Stay
01-11-1947	*The Warrior*	(Metropolitan Opera House, NY)
06-15-1946	*One World Flight*	Departure
01-14-1947	*One World Flight*	Introduction
01-21-1947	*One World Flight*	England
01-28-1947	*One World Flight*	France, Denmark, Norway
02-04-1947	*One World Flight*	Sweden, Poland
02-11-1947	*One World Flight*	Soviet Union

Broadcast Date	Series/Special Title	Episode Title
02–18–1947	*One World Flight*	Czechoslovakia
02–25–1947	*One World Flight*	Italy
03–04–1947	*One World Flight*	Egypt, India
03–11–1947	*One World Flight*	China
03–18–1947	*One World Flight*	Philippines
03–25–1947	*One World Flight*	Australia
04–08–1947	*One World Flight*	New Zealand
04–15–1947	*One World Flight*	Conclusion
04–08–1947	Committee for the First Amendment	Hollywood Fights Back
07–10–1949	United Nations Radio	Citizen of the World
09–11–1949	United Nations Radio	Could Be (rebroadcast 10–23–1949)
03–26–1950	United Nations Radio: *The Pursuit of Peace*	Document A/777
05–07–1950	United Nations Radio: *The Pursuit of Peace*	Fear Itself
11–04–1951	United Nations Radio: *Windows on the World* (three parts, to 11–06–1951)	
10–04–1955	United Nations Radio: *The Charter in the Saucer*	
11–23–1958	Tribute to Carl Sandburg	
04–29–1961	Memorandum to Jeremiah	
05–01–1961	United Nations Radio: *Die Erklaerung der Menschenrechte*	UNO Dokument A/777
02–12–1962	Ann Rutledge	
04–18–1963	*Personal Report* (WNDT-TV, NY)	Norman Corwin interview with Mildred Freed Alberg

Broadcast Date	Series/Special Title	Episode Title
08–20–1963	Studs Terkel Almanac	Overkill and Megalove
10–26–1965	Writers at Work (KPFK radio, Los Angeles)	Norman Corwin interview with Francis Roberts
07–08–1967	Profile: Isaac Stern (KFAC, Los Angeles)	
07–16–1967	Profile: Nelson Glueck (KFAC-FM, Los Angeles)	
08–19–1967	Interview with Norman Corwin, August 1967 (KCOP-TV, Los Angeles)	
09–17–1967	Profile: David Ben-Gurion (KFAC, Los Angeles)	
02–15–1968	Norman Corwin interview with Pete Seeger (KFAC, Los Angeles)	
12–10–1968	Yes, Speak Out, Yes	
02–28–1971	Murder in Studio One (WPRB, Princeton, NJ)	
10–05–1975	Norman Corwin interview with Steve Markham (KFAC-FM, Los Angeles)	
1975–1976	Thirteen by Corwin (NPR series that rebroadcast some of Corwin's most famous shows, remastered from the original transcription discs. Corwin wrote an introduction to each program, which was read by a different celebrity each week. Aired Sundays on KCSN as part of Don't Touch That Dial. Only the first two dates of broadcast could be verified.)	

Broadcast Date	Series/Special Title	Episode Title
11–16–1975	*Thirteen by Corwin*	They Fly through the Air
11–23–1975	*Thirteen by Corwin*	Radio Primer
	Thirteen by Corwin	Descent of the Gods
	Thirteen by Corwin	Mary and the Fairy
	Thirteen by Corwin	El Capitan and the Corporal
	Thirteen by Corwin	The Undecided Molecule
	Thirteen by Corwin	The Odyssey of Runyon Jones
	Thirteen by Corwin	My Client Curley
	Thirteen by Corwin	New York: A Tapestry for Radio
	Thirteen by Corwin	Cromer
	Thirteen by Corwin	Untitled
	Thirteen by Corwin	The Long Name None Could Spell
	Thirteen by Corwin	Could Be
06–18–1976	Interview with Norman Corwin, (KGIL-AM Radio, San Fernando Valley, CA)	
08–10–1976	Norman Corwin interview with Chuck Schaden (WBBM, Chicago)	
02–16–1977	Lincoln program (KCET-TV, Los Angeles)	
04–01–1978	Network at 50	
05–29–1979	*Sears Radio Theatre*	The Strange Affliction
1982	*Chicago Radio Theatre*	The Curse of 589
10–11–1982	*Sunday Show*	Norman Corwin interview with Connie Goldman
07–04–1983	NPR *Morning Edition* segment	
1983–1984	NPR *All Things Considered*	Six by Corwin (Holiday Series)

Broadcast Date	Series/Special Title	Episode Title
05–29–1983	*Holiday Series* (NPR)	Memorial Day
07–04–1983	*Holiday Series* (NPR)	July 4th
09–05–1983	*Holiday Series* (NPR)	Labor Day
10–12–1983	*Holiday Series* (NPR)	Columbus Day
11–24–1983	*Holiday Series* (NPR)	Thanksgiving
01–01–1984	*Holiday Series* (NPR)	New Year's Day
09–12–1984	*Ray Briem Show* (KABC radio, Los Angeles)	Norman Corwin interview
05–07–1985	*Newsbreak with Charles Osgood* (CBS Radio Network)	Norman Corwin interview
08–24–1986	WIBA Radio, Madison, WI	Norman Corwin interview, "Life in the Past Lane"
08–19–1988	KPFK Radio, Los Angeles	Norman Corwin interview with Ray and Kathy Straczynski
09–26–1990	*The Radio Show*	Norman Corwin interview with Tom Snyder
12–12–1990	*The Connection* (WBUR Radio, Boston)	Norman Corwin interview with Christopher Lyddon
12–15–1991	Anniversary special, NPR: *Bill of Rights: 200*	
11–20–1993	NPR *Morning Edition* segment	
12–03–1993	*The Plot to Overthrow Christmas* (KUSC)	
12–23–1993	KIEV Radio, Glendale, CA	Norman Corwin interview, "Still Going Strong"
05–05–1995	Commemoration of V-E Day (WBEZ Radio, Chicago, IL)	

Broadcast Date	Series/Special Title	Episode Title
01-30-1997	*More by Corwin*	The Writer with the Lame Left Hand
03-05-1997	*More by Corwin*	The Curse of 589
07-04-1997	*More by Corwin*	Our Lady of Freedoms
11-06-1997	*More by Corwin*	The Secretariat
12-31-1999	*More by Corwin*	Memos to a New Millennium

TELEVISION PROGRAMS

Broadcast Date	Series/Special Title	Episode Title
03-20-1964	*Inside the Movie Kingdom* (NBC)	
1965	*FDR* (NBC series on the life of Franklin Delano Roosevelt, episodes 1 and 26)	
01-08-1965	*FDR*	Making of a Man
07-23-1965	*FDR*	Going Home
12-23-1969	*The Plot to Overthrow Christmas* (KCET)	
1971–1973	*Norman Corwin Presents* (Canadian Broadcasting Corporation television series produced by Corwin for Westinghouse Group W in 1971–1972)	26 episodes (aired in syndication, so each episode aired on many different dates. Many episodes were written by Corwin, adapted from his radio works; some episodes were written by others.)
	Norman Corwin Presents	Two Gods on Prime Time (Corwin)
	Norman Corwin Presents	The Undecided Molecule (Corwin)
	Norman Corwin Presents	Soliloquy for Television (Corwin)
	Norman Corwin Presents	The First Big Try (Corwin)
	Norman Corwin Presents	The Discovery (Corwin)

Broadcast Date	Series/Special Title	Episode Title
	Norman Corwin Presents	A Letter from an Only Child (Don Balluck)
	Norman Corwin Presents	Hold That Line (James W. Nichol)
	Norman Corwin Presents	Crown of Rags (Howard Brown)
	Norman Corwin Presents	The Blue Hotel (Corwin's adaptation of Stephen Crane story)
	Norman Corwin Presents	Reunion (Arthur Joel Katz's adaptation of John William Corrington story)
	Norman Corwin Presents	Matter of Life and Death (Robert Pressnell, Jr.)
	Norman Corwin Presents	The Better It Is, The Worse It Is (Charles M. Cohen)
	Norman Corwin Presents	A Son, Come Home (Ed Bullins)
	Norman Corwin Presents	The Pursuit (Corwin)
	Norman Corwin Presents	Pappy's Oasis (aka Bandit) (Alvin Sargent)
	Norman Corwin Presents	Odyssey in Progress (Corwin)
	Norman Corwin Presents	Aunt Dorothy's Playroom (Don Balluck)
	Norman Corwin Presents	The D.J. (Charles M. Cohen)
	Norman Corwin Presents	Bingo Twice a Week (Sol Saks)
	Norman Corwin Presents	A Foreign Field (Norman Katkov)
	Norman Corwin Presents	Jefferson's Crush (Corwin)
	Norman Corwin Presents	The Joy of Living (William F. Nolan)
	Norman Corwin Presents	The Moat Farm Murder (Corwin)
	Norman Corwin Presents	The One Man Group (Corwin)
	Norman Corwin Presents	Please, No Flowers (Corwin adaptation of Joel Ensana story)

Broadcast Date	Series/Special Title	Episode Title
	Norman Corwin Presents	You Think You Got Troubles (Corwin)
06–11–1974	*Judgment* (ABC)	The Court Martial of the Tiger of Malaya, General Yamashita
04–01–1978	Network at Fifty (CBS)	An ode commemorating CBS's 50th anniversary, read on the air by Walter Cronkite
02–05–1979 to 04–09–1979	*Academy Leaders* (KCET series of Oscar-nominated short films narrated by Corwin)	10 episodes (Mondays, repeated on Saturdays; reran on KCET in October)

BOOKS, INCLUDING PUBLISHED SCRIPTS, SCREENPLAYS, AND WORKS IN ANTHOLOGIES

1929   *So Say the Wise*. Compiled by Hazel Cooley and Norman Corwin. NY: George Sully.

1939   *Best Broadcasts of 1938–1939*. Max Wylie. NY: Whittlesey House. ("Seems Radio Is Here to Stay")

Columbia Workshop Plays: Fourteen Radio Dramas. Selected and edited by Douglas Coulter. NY: McGraw-Hill. *(They Fly through the Air)*

The Plot to Overthrow Christmas: A Holiday Play. Mount Vernon, NY: Peter Pauper Press.

"Seems Radio Is Here to Stay": *A Columbia Workshop Production*. NY: Columbia Broadcasting System (CBS).

They Fly through the Air with the Greatest of Ease. Weston, VT: V. Orton.

1940   *Ann Rutledge and Lincoln*. NY: Batten, Barton, Durstine & Osborn.

Best Broadcasts of 1939–1940. Max Wylie. NY: Whittlesey House. ("My Client Curley")

New Walls of China. NY: Trans-Pacific News Service.

1941   *26 by Corwin*. NY: CBS

We Hold These Truths. Norman Corwin and J. Stewart. NY?: n.p.

The Writer's Radio Theatre. Compiled by Norman S. Weiser. NY: Harper. ("Words without Music: A Group of Great Literary Works Tied Together into a Half-Hour Radio Script.")

1942 *Thirteen by Corwin: Radio Dramas.* NY: Henry Holt.

This Is War!: A Collection of Plays about America on the March. NY: Dodd, Mead. (*This Is War* and *The Enemy; Concerning Axis Propaganda* and *To the Young; Yours Received and Contents Noted*)

To the Young. NY: Writers' War Board.

We Hold These Truths: A Dramatic Celebration of the American Bill of Rights, including an Address by Franklin D. Roosevelt. NY: Howell, Soskin.

1943 *Forever and a Day,* RKO Pictures.

"The Odyssey of Runyon Jones" in *The Fireside Book of Dog Stories.* Edited by Jack Goodman. NY: Simon & Schuster.

The Three Readers. Edited by Clifton Fadiman et al. NY: Readers Club. (*Daybreak*)

War Poems of the United Nations. Edited by Joy Davidman. NY: Dial Press. ("Lyric Passages")

The World We Are Fighting For: "Between Americans" #18 [script]. With R. E. Lee, J. Lawrence, R. Collins, and C. Sweeten. Los Angeles: Distributed at Bullock's Department Store, where KFI broadcast the series.

1944 *The Girl Lincoln Loved.* NY: Batten, Barton, Durstine, & Osborn.

More by Corwin: 16 Radio Dramas. NY: Henry Holt.

Off Mike: Radio Writing by the Nation's Top Radio Writers. Edited by Jerome Lawrence. NY. Essential Books. ("Re Me")

Once Upon a Time, Columbia Pictures. With Lucille Fletcher.

1945 *From D-Day through Victory in Europe: The Eye-Witness Story as Told by War Correspondents on the Air.* Edited by Paul Hollister and Robert Strunsky. NY: CBS. ("On a Note of Triumph")

On a Note of Triumph. NY: Simon & Schuster.

Prayer. Utica, NY: Coggeshall.

Radio Drama in Action. Edited by Erik Barnouw. NY: Farrar & Rinehart. ("London by Clipper" and *An American in England* episodes)

Set Your Clock at U-235: A Dramatization of the Theme of the 1945 Forum of the New York Herald Tribune (aka *Responsibility of Victory*). NY?

Selected Radio Plays of Norman Corwin. With L. Untermeyer. NY: Editions for the Armed Services.

This Way to Unity, for the Promotion of Good Will and Teamwork among Racial, Religious, and National Groups. Edited by Herrick and Askwith. NY: Oxford Book. (Untitled)

1946   *Best One-Act Plays of 1945.* Edited by Margaret Mayorga. NY: Dodd, Mead. *(On a Note of Triumph)*

Footnote on One World: Address Delivered in the Sydney Town Hall, Sunday, 29th September, 1946. Sydney: Australian Broadcasting Commission.

The Saint's Choice of Radio Thrillers. Edited by Leslie Charteris. Hollywood, CA: Saint Enterprises. *(The Moat Farm Murder)*

While You Were Gone: A Report on Wartime Life in the United States. Edited by Jack Goodman. NY: Simon & Schuster. ("The Radio")

1947   *One World Revisited.* NY: Common Council for American Unity.

Radio's Best Plays. Selected and edited by Joseph Liss. NY: Greenberg. *(Daybreak)*

Untitled and Other Radio Dramas. NY: Henry Holt.

1948   *Words to Live By: A Little Treasury of Inspiration and Wisdom.* Edited by William Ichabod Nichols. NY: Simon & Schuster. ("The Rights of Man")

1950   *Modern One-Act Plays.* Edited by Francis J. Griffith and Joseph E. Mersand. NY: Harcourt Brace. *(My Client Curley)*

Theatre Arts Anthology: A Record and a Prophecy. Edited by Rosamond Gilder. NY: Theatre Arts Books. ("The Sovereign Word: Some Notes on Radio")

1951   *The Blue Veil*, RKO Pictures.

1952   *Dog in the Sky: The Authentic and Unexpurgated Odyssey of Runyon Jones.* NY: Simon & Schuster.

The Plot to Overthrow Christmas. NY: Holt.

1953   *Scandal at Scourie*, Metro-Goldwyn-Mayer.

1955   *Lust for Life.* Metro-Goldwyn-Mayer.

1958	*The Naked Maja.* Metro-Goldwyn-Mayer.
1959	*The Story of Ruth.* Twentieth Century–Fox Film Corporation.
1960	*The Rivalry.* NY: Dramatists Play Service.
1961	*The World of Carl Sandburg: A Stage Presentation.* Norman Corwin & Carl Sandburg. NY: Harcourt, Brace & World.
1962	*Chinese Wall.* Los Angeles: Theatre Group (Organization) and University of California, Los Angeles.
1963	*Overkill and Megalove.* Cleveland: World.
1965	*New Dimensions in Literature: Introduction to Drama.* Edited by Louise G. Stevens. Wichita, KS: McCormick-Mathers. *(My Client Curley)*
1966	*I Have Seen War.* Edited by Dorothy Sterling. NY: Hill & Wang. ("On a Note of Triumph")
1969	*Prayer for the 70s.* N. Corwin, S. Bass, & A. Goodman. Garden City, NY: Doubleday.
1970	*The Future Is Now: All-New All-Star Science Fiction Stories.* Edited by William F. Nolan. Los Angeles: Sherbourne. ("Belles Lettres, 2272")
1972	*A Dialogue between Conscience and Man.* Los Angeles: University of Judaism.
1978	*Holes in a Stained Glass Window.* Secaucus, NJ: Lyle Stuart.
	Jerusalem Printout. Bloomington, IN: Raintree Press.
1979	*Network at Fifty.* Northridge, CA: Invierno Press.
1981	*A Date with Sandburg.* Northridge, CA: California State University, Northridge, Libraries, Santa Susana Press.
	Greater Than the Bomb: The First Publication in English of a Radio Program Broadcast Internationally in 1950 and Repeated Many Times Since. Northridge, CA: California State University, Northridge, Libraries, Santa Susana Press.
1983	*Trivializing America.* Secaucus, NJ: Lyle Stuart.
1986	*America at War: The Home Front, 1941–1945.* Edited by Richard Polenberg. Upper Saddle River, NJ: Prentice-Hall. ("We Hold These Truths")

1987   *Making America: The Society and Culture of the United States.* Edited by Luther S. Luedtke. Chapel Hill, NC: University of North Carolina Press. ("Entertainment and the Mass Media")

1991   *The Bradbury Chronicles: Stories in Honor of Ray Bradbury.* Edited by William F. Nolan. NY: Penguin. ("The Muse")

1991   *A Western Harvest.* Frances Ring. Santa Barbara, CA: Daniel and Daniel. (reprints of several of Corwin's *Westways* columns)

1992   *The Ageless Spirit.* Edited by Phillip L. Berman and Connie Goldman. NY: Ballantine. (Untitled essay by Corwin)

1993   *Conartist: Paul Conrad, 30 years with the* Los Angeles Times. Norman Corwin; introduction by Shelby Coffey III. Los Angeles: Los Angeles Times Syndicate Books.

1994   *Norman Corwin's Letters.* With A. J. Langguth. NY: Barricade Books.

Years of the Electric Ear: Norman Corwin. With D. Bell Hollywood, CA: Directors Guild of America.

2006   *The Blue Veil (1951): Shooting Script.* With F. Campaux. Alexandria, VA: Alexander Street Press.

2009   *Norman Corwin's* One World Flight: *The Lost Journal of Radio's Greatest Writer.* With M. C. Keith and M. A. Watson. NY: Continuum.

(2011) *Memos to a New Millennium: The Final Radio Plays of Norman Corwin.* With M. J. Kacey. Duncan, OK: BearManor Media.

ARTICLES, INTRODUCTIONS, AND PUBLISHED REVIEWS

Selected items in the Corwin Collection, as annotated by Norman Corwin. Norman was a popular forewordist, and a complete list of introductions, forewords, and essays would number in the hundreds.

"Editorials". While Corwin was in his teens, he wrote a number of parodies. This file contains five parodies Corwin wrote in the late 1920s, in which he sought to demonstrate how five prominent Americans would have described a game in the baseball World Series if they were reporters covering that game. Those who were parodied include Carl Sandburg, William Randolph Hearst, Alfred Kreymborg, Vachel Lindsay, and H. L. Mencken. Corwin wrote these while employed for the

Greenfield Recorder, but it is not known whether these were ever published in that paper.

Aerial Armada. In 1931, while working as a reporter for the *Springfield Republican*, Corwin experienced his first flight in an airplane while covering a national exhibition tour of the U.S. Army Air Force during the Massachusetts leg of its tour.

You'll Hear from Them Later. A photocopy of a newspaper clipping from the *Springfield Republican*, around 1931. The clipping contains a front-page photo of a bell foundry in England, with a caption. Corwin wrote the caption for this photograph.

Petition after Victory. "Petition after Victory" was the title of a poem by Corwin, written in the form of a prayer, that was originally published in *Colliers* magazine in November 1944. It was later incorporated into "On a Note of Triumph" in May 1945.

Airborne. A letter to Corwin from Richard L. Field, associate editor of *Holiday* magazine, regarding an article by Corwin titled "Airborne," which he wrote for the magazine in 1946.

You Are Going on a Long Journey. Following the *One World Flight* of 1946, Corwin wrote an article for *McCall's* magazine titled "You Are Going on a Long Journey," which summarized the high points of the trip while meditating on its meaning.

Eulogy for FDR. Photocopy of an excerpt from a book titled *Masterpieces for Radio and Declamation*, compiled and edited by Robert Goodman and published by Liberty Publishing Company in 1952, which contains the text of a eulogy Corwin wrote in 1945 at the request of CBS upon the death of President Franklin D. Roosevelt.

Boys from *The New Yorker*. In 1953, for the twentieth anniversary issue of *Daily Variety*, Corwin wrote an article titled "The Boys from *The New Yorker*." In this article, Corwin criticized the views of *New Yorker* film critic John McCarten.

The Pursuit of the Pursuit of Happiness. Materials related to article Corwin wrote in 1969 for the inaugural issue of the *PHP (Peace and Happiness through Prosperity)* magazine entitled "The Pursuit of the Pursuit of Happiness." *PHP* was an English language magazine published in Japan.

Speculation on Speculation. For the November 1969 issue of the program guide for public television station KCET, Corwin wrote an article titled "Speculation on 'Speculation,'" which was an appreciation of the work of commentator Keith Berwick.

Introduction. Issue no. 2 of the *ISOMATA Review*, published in summer 1973. Corwin wrote the introduction.

Corwin on Media. Explanatory notes on the ninety-five monthly columns Corwin wrote for *Westways* magazine between January 1973 and November 1980. Includes a chronological breakdown and an alphabetical list by title.

Album Liner. Materials related to Frank Bresee's 1975 double-record album of *The Golden Days of Radio*, for which Corwin wrote the album liner.

Don't Write This Man. File contains various versions of "Don't Write This Man" (also published as "How Old Would You Say This Man Is?"), a tribute Corwin wrote about his father, Samuel, shortly before the latter's 100th birthday in 1975. The piece, originally published in the *Los Angeles Times*, later appeared in the Winthrop [MA] *Sun* and in the magazine of the AARP, *Modern Maturity*.

Preface. In 1981, Corwin wrote a preface for William E. Ewald's compendium of 16mm short films entitled *100 Short Films about the Human Environment*. This file includes a letter from Ewald to Corwin and a photocopy of Corwin's preface from the publication.

The Hot Cold Reading. Typescript of "The Hot Cold Reading," a reminiscence about Welles that Corwin wrote for the Museum of Television and Radio, and a release for a seminar by Corwin: "Working with Orson Welles." 1992

Foreword. File contains material relating to the foreword Corwin wrote for Ron Lackmann's encyclopedia of radio *Same Time . . . Same Station* (Facts on File, 1993).

Dead for a Ducat. In 1998, Corwin wrote an article for publication in the *Journal of Radio Studies*, titled "Dead for a Ducat." In the article, Corwin lamented the manner in which radio was supplanted by television. This file contains a typed manuscript of the article, as well as handwritten notes and an earlier typed version of this same article.

Foreword. File contains the foreword Corwin wrote to Arthur Anderson's history of children's radio programs, *Let's Pretend*. 2004

Not dated

On the Firing Line. File contains clippings from "On the Firing Line," a humorous column of poetry and observations Corwin wrote for the *Springfield Union* while still working as a reporter for the *Springfield Republican*.

Contagions and Conspiracies. "Contagions and Conspiracies" was the title given to an essay that Corwin wrote for *Westways* magazine, and which examined different societal attitudes, and the conditions that allowed them to spread.

Tangled Weave. File contains the typescript of an article Corwin wrote for publication in a brochure on *The Rivalry*, for sale at performances of the play.

PART ONE

VOICE

Norman Corwin as Sound Auteur

1

RADIO'S "OBLONG BLUR"

On the Corwinesque in the Critical Ear

Neil Verma

In June of 1947, writer Philip Hamburger published a profile of Norman Corwin billed as "The Odyssey of the Oblong Blur" in the *New Yorker*, perhaps the most vivid article to appear in any national publication about Corwin during the years in which he was the most recognized radio dramatist in the United States.[1] One of Hamburger's best-remembered profiles in a seven-decade career at the magazine, "Oblong Blur" was soon used as the title of his first published anthology, which set Corwin's life alongside similar pieces on Judge Learned Hand and UN Secretary General Trygve Lie, among whom the CBS broadcaster hardly felt out of place.[2] But that stature would not last. Just as 1947 was a tipping-point year for cultural politics in the United States—something in which Corwin was personally and professionally bound up, as Thomas Doherty's chapter in this volume lays out—it was also a pivotal year for attitudes toward Corwin's work, coming at the tail end of an almost unbroken string of triumphs during the age of live radio (see chapters by Cummings and Crook) and near the beginning of a phase when he would adapt his values and styles to recording arts, film, and television (see Smith, Watson, and VanCour chapters) over an enduring career that took his sonic sensibilities into a variety of authorial situations across the creative industries. In 1947 Corwin married Katherine Locke; he aired his *One World Flight* recordings of the voices of people he met around the globe; he codirected and produced *Hollywood Fights Back* for the Committee for the First Amendment to fight the blacklist; and he also published a book of his radio plays, which would be the last such anthology to appear for sixty-eight years.[3]

Who was Corwin to Hamburger and other critics around 1947? As *Variety*'s radio editor Bob Landry noted at the time, the history of critical columns about radio during the golden age of the medium was largely the story of half-hearted efforts launched and then abandoned by a wide array of periodicals: *PM, The Saturday Review of Literature, Life, Newsweek, McCall's, American Mercury, The Nation,* and *The New York Daily News* among others.[4] Combing through these for reflections on style turns up just a few essays about a smattering of shows. For Landry, a true radio criticism was not even possible. With 65,000 units of time technically for sale every day on American airwaves, sheer abundance prevented a discourse that could engage the narratives on the airwaves at a granular textual level, and any critical reflection would necessarily be retrospective—the show under review may already be over for good, disappeared into ether—and thus less useful to the public than a theater, book, or film review might be.

Corwin's work was a rare exception. His high-profile broadcasts were backed by CBS and the federal government, and his daring plays drew upwards of 60 million listeners from Pearl Harbor to V-J Day, among them many reflective intellectuals. He was, at 35, in the words of *Time* magazine, radio's "boy wonder."[5] His works earned frothy praise from the likes of Carl Van Doren, who compared Corwin to playwright Christopher Marlowe, and Carl Sandburg, who called Corwin's V-E Day show "On a Note of Triumph" one of the all-time best American poems.[6] But such acclaim was not entirely universal. That same broadcast drew scorn from *Harper's* columnist Bernard De Voto, who called it a "mistake from the first line" full of "pretentiousness" and "bargain-counter jauntiness" in a review that repeatedly cudgeled the play's "bad writing."[7]

Perhaps both assessments are right. After all, the notion that poetry belongs on the bargain counter (and the bargain counter in the poetry) might describe Corwin's whole literary philosophy. In a discussion with Douglas Bell, he put it this way: "I have very small patience with writers who need to be interpreted by a board of interpreters before you can understand what the hell they are talking about."[8] Corwin went so far in the other direction that it sometimes comes across as a fault. In one of my interviews with him, Corwin insisted on an aesthetic of intelligent clarity in his approach: "You're talking to adults smarter than you, and one's obligation is to be understood. I have no patience for the obscurantists."[9] In his 1983 book *Trivializing America,* he joked that Americans have a special capacity for oversimplifying in their writing, "since we are constantly inspired to keep at it by the examples of advertising and government."[10]

The remarks of both detractors and devotees like De Voto and Sandburg also illustrate another point: for many of his contemporaries, it was awfully hard to react to Corwin's habit of excess without mimicking it. Hamburger's profile caught this bug. Shuttling between the satirical and the unctuous, "The Odyssey of the Oblong Blur" tells a gauzy tale of Corwin's first encounter with radio, when he and his older brother Al built a crystal set out of a box of Quaker Oats, and relates tall tales of Corwin's artistry, like the time he spent two days trying to simulate the sounds of depth charges and submarine control levers to the satisfaction of a Navy vet. The profile outlines how Corwin came to the CBS network in the heyday of experimental radio during the late 1930s; notes memorable plays like "The Plot against Christmas" (with various figures in Hades conspiring against Santa Claus), "The Odyssey of Runyon Jones" (about a boy searching the afterlife for his dead dog), and "Ann Rutledge" (about Lincoln's lost love); and takes us through his career until the One World Flight project, which enabled him to travel to seventeen countries and fly 37,000 miles to record voices—"His object: to see if the postwar world was One World. His method: to record what he heard on a wire four thousandths of an inch in diameter," as Hamburger put it.[11] But to the reader today, even Corwin's miniaturization of the globe is obscured behind Hamburger's own overdone literary exercise, for not only did he write the profile as a radio play, but he wrote it *in the style of Norman Corwin*. Here is the opening:

> *Narrator.* Hark!
> (Music: *Introductory cue; violins super-agitato)*
> Leave us rip our cerebellums
> From the skull itself
> And fly as on a carpet magic
> To Boston, Massachusetts
> *(Music: Reminiscently sentimental; with schmalz)*
> May 3, 1910!
> Lincoln dead, Garfield shot, McKinley gone.
> The carriage has lost its horse!
> The lamp no more drools dripping wax!
> Cyrus Field has long since laid his cable!
> Aye! The Wright Brothers, silent and alone upon a sandy spit at Kitty Hawk,
> Have some time previous sent skyward the fatal instrument of winged flight.
> *(Music: Full orchestra; tremendous paean.)*
> We're starting out this way,
> Since it's a festive day.
> A child is being born
> As from a golden horn
> And Heaven sings and sings
> As Stork a Poet brings!
> *Little Guy (interrupting).* Hey, Mister, this isn't clear.
> Just *what* is going on here?
> *Narrator.* Hold on, Little Guy, and you will see,
> How Norman Corwin came to be![12]

CRITICAL EARSPACES

Hamburger's mimicry of Corwin's style poses the problem of what that style is, how it came to be, and, most importantly, how we should conceptualize sonic style in the first place. Despite a revival in thought about narrative audio prompted by the recent rise of podcasts as well as a renewed interest in Corwin as an audio artist (perhaps the most important practitioner of narrative-driven audio in U.S. history), overt thoughts on the question of what we might call the "Corwinesque style" have been muted. One reason is style's intimate connection to authorship, the rusted old sedan of theory, one that is today all but abandoned at an impasse between poststructuralist skepticism on the one hand and stale auteur studies on the other, something this book tries to overcome by emphasizing a model of "sound authorship" that follows Corwin's blur of production through a variety of media industry architectures.

Another reason is that both the public and broadcasters tend to neglect audio heritage. Many admired practitioners of the audio arts today suffer from an amnesia about the origins and histories of their own techniques and sensibilities. Read the best-selling recent books on radio technique and you will find virtually no references by authors or celebrity broadcasters to Corwin or the hundreds like him who made brilliant radio in generations past. The "New Masters" of radio seem uninterested in the "Old" ones; it is as if no one had thought to tell radio stories before *This American Life*.[13] Testimonials in the press that followed Corwin's death in 2011 also illustrate the problem. While many commentators celebrated his life and role in the war effectively, lauding Corwin as the greatest at his craft, none had a serious or precise way of talking about that craft. Few major papers carried quotes from his scores of hit radio plays, let alone serious explorations of what made them groundbreaking.

The result was Corwin without the Corwinesque. Obituaries lacked precisely the drama and literary vanity to which Sandburg, De Voto, and Hamburger all responded back in the 1940s.[14] All three of those writers had an "ear" for Corwin, a sonic shorthand that underlies both the way they praise and blame him. The *New Yorker* piece, for instance, uses rapid-fire messages from contemporaneous literary figures from William Saroyan to Arch Oboler, as well as choruses of voices and anthropomorphized objects—cities, buildings, a crystal set—that deliver soliloquys. All that had a certain ring for Corwin's 1940s audiences and critics. But who would get the joke now? Collective experience of Corwin's sound has passed from living memory. All this is to say that the question of the Corwinesque—a term that appeared nowhere until producer Norman Lear dreamed it up in the foreword to a recent edition of Corwin's notebooks published by Michael C. Keith and Mary Ann Watson —only makes sense if we recognize its inherent historical and contextual contingency, its existence in a field that responds to its elements only selectively.[15] The question of Corwin is thus the question of which Corwin matters to whom, when, and why, which is the only way any artistic legacy ever "comes to be." That is the central argument of this chapter.

So what was the Corwinesque around 1947? What is it nowadays? What might it become in the future? In this chapter, I focus on a few of Corwin's critics to explore the "critical earspaces" in which Corwin's work existed and continues to exist, the plural discursive-receptive worlds in which his sonic creativity becomes intelligible at particular moments in time. Rather than seeking a final theory of the Corwinesque style that fits all times, audiences, and situations, this chapter will propose that certain strains of Corwin's work are "hearable" only through the assumption of critical imaginary tuned to particular frequencies. To foreground that process, I'll use Hamburger's article as a starting point for three studies of how Corwin's aesthetics form the "anatomies of criticism" in which they come to be understood, assessed, and ascribed value. Only by attending to that process can critical commentaries undergird a modernized model of the media author, particularly one like Corwin, whose career crossed so many fields. In what follows, I take inspiration from Shawn VanCour's recuperation of Rudolf Arnheim's approach to style historiography outlined in his chapter in this volume, emphasizing that style is a construct of the historian that comes into being at certain levels of magnification, where the presence of a particular technique matches a perceived way of making that is conditioned by medium and subject. While VanCour follows this insight to see how style-concepts are applied in different times and media by authors, this essay follows another track, mapping how critical ears and minds select different levels of magnification with which to focalize the oblong blur of the Corwinesque.

A HIGH WIRELESS ACT

In its profile, the *New Yorker* evinced more irritation with one aspect of Corwin's style than any other: overwriting. Hamburger pokes fun at Corwin's unreasonable demands of sound (*"Music: a universal theme, oscillator beneath, denoting pain of the world and bigness thereof, fading"*) and apes how he lets childish alliteration run amok, as when the members of the audience are called "Sons of a Sun spinning sadly through space."[16] Many critics disapproved of what they saw as a lack of restraint, although Corwin actually restrained himself often. In the published version of *On a Note of Triumph* for instance, one finds unaired sections reflecting on gruesome firing squad sequences, even a vision of the riders of the apocalypse— "unblushing phrases" restored to the text "for the sake of my conscience," the author explains.[17] Still, Corwin's penchant for overwriting was a widely understood issue. In his lifetime, the author neither denied it nor conceded that it required apology. "I was unafraid to give Apollo a good long speech in 'Descent of the Gods,'" he told Douglas Bell. It was Apollo, after all.[18] Corwin might have always been this way. According to biographer R. LeRoy Bannerman, as a senior in high school he submitted to his English teacher an abstruse treatise of polysyllabic wordplay entitled "Words," simply so that he could be summoned to the front of the class to parse passages of Corwin for a teacher who had parsed passages of Milton for him.[19]

But there is another way of thinking about Corwin's overwriting. Among many of his contemporaries in the industry, his verbal excess was understood as a challenge to technicians and actors just for the sake of it, launched in the spirit of the experimental era of broadcasting as an attempt to break new ground. In the script for "New York: A Tapestry for Radio," for example, a date scene contains this befuddling note: "*Music: Love on brownstone stoop at three in the morning after an evening at the RKO Proctor Theater and a long walk in the park. It sustains, behind.*"[20]

There is an even better example of an "aesthetic of challenge" in "The Undecided Molecule," a play concerning a particle that refuses to select his destiny before the Court of Physiochemical Relations. This sets up a verse play riddled with triple internal rhyming schemes and hurdles of enunciation. Here are some lines Corwin gave to a representative of the Minerals, making his case for why the molecule should elect to join his Kingdom:

> *Mineral Spokesman.* If he wishes to be a worker, he
> Can serve in a column of mercury,
> If he'd rather be gay and giddysome,
> There's radium, uranium, iridium.
> O tantalum, tungsten, talcum, tin,
> Ipsy, pipsy, bitters and gin,
> Alto sax and carpet tacks,
> Rackety rax borax—
> Merrily, beryly, chalybite, chin,
> Tripolite, zinc and kaolin . . .
> *Judge.* Are these football yells necessary?
> *Mineral Spokesman.* Yes sir—Very.
> *Judge.* What do they mean?
> *Mineral Spokesman.* Well, amphibole, sphene and pyroxene,
> Being amygdaloidally idiochromatic,
> May create a stalactitic static
> Affecting the schlenohedral speed.
> *Judge.* That clears it up very well indeed.
> Proceed.[21]

Is the schoolboy still showing off? Perhaps, but to say the passage is overdoing it misses the point that when set in the live radio medium, lexical exhibitionism such as this takes on an aesthetic valence that it does not bear in schoolbooks.

Corwin's lines are deliberately composed to be easy to botch when vocalized, which is why it is impressive when they are delivered smoothly—listening to them is like watching a tightrope walker—particularly in a play that stands or falls on steadily paced delivery across the duration of the broadcast, with any flubs interfering with a smooth rhythm. The style doesn't *resort* to overworked literary calisthenics and tongue twisters; it *depends* upon them. It says at the sonic level, "Look at me trying so hard I might blow it." That comes through only if we read Corwin's words as fundamentally radiophonic rather than written for the page. Indeed, it may be incorrect to evaluate Corwin's aesthetic as *poetic*; on that matter both friend Carl Sandburg and foe Bernard De Voto are incorrect—Corwin couldn't have written "a great American poem," and his works can't be "bad writing" because they are not "writing." "So dependent is this poetry on the ear," wrote one critic in 1944, "that it seems almost a mistake to read it in the cold glare of print."[22] Think of the Corwinesque as broadcasting rather than literature, and it transforms, with many of its liabilities coming across as dares.

If this is right, that the Corwinesque relied at a certain moment in its history on a show of its own bravery, then perhaps it clarifies where Corwin fits among his peers as a radio director. William N. Robson, director of *The Man behind the Gun* and *Escape*, among many other radio programs, was known to run demanding rehearsals to control for errors during broadcast. *Columbia Workshop* director Earle McGill cared most about microphone calibration, claiming that actors were interchangeable. William Spier, director of *The March of Time* and *Suspense*, filled dramas with thick underscore, reflecting his expertise in music, to control mood and pace. But in all three cases, listeners were not supposed to peer past the play at the work behind it. In their own ways, each of these outstanding directors diverted attention from the fact that he could lose control over the material heterogeneity of the broadcast at any time. The idea was to convince listeners to subscribe wholeheartedly to an illusion so thorough that every technique appeared to be the listener's imagination at work. Execution trumped conceptualization.

Corwin's plays were just the opposite, opening up their own process, specifying what might go wrong just before it does. That's why it's easier to compare Corwin to *Lights Out*'s Arch Oboler, *The Columbia Workshop*'s Irving Reis, *Studio One*'s Fletcher Markle, or *The Mercury Theater on the Air*'s Orson Welles, all of whom also foreground the possibility of mistake, than it is to compare him to McGill, Spier, or Robson, despite Corwin's being professionally tied more closely to the latter three.

Buffoonish yet soaring, it is no surprise that many saw the Corwinesque involving an aesthetic of speed. In a 1945 review of a Corwin anthology, for instance, UCLA professor William Matthews wrote of what he perceived to be a "frontier spirit" that resulted in part from Corwin's difficult language delivered at a rapid rate.[23] For Matthews, it was impossible to call Corwin a genius in the traditional sense, because his tendency was to "rush breathlessly" from one idea to another, an aesthetic of pace that outran itself and resembled a "an exciting storm." Thanks to this spirit, even when the prose was purple, the defect came across as that of an innovator.

To keep that up, Corwin had to innovate constantly. Perhaps that is why his plays took on so many forms—the letter ("To Tim at Twenty"); the soliloquy ("A

Soliloquy to Balance the Budget"); the poetic essay ("Daybreak"); the treatise ("Anatomy of Sound"); the pageant ("Unity Fair"); the bible story (a trilogy of "Samson," "Esther," and "Job"); the literary biography (a trilogy of "Whitman," "Sandburg," and "Wolfe")—and why he pursued generic hybridity throughout his career. In his first *Variety* review in 1937 Corwin was called a mixture of "the press agent and the poet"; in 1944 Milton Kaplan pointed out that he uniquely used both prose and poetry so that the former could speak in specificities and the latter in generalities.[24] To be an experimental writer in Corwin's way in the 1940s was to be a compound of sonic substances audibly undecided.

If many of Corwin's contemporary critics were attuned to speed, excess, and reflexivity, they also were equally fascinated with his brevity. As Glenn Christiansen of Lehigh University explained in a 1947 analysis, Corwin's use of puns and music was an important form of shorthand, a way of giving sound the "unusual burden of words" or intensifying meanings to give the broadcast a logical fabric that "does not ravel."[25] Unlike De Voto, Christiansen saw within this verbiage the corollary of Corwin's much admired succinctness. In other words, the same groan-inducing instinct that allowed Corwin to call one realm of the dog afterlife "cur-gatory" drove him to produce compressed proverbs that impressed the ear: "Good things don't come running when you whistle for them" and "There are no barefoot pleasures in these hobnail times." Christiansen continues:

> This power of words enables him, in the same script, to epitomize the spiritual worth and physical worthlessness of the human brain in two sharply antithetical words— "This majestic mush." He knows the power of simple words; at the end of whimsical directions to a designer who is to turn out a brain, he brings the reader up short with the direction, "It must be made of air and dust and water and a little passion and a little pain."[26]

Like his overwritten tongue twisters, innovation, and reflexivity, it seems that at least a few critics understood Corwin's approach to simplicity to embrace the danger of failure and inscrutability. How, after all, shall the poor technician produce a brain out of air, dust, and water anyway?

For the critical ears of 1947, to sum up, the key to the Corwinesque was to be seen to be walking a high literary wire without a net. Nothing confirmed that better than a fall. I'd wager many listened for a lousy line or overdone tune as part of the pleasure of it all, as a confirmation that the broadcast was truly experimental, breaking new ground. Moreover, the high-wire act of the Corwinesque relies on a kind of listening-for-risk that was inherent in the radio of the 1940s and is impossible for us to enter into now, because we can't listen to Corwin's work new, fresh, or live. One deep aspect of the Corwinesque of the 1940s—the possibility, even anticipation, of imminent artistic failure, up above an enormous audience out there in the dark—seems lost for good.

COALITION AND COLLATION

Of course, while contextual listening is important, the earspace of the 1940s has no monopoly on Corwin or on the Corwinesque. Even if Sandburg, Matthews, De Voto, and Christiansen listened "in the moment" with an ear for Corwin's personal voice, the ontology of the work of Corwin (or of any other media author) cannot be reduced to the impressions of the original audience, no matter how well informed. To do so would fetishize that audience in the same way critics used to fetishize the author as a limiting being who has the final say on meaning. Substituting a godlike original audience for the godlike author is unworkable for a number of reasons—in the first place because the line between "original" earspace occupied by Corwin's plays and their "later" iterations is awfully unclear.

When does the Corwin era stop and the post-Corwin era begin? 1947? 2011? Maybe 2015, with the publication of Michael James Kacey's edition of Corwin's most recent volume of plays, *Memos to a New Millennium*? I would argue that conveying a sense of present that configures Corwin as a past figure is a rhetorical matter, not a chronological one. It is an argumentative stance that asserts a "retro-auditory" relationship where an ongoing one had existed. In Milton Kaplan's 1949 book *Radio and Poetry*, easily the most substantive critical survey of radio writing in the United States, Corwin's philosophy and process are still spoken of in the present tense.[27] But in 1950, critic Gilbert Seldes (who produced Corwin's first directorial program, *Living History*, in 1939) already speaks of Corwin's work in the past tense, describing him as an "admirable carrier for liberal patriotic ideals" with a "poetic sense of the dignity and worth of individual life." Seldes goes on:

> For a time Corwin held the fate of the documentary in his hands. [...] He was the political conscience of the broadcasting industry. [...] Few were aware that he used a fact, a position in latitude and longitude, or the gross annual tonnage of flatboats over the Rhine, as a poet might, to startle, to set the imagination working, to make the heart beat faster—never as a fact in relation to other facts.[28]

For Seldes, the Corwin age is already beyond recovery, and as it enters the twilight of public memory, its most prominent properties have already begun to change. Note how Corwin's high-wire-act qualities are neither denigrated nor appreciated—they simply don't register—and how a variegated body of work that includes operetta and comic satire is reduced to its war-themed programming. This focus would hold true in subsequent decades. When Studs Terkel interviewed Corwin in 1968, he focused on the war broadcasts too, quoting directly from *On a Note of Triumph*, "They Fly through the Air with the Greatest of Ease" and "Untitled," a play whose words from the war dead had "worn very little" for the Vietnam-era generation, in Terkel's estimation.[29]

Both Seldes and Terkel considered Corwin to be also a documentarian, a title that had only intermittently been applied to his works in the 1930s and '40s but became attached more strongly later and sticks to them today. One result of that reclassification is already evident in Seldes's comments. As long as Corwinesque broadcasts are measured by standards of documentary rather than those of literature (or, better, those of something we can't quite name), they can more easily be found suspicious. At one point Seldes accuses Corwin of taking documentary "into the moonlit garden," a seducer who offered a "romantic interlude" that may have been honorable but spoiled the form's good name nonetheless.[30]

Seldes goes on to criticize Corwin for disempowering independent thinking by his audience, presenting complexity through symbols, and using characters to represent groups who "became as stereotyped in their way as the familiar characters of other radio programs. [. . .] [T]hey were more voices than people." Hamburger's 1947 article had already hinted at this same critique. His quasi-Corwinesque narrator summons various needed characters to the microphone when their testimony is required, many of them "types" that holler "Present" as they appear. When information about Corwin's plays is needed, for instance, The Historian arrives and rattles off a list. The Technician and The Executive likewise testify to Corwin's work ethic.

As these critiques indicate, in an earspace that figures Corwin as something of "the past" (a period beginning perhaps with Seldes and continuing up until today), a certain strain of the Corwinesque tends to fluoresce, one rooted in Corwin's famous documentary attempts to glorify the "common man" or "little guys"—farmers, GIs, factory workers—by drawing their voices to a sonorous space and national coalition, making these two types of imaginary spaces mirror and rationalize one another. The paramount example is "We Hold These Truths," which celebrated the 150th anniversary of the Bill of Rights only days after Pearl Harbor and has grown in importance in recent years after long being hidden in the shadow of *On a Note of Triumph*. One key passage in "We Hold," as I have argued elsewhere, allows us to hear Americans of the revolutionary period (widows, blacksmiths, politicians) speak from a series of shallow locations in a quick succession and a similar group in the present (workers, Okies, businessmen, mothers) as a way of building mystical union through time.[31] The same technique was used in the plays "Psalm for a Dark Year" and "Unity Fair" to bind together different regions and nationalities into sonic coalition. In a 1945 article in the *Saturday Review of Literature* about *On a Note of Triumph*, drama critic John Mason Brown writes of how Corwin welds together a series of locations and "stereotyped" vocal materials into a story: "It is hard to describe the power of his images, the variety of his rhythms, the driving conciseness of his phrases, and his happy mixture of the colloquial and the eloquent."[32]

The style has had many names over the years, with writers reaching for metaphors from mural painting to montage, horizontal drama, mosaics, and cantata. In my work I have used another word: *kaleidosonic*. In kaleidosonic radio, we segue from place to place, experiencing shallow scenes as if from a series of fixed apertures, thereby giving time periods expressive existence. Corwin tended to speak of this strain of his work more proudly in his later years. One of his favorite works was 1943's "The Midwest: Breadbasket and Arsenal," a broadcast whose introductions switches between announcers at hubs in Chicago, Duluth, Cleveland, Detroit, and St. Louis, bringing us the voices of a Nebraskan beef farmer, a chief steward of the CIO at the Studebaker plant, the president of a steel company, and a British refugee. The broadcast also collages readings of newspapers in Downer's Grove, Illinois, Waterloo, Indiana, and Montevideo, Minnesota, while offering statistics on the productivity of the region, emphasizing its production of tractors, steel, wheat, eggs, food, and guns. Philip Roth, who claims that listening to Corwin was one of the most thrilling events of his childhood (the published edition of *On a Note of Triumph* was, apparently, the first book he ever bought), testifies to the power of the technique in one of his interviews: "The names would just wash over me, and I'd think 'This is a great country.'"[33]

Kaleidosonic style can be contrasted with what I refer to as "intimate style," in which the listener is attached to a character who moves through deep scenes slowly over time, as a way to give space expressive existence. A good example of intimate style is Corwin's *American in England* series (touched on in Crook's chapter in this volume), in which the horizon of wartime is shaped by a proximal relation to a surrogate narrating entity "nearby"—actor Joseph Julian, who takes us on a tour of fortified England during the blitz, meeting everyday people.

Together these two styles of sonic creativity form what I call a "theater of space and time" associated with the late Depression and war years on American airwaves. Not only did Corwin use both intimate and kaleidosonic styles, but he often made them interlock. The opening section of "On a Note of Triumph" is a good example. In the space of just four minutes, we hear a song of Hitler's death, along with versions of that song vocalized by Serbs, Danes, and Greeks; then come expressions of relief at the fall of Berlin from a mother in Mississippi and a wife in Bridgeport; next we hear a New Hampshire congregation, a rabbi in Oklahoma, and a bishop in a cathedral chanting to God; then there are crowds in Times Square, Piccadilly, and Nevsky Prospect. After that kaleidosonic sequence, the narrator takes us up into the stratosphere in search of a faint whisper behind the celebratory din, "a modest voice, as sensible and intimate to you as the quiet turning of your own considered judgment." Eventually, we come to an ordinary GI overseas: "This boy, that boy, any boy at all with war still thumping in his ears," who speaks to us first as an intimate individual asking questions about the victory. In his 1945 published edition, Corwin disrupts this intimacy with literary reflections that abandon the boy ("War has the voice of a million muzzles"; "All creatures living in the earth and air, entire censuses of the seas have felt the shock"), but on air he resists, and lets us occupy a tiny acoustic environment as part of an imagined dyad with the hero of the hour in a moment of quiet copresence.

This connection between the large context and the individual being, between the near and the simultaneous, is Corwin's way of speaking the languages of space and of time all at once. That capability underlies Corwin's glorification of the common man, who is really Corwin's public refracted through the ether. This was his great discovery as an artist. In 1939, Archibald MacLeish wrote, "The situation of radio is the situation of poetry backwards. If poetry is an art without an audience, radio is an audience without an art."[34] Corwin understood something else. In radio, the audience *is* the art.

Or so it has come to seem from a distance. I am not alone among radio historians in foregrounding these aspects of Corwin's work: Matthew Ehrlich has emphasized Corwin's "murals and polemics," and Bruce Lenthall has associated these aspects of Corwin's style with his "modernism of the air."[35] At a dinner celebrating Corwin's seventy-fifth birthday in 1985, Norman Lear insisted that Corwin's passion was to "expand the universe of sounds heard and feelings felt by radio listeners"[36] I'd suggest that this model of the Corwinesque is particularly meaningful to us now because its content—the voices of the subordinated, the downtrodden, the average—is both a reminder of an idealized era of 1930s liberalism and a way of connecting Corwin's aesthetic with subsequent media forms.

Robert Altman's multitrack film aesthetic of the 1970s is a clear descendant of the kaleidosonic style—the director is famous for claiming that he learned drama from Corwin, even that he memorized *On a Note of Triumph*.[37] On radio today, *This American Life* is intimate on the small scale, often following a series of deep and long narratives, but kaleidosonic in the large scale by arraying narratives together thematically. *Radiolab*, by contrast, is kaleidosonic in its architecture, featuring fast, shallow segments that empower its aesthetic of wonder as it moves wildly around space and time (not unlike a vivid episode of *The March of Time*), while also providing a highly intimate glue in the closely miked studio banter of its hosts, which is designed to feel proximal and familiar (for more on *Radiolab*, see Russo's chapter later in this volume). Even prominent television programs use these kaleidosonic and intimate sound aesthetics to some degree. Think of how *The Wire* and *Game of Thrones* distribute and collect voices across spaces in world-making portraits; think of how our ears hear the nasal exhalations of Tony Soprano on *The Sopranos* so very well, or the coughing Walter White on *Breaking Bad*— another oddly otolaryngeal antihero in the new "golden age of TV."

That we even notice the intimate/kaleidosonic relationship in studies of classic radio today also has a lot to do with the technology behind today's critical earspace. Today it is easy to listen "distantly" to classic radio through formats that allow us to pause, rewind, categorize, and remix vast amounts of golden age audio in a way that was impossible in 1947. However, both admirers like Brown and skeptics like Seldes are incorrect when they ascribe kaleidosonic aesthetics to Corwin uniquely. That "people's radio" form of the Corwinesque was not only his; it reflected a broadly shared vocabulary of radio dramaturgy, a way of talking about time and space that characterized many programs of that time. For other uses of the kaleidosonic, consider the works of Stephen Vincent Benét or *Cavalcade of America*. For examples of the intimate style, listen to any first-person-style play from *The Mercury Theater on the Air*. What made Corwin special among these dramatists was how he made these styles complementary at key rhetorical moments. And just as airing a *coalition* of voices was an epistemological act that reinvented those whom it depicted in 1945, our use of a new *collation* of recordings today redraws the parameters of what those sounds can mean, amplifying things hitherto inaudible.

THE LONG WAIT

It may have taken until the digital age to really understand how Corwin used kaleidosonic passages in his broadcasts to glorify the "common man," but it wasn't too long after 1947 that Corwin's dedication to an aesthetic of political pluralism had become a liability on two fronts. It seemed seditious to red-baiters, especially at points where he extended it into the international realm, as other chapters in this book explore. It also seemed phony to leftists. In a 1946 article on populist realism, writer James T. Farrell called Corwin's populist work "tendentiously organized," relying on editorialization to foster conviction rather than on character.[38] Around that time, *The Nation*'s Lou Frankel wrote an editorial on Corwin's *One World* series that saw it as an undignified failure. Although it was an earnest attempt "to let every working stiff, every white collar man and housewife and fighting man in America hear just what his opposite number in other countries had to say," to Frankel's ears it came across as cold. "It is as if the late John Barrymore decided, without warning, to play Hamlet in pantomime."[39] The tide had clearly turned. Hamburger's *New Yorker* profile mocked Corwin's faith in building sonorous coalitions. Throughout the piece, the narrator summons various character "types" to the microphone, including a character referred to as The Great Globe Itself as well as the Chorus of One Hundred Little Guys from Everywhere in the World, which returns from time to time to deliver couplets. The piece even ends with a monologue by the Common Man, bemoaning how Corwin talked over, past, and through him: "you ought to think about what the words mean before you use them."[40]

Rereading that passage with its moral superiority reminded me of another coda, this one to a Corwin play that is perhaps the most difficult in his body of work: 1944's "Untitled," a grim story widely republished in magazines and newspapers, one that might stand as Corwin's major statement about war had it not soon been overshadowed by *On a Note of Triumph*. The play concerns the life of a war casualty named Hank Peters, played by Fredric March. We hear about his record from his mother, teachers, girlfriend, pals, and even the Nazi soldier who fired the shell that killed him. The play ends with Peters speaking, as he lies "fermenting in the wisdom of the earth," about what peace will mean when it comes. The monologue concludes this way:

> Let me tell you—
> From my acre of now undisputed ground I will be listening;
> I will be tuned to clauses in the contract where the word Democracy appears
> And how the freedoms are inflected to a Negro's ear.
> I shall listen for a phrase obliging the little peoples of the earth:
> For Partisans and Jews and Puerto Ricans,
> Chinese farmers, miners of tin ore beneath Bolivia;
> I shall listen how the words go easy into Russian
> And the idiom's translated to the tongue of Spain.
> I shall wait and I shall wait in long and long suspense
> For the password that Peace is setting solidly.
> On that day, please to let my mother know
> Why it had to happen to her boy.[41]

The dead are frequently active, involved, speaking characters in Corwin's plays. From "The Odyssey of Runyon Jones" to "We Hold These Truths" and even a comedy like "L'Affaire Gumpert," there are many occasions in which the voices of the dead arise at a powerful dramatic moment to wield irresistible force in the world of the living. In "Untitled," Peters's death is more than a patriotic act, but also a kind of background moral condition that can and ought to rest heavily on our everyday doings. Death is a thing always awaiting its justice, its narrative, its return to its mother.

I have a hunch that this feature is destined to grow in importance over time for those of us who study it and think about Corwin's work. If the work of Kate Lacey, Elena Razlogova, and others is any indication, the ethics of listening and the moral economies it manages are a vital emerging area for media studies broadly and for radio scholars in particular.[42] That development refreshes what Corwin may come to represent in a future earspace.

In a 1943 article in *Variety*, Corwin wrote of radio's role in what he called "the making of this earth as a fit place in which to live and work," of a medium that affords the word not just authority and power but also "dignity."[43] *That* Corwin, the one for whom sound is a medium of dignification, is still speaking; he is growing louder as his words are no longer broadcast through terrestrial space but through time. Now that Corwin himself has come to repose in the wisdom of the earth, after more than a century walking upon it, our question will be what relationship we ought to have with the dead who really do keep on sounding after they are gone—what obligations we owe their vision (now quaintly antique, painfully so) to the little people of the earth—as their voices echo in clouds of data.

But "Untitled" isn't just about the way the dead can and ought to speak to the living, which has been an animating question in theory of recorded sound for decades. It is also, and strangely, about how the dead *listen* to the living. Corwin always wanted his dramas to draw from his listeners, to echo them, as if the plays had a consciousness of their own. How will we listen to these plays in the future, and can they still listen to us and return us to ourselves? I'd like to conclude my odyssey into three critical earspaces that focus the blur of the Corwinesque—the past, the present, and the future—with a fourth: the idea that these plays and the moral force that underlies them are *themselves* another earspace, one critiquing any world into which they resound. Way down in his own acre of undisputed ground, imagine Corwin in a long and mysterious suspense, his ear turned upward in our direction.

NOTES

1. Philip Hamburger, "Norman Corwin," *New Yorker* (April 5, 1947): 36–49.
2. Philip Hamburger, *The Oblong Blur and Other Odysseys* (New York: Farrar, Straus, 1949). All subsequent references to the article will use this edition, for finer pagination.
3. The latter is one of the last things he worked on before his death and contains a number of plays he produced in collaboration with Mary Beth Kirchner for NPR: Norman Corwin, *Memos to a New Millennium: The Final Radio Plays of Norman Corwin,* ed. Michael James Kacey (Albany, GA: BearManor Media, 2015).
4. Robert J. Landry, "The Improbability of Radio Criticism," *Hollywood Quarterly* 2 (October 1946): 70–78.
5. "Prizes for Corwin," *Time* (March 4, 1946): 62.
6. Christopher H. Sterling, *Biographical Dictionary of Radio* (New York: Routledge, 2013), 71; Denis McLellan, "Norman Corwin Dies at 101: Radio's Poet Laureate," *Los Angeles Times* (October 19, 2011), http://articles.latimes.com/2011/oct/19/local/la-me-norman-corwin-20111019.
7. Bernard De Voto, "The Easy Chair" column, *Harper's* (July 1, 1945): 33.
8. Norman Corwin and Douglas Bell, *Years of the Electric Ear* (New York: Scarecrow Press, 1994), 25.
9. From my phone interview with Corwin, August 23, 2008.
10. Norman Corwin, *Trivializing America* (Secaucus, NJ: Lyle Stuart, 1983)
11. Hamburger, *Oblong Blur,* 91.
12. Ibid., 76–77.
13. See, for example, Jessica Abel, *Out on the Wire: The Storytelling Secrets of the New Masters of Radio* (New York: Broadway Books, 2015); and John Beiwen and Alexa Dilworth, *Reality Radio: Telling True Stories in Sound* (Chapel Hill: University of North Carolina Press, 2010).
14. See introduction to this volume.
15. Norman Lear, "Foreword," *Norman Corwin's One World Flight: The Lost Journal of Radio's Greatest Writer,* ed. Michael C. Keith and Mary Ann Watson (New York: Continuum, 2009), ix–x.
16. Hamburger, *Oblong Blur,* 78, 79.
17. Norman Corwin, *On a Note of Triumph* (New York: Simon & Schuster, 1945), 7, 63–64.
18. Corwin and Bell, 76.
19. R. LeRoy Bannerman, *On a Note of Triumph: Norman Corwin and the Golden Years of Radio* (New York: University of Alabama Press, 1986), 17.
20. Norman Corwin, *Untitled and Other Radio Dramas* (New York: Henry Holt, 1947), 333.
21. Corwin, *Untitled,* 23.

22. Milton Kaplan, "Radio and Poetry," *Poetry* 64, no. 5 (August 1944): 273.
23. William Matthews, "Radio Plays as Literature," *Hollywood Quarterly* 1, no. 1 (October, 1945): 40–50.
24. "Poetic License" *Variety* (November 3, 1938), 36; Kaplan, 272.
25. Glenn J. Christiansen, "A Decade of Radio Drama," *College English* 8, no. 4 (January 1947): 183.
26. Christiansen, 184.
27. Milton Allen Kaplan, *Radio and Poetry* (New York: Columbia University Press, 1949).
28. Gilbert Seldes, *The Great Audience* (New York: Viking, 1950), 120.
29. From an uncatalogued Studs Terkel interview with Norman Corwin, circa 1968. Thanks to Allison Schein at the Studs Terkel Archive / WFMT Chicago for providing audio.
30. Seldes, 121.
31. Neil Verma, *Theater of the Mind: Imagination, Aesthetics and American Radio Drama* (Chicago: University of Chicago Press, 2012), 57–90.
32. John Mason Brown, "Seeing Things: On a Note of Triumph," *Saturday Review of Literature* (May 26, 1945): 25–26.
33. Claudia Roth Pierpont, *Roth Unbound: A Writer and His Books* (New York: Farrar, Strauss and Giroux, 2013).
34. From a letter published in *Furioso* 1, no. 1 (1939): 1–2.
35. See Matthew Ehrlich, *Radio Utopia: Postwar Audio Documentary in the Public Interest* (Chicago: University of Illinois Press, 2011), 24–45; Bruce Lenthall, *Radio's America* (Chicago: University of Chicago Press, 2007), 175–200.
36. Norman Lear, "The Life of the Mind," in *13 for Corwin*, ed. Ray Bradbury (Fort Lee, NJ: Barricade Books, 1985), 20.
37. See Gayle Sherwood Magee, *Robert Altman's Soundtracks: Film, Music and Sound from MASH to A Prairie Home Companion* (New York: Oxford University Press, 2014), 22. See also "Altman, Audience, Corwin," *Studio 360* (WNYC New York), December 27, 2003.
38. James T. Farrell, "Social Themes in American Realism," *English Journal* 35, no. 6 (June 1946): 312.
39. Lou Frankel, "In One Ear," *The Nation* (February 15, 1947): 137.
40. Hamburger, *Oblong Blur,* 93.
41. Corwin, *Untitled,* 83.
42. Kate Lacey, *Listening Publics: The Politics and Experience of Listening in the Media Age* (Malden MA: Polity Press, 2013); Elena Razlogova, *The Listener's Voice: Early Radio and the American Public* (Philadelphia: University of Pennsylvania Press, 2011); Ian Whittington, "Radio Studies and 20th Century Literature: Ethics, Aesthetics and Remediation," *Literature Compass* 11, no. 9, (September 2014): 634–48.
43. Norman Corwin, "Confessions of an Optimist," *Variety* (July 14, 1943): 32.

2

NORMAN CORWIN AND THE BLACKLIST

Thomas Doherty

If radio auteur Norman Corwin was not officially blacklisted—admittedly, something of a non sequitur given that the defining qualities of the blacklist were deniability and intangibility—it was not for lack of trying. The Hollywood life of the blacklist era, a sorry interregnum in the history of American entertainment, might be dated from November 25, 1947, when Eric A. Johnston, president of the Motion Picture Association of America, announced that henceforth the major studios would not "knowingly employ a Communist," to the release of *Spartacus* in December 1960, when one of the most infamous blacklistees, screenwriter Dalton Trumbo, was awarded his first screen credit in thirteen years. Throughout these years, Corwin remained stubbornly and steadfastly left of center, indeed a man who might rightly be suspected of being, in the loaded jargon of the day, a fellow traveler, someone who was reliably on board with the positions of the Communist Party if not, to use another Cold War circumlocution, a card-carrying Communist. Most audaciously, even during the depths of the blacklist era, he continued to embrace the Hollywood Ten and others deemed persona non grata by the studios, the radio and television networks, and, it must be admitted, a goodly portion of the American public. At a time when most artists avoided contact with the controversial causes and toxic talent, running for cover or rushing for clearance, Corwin refused to shun—and often courted—the ideological pariahs.

To say that Corwin was not blacklisted is not to say he was free and clear of hardships and pressures or that his political stance did not cost him opportunities and income. "During the dark days of blacklisting, Corwin was never denied gainful employment, but its effect followed him closely" is the measured appraisal of Corwin biographer R. LeRoy Bannerman. "He frequently faced unexpected and inexplicable stalemates in negotiations for work. He would be summoned, and favorably evaluated, but the next logical step was never taken."[1] How many of the speed bumps in a heretofore fast-track career can be attributed to the blacklist and how many resulted from the normal operations of what is a maddeningly stop-and-go business in even the best of times is hard to gauge.

Still, despite the oppressive atmospherics of the early years of the Cold War, Corwin remained one of the few high-profile artist-activists in the motion picture or broadcasting media who worked regularly without recanting his beliefs and snubbing his politically inconvenient associates. One does not see in Corwin's curriculum vita the long gaps between credits that one sees in the work of so many of the actors, writers, and directors who were named in testimony before the House Committee on Un-American Activities (HUAC) or listed in the pages of *Red Channels: A Report on Communist Influence in Radio and Television*. Corwin never named names—indeed, he was never subpoenaed to testify before HUAC or any other congressional committee. He never published a mea culpa for his activist past or present, and he never felt compelled to go into self-exile in Mexico or Europe. In the context of the times, and especially in light of his brazen left-of-centerism, he came through the scoundrel time amazingly unscathed.

Given his credentials and fame, Corwin certainly personified the kind of high-value target that an ambitious anti-Communist congressman or self-appointed guardian of the realm would have wanted to take down. From 1938, when the twenty-seven-year-old aspiring poet-playwright-writer left the publicity department at Twentieth Century-Fox in New York to break into big-time radio, until the late 1940s, when a new broadcast medium began to supplant the old one, Corwin was lauded as the maestro of the airwaves, the highbrow virtuoso in a lowbrow medium, the golden boy of radio's golden age. At CBS, he was the prize jewel and trophy artist for a network that typically ranked a distant also-ran in the ratings behind the monolithic NBC empire. "Columbia's gem," the trade press dubbed him.

Tellingly too, in an age in which radio art went out over the air and vanished in the ether, Corwin's prose was accorded a special stature and permanence: it was recorded, rebroadcast, and preserved—and not just on transcription discs. Collected and bound between covers, his radio plays garnered respectful reviews from critics grateful to find a modicum of class in a déclassé medium. In a laudatory review of *Thirteen by Corwin*, a baker's dozen of his radio plays published in 1942, the *New York Times* book critic Ralph Thompson alluded to the snooty airs assumed by literary types who deigned to hearken to radio. "Norman Corwin has the touch," admitted Thomson, "and even members of a certain Benevolent and Protective Order, who are sworn to throttle radio authors and lynch radio announcers on sight, should relent somewhat upon reading *Thirteen by Corwin*," adding good naturedly, "Take it from one of the oldest living members of the B.P.O. of Radio-phobes."[2] Nobody called Corwin's sophisticated dramas "soap operas."

More than Corwin's literary credentials, however, critics turned their ears to the ways he orchestrated the chamber music of radio: here was a writer-producer-and-sometime-narrator whose plays had to be heard to be savored. From his very first breakout hit, *The Plot to Overthrow Christmas,* broadcast on Christmas Day 1938, Corwin was appreciated as a unique talent and singular voice of the medium—an auteur before the concept was applied to motion picture directors, much less radio playwrights. In 1939, reviewing Corwin's six-part series *So This Is Radio, Variety* critic Robert Landry had already tagged him as "one of radio's most virile mentalities," an artist who made no concessions to the alleged hoi polloi gathered around their Philcos.[3] Again and again, it was Corwin's mastery of the auditory atmospherics of radio that impressed his listeners. "In the most literal sense of the word he is air-minded," observed John Mason Brown in a lengthy appreciation in *Saturday Review* in 1945. "He is a radio writer as surely as a man who only writes novels is a novelist, or one who concentrates on plays is a dramatist."[4] Corwin himself invented a job description for his creative niche: "I was a radiowright—a new species."[5]

Corwin's radio chops were inseparable from his political affinities. Almost all his works exude traces of the New Deal populism and Popular Front loyalties that shaped his outlook in the 1930s. Though never as radical as some of the cadre—unlike folksinger Woody Guthrie, he would never have scrawled "this machine kills fascists" on a radio microphone—he used the lights and wires in the radio box to advance a like-minded agenda. "For the past five years, Corwin has been the most consistent producer of anti-fascist radio plays and he has written most of the scripts himself" noted an approving critique in the *New Masses,* the Communist literary-cultural weekly, in 1944. "Corwin's credo is a simple, yet dynamic one: to use his talents in the interest of the people."[6] Corwin was firmly, as his comrades, Communist and not, might have said at the time, "a man of the Left." He also walked the walk outside the radio booth, acquiring a prominent public profile as an activist, artist, and educator.

At the outbreak of World War II, Corwin was battle ready. "There is a desperate necessity to explain this war to the people," Corwin wrote in 1942. "They are earnest. They want to fight, and they want to be sure what they are fighting for and what they are fighting against."[7] Corwin felt duty bound to tell Americans—as director Frank Capra was doing on film for the U.S. Army—why we fight. His theater of operations was the radio soundstage, where he spent the duration overseeing a series of prestigious command performances that neatly bracketed the war years. On December 15, 1941, as American battleships still smoldered in Pearl Harbor, Corwin helmed a timely commemoration of the 150th anniversary of the Bill of Rights entitled *We Hold These Truths.* Featuring a cast of all-star names and simulcast over all the major radio networks, it dramatized the adoption of the first ten amendments to the U.S. Constitution. FDR himself was the final voice in the Corwin-conducted chorus.

Throughout World War II and on into its immediate aftermath, Corwin's progressive impulses and booming paeans to the strong backbone and bedrock decency of the Average Joe–made–GI Joe were in perfect synch with the values promulgated by the Office of War Information (OWI) and the idealism fostered by the founding of the United Nations. Speaking of Corwin's war work, screenwriter Philip Dunne, himself then in harness with the OWI, figured the network man was doing a better job than the government men. "[O]ver at CBS Norman was doing the same sort of thing on his own, and probably doing it more effectively than we were," he recalled in 1991.[8]

The zenith of Corwin's wartime radio career was the aptly titled *On a Note of Triumph,* broadcast by CBS on V-E Day, May 8, 1945, at 9:00 P.M., rebroadcast the following Sunday, and released in book form later that week by Simon & Schuster. An eloquent distillation of wartime grit and postwar aspirations, the project had been in the works for months, timed to debut at the moment of victory in Europe. "Without equivocation, chalk this up as one of the high-water marks in radio listening, a fitting, joyous climax to a memorable day in history," gushed *Variety,* no easy mark for over-the-air sentiment.[9] *Billboard* blocked out space for a special editorial brimming with superlatives. "*Triumph* was the single greatest—and we mean greatest in its full meaning—radio program we ever heard," it wrote under the headline "Corwin for Everyone," demanding that CBS relinquish its copyright and make the show public domain.[10] Decades later a generation of Americans could still recite the clarion fanfare of the opening lines: "Take a bow, G.I., / Take a bow, little guy. / The superman of tomorrow lies at the feet of you common men of this afternoon."[11]

For a brief moment, in the postwar afterglow, the times seemed no less propitious for Corwin's brand of forward-looking uplift. Nineteen forty-six was the year of William Wyler's *The Best Years of Our Lives* and a burgeoning genre of Hollywood social problem films, message-mongering entertainments very much in tune with Corwin's progressive sensibilities. To be sure, Winston Churchill's warning that an iron curtain had descended across the European continent dampened the promise of a bright new dawn, but Corwin remained passionately committed to a one-worldly vision of postwar Allied cooperation.

Corwin's first major postwar production was a forthright articulation of his utopian zeal for a better world built up from the wartime ruins. Premiering on January 14, 1947, and broadcast over thirteen weeks, *One World Flight* played as an audio slide show of the round-the-world trip he had taken the previous year as the first winner of the Wendell Willkie Memorial One World Award global tour. On February 18, 1946, at a special awards ceremony held at the Waldorf-Astoria Hotel and broadcast over CBS, New York mayor Fiorello H. LaGuardia presented the award to Corwin for his contribution to "the ideal of international unity" and "inspired writing," christening him "the first of the Willkie travelers who circle the globe" to further the late statesman's "dream for all mankind."[12]

Naturally, Corwin took along a microphone and recording equipment. He returned with over one hundred hours of recordings—both from world leaders and ordinary people on the street—and ambitious plans for a series of programs to report his findings and pontificate accordingly. "No one doubts the educational value of the Corwiniana in the offing," reported *Variety*, which could never resist coining a neologism, but the word *educational* was seldom a compliment in the trade paper of record.[13] "We don't intend to produce an austere social tract," Corwin assured potential listeners who might have grown weary of his hectoring. Rather he billed the show as a kind of radio travelogue designed to "take listeners along on the trip, giving them the sense of world flight."[14] Predictably, despite his protestations, Corwin remained an incorrigible radio evangelist. *One World Flight* would be didactic, universalist, and suspiciously open-minded about the socialist alternative to American capitalism.[15]

Little wonder, given the emergent geopolitical realities, that the series was met with a response new to Norman Corwin: mixed reviews. Suddenly, the radiow-right with perfect pitch was out of tune with the zeitgeist. To the ears of many critics, the series seemed tendentious and hopelessly naïve. After listening to the first three shows, *New York Times* media critic Jack Gould rendered a harsh verdict. "*One World Flight* frankly is sympathetic to the Soviet Union and might be construed as either a good or bad editorial, depending upon the individual listener's point of view," wrote Gould. "The broadmindedness of CBS on political issues would seem unassailable in this case." By then, the last thing CBS wanted to be lauded for was its broadmindedness in regard to pro-Soviet editorials aired over the network. Gould was no flag-waving red-baiter—he would be a strong voice against the blacklist and HUAC/McCarthyism throughout the Cold War—but that did not mean he had any patience for the gullibility of the fellow traveler.[16]

Broadcast on a sustaining basis (that is, without a commercial sponsor, as a kind of loss leader, sometimes with hopes that a respectable following would ultimately lure a sponsor), *One World Flight* was saddled with a lethal time slot: Tuesdays at 10:00 P.M., opposite the ratings powerhouse Bob Hope on NBC. Corwin's liberal fan base groused that CBS was setting him up for a fall, to which a CBS executive countergroused: "We gave Corwin carte blanche, invested lavishly in time, staff, and preparation expenses. We broke our own policy against recording [that is, prerecorded content] in order to facilitate a good show. All this adds up to a considerable outlay and a first-class gesture to socially conscious broadcasting." *Variety*'s report on the CBS-Corwin contretemps concluded with a gloomy forecast of Corwin's future in the company that had for so long coddled him: "CBS, after years of 'showcasing' Corwin as its top concession to liberalism now finds itself stuck with him—and wishes it wasn't."[17] Few concessions to liberalism were to be made that year, either at CBS or on Capitol Hill.

Nineteen forty-seven was in fact the tipping point year, the year the nascent Cold War came to, or was declared on, American entertainment. In May 1947 a subcommittee of the House Committee on Un-American Activities, under the gavel-pounding chairmanship of J. Parnell Thomas (R-NJ), journeyed to Hollywood for a set of closed-door hearings that would serve as an on-the-road tryout for the major production slated to premiere in Washington later that year. Government watchdogs—from the FBI and Capitol Hill—were now listening to radio and watching movies, antennae alert for any whisper of Communist rhetoric.

Even before the HUAC subcommittee hearings, by way of backhanded tribute, Corwin was being targeted by anti-Communist investigators. In April 1947, a headline in *Variety* foretold the troubles to come: "Probers Move In on Radio; Seek Corwin Scripts." The previous week HUAC had subpoenaed all thirteen of the scripts from Corwin's *One World Flight* series. "In the past, the committee had requested scripts of news commentators but this marks the first time in the current and as yet unsuccessful drive to pin the Red rap on showbiz personalities that a network dramatic show has come under the D.C. probers' o.o. [once over]," the trade paper observed.[18] CBS meekly forked over the scripts.

Throughout the summer and fall of 1947, the entertainment industry braced for the upcoming HUAC hearings in Washington. However, even as Hollywood awaited its date on Capitol Hill, a group of artists from the studios and networks was galvanized into action. Outraged at the accusations, they formed a committee of their own. If the idea for its name was not first proposed by Corwin, it was certainly Corwinesque in temper: the Committee for the First Amendment.

As with so much else in blacklist history, memories diverge on the origins of the group. When and where the idea was first hatched is hazy—some say over a table at Lucey's Restaurant, the popular star hangout across from Paramount Pictures; others, after a round of frenzied crosstown phone calls. Even the makeup of the principal instigators is disputed. In *Hollywood on Trial,* the first book on the HUAC hearings, published in 1948, screenwriter Gordon Kahn credits directors William Wyler and John Huston, screenwriter Philip Dunne, and actor Alexander Knox with the idea for the group.[19] Huston, who should know, remembered it differently: "The original founders were William Wyler, Philip Dunne, Norman Corwin, Billy Wilder, and myself," Huston stated in April 1948, when memories were still fresh. "We five collaborated on every written line, I believe, from the original manifesto to the last paid advertisement appearing in the Trade papers." Huston also credited his four colleagues and himself with concocting the two highest-profile actions taken by the committee: "We were also entirely responsible for the trip to Washington, and for the various radio programs."[20] For his part, Corwin never claimed to be a principal organizer and said he took his cues from Huston.[21]

Once the idea for an anti-HUAC committee circulated around Hollywood, a cast of glamorous volunteers eagerly signed on: first numbering in the dozens and soon in the hundreds, with the original membership roster put at 135. A steering committee was formed, comprising Huston, Wyler, Dunne, actor Shepperd Strudwick, and talent agent M. C. Levee. Colin Miller, an assistant to Charles Einfield, president of Enterprise Films, brought in his entire staff to handle publicity for the committee, a crew that included David Hopkins, son of former FDR advisor Harry Hopkins.[22] Restaurateur David Chasen lent his landmark eatery as an informal command center; scores of people met at Chasen's every day to plot strategy, with the likes of Ava Gardner pouring coffee. Sam Jaffe, the prominent talent agent, opened his office to Corwin to write scripts for the two radio shows planned for coast-to-coast broadcast.[23] As remembered by the original members, the pitch-in, can-do spirit of the committee partook of the let's-put-on-a-show spontaneity of a vintage MGM musical.

Corwin did not need to wait for a consensus to express his feelings about HUAC. On August 5, 1947, he fired off a letter to Walter Davenport, associate editor of *Collier's Magazine*, to take issue with an article Davenport had written on the HUAC investigation. The editor had wondered why, if certain stars and artists were not Reds, they should "earn such dubious distinction" as to be so charged by a congressional body. Corwin was having none of it. "It is my considered conviction that the Un-American Activities Committee is the single most dangerous force in America today—more so than sporadic Red or Fascist individuals or groups who are at least obliged to operate without congressional immunity," he wrote. "To be called a Red by this committee is usually less ground for suspicion of subversive activity than it is a tribute to the steadfastness and effectiveness of one's fight for democratic principles."[24]

Corwin expressed similar sentiments for the public record. He told the *Hollywood Citizen's News* that he resented not being subpoenaed by HUAC, that the forthcoming hearings were nothing but a publicity stunt. "The Committee's attack on Hollywood . . . is designed to scare the hell out of the industry," Corwin said. Its real purpose was to intimidate producers and thereby exert "thought control" over the content of Hollywood films. HUAC, he sneered, was "a jackal feeding on civil liberties."[25]

As the Hollywood committee coalesced, the Washington committee finally announced a firm starting date for the hearings and initiated the necessary preliminaries. On September 23, HUAC began sending out subpoenas to witnesses—forty-three in all. Some of the chosen were willing enough to testify, being in tune with, or at least pretending to be in tune with, HUAC's goals. Nineteen others were not so friendly, indeed outright hostile, an attitude that soon earned them the sobriquet "the Unfriendly Nineteen."

With the date for the start of the hearings nearing, the Committee for the First Amendment (CFA) formulated a precision game plan: its overruling strategy was to oppose HUAC while not getting too cozy with the Unfriendly Nineteen. Wyler was particularly adamant that the CFA not be vulnerable to the charge that it was a Communist front group, rightly suspecting that most of the Unfriendly Nineteen were dutiful members of the Communist Party USA. Huston, Wyler, et al. sought to walk a fine line: to oppose HUAC without embracing the Communists, who also opposed HUAC. Though the Committee for the First Amendment and the Unfriendly Nineteen shared a common enemy, they were not comrades in arms.

Corwin boldly undercut the strategy by refusing to keep the Unfriendly Nineteen at arm's length. On October 16, 1947, the week before the Thomas committee hearings, he spoke at a mass meeting held at the Shrine Auditorium in Los Angeles and sponsored by the Progressive Citizens of America. Eighteen of the subpoenaed unfriendlies also spoke. The assembly passed a resolution addressed to Speaker of the House Joseph W. Martin, Jr. (R-MA) calling for the abolition of the House Committee on Un-American Activities "where there still remains the freedom to abolish it."[26]

Speaker Martin did not heed the demand. From October 20 to October 30, 1947, HUAC held the first of its soon-to-be notorious hearings into alleged Communist subversion in the entertainment industry. Unfolding under the klieg lights of five commercial newsreels and before the radio microphones of the national networks, it set the pace for all the great political-media sensations of the postwar era. In the end, thirty-nine witnesses would be called. Of the original nineteen unfriendlies, the Thomas Committee called only eleven. All except German playwright Bertolt Brecht refused to answer the committee's key question: "Are you now or have you ever been a member of the Communist party?"* The ten unfriendlies stood on their First, not Fifth, Amendment rights: that is, they refused to answer on the grounds that the question violated their rights of freedom of expression granted under the First Amendment to the U.S. Constitution, not the right against self-incrimination enshrined in the Fifth.

Infuriated at the recalcitrance and—in the cases of screenwriters John Howard Lawson and Albert Maltz—vituperative defiance of the Ten, HUAC charged them with contempt of Congress, which in due course was voted on and affirmed by the full House of Representatives. The Unfriendly Ten—soon to be called the Hollywood Ten, although at the time Hollywood wanted no part of them—would eventually be tried, convicted, and sent to prison for six months to a year.

Meanwhile, the Committee for the First Amendment was plotting two distinct kinds of airborne assaults. On the afternoon of Sunday, October 26, the day before the second week of hearings was to resume, twenty-six members of the committee arrived in Washington by chartered plane to attend and protest the hearings. Fronted by Humphrey Bogart, the group held press conferences, lobbied sympathetic congressmen, and petitioned Speaker Martin to terminate the investigation. Schmoozing with the starstruck Washington press corps, the celebrities did their best to siphon publicity away from Thomas's show.

---

* In homage to the preinflationary stakes of the radio quiz show, the inquiry was dubbed "the $64 question." In 1955, the ante would be upped exponentially in the age of television with the broadcast of *The $64,000 Question.*

Corwin was not on board the plane, but he was fully on board with the agenda. Appropriately, his signature contribution came on home turf: wrangling and writing two radio shows, each titled *Hollywood Fights Back!* Corwin was showrunner for the Los Angeles side of the broadcasts, and CBS radio producer William N. Robson, for the New York end. "I did not initiate the program but was approached by Huston or Wyler, or both, to help assemble it," Corwin recalled in 1987. "My contribution was not a terribly creative one. It was largely that of helping to produce it and guiding it to the microphone."[27] That estimation seems unduly modest: both shows bear all the imprints of Corwin's ethereal touch: clarion rhetoric, orchestral bombast, and a choir of voices speaking in the many accents of the common man—or, in this case, the Hollywood star.

Broadcast over ABC at 4:30 P.M. on two successive Sundays, the first on October 26, after the first week of hearings, and the second on November 2, after the hearings had suddenly adjourned the previous Thursday, the shows aired the goals and gripes of the CFA to a nationwide listening audience. One after the other, an array of show business stars, directors, and playwrights, reinforced by four United States senators, spoke for a total of thirty minutes. The direct-address orations asserted the American fidelity to freedom of expression and bewailed the threat to constitutional democracy posed by HUAC's techniques.

Besides his production skills and prose, Corwin added his voice to the first program, a testament to his marquee status alongside such heavyweights as Judy Garland, Gene Kelly, Danny Kaye, and Frank Sinatra. His appeal was inserted between that of actress Paulette Goddard and a soldier who was already a household name, if not yet a Hollywood star:

> This is Norman Corwin. Whenever an investigator in this country challenges a man's rights to think his own thoughts, he is discrediting every fighting veteran of World War II. For, among other things, that war was fought to get rid of fear and intimidation.
>
> Here now is one of the famous veterans of that war, America's most decorated soldier—Audie Murphy.

Murphy obliged with a ringing endorsement of the creed of committee:

> You know during the war every guy in uniform dreamed of the day when he could stop squeezing triggers and come home. You get so fed up on fighting that you never want to do it again. There's one kind of fighting that has to go on always. You can't ever take a furlough from this fight to preserve human liberty. I think the methods used by the Thomas-Rankin committee are a challenge to those liberties and I think we should use every fair and constitutional means to fight those methods.

The second show was of a kind, though far more upbeat: Chairman Thomas had ended the hearings a day early and the CFA was not shy about taking credit for the sudden adjournment. The moment marked the giddy summit of optimism for opponents of HUAC: Chairman Thomas and his henchmen, they felt, were on the run.

For either show, Corwin sought, but could not nab, Brooklyn Dodgers manager Branch Rickey and the most famous name in baseball that year, Jackie Robinson, who the previous April had just broken the color barrier to become the first African American player in major league baseball. Corwin had even prepared a suitably metaphoric script for Robinson:

> My name is Jackie Robinson. I'm a ball player. All of us think of baseball as the great American game. You get your chance at bat and then you play in the field. Well, that's the way it should be even in law. That's the way the Constitution says it's got to be. . . . But here in Washington it seems to be all hitting and no fielding. If there's something to be gained from calling a man names and not letting him ask you how come, or wherefore, or even answer back. . . . Well, it's a mighty new way of playing the game to me. I hope it doesn't catch on.[28]

Decades later, Corwin reflected on his role in the shows. "What we did was to get as much as we could from the participants, to find out exactly how they felt and allow them to make their own statements," he recalled. "Where they felt they might like some help in the writing of it—the rounding and polishing of what they had done—I, among others, contributed. William Robson was also a part of that." All in all, he felt the two radio blasts at HUAC were "a striking pair of programs, very powerful, and which I hope one day will be recognized as an important document of that period. It was probably the only time that the embattled community in Hollywood *did* fight back."[29]

Though some in Hollywood did indeed fight back, the counteroffensive against HUAC and the blacklist was a losing battle. On November 25, 1947, Motion Picture Association of America president Eric Johnston emerged from a meeting with the major studio executives at the Waldorf-Astoria hotel in New York to make a momentous announcement. An aide handed out press releases to waiting reporters, and Johnston himself reiterated the crucial parts of the policy before the radio microphones and newsreel cameras. "Members of the Association of Motion Picture Producers deplore the action of the 10 Hollywood men who have been cited for contempt by the House of Representatives" began the statement. But the association would not just deplore, it would act:

> We will forthwith discharge or suspend without compensation those in our employ, and we will not re-employ any of the 10 until such time as he is acquitted or has purged himself of contempt and declares under oath that he is not a Communist. On the broader issue of alleged subversive and disloyal elements in Hollywood, our members are likewise prepared to take positive action. We will not knowingly employ a Communist or member of any party or group which advocates the overthrow of the government of the United States by force or by any illegal or unconstitutional means.[30]

What soon became known as the Waldorf Statement marked the formal implementation of the blacklist in Hollywood.

Nonetheless, despite the near-universal opprobrium directed at the Hollywood Ten and the other pariahs, Corwin remained staunchly committed to their cause. In December 1947, in an essay in a special issue of the *Screen Writer*, the house organ of the besieged Screen Writers Guild, he derided the House Committee on Un-American Activities as "a political surrey with a lunatic fringe on top" and blasted "the tyranny of illegal, unconstitutional, and unmoral attempts to impose a thought control of rigid conformity, by means of intimidation, innuendo, and naked slander." The radiowright was proud to share common cause with his kinsmen in a rival medium. "One might ask what an assault on the freedom of the film industry has to do with a radio man," he asked so he might answer. "A threat to the freedom of expression of [director] Lewis Milestone and [actor] Larry Parks [two of the original nineteen 'unfriendlies' subpoenaed by HUAC] is a threat to the freedom of the radio industry, the printed page, and the spoken word, a threat to the rights of conductors and painters." Corwin's essay had a resonant call-back title: "On a Note of Warning."[31]

Corwin also remained committed to the causes of other no less dubious characters, the most famous of whom was running for president of the United States: Henry A. Wallace, FDR's third-term vice president, stood as standard bearer on the third-party ticket of the Progressive Party. In lockstep with the Communist Party USA (CPUSA) line on foreign policy, Wallace was the darling of what remained of the true-believing veterans of the Popular Front. Out of deference to Wallace, the CPUSA did not field a candidate that year, and its ranks supplied many of the foot soldiers for the logistical infrastructure of the campaign. These facts were not secret.

In 1948, Corwin enthusiastically backed Wallace, attending his nominating convention in Philadelphia and coordinating the radio outreach for the quixotic campaign. Corwin's responsibilities included producing spot announcements on radio, record albums of campaign speeches, and musical programs. But though Broadway personalities and folksingers were in abundance at the convention, no motion picture star or brand-name radio talent—Corwin excepted—ventured near the site. Observing "the complete dearth of film talent" in the Wallace campaign, *Variety* blamed the obvious culprit: the HUAC probe.[32]

Wallace lost the election, but Corwin did not lose heart. On Friday, November 26, 1948, he was a proud participant in a "Thanksgiving meeting with the Hollywood Ten," a confab held at the El Patio Theatre. "In Hollywood, let us show our thanks by a return to a free democratic screen with equal opportunity for all" read the ads trumpeting the event. "On Thanksgiving Day, anniversary of the blacklist, we call upon the film industry to revoke the blacklist." Corwin's name came first in a list of artists in solidarity with the Hollywood Ten, at the time of their peak radioactivity.³³ Doubtless Corwin was listed first due to name recognition: no marquee star in film or radio would have dared to be seen in such company.

On June 8, 1949, Corwin's name was again prominently highlighted—though on a list he did not sign voluntarily. At the espionage trial of Judith Coplon, a former analyst for the Department of Justice and an accused Soviet spy, Corwin's name popped up in confidential FBI reports that the government had turned over to Coplon's defense attorney. In open court, and thence into the national media, he read from the documents in which an informant had identified Corwin (along with a slew of other Hollywood activists) as at least a fellow traveler if not an outright Communist. "Although the FBI was not guilty of publicizing the names at the Coplon trial, it was its unverified lists supplied to the State Dept. that put the smear on Fredric March and Florence Eldridge, Edward G. Robinson, Helen Hayes, Dorothy Parker, Norman Corwin, and a flock of others," noted an angry account in *Variety*.

Being typeset next to words like *espionage, spy*, and *Communist* demanded a speedy response. The next day, Corwin vehemently denied the charge in a statement issued to the New York press and in a telephone interview with the *Springfield Daily News*. "I am not a Communist. I am not a fellow traveler," he declared. "But I do have contempt for irresponsible smear lists, whether issued by career crackpots or 'Chicken-Little' agents." Describing Corwin's tone as "crisp and angry," the article quoted him as saying "the full idiocy of the list is indicated by one detail concerning Fredric March and the Communists." Corwin explained that March had simply read a poem entitled "Set Your Clock at U-235"—written by Corwin—at a Madison Square Garden rally on the question of whether the atomic bomb was to be used for peace or war. The poem had earlier appeared on the front page of *New York Herald-Tribune*, an impeccably Republican newspaper. "What, do you suppose could be Communistic or subversive in that?" he demanded.³⁴

Corwin and his compatriots may have found some consolation in the public backlash that greeted the revelations from raw FBI files. President Truman condemned the practice at a press conference, and newspaper editorials weighed in on Hollywood's side. "Suppose the FBI reports had contained the names of several cabinet members, a judge or two, and the senator and congressmen who handle the Justice Department appropriations," speculated an editorial in the *Chicago Sun-Times*. "Can anybody believe that the Department would have chosen, in that case, to disclose the reports? But Fredric March, Dorothy Parker, and Norman Corwin and the others—that was different. The Department didn't mind letting THEM be smeared."³⁵

The drip-drip-drip of Corwin name-dropping continued unabated. On June 8, 1949, the same day his name was read in open court in Washington, DC, the California State Senate Committee on Un-American Activities, basically a Golden State version of HUAC, chaired by state senator Jack B. Tenney (R-Los Angeles), tagged Corwin along with several hundred others as being "typical of the individuals within the various Stalinist orbits." Most people on the list quickly denied the charges—Tenney "must be a sick man or he wouldn't rush to the press to indict good citizens," said Edward G. Robinson—but the *Los Angeles Times* could not reach Corwin for a comment. Its reporter did reach the employer who had once lavished "Columbia's gem" with praise and who now responded with a tepid, carefully worded statement. "Norman Corwin has not been on the Columbia Broadcasting staff for more than a year," said CBS. "However, he has recently been engaged to be heard on July 10. We do not believe that Norman Corwin is a Communist or a fellow traveler."[36] On June 23, a final report by the Tenney committee reiterated its condemnation of twenty-one on the original list—including Corwin—"as persons who had failed to make any attempt to disprove or repudiate activities and affiliations cited in former reports." That is, the accused had not, in the Tenney committee's eyes, been sufficiently vehement in denying the charges. The *Los Angeles Times* contradicted the Tenney committee's claims, noting that Corwin and others of the twenty-one had indeed denied, in print, the charges the day after the initial report was released.[37]

Because HUAC, the Tenney Committee, and FBI files leaked in federal court had named Corwin, it seemed almost inevitable that his name would also surface in testimony before the other major legislative body investigating Communist infiltration in the entertainment industry, the Senate Internal Security Subcommittee chaired by Senator Pat McCarran (D-NV). On December 17, 1949, the McCarran committee released closed-door testimony taken the previous September from a former FBI agent named John J. Huber. Huber cited Corwin in a list of celebrity drawing cards—other familiar names included Charles Chaplin, John Garfield, and Edward G. Robinson—who lured guileless citizens to Communist front groups in order to seduce them into the party. Huber expressed surprise that Corwin would be hired by the United Nations to write scripts because "Corwin was known in the Communist Party as a person who would always follow the party line. He appeared and spoke at many meetings and he never deviated from the party line. His name was connected with the party's biggest and most useful fronts."[38]

Not satisfied with exposing Corwin during the hearings, Senator McCarran took his animus to the floor of the United States Senate. In March 1949, Corwin had been hired as chief of special projects for United Nations Radio, a fact that McCarran believed reflected poorly on the judgment of the world body. "Mr. Corwin is cited as a Communist and subversive by the Attorney General of the United States," McCarran asserted. "Mr. Corwin is or has been a member of a long list of Communist-front organizations." Corwin fired back: "McCarran is a political mad dog who wrote admiringly of his friend, dictator Francisco Franco, a comrade of Hitler and Mussolini."[39]

In the anti-Communist sweepstakes of the Cold War, the competition between investigative bodies was fierce and the overlapping jurisdictions sometimes murky, but all of the major legislative groups (HUAC, the Tenney committee, the McCarran committee) and the most prominent executive branch agency (the FBI) managed to single out Norman Corwin as a person of dubious loyalty. However, for a worker in the broadcasting trade, the most damning forum to have one's name boldfaced in was the magnum opus of a civilian outfit named American Business Consultants. Their business was blacklisting.

On June 22, 1950, along with 150 other artists in the broadcasting industry, Corwin's name was listed in *Red Channels: A Report on Communist Influence in Radio and Television*, the first official guidebook to alleged subversives in the two broadcast media. An all-too-convenient index culled from anti-Communist newsletters and its own primary research, *Red Channels* was a compendium that codified the names of the politically suspect—men and women who had signed too many petitions, spoken at too many rallies, or written too many checks to too many left-of-center causes. Whereas the MPAA's Waldorf Statement in 1947 was the official starting gun for the motion picture blacklist, the publication of *Red Channels* was the red-letter day for the blacklist in radio and television. Most of the names had been bandied about for years—uttered in HUAC testimony or dropped by right-wing columnists—but by putting them in a bound volume, alphabetically listed, with activities enumerated, *Red Channels* gave a weight and authority to the accusations and thereby became a convenient go-to sourcebook for sponsors and producers desperate to duck incoming fire from anti-Communist pressure groups. The name of the volume that named so many was itself a piece of brilliant marketing, conjuring images of crimson propaganda wafting through the airwaves.

Red Channels red-tagged Corwin with participation in nine organizations deemed unpatriotic, dating from 1941, when he signed a statement for Russian War Relief, Inc., to 1949, when he participated as sponsor and panel speaker at the Scientific and Cultural Conference for World Peace. The rest of the accusations were of the same stripe: participation in a dinner at the American Russia Institute in 1944, when the United States and the Soviet Union were allies, and membership in the National Council of American-Soviet Friendship in 1946 and 1947, when the two countries were no longer allies. At least one of the organizations *Red Channels* labeled as "espousing Communist causes," and which it cited Corwin for joining, emphatically did not fit the volume's own criteria: the Committee for the First Amendment.[40]

Characteristically, Corwin's counterblast at *Red Channels* was sparked not by his own listing but by the plight of the actress Jean Muir, who was fired from the radio and television serial *The Aldrich Family* due to her listing. "By this time it should be clear to the smearees listed in *Red Channels* and various other shitpiles that the time for action arrived long ago," he wrote NBC announcer Ben Grauer. "The issue is a naked, bold, economic lynching—a blacklisting so black-and-white, if you don't mind the color scheme, that at least the besieged liberal has some ammunition if he cares to fire."[41] Corwin hoped some sort of coordinated legal action could be mounted collectively by the 151 "smearees," but nothing ever came of it.

In 1951, Corwin's name came up—again—during a second round of HUAC investigations into Communist influence in American entertainment. On March 8, 1951, the committee, now chaired by John S. Wood (D-GA), interrogated Stalinist critic V. J. Jerome, chairman of the National Cultural Commission of the CPUSA. A dedicated party-liner working the media beat for the *New Masses* and the *Daily Worker*, Jerome had allegedly been responsible for setting up Communist cells in Hollywood in 1936–1937. Jerome refused to answer most of the committee's questions on grounds of self-incrimination, but at one point he was asked whether as "cultural commissar" he had overseen the establishment of Communist cells in radio and television.

"Wasn't Norman Corwin directed to infiltrate and form Communist Party cells in radio?"

"I have no knowledge of that," Jerome replied. The answer was not an outright denial, and the charge hung in the air.[42]

On April 1, 1952, in a closed-door session of the McCarran committee, Corwin's name surfaced yet again during the reluctant testimony of radio writer Millard Lampell. A prolific author of novels, song lyrics, radio scripts, and screenplays, Lampell had been hauled before the subcommittee to be grilled about his role in alleged Communist infiltration of the Radio Writers Guild. Like Corwin, he had written radio scripts for the United Nations.

Under aggressive interrogation, Lampell stood on his Fifth Amendment rights against self-incrimination. When not refusing to answer outright, he bobbed and weaved around the queries.

"Did you co-author with Norman Corwin a radio show entitled 'Hollywood Ten'? Specifically a show that was not broadcast but that was written in defense of the Hollywood Ten?" he was asked.

"I have no recollection of ever having written any radio broadcast with Norman Corwin that was not broadcast," replied Lampell, a cagey answer that was not an admission, a denial, or a refusal to answer on grounds of self-incrimination.[43]

Throughout the late 1940s and early 1950s, during the most oppressive years of the blacklist, Norman Corwin's name was dropped in all the wrong places—by anti-Communist investigative committees in both houses of Congress, in the like-minded Tenney committee in California, in federal court in leaked FBI documents, and in the scarlet pages of *Red Channels*. All the accusations were followed avidly by the national press.

Finally, on February 19, 1953, Corwin decided to confront face to face one of the main sources of many of his problems. Having heard from friends that he was under investigation by the FBI, he walked into the Los Angeles Field Office of the

Federal Bureau of Investigation to clear the air and lay his cards on the table. Accompanied by his lawyer, Corwin came armed with an extensive set of documents—prepared at the behest not of the FBI but of MGM, which had required a background check before it would hire him as a screenwriter. The FBI had indeed been investigating him due to his sensitive position overseeing radio programs for the United Nations.

According to Corwin's FBI file—a cache of memoranda, official reports, and clippings running 519 pages—Corwin asked that the agency make photostatic copies of his MGM material. One of the documents was an extensive list of all the organizations he had lent his name to. "This document runs seven pages in length and includes some two hundred different organizations starting with the American Bible Society and ending with the Maine Methodist Conference," reads the FBI's straight-faced account. Corwin wanted the agency to understand that he lent his name to all kinds of seemingly worthy causes and was never too particular about scrutinizing the agenda of a seemingly upright group. The list did not include any suspect organizations—like the Committee for the First Amendment—but was submitted, said Corwin, "to indicate something of the largess in allowing my name to be used. I did not suspect anything about any of these people and it was later that some of these showed up to be under suspicion."

Corwin submitted two other documents that he dubbed Exhibit B, a list of his awards, and Exhibit C, a list of complimentary letters he had received in the course of his career. "[I]f the criterion is to whether man's ideology is disloyal or turning to disloyalty, [then] these exhibits are interesting evidence that a vast area of American life felt entirely to the contrary; it felt that my work was inspiring to a higher loyalty in the sense of the best Americanism; and in its contribution toward the understanding and glorification of American principles and traditions."

At this point in the meeting, Corwin made a declaration that the Hollywood Ten had refused to make to a government official. His lawyer spoke the words for him. "We would like to state, as he has stated under oath, that he, Corwin, has never been a member of the Communist Party or Communist Political Association. He also could not be called a fellow traveler because he differentiated from the Communist Party beginning with the Communist intervention in Finland." Corwin expanded on his deviations from the party line and cited the bad notices his work had received in the *Daily Worker*.

On March 16, 1953, Corwin contacted the FBI again, with some clarifications and expansions. He provided an expanded list of his organizational affiliations, including the "suspect" groups, noting—with ironic understatement—that "one has learned to be cautious about what he sponsors these days, but the necessity was not so apparent then." He declared that he had since ceased to participate in the suspect groups "for I found that they were so purged of liberals as to be ineffective as liberal organizations."

Corwin then delivered an avowal of his beliefs and a recap of his career. Fraught with mounting frustration, the statement is worth quoting at length:

> In the past 15 years I have been a publicity writer, a writer-director-producer for CBS, a movie writer, a free-lance writer, and a part-time member of the staff of the United Nations. In the course of this work, my travels have taken me countless times back and forth between West and East coasts; a hundred times up and down these coasts; thrice to Europe; once around the world. I have produced from 150 to 200 broadcasts, including many all-network and international programs; written several books and scores of articles; delivered perhaps a hundred speeches; received perhaps fifty thousand letters and sent out maybe twenty thousand.

After the list of credentials, Corwin throws down a challenge:

> And out of all this activity, the many broadcasts and speeches and letters, there is not only nothing faintly resembling disloyalty to the United States, but on the contrary there is overwhelming evidence, which I will be glad to produce to authorized parties at any time, that my work has inspired loyalty, not the opposite of it; that my writings have served to strengthen America, not subvert it.

To clinch his case, Corwin appended a list of seven pivotal positions he held in defiance of doctrinal CPUSA policy—including, crucially, his support for Britain and Finland during the period between the Hitler-Stalin Pact of August 1939 and the invasion of Russia by the Nazis in June 1941. Only an authentic liberal, not a party member or fellow traveler, would have held such positions.[44]

For any other artist-activist in the entertainment industry such repeated tarring with the Communist brush would have terminated a career. Corwin always considered himself—in context—to have been luckier than many of the names named alongside him. After all, there are degrees of victimhood and, in any mapping of the real estate of blacklist hell, Corwin resided in the first circle not the lowest depths. In October 1950, responding to an inquiry from the American Civil Liberties Union about his listings in *Red Channels* and the blowback on his career, Corwin took issue with the accuracy of several of the listings ("I am cited as a toastmaster of an American Youth for Democracy dinner in San Francisco on November 11, 1950. I was in New York on that date.") but asserted he suffered no adverse career consequences. "To date, the listing has had no appreciable effect on my work but this, I believe, is because radio stations and personnel, being pretty well familiar with my programs on American and International affairs for ten consecutive years, recognized in my case, as in others, the utter trashiness of Fitzpatrick's *[sic]* slander."† He added an important caveat: "I am under no illusions, however, that were I sponsored by General Foods, this listing might

---

† Corwin misspoke. He meant Theodore C. Kirkpatrick, managing editor of *Counterattack*, the right-wing newsletter that published *Red Channels*.

not have damaged me. It just so happens that I have never been interested in sponsorship."[45]

However, in mitigating the impact of *Red Channels* and similar listings on his career opportunities, Corwin was too naïve. Unbeknownst to him, he had been considered for a job as a screenwriter at RKO in the late 1940s. As was customary, studio head Howard Hughes tasked RKO's Research Department with conducting "quite an extensive inquiry into Corwin's background and activities." The results ended the employment possibility. "According to Hughes," reported a confidential FBI memorandum recounting an interview with the not-yet-reclusive millionaire at the Desert Inn in Las Vegas, where he was residing incognito, "the inquiry uncovered considerable information reflecting that Corwin has in the past been the sponsor, member of, or otherwise associated with numerous organizations which are outright Communist organizations or Communist fronts."[46] Corwin lost more career opportunities than he knew.

In later years, looking back on the era, Corwin considered himself not to have been blacklisted but, in another of the eerie coinages of the age, *graylisted*, a zone where victims were "underworked" but not totally barred from gainful employment. "In my case the economic impact was felt, but it was not grave," Corwin recalled to interviewer Douglas Bell in 1986. "I wrote a book during that period, worked on some films. I did have revenue." Typically, he put the greatest cost in emotional terms. "The main impact was on my spirit. I grieved for America." But though Corwin might grieve, he still earned a living under his own name and worked regularly—though not at the pace of his prime years of bankability. "The blacklist was an iron curtain of the worst kind, impenetrable for most people," Corwin observed, knowing its full force had not descended on him.[47]

Luckily, the workaholic wordsmith who never knew writer's block had other options. Increasingly, Corwin turned to the stage and motion picture work. In 1955, *Variety* described him not quite ironically as "a fugitive from radio."[48] In 1956, when the blacklist was still rigorously enforced in Hollywood, and many of his political soul mates were either unemployable or using pseudonyms, Corwin wrote the screenplay for Vincente Minnelli's prestigious biopic of Vincent van Gogh, *Lust for Life* (1956). The film was released to ecstatic reviews and earned Corwin an Oscar nomination for best adapted screenplay. That same year, by way of comparison, Dalton Trumbo, the most notorious of the Hollywood Ten, was still working under pseudonyms: he could not show up to the Academy Awards ceremony to accept the Oscar for Best Story for *The Brave One* (1956), which he wrote under the moniker "Richard Rich."

In tandem with the blacklist, other cultural forces were working to get Corwin scratched from the radio A-list. By 1947, the shelf life of his Popular Front sympathies had expired: the internationalist outlook, progressive utopianism, and presumption that he was the spokesman for the Little Guy got an increasingly frosty reception as the Cold War settled in. Just as bad, Corwin's distinctive auditory style—which had once sounded so fresh, robust, and inspirational—was beginning to sound tinny and off key. A profile of Corwin, written in April 1947 for the *New Yorker*, was an early warning sign that his golden moments—like those of radio—had already passed. The article marked the first time a radio writer had been accorded the honor of recognition by the flagship magazine of uptown Manhattan literary culture, but it was also a snarky put-down of Corwin's audio oeuvre. Rendered in the form of a vintage Corwin radio play, the profile was more satire than homage, capturing with spot-on accuracy the most pretentious and dated of Corwin's narrative devices and stylistic tics.

In her biography of CBS president William S. Paley, Sally Bedell Smith relates an anecdote that has become emblematic of Corwin's declining fortunes in the postwar radio atmosphere—and the cultural-corporate shift from a New Deal ethos where the airwaves were to be operated for "the public interest, convenience, and necessity" to a business model devoted to unbridled commerce. Corwin and Paley encounter each other while traveling by train from Pasadena to New York. Paley invites Corwin to dinner—those being the days of luxurious transcontinental railway travel—and two discuss the topic they have in common. Paley advises Corwin—advice that strikes Corwin as marching orders from the boss—to write for a broader public, to make certain that most of the 90 million radio families in America have their dial tuned to CBS.

"The handwriting was on the wall, as far as radio was concerned," reflected a rueful Corwin. "It was now spelled out in fresh ink, in Paley's hand.... I knew that to set out with the express aim of 'reaching as many sets as possible' would mean studying to write soap opera, or gags, or programs of towering innocuousness."[49] The poet laureate of the airwaves was temperamentally unable to bend his talent to jingles, schmaltz, and wisecracks.

Like the Hollywood director Frank Capra, who never regained his instinctive bond with the John Doe moviegoers of America after World War II, Corwin was out of synch with his audience—or the needs of a network with its trademark eye now focused on television. Whether Capra-corn or Corwiniana, the postwar world would be less tolerant of progressive opinion and less willing to air programming unlikely to turn a profit. Muted by the blacklist, by commerce, and by changing tastes, perceived as standard bearer for old-time radio technique, out of step in aesthetic style and political temper with the times, Corwin ended his radio days on his own terms, but not, alas, on a note of triumph.

NOTES

1. R. LeRoy Bannerman, *On a Note of Triumph: Norman Corwin and the Golden Years of Radio.* New York: Carol Publishing Group, 1968: 219.

2. Ralph Thompson, "Books of the Times: *Thirteen By Corwin*," *New York Times*, January 29, 1942: 17.
3. Robert Landry, "So This Is Radio," *Variety*, July 26, 1939: 36.
4. John Mason Brown, "Seeing Things: On a Note of Triumph," *Saturday Review*, May 26, 1945: 22.
5. Quoted in Sally Bedell Smith, *In All His Glory: The Life and Times of William S. Paley*. New York: Simon & Schuster, 1990: 268.
6. Lee Lawson, "Review and Comment: Norman Corwin," *New Masses*, June 27, 1944: 24–25.
7. Quoted in Gerd Horten, *Radio Goes to War: The Cultural Politics of Propaganda during World War II*. Berkeley: University of California Press, 2002: 48.
8. Douglas Bell, *An Oral History with Philip Dunne*. Beverly Hills, CA: Academy Foundation Oral History Program, Margaret Herrick Library, Academy of Motion Picture Arts and Sciences, 1991: 230.
9. Rose, "Corwin's V-E Day 'Note of Triumph' Is Hailed As Milestone in Radio," *Variety*, May 16, 1945: 24.
10. "Corwin for Everyone," *Billboard*, May 19, 1945: 4.
11. Terry Teachout, "Norman Corwin, RIP," *Arts Journal* weblog, October 19, 2011. http://www.artsjournal.com/aboutlastnight/2011/10/tt_norman_corwin_rip.html.
12. "Corwin '1-World' Award; Goes to Coast Sunday," *Variety*, February 20, 1946: 28.
13. "Corwin's Projected CBS Series Implements Paley's 'Program Primer,'" *Variety*, November 13, 1946: 24, 34.
14. "Large Crews Race Clock for Preem of Corwin 'One World Flight' Jan. 14," *Variety*, January 1, 1947: 23.
15. Corwin's personal account of the flight can be found in Michael C. Keith and Mary Ann Watson, eds., *One World Flight: The Lost Journal of Radio's Greatest Writer*. New York: Continuum, 2009.
16. Jack Gould, "One World Flight," *New York Times*, February 2, 1947: X11. On the other hand, Jerry Franken in *Billboard* gave the show a warm greeting. "It is a superb example of the great work radio documentaries, in the hands of an outstanding writer, can do," he wrote, a paean to world peace "devoid of arty, phony theatricalism." Jerry Franken, "Superb Corwin Preem Reveals Bigotry, Ignorance Rampant," *Billboard*, January 25, 1947: 8.
17. "CBS Fiddles As Liberals Burn; Network Dissolves 'One World' into Schism of Faith, Hope, and McCarthy," *Variety*, January 29, 1947: 25.
18. "Probers Move In on Radio; Seek Corwin Scripts," *Variety*, April 23, 1947: 23.
19. Gordon Kahn, *Hollywood on Trial: The Story of the Ten Who Were Indicted*. New York: Boni & Gaer, 1948: 135.
20. John Huston to Harry L. Kingman, April 23, 1948. (John Huston papers, Margaret Herrick Library, Academy of Motion Picture Arts and Sciences.)
21. According to blacklist historians Larry Ceplair and Steven Englund, "Dunne, Wyler, and Huston *were* the Committee for the First Amendment." Larry Ceplair and Steven Englund, *The Inquisition in Hollywood: Politics and the Film Community, 1930–1960*. Chicago: University of Illinois Press, 2003 [1979]: 275.
22. "Protest Group to Fly to Capital," *Los Angeles Times*, October 25, 1947: 3.
23. Sam Jaffe was a prominent Hollywood agent who should not be confused with the popular character actor of the same name.
24. A. J. Langguth, ed., *Norman Corwin's Letters*. New York: Barricade Books, 1994: 102–103.
25. "Communist Witnesses to Defy Communist Quiz," *Hollywood Citizen's News*, October 16, 1947, cited in Corwin's FBI file.
26. "Meeting Demands End of House Inquiry Group," *Los Angeles Times*, October 16, 1947: A18.
27. Douglas Bell, *Years of the Electric Ear: Norman Corwin*. New Jersey: Directors Guild of America and Scarecrow Press, 1994: 132.
28. Teletype from Norman Corwin to Jim Beach, October 24, 1947. (Norman Corwin papers, Special Collections, Thousand Oaks Library, Thousand Oaks, CA.)

29. Bell: 132–133.
30. Norman Corwin, "On a Note of Warning," *Screen Writer* (December 1947): 4–6.
31. "Johnston Gives Industry Policy on Commie Jobs," *Daily Variety,* November 26, 1947: 1.
32. "Wallace's 'Cast' Includes Many from Show Biz," *Variety,* July 28, 1948: 2, 20.
33. "Let Us Give Thanks" [advertisement], *Daily Variety,* November 24, 1947: 9.
34. "Norman Corwin Disgusted by Data on Communists," *Springfield Daily News,* June 9, 1949, cited in Norman Corwin's FBI file. Corwin may have spoken to the *Springfield Daily News* for sentimental reasons; in the 1930s, he served a brief stint as a reporter for the *Springfield Republican.*
35. "Robinson, March on FBI Red List," *Daily Variety,* June 9, 1949: 1, 8; "H'wood as 'Red' Scapegoat No Longer Paying Off; Loose Labelling Misfires," *Variety,* June 22, 1949: 1, 23; "Film Figures Deny Being Members of Communist Party," *Daily Variety,* June 9, 1949: 9.
36. "Roll Takes in Many of Prominence," *Los Angeles Times,* June 9, 1949: 1, 20; "Comment of Those Named in Inquiry," *Los Angeles Times,* June 9, 1949: 1, 20, 22.
37. "Tenney Group Report Strikes at 21 Critics," *Los Angeles Times,* June 24, 1949: 19.
38. "Red Sabotage Plot in War Disclosed: Undercover Agent Asserts U.S. Armament Plants Were Targets," *Los Angeles Times,* December 18, 1949: 10.
39. Quoted in Keith and Watson: 203.
40. *Red Channels: The Report of Communist Influence in Radio and Television.* New York: American Business Consultants, 1950: 9, 41–42.
41. Langguth, *Norman Corwin's Letters:* 128–129.
42. Herb Golden, "Jobs Blues for Hollywood Reds," *Variety,* March 14, 1951: 55.
43. "Claim Reds Run Radio Writers Guild; Lyon, Lampell Won't Answer Queries," *Variety,* August 27, 1952: 1, 34. Lampell's April 1, 1952, testimony was released to the public on August 26, 1952.
44. Quotes are from "Statements Made and Documents Furnished by Norman Corwin" in Norman Corwin's FBI file.
45. Norman Corwin to Patrick Murphy Malin, October 25, 1950. (Norman Corwin papers, Special Collections, Thousand Oaks Library, Thousand Oaks, CA.)
46. Office Memorandum, February 27, 1953, from Norman Corwin's FBI file.
47. Quoted in Bell: 131.
48. "MGM's Big Made-with-Words," *Variety,* October 5, 1955: 18.
49. Smith: 267–268.

3

NORMAN CORWIN AND THE BIG SCREEN

Artistic Differences

Mary Ann Watson

Norman Corwin's complicated relationship with the film industry began with his first job as a cub reporter at the *Greenfield Recorder*, a small-town daily in Greenfield, Massachusetts. In 1929, in addition to his regular duties, he took on another role. "I became a film critic at the age of nineteen and ran a column headed 'Seeing Things in the Dark,'" he recalled. "It was pretty cheeky of a nineteen-year-old to sit in judgment of movies from Hollywood. After filing two or three of my reviews that were extremely negative, the proprietor of the local movie house made it known that I was persona non grata as a freebie, and that henceforth the paper would have to pay for my seat, which they did."[1]

Corwin's next link to the silver screen came from the other side. In 1936, through the intercession of his big brother Emil, who worked in the publicity department of the NBC radio network, Norman was hired by Twentieth Century-Fox Films to work in public relations. It was not his dream job, but he was good at it. Each week Corwin prepared fifteen minutes worth of promotional copy that was distributed to radio stations throughout the country. Local on-air personalities would read the material plugging Twentieth Century-Fox movies and their stars.

In the midst of the Great Depression, Americans were flocking to the movies to escape reality for a while. Corwin made sure they knew about the latest and greatest of Fox's biggest celebrities, including Shirley Temple, Bill "Bojangles" Robinson, Don Ameche, Tyrone Power, and Sonja Henie. Another aspect of Corwin's $50-per-week position was representing the studio when stars, producers, and directors arrived in New York on transoceanic liners. Corwin would meet them and then accompany them by taxi to their hotels.

"Corwin's job thrust him more and more into refined circles," writes his biographer LeRoy Bannerman. "New York offered sophisticated surroundings that challenged Corwin's New England conservatism."² Decades later Corwin reminisced: "The boon of free meals was a new experience, a luxury that seemed to me at the time to be verging on decadence because I ate in posh restaurants that I would not have patronized on my own power. It was no longer chow at the hash joint or dinner at the diner. It was eating—eating underscored." Norman thought it was wonderful to get fed and paid to watch movies, but he understood that PR was "not one of man's grander enterprises."³

While Corwin was working for the studio, he was also working on his own ideas for a poetry program for radio. The young man's artistic identity was emerging. It had experimentalism at its core. At the age when the need to make sense of life grows strong, Corwin developed what novelist Joseph Conrad called "the inward voice that decides."⁴

Corwin pitched the *Poetic License* series to station WQXR. They could not pay him but offered airtime in the world's most important city of possibilities. Norman's innovations with the spoken word were welcomed and—again with Emil's intercession—soon caught the notice of someone with clout. Emil's friend and NBC colleague Ted Church knew Kitty Crane, secretary to William B. Lewis, the vice president of programming at CBS. She prevailed upon her boss to listen to an episode of *Poetic License*. He was impressed.

On April 12, 1938, Norman wrote to his parents: "Dear Ma and Pa: This is one of the last letters I'll be writing on this stationery, because this very afternoon I signed a contract with the Columbia Broadcasting System to serve as a director of dramatic programs. My salary is $125 a week, with automatic raises of $25 a year if my contract options are renewed at the end of each year. . . . I'm modifying my enthusiasm until I have a chance to learn the ropes at CBS and get the feel of things."⁵

A stipulation of Corwin's employment was that the network-owned talent agency, Columbia Management, represent him for outside work, with a 20 percent share of his earnings. It wasn't until December 1939 that Norman learned the agency was soliciting assignments for him in feature films. "While I appreciate all that you are attempting to do in my behalf," he wrote in a missive of protest,

> I would appreciate consultation before any letters are sent out to film companies regarding my availability to work in pictures. The truth of the matter is that I am not now seeking picture work and do not want to be represented as doing so. I would infinitely prefer to wait until some company is attracted to the prospect of taking me on for certain potentialities which they may recognize out of my radio work. . . . Thus your letters about me to [David O.] Selznick and RKO, while very generous in their intent, are a source of potential embarrassment to me. I hope no other letters of a similar nature have gone to other studios.⁶

The following year Corwin's fame and artistic accomplishments in radio continued to rise. His seminal efforts for *Columbia Workshop* were a tour de force. This included Corwin's adaptation of Stephen Vincent Benét's *John Brown's Body*, which featured the actor Charles Laughton. A close friendship grew between the two men. When Laughton returned to the West Coast, he prevailed upon RKO producer Erich Pommer to hire Corwin to adapt to the screen a recently acquired property, the play *Two on an Island* by Elmer Rice.

Corwin spent three months, from late June to late September 1940 in Los Angeles, staying in the guesthouse at the Brentwood home of Charles Laughton and his wife, actress Elsa Lanchester. While in California, Corwin continued to write scripts for the CBS radio series *Forecast*, which was broadcast from Los Angeles. His correspondence from the time reveals his mixed feelings about working in feature films.

After two weeks, he wrote to his parents, "The work here is leisurely compared to the pace of radio. . . . It's the difference between doing a show every week and working on maybe two or three pictures a year."[7] In mid-July Corwin wrote to the radio critic of the *New York World-Telegram*, "The work out here is tremendously absorbing. . . . I miss the impact of people and the immediacy of interpretation which comes out of directing (radio) but, on the other hand, I am again tapping those inward circuits of expression which, as you well know, all writing is based on."[8]

By mid-August he had made a decision, which he shared with his parents, "About myself and Hollywood: I have turned down a long-term offer for the second time. For good and sufficient reasons. I may in the future turn down salaries three or four times my radio salary to achieve what I believe in the end will profit me both artistically and economically."[9]

Corwin cheerfully described a typical workday to his father: "Up at eight, breakfast in the garden, a twelve-mile drive to work, arriving in the office about 10. I open mail, do a little work on the script, go to lunch on the studio lot," he reported. "After lunch there may be a conference with the producer. We discuss points raised in the script, go over material, outline story and character development. . . . We are frank with each other and sometimes will argue a single point for a half-hour. We find that we're 50 percent right usually and never have the slightest unpleasantness."[10] But the truth was that Corwin didn't enjoy the committee nature of movie-making. "It was hard to endure Hollywood's assembly line scrutiny," Bannerman wrote, "having experienced the freedom and individual control of radio."[11]

While Corwin was in Hollywood justifying his artistic choices, William B. Lewis was reminding him that CBS treasured his individual vision. He wanted to know what would make the writer-producer-director happy. Corwin, discouraged with the "soft and easy money" zeitgeist of the movie business, told Lewis precisely what he wanted: "I would be interested in any good 26-week setup, even it paid less than movie dividends, providing I could do a show that would make us all happy and self-respecting rather than rich. I mean a whopper of a prestige show, in which I might be given resources and a free hand to write and produce the best goddam show on any air. That sir, would be worth more to me than the Hollywood lucre which, mind you, feel very nice on the inner lining of the pocket."[12] They had a deal.

The *Twenty-Six by Corwin* series fulfilled all the high expectations. The artistic range of the plays astonished critics. Literary critic Clifton Fadiman claimed that Corwin "writes as if he's several men."[13] But Corwin did much more than write the scripts for his radio productions. He was the producer, the director, the midwife—an architect of the air, inventing and refining techniques of audio storytelling.

During the war years, the radio industry grew in strength and prominence and helped foster a national spirit of cooperation. Patriotic themes permeated the airwaves, and so did the works of Norman Corwin. His themes of the magnificence of the common man and woman touched a responsive chord in the American people.

Between 1941, with *We Hold These Truths*, and 1945, with *On a Note of Triumph*, Corwin enjoyed unprecedented free rein over his work. His programs were offered to all CBS affiliate stations on a sustaining basis, meaning that in exchange for carrying all the network's sponsored programming, they were given the sustaining broadcasts free of charge. So, Corwin could create without commercial interference or the requirement to clear his ideas with his employer. It was a rare set of circumstances that suited his personality and artistic temperament. Reflecting on his career in his eighth decade, Corwin said. "Sure, in a collaborative medium many opinions and judgments come into play, but ultimately it comes down to the imprint of a single person with authority. When it doesn't, the results show. It becomes a mess. For good or ill, there's something to be said for the auteur."[14]

We Hold These Truths, a reflection on the 150th anniversary of the ratification of the American Bill of Rights, aired on all four radio networks (NBC red and blue, CBS, and Mutual) on December 15, 1941, just a week after the Japanese attack on Pearl Harbor. The broadcast, which featured a stellar cast, including Jimmy Stewart, Orson Welles, Lionel Barrymore, and President Franklin Delano Roosevelt, reached the largest audience ever assembled for a radio drama. Corwin's words, celebrating and elucidating freedom, stiffened the resolve of a country being asked to sacrifice so much to preserve it.

The following afternoon, December 16, 1941, Corwin and his agent Nat Wolff kept an appointment with the head of production at Metro-Goldwyn-Mayer, Dore Schary. Motion pictures were knocking again. The triumph of the night before raised the financial stakes for Schary to lure the radio writer into film. So MGM offered a seven-year contract at twice his original offer, which would nearly quadruple the amount Corwin was making at CBS. "It was tempting," wrote Bannerman, "but Corwin weighed the artistic restraints which he knew were inevitable in the motion picture industry. He chose to remain in radio."[15] The CBS brass was relieved.

During the time between *We Hold These Truths* and *On a Note of Triumph*, Corwin experienced disappointments with Hollywood. RKO scrapped the *Two on an Island* project that he had worked on with Erich Pommer. Also, Columbia Pictures optioned Corwin's radio play *My Client Curley*, based on a whimsical story by Lucille Fletcher about a singing and dancing caterpillar. Corwin did not write the screenplay, but he was handsomely paid for a one-day script conference in Hollywood. When the resulting feature-film adaptation *Once Upon a Time*, starring Cary Grant and Janet Blair, opened in 1944, however, Corwin discovered not much of his consultation was put to use.

"Let me say this about *Once Upon a Time*," Corwin remembered.

> That picture opened in Radio City Music Hall, and I believe it had the shortest run of any picture to ever play that house. I met Grant at a dinner party one night about a year later. He did everything charmingly. He charmingly and sheepishly apologized for that picture. It violated every instinct that I had about my own script. Instead of being a nebbish agent, as in my original, Cary played a producer whom we meet in black tie. This completely torpedoes the original premise.... Also the kid was miscast. He was a whining kid, completely unlike the boy I conceived for *My Client Curley*, who was charming.... Nothing was right.[16]

Working the aural medium, Corwin contributed mightily to the force of radio as a weapon in the arsenal of democracy with series such as *This Is War!*; *An American in England*, with Edward R. Murrow; and *Passport for Adams*, starring Robert Young as a small-town newspaper editor on a goodwill mission to countries favoring the Allied cause. Several plays in the 1944 *Columbia Presents Corwin* series also rallied the war effort, including *Untitled*, a poignant story of young soldier killed in combat.

Toward the end of 1944, with an Allied victory in Europe apparently assured, CBS asked Corwin to prepare a program celebrating the anticipated event. On May 8, 1945, just after the collapse of Germany, CBS aired *On a Note of Triumph*, an epic aural mosaic. This program is considered to be the climax of the luminous period in the history of radio when writing of high merit, produced with consummate skill, was nurtured—as well as protected from commercial interference.

After the broadcast, phone calls and letters of praise flooded the network, including a letter from Carl Sandburg calling *On a Note of Triumph* "one of the all-time great American poems."[17] The script was released by Simon & Schuster in book form and sold out so quickly that the publisher rushed a second printing the following week.

Corwin enjoyed the many honors showered upon him in the months following the end of the war. A particularly significant one was reported in *Time* magazine in 1946: "Norman Corwin, radio's 35-year-old wonder-boy enjoyed a week befitting his prestige. He won the Wendell Willkie Award—a trip around the world sponsored by the Freedom House and the Common Council for American Unity.

Skipping lightly over all other U.S. writers and artists, the organization thought Corwin's *On a Note of Triumph* was the best contribution to the concept of One World in the field of mass communication."[18]

The award was created as a living tribute by the friends of Wendell Willkie after his death from a heart attack in 1944 at the age of 52. President Roosevelt named Willkie, his Republican opponent in 1940, to serve as his personal ambassador at large in 1942. Willkie's mission was to go around the world, still in the throes of war, to meet with the Allies. Corwin accepted the Willkie Award on one condition: that it would be a working trip for CBS.

Thomas Doherty writes compellingly in this anthology of the significance and political aftermath of the *One World Flight* documentary series. In his chapter "Norman Corwin and the Blacklist," Doherty also chronicles Corwin's brave, principled involvement in the anti-HUAC movement and the resulting *Hollywood Fights Back!* radio programs. Corwin's devotion to the First Amendment trumped any of his misgivings about the shortcomings of the movie business.

Just weeks after the two broadcasts of *Hollywood Fights Back!* aired, *Variety* reported that Corwin had been granted a leave of absence from CBS to work on outside projects, which fueled speculation that Corwin would be leaving radio to work in films. The rumor proved true. In November 1947, Corwin began work on the scenario for a significant motion picture, a screenplay based on Robert Penn Warren's novel *All the King's Men* about a Southern demagogue.

It was not a good experience, though, for someone who was still a neophyte writing for the big screen and unaccustomed to being told he needed help. When the film's producer, Robert Rossen, decided he should collaborate with Corwin on the final script, Corwin's attorney objected and Corwin left the project. He wrote to a friend: "I have just finished a screenplay after grappling with its problems for four months, and I am glad to be rid of it. I find the film processes so pitted with assembly line psychology and commercial considerations that the joy of creation is reduced to a quality of routine."[19]

The film, with Rossen's script, became a box office hit and won three Academy Awards, including Best Picture of 1948. In the early 1990s, when Corwin was interviewed for the Directors Guild, he talked about the advice he received from the lawyer:

> He was a counselor in my life at that time, a man for whom I had a great deal of respect and affection. He was a very important man, on the board of directors at Twentieth Century-Fox ... at one time business manager for Salvador Dali. ... I listened to him when I should have listened to my better sense. He took it strictly from a public relations aspect. His argument was that I was known as my own man—I was my own writer-director-producer. I had never written collaboration in my life, so to acknowledge that I needed a collaborator on this script would be to show a certain weakness. I regret that I listened to him.[20]

Film critic Leonard Maltin also asked about Corwin's decision to leave *All The King's Men*. "I struck out on that," Corwin said without hesitation. "I failed so miserably that I did not contest for one minute Bob Rossen's decision. I have no defense; sometimes we screw up and I just screwed up."[21]

By the time Corwin's name appeared in *Red Channels* in June 1950, television was well into eclipsing radio as the dominant medium in American life, but TV and its corporate parentage held little appeal for Corwin. With his network radio career essentially ended, Corwin and his wife Kate had settled in Los Angeles, and he devoted himself to writing screenplays. Three scripts he was commissioned to write, though, never were produced because of problems with financial backing.

Corwin's frustration and skepticism about the film industry at the time was evident when he wrote to CBS producer Davidson Taylor and his wife, Mary Elizabeth, in the spring of 1948: "Last week I was admitted to the presence of God, in the form of an interview with L. B. Mayer. He offered me *Raintree County* to adapt for the screen—Metro's most expensive current property—along with the flattering unction that I was the only man in America who could do it. I then went home and read the book—all 1,060 pages of it.... I'm pretty certain I will turn the offer down. Not because the book is not good and juicy and could make fine movie, but because I am tired of working for indecisive producers, who blow hot and cold and change their whores in midstream."[22]

Corwin's first sole feature-film writing credit was for the 1951 RKO release *The Blue Veil*. It was an adaptation of a French story by François Campaux of a woman unable to have children who took the "veil" of a nurse and governess to other people's progeny. It starred Corwin's good friend Charles Laughton and Jane Wyman, who won the Golden Globe Award for Best Actress and received an Academy Award nomination for her performance.

Corwin had been hired to rewrite an unacceptable screenplay. He explained in a letter to friend that the original script of *The Blue Veil* was "a basket case which was delivered to me as a patient in an auto accident might have been rushed to an emergency ward." "I saved it from disaster for two reasons," he continued, "because I liked the producers as friends and because I needed the money. I learned something from the picture too; and it was no disgrace to anybody involved."[23] The *New York Times* review by Bosley Crowther, however, was unkind to *The Blue Veil*, calling it "a whoppingly banal tear jerker." Corwin's scenario offered, he wrote, "little in the way of wit, grit or, for that matter, real substance."[24]

In 1952, Corwin rewrote the screenplay *Scandal at Scourie*, a 1953 MGM release. The initial story idea came from a magazine article entitled "My Mother and Mrs. McChesney" that told the true story of the adoption of a Catholic orphan by a Protestant couple who endured bigotry in their Protestant rural community in eastern Canada. Again, Corwin was not the original writer, but, in his words, he was given "a crippled script, maimed by two professional veteran screenwriters."[25]

Scandal at Scourie was the last of eight feature films that starred the powerhouse Hollywood duo of Greer Garson and Walter Pidgeon. Yet the film disappointed at the box office, due in part to MGM's spiritless promotion. "I recall that the picture opened in New York City at the Little Carnegie. That will give you some idea," Corwin said. "The Little Carnegie was a theatre on 57th Street, that, I think, seated about 300 people. So something was afoot there. That was strange.... Greer and Metro had a falling out around that time, and the studio, in an expression of impatience with her, decided it would not get behind the picture.... Curious thing, cutting off one's nose to spite one's face."[26]

Corwin had little patience for Hollywood infighting, but his next project would be more placid. It began with a call from John Houseman to take a meeting about a picture that Vincente Minnelli would direct. Houseman, like Corwin, also joined CBS in 1938. He was a protégé of Orson Welles on *The Mercury Theatre on the Air*. Corwin was told that MGM had a ten-year option on *Lust for Life*, Irving Stone's 1934 novelized biography of Vincent van Gogh, which was nearing its end in 1955.

"We needed a writer with the skill to select and arrange the words and events of Vincent's life with a sense of structure and poetry," wrote Houseman in his memoir *Unfinished Business*. "I called Norman Corwin, who had done much of this kind of writing during the great days of radio. He was familiar with the material and, within a few weeks, working twelve hours a day, we were able to present the studio with a shooting script."[27]

Although the book had been rejected by seventeen publishers before Longmans, Green & Company accepted it, *Lust for Life* became an immediate bestseller. Stone termed his work "bio-history." His method involved immersing himself in the native environment of his subject and exhaustively researching all the primary source materials he could use as the basis to create dialogue, both reconstructed and imagined. The result was not true history but interpretation in novel form.

The book popularized the work of van Gogh with the American public. Then a spectacular retrospective on van Gogh's oeuvre at the Metropolitan Museum of Art and the Art Institute of Chicago in 1949–1950 generated hundreds of thousands of new enthusiasts. Corwin himself was among the crowds. As a result of the van Gogh exhibition, Houseman said with hyperbole, "Reproductions of his 'Sunflowers' hung in every students' dormitory in America."[28] Also, the 1952 movie *Moulin Rouge*, about the life of painter Toulouse-Lautrec, directed by John Huston, was a well-reviewed and highly profitable undertaking that changed Hollywood's conventional wisdom that films about artists were not good box office.

The timing was right for the project on van Gogh, but two unsuccessful attempts had already been made to adapt it, one by Dalton Trumbo and one by Irving Stone himself. Houseman asked Corwin to give it a try. "Houseman asked me if he should send me the two screenplays," Corwin remembered. "I said no, just send me the book—and when I read the book I was astonished at the life of van Gogh, and I have always been grateful to it, although I departed from the book because I felt that nobody knew van Gogh better than van Gogh himself, and I was interested in presenting the best of the man and not the worst of him."²⁹

Corwin did away with most of Stone's structure, such as the hallucinations of a seductive young woman who appeared to van Gogh and illuminated his sexual impulses and disturbances. Instead, the screenplay retained the title *Lust for Life* but delved more deeply into the relationship between van Gogh and his younger brother, Theo. Corwin used the primary source of the letters between the siblings.

The deep bond between the van Gogh brothers was something the scriptwriter understood and related to completely. In 1928, Corwin had written to his father about his sons, "Nowhere outside of fiction have I ever come across three fraters who were so closely interested each other's welfare or more proud of each other's accomplishments."³⁰ Norman's siblings were a tonic to his chronic self-doubt. For a while, during the early years of his time at CBS, Norman and his brother Emil both moved into the apartment of Alfred and his wife, Freda. It became their task, Bannerman writes, "to fuel his ego, to lend encouragement, to lift his spirits. Always upon returning home, he seemed depressed, feeling the week's effort had missed its mark. They would assure him the program had been excellent, but he was never quite satisfied. This impatience for perfection was peculiar to his character and was evident throughout his career."³¹ In the following decades, when the siblings were apart, correspondence never faltered. Van Gogh's struggle for confidence in his art and the role of his brother and his wife in helping him believe in his own excellence was not uncharted psychological territory as Corwin worked on the screenplay.

Van Gogh's correspondence with the artists Anthon van Rappard and Émile Bernard also informed Corwin's work, as did *The Intimate Journals of Paul Gaugin*. Every key line of dialogue was cross-referenced with one or more sources that would justify it in the script. "This index will serve not only as a guide to ourselves, through the labyrinth of documentation," Corwin wrote to John Houseman, "but will [also] take care of . . . the studio's need to keep track of every last isotope."³²

At a showing of *Lust for Life* on the eve of Corwin's one-hundredth birthday, he recalled, "The novelist, Irving Stone, thought I had demeaned the book by turning to the letters as my source."³³ But his painstaking study of the historical record, Corwin believed, "is why I think that the movie is truer than any other film made about a painter."³⁴

The changing nature of American radio was a still a personal loss for Corwin as he labored in Hollywood. His artistry no longer had a natural home base. It was a loss too for those who loved the theatre of the mind and hoped he would continue to keep the torch burning. In an intimate three-page, single-spaced letter written in 1955 to Marianne Roney, an executive of Caedmon Records, a company that specialized in spoken-word discs, Corwin revealed his internal turmoil about his move into feature films. He was responding to a letter in which she said, "I see you wasting yourself."

"Your impulse to shake me until my fillings loosen and some sense gyroscopically spins into my head," he responded,

> is based on the presumption—flattering to the beast because of the implicit value you put on his time and talent—that I am wasting my time.... It is not the first time I have been reception committee to that and associated thoughts; but the cause and effect, the interwoven circumstances of time, place, economy, politics, damaged amour-propre, upheavals and readjustments, impatience, the need to support no less than seven persons including two children, my wars against me on several fronts at once, my affinity for pressure, which is the only discipline to which I have ever consistently yielded, my having to abandon one medium which I had mastered to the satisfaction of listeners internationally (or rather which abandoned me)—all these things and others lumped together, boiled down, the essence extracted, make for an attitude and a rationale.

He defends himself against Roney's blanket criticism of Hollywood:

> Is it a whorehouse? I think not. It is a factory-sized atelier, abused by many but used by many more; that it pays better than radio or recordings is not to be held against it. Would that other industries paid their artists better, not that movies pay their artists less. I have learned things from working on movies that make me a better craftsman and dramaturgist. It has opened my eyes and made me use them in my work, whereas before I had only used my ears.

Corwin told Roney of his excitement for his current project:

> Now for the first time comes a picture that challenges the ass off me.... Houseman had said to me: "Abandon convention. Apply to it the same bold creativity that you brought to radio." ... The subject is sublimely heroic and tragic and beautiful. I feel privileged to tie the shoestring of van Gogh as a man and a writer, let alone a painter. I have just spent a month of my own time already, digesting just a pie-shaped corner of the literature on Vincent and I have been enriched by it.[35]

The subject of the film, the director, and the writer were all men determined to remain true to their own artistic visions. All received criticism in their time—van Gogh for haste and impulsiveness; Minnelli for the artificiality of spectacle; and Corwin for purple prose. This confluence of auteurs resulted in an extraordinary motion picture. Corwin's love of language, pacing, cadence and sound sensibilities gave Minnelli the foundation to frame van Gogh's physical world as a window to his interior landscape.

Houseman, Minnelli, and Corwin all immersed themselves in the life of van Gogh and his letters. Early in the script development process, Corwin sent Houseman a ten-page single-spaced memo offering ideas on the story trajectory and themes. He separated the qualities of van Gogh's character into two categories. The first was

Developing Elements, the areas in which there is a definite progression, such as Vincent's evolving power of spontaneous expression. From an inarticulate, uncertain, and hesitant boy who "fumbles and grasps," Vincent matures. "In spite of a complete lack of literary pretension," Corwin observes, "his letters become masterly."

The second category was Constant Persistent Elements, which include Vincent's loneliness, humanity, money troubles, and ragged appearance. Another persistent element was his resistance to compromise. Corwin wrote of the artist, "He remains just as austere toward principles as he was soft toward human frailty, and in doing so he represents a phenomenon of integrity and persistence. He never wavers from this."[36] Those who have studied the life and career of Norman Corwin could describe him in just this way.

Correspondence between Corwin and John Houseman reveal that as the script progressed in the United States, pages were sent to Houseman on location in Europe. In many cases, Corwin acknowledged that improvements had been made in his original. But often he questioned the need for changes or additions. For example, in a letter to Houseman dated July 28, 1955, Corwin wrote:

> pg.103. Vincent's second speech: I see I have been outvoted on the "You said in your letters that you needed peace." I go down in flames still protesting that it drags in a dead cat that has never been mentioned before, in fact it runs against the grain of everything Gauguin has ever said. We have been very careful to build him up as a strong, scoffing, contemptuous, above his environment. By saying "you needed peace" we make him [identify] with Vincent's need and a partner in his neurosis.... I disagree with you thoroughly on this one.[37]

Producer Houseman writes of "our great caravan" of twenty to thirty vehicles carrying the cargo of moviemaking equipment on the "long trek along the highways of France, Belgium, and Holland." "Occasionally Minnelli would become so entranced by something he saw during the day," Houseman recalled, "that Jud [Jud Kinberg, Houseman's production associate] and I would sit up all night writing a new scene that would be shot in this new location. When these were viewed in Culver City they invariably evoked cables of protest—either from Norman Corwin, who accused us of mutilating his script, or from the production department, which resented every additional hour we spent on location."[38]

Kirk Douglas had been cast as van Gogh early in the project, a part he had long wanted to play. His resemblance to the artist was remarkable, but he also was consumed with the intensity of the character. It was Corwin's idea, though, to have Anthony Quinn play Paul Gauguin. When Quinn read the script, he demurred, indicating the part was too small for him. Norman scolded, "For God's sake Tony, it's not a side of ham."[39]

Corwin's screenplay dealt with final twelve years of van Gogh's life, from his missionary work with miners to his death at age thirty-seven from a presumed self-inflicted gunshot.[40] Instead of the traditional three-act narrative of feature films, however, Corwin broke his story into four sections that coordinated with the phases of van Gogh's work—the black-and white drawings from the mining district, the Dutch drawings and paintings of rural laborers, the impressionist landscapes of Paris, and the nature portraits of Southern France.

Another affinity Corwin shared with his subject was a respect and admiration for those who toiled at physical labor. The "majesty" of work was the subject of one of Corwin's essays in his 1978 book *Holes in a Stained Glass Window*. "It is work that rules the earth, and always has, since man took his first habiliments for what, for better or worse, we call civilization. There is nothing that we wear, use, eat, nothing on our shelves, in our closets, files, vaults, nothing that we read or see or even *know,* that does not represent the work of people living and dead," he wrote. "The buttons on a shirt, no less than the pyramid of Cheops, symbolize labor. The faucet that washes the dinner dishes had to be tapped, impounded, purified, pumped, and piped. The pen in hand, the paper on the desk, the desk on the floor, the floor on the foundation—all are made not grown. And the oldest work of all, of course, is agriculture. Endless sowing, planting, reaping, threshing, harvesting. Man's needs have made working gardens out of steppe, upland forest, sacred mountains, and weed-beds of the sea."[41]

Van Gogh's elevation of workers by committing their essence to canvas spoke to Corwin of the painter's true character. In one of Vincent's letters to Theo that Corwin uses in the screenplay, the older brother asks, "Do you realize, Theo, that what I'm doing is new? In the paintings of the Old Masters did you ever see a single man or woman at work? Did they ever try to paint a laborer or a man digging?" Of his technique, van Gogh tells Theo, "I've been trying to find a pattern. I'm trying not so much to draw hands as gestures. Not so much faces as the expressions of people. Men and women who know the meaning of toil. . . . They have honestly earned their food."[42]

The use of van Gogh's paintings in *Lust for Life* was a critical issue as Corwin began his work. "The pictures are so closely wrapped around his life," he wrote to Houseman. He cautioned moderation in their use, though, "lest we resemble a catalogue. . . .The point I am trying to make is that not even the greatest painting ever made can justify an arbitrary and un-organic, unintegrated use of it in what is first and last a story on screen, a drama." Corwin likened the alignment of the visuals to the story to "the synchronizing of film and soundtrack."[43]

In *The Films of Vincente Minnelli*, author James Naremore notes, "Minnelli wanted to photograph the original canvases" to "bring the audience close to the surface of van Gogh's work."[44] In today's world the proposition would seem preposterous given the current value of the artwork. The logistics of handling the paintings would be a curator's nightmare, and the insurance premiums would be astronomical.

But in 1955 Corwin identified twenty van Gogh paintings that would be essential to the story. He sent the list, along with the names of the owners of each artwork to producer John Houseman. He also wrote, "It is important to bear in mind that these canvases must be shot *without frames* [emphasis Corwin's]. In some cases, they should be seen with hands holding them, as though being inspected by Gauguin, Tanguy, Theo, or Vincent himself. In others they can be stood on the floor, as though from the aspect of someone inspecting them in a house or gallery. I assume we will have ample time to discuss the integration of this material into the script, after we have made inquiries as to the availability of the above titles."[45]

Corwin's passion for his work on *Lust for Lust* was laid bare in a lengthy letter he wrote to Vincent van Gogh's nephew and namesake, V. W. van Gogh, the son of Theo and Johanna, who was born six months before his uncle's death. The younger van Gogh had decided not to cooperate with MGM on the use of paintings he owned in the production of the movie. "A few months ago," wrote Corwin,

> I was asked by a film company to write the screenplay of a film based on the life of Vincent van Gogh. At first I shared the apprehension of so many people in the arts, that the approach to this, like so many other film biographies might be false; that wholesale and antic license would be taken with facts, that the film would use paintings as mere props, and destroy their value and beauty for audiences. I was soon disabused of this notion. I found the approach to be thoroughly serious and reverent; that no expense was spared to seek out the highest authorities and the most authentic sources of information.

After assuring V. W. van Gogh of the studio's good intentions, Corwin personally appealed to considerations of legacy.

> I was disturbed by the fact that so many times in Vincent's letters, he movingly underscores the wish to have his paintings *seen* [emphasis Corwin's] by many people.... I do not speak for the studio which is making the picture, but for myself as an individual. I am thinking of the millions—literally millions of people in the world—in Alaska and Oceania, in Africa and the Orient, who have never seen a van Gogh painting and never in their lives will see one, or hear him spoken of, unless it is through the medium of a widely circulated motion picture.
>
> ... I am thinking of the legion of half-informed or ill-informed who know only of the most tragic events about Vincent's life and have in their minds a picture of unrelieved sordidness—and how important and valuable it would be to bring the portrait into a true perspective—so that millions more can love and revere Vincent's memory instead of being only dimly aware that he was a painter who cut off an ear in a seizure of madness.

Corwin closed by saying,

> I urge you to reconsider your decision before it is too late.... For Vincent belongs to the ages and the world, his expansive mind chafed at limitations.... I apologize for

the length of this letter, but the issue is so vast, and the time is so short, that I wished to put before you as fully as possible, and in the frankest spirit, my reasons for urging you to open the door to cooperation. Millions of people still in the womb of time will thank you.[46]

Corwin's eloquence, however, was unpersuasive.

A great many other private collectors and organizations did, however, allow two hundred of van Gogh's paintings to be captured on film by visiting crews. The *Harvard Crimson* review of *Lust for Life* noted, "From Fogg [Harvard Museum of Art] to Moscow, van Gogh's paintings were sought and photographed. The camera could not adequately show his thick daubs of paint, but it does capture his magnificent coloring, including the electric yellows with which he described a world he thought illuminated by the brilliant light of God and His sun."[47] The intense light needed for motion picture cameras could have damaged the paintings, so portrait cameras were used to make low-light time exposures. Then enlarged transparencies were backlit and filmed again with special lenses.

Each section of the film was given a dominant color scheme by Minnelli and his cinematographers F. A. Young and Russell Harlan. The director fought to achieve the look he envisioned. Minnelli believed that CinemaScope was the wrong format because wide screen did not correspond to the shape of a canvas. He lost that battle with MGM, but he won the fight to forgo the Eastman color process that resulted in colors "straight from the candy box, a brilliant mixture of blues, reds, and yellows that resembled neither life nor art."[48] His preference was to use a defunct film stock that produced softer, subtler tones, and the studio acceded to the more expensive option.

At the time *Lust for Life* was in progress, Corwin said, "My able associate and dialogue writer is Vincent van Gogh."[49] Years later, though, in the early 1970s, when an old criticism of Corwin resurfaced, he was not so categorical about the words being taken directly from the painter's mouth. While working on Corwin's biography, Bannerman wrote an academic journal article on his subject, in which he quoted well-known radio and TV writer Max Wylie suggesting that Corwin's body of work dealt primarily with "symbolic representation" in his characters and offered only "glimpses of real human interaction" in his work.

After reading a draft of the piece, Corwin sent Bannerman a complimentary letter on the article, but he took umbrage with the criticism.

> The quote from Max Wylie on page 8 was of particular interest to me, because I either never ran across it, or forgot it. Max's was not the only comment of that kind, and they are all firmly rooted in a common misconception: that I was (or am) incapable of writing people [Wylie's underscoring] or than showing more than a glimpse of "human interaction." Misapprehension is the polite term, bullshit is the impolite. . . . Gauguin and van Gogh, and Theo did not write themselves. If I did not create those characters on the screen, who else did?[50]

In *Lust for Life,* wrote film reviewer Mark Gabrish Conlan, Corwin offered "the complexity of life rather than the neatness of fiction." Van Gogh suffers for his auteurism. He is portrayed as "a workaholic with a profound sense of guilt that he couldn't make a living from his painting even while he had no inclination, desire, or even ability to the change his style to make his work more salable."[51] It was a suffering that Corwin fully understood.

The contemporaneous reviews of *Lust for Life* were mixed. *Variety* was underwhelmed: "This is a slow-moving picture whose only action is the dialog itself. . . . *Lust for Life* is largely conversation."[52] Bosley Crowther, film critic for the *New York Times* was enamored of the "pictorial color continuities, planned like a musical score." Crowther said the artistry of the color, though, did "not discredit the acting of Mr. Douglas or the quality of the script prepared by Norman Corwin. . . . Both the script and the performance of this picture have a striking integrity in putting forth salient details and the surface aspects of the life of van Gogh."[53]

The dramatic highlight of the film is when Gauguin arrives in Arles to stay with Vincent, who has dreams of creating a "Studio of the South" artist colony. But the men have wholly different approaches to art. Gauguin is also eccentric and passionate, but he is more intellectual and disciplined in his painting. Corwin captures the rub of the conflict in one perfect, angry exchange. Gauguin's chiding reaction to van Gogh's quick, thick brush strokes is "You paint too fast." Vincent shoots back, "You look too fast."

Corwin explained that exchange:

> Theo worked for the art dealer Groupil in Paris. At one point Theo wrote Vincent that a dealer said, "Tell your brother that he paints too fast." Vincent wrote back, "Tell your friend that he looks too fast." I saved that exchange for a scene between van Gogh and Gauguin, who was patently jealous of his friend's output. Van Gogh would go out in all kinds of weather and would set up a wind defying easel and paint outdoors. Van Gogh turned out a canvas a day for a long time. Gauguin just sat in that "yellow house" in Arles which he shared with Vincent and painted.[54]

Lust for Life received four Academy Award nominations: Corwin for Best Adapted Screenplay, Kirk Douglas for Best Actor, Anthony Quinn for Best Supporting Actor, and a team of five men for Best Color Art Direction. Even though Minnelli was not nominated for Best Director, for the rest of his life he regularly named *Lust for Life* as his favorite among his films.

Only Quinn took home the Oscar. Kirk Douglas's loss to Yul Brenner for *The King and I* was shocking to those who admired his brave, passionate performance of van Gogh's neuroses. It was a devastating disappointment for Douglas who still believes it was the best work of his long career.[55]

In the years and decades that followed, *Lust for Life* entered the pantheon of classic motion pictures. Sixty years after its debut, *Lust for Life* is still shown frequently on cable networks and widely studied in schools of art and film. In 1956, Corwin had good reason to believe that his transition to motion pictures held unlimited promise.

Corwin's next film project was also about a painter, Spaniard Francisco Goya. The title, *The Naked Maja,* refers to one of a pair of paintings; the other is *The Clothed Maja.* One shows a nude woman reclining on a bed of pillows with her arms behind her head. She has an unembarrassed, bold, forward gaze. Visible pubic hair made the painting that was completed in 1800 an object of total profanity in its time.[56] The companion picture, completed in 1805, shows the same woman, identically posed but clothed in a clinging white dress with an embroidered jacket.

The identity of the woman in the paintings, which now hang in the Prado Museum in Madrid, Spain, is not certain. Some art historians believe she is the mistress of Prime Minister Manuel de Godoy because he commissioned the artwork. Others are of the opinion that she is a composite of female figures in the mind of the artist, or perhaps his mistress. Another theory, which is proffered in the film, is that she is the Duchess of Alba, who might have been a lover of Goya's.[57]

In February 1957, producer Geoffredo Lombardo of Titanus Film of Rome struck a deal with Alfred Lewin to coproduce, write, and direct the company's project on Goya. Lewin, an accomplished Hollywood hyphenate, had written the screenplays for several successful motion pictures, including *The Picture of Dorian Gray* (1945). Ultimately, though, Henry Koster took on the directing duties. His experience with directing major productions included *The Bishop's Wife* (1947), *Harvey* (1950), and *The Robe* (1953).

The initial script was written by Lewin, based on a story by Talbot Jennings and Oscar Saul. The details of Corwin's involvement with the project are sketchy. There are no files regarding *The Naked Maja* in Corwin's meticulously kept collection of papers. His daughter believes the project was so painful for her father that he "couldn't bear to keep materials that documented his association with it."[58] If *Lust for Life* was the zenith of Corwin's motion picture career, this film was its nadir.

Copies of various versions of the screenplay at the Margaret Herrick Library at the Academy of Motion Picture Arts and Sciences, however, offer an approximate timeline of the script development. A 230-page "temporary complete screenplay (GOYA) by Albert Lewin" is dated August 1, 1957. A 280-page "temporary complete composite screenplay by Albert Lewin" is dated October 1, 1957. Considering that a typical screenplay for a feature film is in the neighborhood of 120 pages, an observer might infer that the increase of fifty pages from the first to the second draft of an already lengthy script suggested problems with the story.[59]

The lead role of Goya was given to Anthony Franciosa at the outset of the project. A New York–trained method actor, Franciosa had been nominated for a Tony Award for his portrayal of a Korean War veteran with a morphine addiction in *A Hatful of Rain*. He reprised the part in the 1957 film version, for which he received an Oscar nomination. His costar, legendary leading lady Ava Gardner, whose untrained acting style relied on instinct, was apprehensive about their pairing. Her instincts in this case were correct.

Director Koster called his work on *The Naked Maja* "one of the most tortuous experiences I had in my time making pictures.... I walked off the picture a couple of times." The toxic environment of the set had much to do with the animosity between the stars. "Franciosa and Ava hated each other," Koster said. "They used to sulk in separate dressing rooms between scenes, refusing to speak to each other." The tension was exacerbated by Franciosa's wife, actress Shelley Winters, who believed her husband was having an affair with Gardner.[60]

In radio Corwin enjoyed great loyalty from actors because he treated them with due respect. "I wasn't a martinet. My productions, I'm glad to say were happy. They were marked by geniality," Corwin recalled. "I had pretty good luck in casting, and that simplified matters. My view of the actor was never that of an instrument that I was playing but of an instrumentalist who was an artist in his own right. If he had a suggestion to make, and I liked it, I was very happy to get it and use it.... The right actor is half the battle or more. After that choice, it is usually just a matter of some minor adjustment in approach. Rarely was the problem of interpretation spread out over several days of rehearsal. We didn't have days; we had hours."[61] When asked about his approach to characterization, Corwin answered: "I was never conscious of any method. I proceeded by instinct, not the product of any method or school."[62]

In spring 1958, with preproduction underway, Corwin joined the team in Rome. The screenwriter who brought van Gogh successfully to the screen was brought in to do the same for Goya. Soon, though, Corwin also found himself in conflict with the leading man. A protracted letter Corwin wrote to Franciosa on April 26, 1958, is a rare document that he kept related to his work on *The Naked Maja* screenplay. The hostility is palpable. A much-excerpted version follows:

> Dear Tony:
>
> I was happy to see you the other day, and delighted to hear about the Spanish music you had found, but by the time you left I was very much disturbed. I think you were too. The cause of the disturbance rests on the mistake I committed in telling you the outline of events beyond the script you had read; the important thing is not what caused it, but the symptoms of misapprehension revealed in your reaction....
>
> Your first reaction to the first pages you received two weeks ago was that all the major characters seemed crystal clear to you except that of Goya. Precisely. In the three-hundred-odd biographies written of this man, Goya remains to us a far greater enigma than any other important figure of his century.... But if I understood you properly, you seemed to think that we should dig this man as soon and as

clearly as we do the Queen, Godoy, the King and Alba. We should spell him out, so that the audience is able to say, "1,2,3, and a, b, c, and now we know he is a certain type, so we can all settle down now and see how he Wins Girl and Loses Girl and Finds Girl."

. . . When I began to outline the third fourth of the story development, you recoiled in seeming dismay. I had volunteered this brief outline in the hope that it would give you some assurance about where we were going, but perhaps even enthusiasm . . . your reaction struck me as unthinking and unjustified. For you seemed to take a bookkeeper's position, counting your total scenes and big moments, against those of Alba and Godoy, and failing to appreciate that a character can develop and evolve even through indirection, involution, regression and pathology. Goya was vain, ambitious, jealous, finally embittered. This is how he is being drawn in *The Naked Maja*. One does not develop all these qualities full blown by page 40.

Tony, I urge you not to make yourself arbiter of how you think Goya should react to given stimulus, such as, say, his deafness. Your idea is that he should rage—that he should throw vases and smash them against a wall in order to test his hearing. That is all right for Stanley Kowalski, but not necessarily Francisco Goya. Beethoven too was an angry deaf man, but there are ways of expressing anger. He jammed his hat down on his head instead of taking it respectfully off when the coach of a Prince passed him on a road. On his deathbed he shook his fist at a lightning storm. How much more magnificent are such gestures than smashing furniture, which any drunken bum can do when angry. I mentioned Kazanism to you when you bellowed out an enactment of how you thought Goya would behave. I yield to nobody in my awed respect for Gadge [nickname for Kazan], but he does tend to break the china when in doubt. It has become his weakest mannerism, not a strength. . . .

The fact remains that I am the writer of record at the moment, and that no page of the script has been written without the deepest and most searching consultation and consideration. My work has yet to be done, and the expected and inevitable flaws of the first complete draft will be attended to at the proper time. But it will profit us all, including yourself, if you understand that the script involved people you have never met, a period you have never been steeped in, a country you have never lived in, a malady that has never plagued you, an aristocracy you have never lived among, atrocities you have never witnessed, and a Duchess you have never laid.[63]

Corwin was accustomed to the world's top-echelon actors clamoring to be in his works. Franciosa's temerity in challenging Corwin while his new script was still in outline form was an unexpected aggravation. Whatever research and script notes existed that were solely Corwin's are gone, though. So, a side-to-side comparison with the final shooting script is not possible.

What we know is that on April 28, 1958—the date of the letter to Franciosa—Corwin was "the writer of record." A 152-page script in the Herrick Library that was stamped on June 17, 1958, is labeled "final shooting script by Norman Corwin and Giorgio Prosperi."[64] How much of that script was a true collaboration is unknown. But after Corwin left Rome, there were additional uncredited rewrites by Koster and Lewin, and even Lombardo contributed. The final story had too many chefs, and Corwin wanted no part of it. He asked that his name be removed from the credits, but the film prints had already been made. So Corwin could not isolate himself from the debacle.[65]

Critics savaged the film. When it debuted, *Variety* opined: "Considering that it was Norman Corwin, who together with Giorgio Prosperi wrote the dialog, the lines are more than disappointing."[66] The *New Yorker* review titled "Smudge," opened with this insult: "Norman Corwin, the old poetaster of radio, and one Giorgio Prosperi have pooled their writing talents to explain the life of Francisco Goya in the Italian-American production called 'The Naked Maja.' The result is a posthumous libel on the painter."[67]

Even when some elements were praised, such as the stunning costuming and lush cinematography of Giuseppe Rotunno, reviewers universally panned the leading man. The *Los Angeles Times* critic Philip K. Scheuer wrote: "Franciosa alternately mopes and moans in his passion, but his voice betrays its New York antecedents and it is hard to imagine him as a great genius."[68] Corwin could take small comfort, though.

At the heart of the failure was "the dreadful script." The *Hollywood Reporter* noted that "the picture bears little relationship to the real life of this remarkable man nor the period of Spanish history in which he lived. . . . It is difficult to understand why the authors avoided the mystery surrounding the fact that Goya painted two identical 'Majas'. . . [which] represent one of the greatest feats of brushwork in the history of art and one of the profoundest enigmas. One wonders why the filmmakers were not tempted to solve it."[69]

The bad review in the *New York Times* was another blow for Corwin:

> An almost incredible hodge-podge of childish notions concerning the life and times of Francisco Goya, the titanic Spanish painter, have been spread upon the screen with an earnestness of performance and a lavishness of color and spectacle that are downright embarrassing in *The Naked Maja*. . . . The drama pays lip service to Goya's deep involvement with his own time. Goya rails at decadence and evil and languishes briefly in jail and "paints the truth" in defiance of tradition, etc. But most of his deeply agonized spiritual turmoil goes on in the arms of Ava Gardner, as the Duchess. Thus, with one stroke, the scenarists, Norman Corwin and Giorgio Prosperi, have rendered the film ridiculous on both main counts, as either a biographical document or and entertaining fictionalized romance.[70]

The faulty history of the movie was even brought up in the halls of Congress. "Bad History Worse Than Obscenities" was the *Variety* headline for an article on a House Postal Operations Subcommittee considering the self-policing practices of the motion picture and publishing industries. Representative Katherine St. George

(R-NY) stated that *The Naked Maja* was a "terrible film" that didn't include a single true historical fact. She complained about the incorrect placement of the Spanish Inquisition in the time of Goya. "They might just as well have had the Mayflower on the Hudson River as a ferry boat."[71]

It was a grinding humiliation for Corwin that he tried his best to rise above. "I felt every decision made on that film was ruinous to the artistic and historical fabric," Corwin recalled decades later. "Nothing of the kind of fidelity and authenticity that I had worked so hard to arrive at in *Lust for Life* was given the slightest welcome on that picture."[72]

There were additional embarrassments, as United Artists, the American distributor of the film, tried to exploit the word *naked* by using billboards with reproductions of the painting, which is not shown in the movie. The Los Angeles police vice squad helped the publicity stunt by ordering that the exposed parts of the woman be blacked out or draped over on the signs.[73] In New York, the painter of the Times Square billboard, James Rosenquist, was asked to make the "private parts" of the Maja smaller.[74] The implied salaciousness suggested a scene in which Ava Gardner was not fully clothed, which never occurred. In fact, as one reviewer pointed out, "The painting itself is only fleetingly visible behind the opening titles."[75]

Corwin could only try to divorce himself from the cinematic train wreck with his skewering humor. "If you should happen to be in the neighborhood of a film named *The Naked Maja*, which bears my name a co-author of the screenplay, kindly do me the favor of not seeing it," he wrote to a friend in publishing. "This is the film on Goya that I was toiling at when I dropped you a line from Rome. . . . Such vulgarization has not occurred in the field of painting since someone cut up a Cezanne still life of three apples, because he could only afford one apple."[76]

The Naked Maja is listed in most Corwin filmographies, but it is an unwelcome and, perhaps, wholly unfair credit. In 1959, he wrote: "In regard to *The Naked Maja*, there is very little I can say without launching into a twenty-page diatribe. I made every effort to have my name taken off the picture, but was unsuccessful. Whole scenes and characterizations were altered without my permission—indeed without my knowledge after I had returned to the United States from Italy. I can only say regretfully that the film was a travesty of a great artist, and I am sorry that I was not able to disassociate myself from it."[77] The presumed decision Corwin made to destroy all his materials related to *The Naked Maja*, save the letter to Franciosa, can be seen as his attempt to be the auteur of his own legacy.

For Corwin, the *Naked Maja* experience was "agonizing," but he maintained a cordial relationship with the director, Henry Koster. The two men worked together the following year on Corwin's biblical screenplay, *The Story of Ruth*. The Old Testament tale was made in 1960 and came out shortly after the release of *Ben Hur*. It was not an epic with a "cast of thousands" though. It was a more modest, character-driven production that required the invention of a story line to fill out the short book in the Bible about the domestic life of a young widow.

Corwin was criticized for the liberties he took. "There were some people—including a very good friend of mine, a rabbi—who were appalled by the suggestion that Ruth had once been in the service of the Moabite religion. But this concept actually came from Jewish sources.... Historically, the film relied on whatever authoritative sources were available to us.... I think my invention was well within the frame of plausibility and logic." Again, the size of the audience was a disappointment. "*Ruth* suffered from a lack of a name cast," Corwin believed. "But I have no apologies to make for that film."[78]

Corwin's final feature-film screenplay was *Madison Avenue*, an adaptation of the 1951 novel *The Build-Up Boys* by Jeremy Kirk, which was a morality tale about the world of public relations. The story concerns an adman fired from his firm who forms his own agency and schemes to steal a top client from his former boss. The high-caliber cast included Dana Andrews, Jeanne Crain, Eleanor Parker, and Eddie Albert.

The script was completed in 1960. Again, Corwin tried unsuccessfully to have his name removed from a project. After being sent the final version of the screenplay by James Fischer, the associate story editor of Twentieth Century-Fox, Corwin wrote back, "I have read and compared it with my original draft and find in it qualitative changes to which I cannot agree. For this reason I must regretfully decline credit."[79]

Madison Avenue was released in the United Kingdom in 1961, but it did not open in American theatres until 1962. The ninety-minute film was not a crowd pleaser. A contemporary review pinpoints the flaws: "It's a terribly snoozy film, despite the fact that it keeps trying to give the impression that it's up-tempo. The characters are cardboard, and soggy cardboard at that. With few exceptions, the dialogue, which is all-important in this type of film and absolutely has to snap and pop, is pedestrian and lacks rhythm."[80] Decades later when asked about *Madison Avenue*, Corwin said plainly, "I don't remember who wrote the book, nor do I remember the picture, nor do I want to."[81]

Hollywood screenwriting was not a good fit for Corwin. Each of his films came to him at the invitation of a producer; they were not original subjects of his choice. As he approached his fifty-second birthday, Corwin wrote to an old friend from his CBS days:

> I have become increasingly conscious of the clatter of the wheels in time's chariot.... I resent the time required to present someone else's work, to correct its flaws, improve its merits, be psychoanalyst and chambermaid to sundry idiots and neurotics in the cast.... If I am a writer, if I can think, if I am a friend of the Phrase, if I have a conscience, then goddam it I should be writing for myself, by myself, even of myself.... If this is a big switch, then maybe it has been too long coming.[82]

After a decade of film work, Corwin entered the next phase of his career; stage plays, books, magazine articles, poetry, special projects for television and radio, and teaching gave him the creative and intellectual freedom to be entirely his own man.

The only professionally satisfying and successful experience Norman Corwin had working in feature films was *Lust for Life*. It was the movie project in which he exerted the most control of his artistic vision. But, more important, he was in many respects writing "of himself." His consanguinity with Vincent van Gogh comprised many attributes, but none more profound than the single-mindedness of bringing to fruition a personally imagined concept infused with the awareness of human need. Van Gogh changed the way people looked at the world; Corwin changed the way people listened to it. Late in his life, when asked to reflect on the whole of his career, Corwin said, "I hate compromise, except in the arena of social action, of course, where it is a necessity. But in art, compromise is an alien force."[83]

NOTES

1. Douglas Bell, *Years of the Electric Ear: Interview with Norman Corwin* (Metuchen, NJ: Scarecrow Press, 1994), 5–6.
2. R. LeRoy Bannerman, *Norman Corwin and Radio: The Golden Years* (University, AL: The University of Alabama Press, 1986), 26.
3. Bell, 16–17.
4. Quoted in Thomas Cotterill, "How Artists Develop their Artistic Vision," *Thomas Cotterill—Philosophical Writer* (blog), July 29, 2012, https://thomascotterill.wordpress.com/2012/07/29/how-artists-their-artistic-vision.
5. A. J. Langguth, ed., *Norman Corwin's Letters* (NY: Barricade Books, 1994), 37.
6. Ibid., 5.
7. Ibid., 47.
8. Ibid., 48.
9. Ibid., 50.
10. Ibid.
11. Bannerman, 55.
12. Langguth, 51.
13. Clifton Fadiman, Introduction, *More by Corwin,* by Norman Corwin (NY: Henry Holt, 1944), ix.
14. Bell, 172.
15. Bannerman, 88.
16. Bell, 138–39.
17. "Norman Corwin, RIP," *Variety,* October, 19, 2011.
18. "Prizes for Corwin," *Time* magazine, March 4, 1946, 62.
19. Bannerman, 198.
20. Bell, 145–46.
21. Leonard Maltin, "Farewell to a Giant: Norman Corwin," *Leonard Maltin's Movie Crazy* (blog), October, 19, 2011, blogs.indiewire.com/leonardmaltin/farewell_to_a_giant_norman_corwin.
22. Bell, 11.
23. Norman Corwin letter to Marianne Roney, (undated) 1955, Corwin Collection, Thousand Oaks Library.

24. Bosley Crowther, "Movie Review: *Ten Tall Men* 1951," *New York Times,* October 27, 1951, http://movies.nytimes.com/movie/review?res=9B02E3DF1F39E23ABC4F51DFB667838A649EDE.

25. Corwin letter to Roney.

26. Bell, 143.

27. John Houseman, *Unfinished Business* (NY: Applause Theatre Book Publishers, 1972), 338.

28. Ibid., 337.

29. Norman Corwin quoted in text by Jeffrey Burbank, "Conversations at the Cinematheque: Norman Corwin for *Lust for Life, 5/1/10,*" May 3, 2010, based on transcribed interview with Patt Morrison, May 2, 2010, at the Aero Theatre, Santa Monica, CA. https://www.facebook.com/notes/aero-theatre/conversations-at-the-cinematheque-norman-corwin-for-lust-for-life-5110/390226414827/. Audio file at http://www.scpr.org/programs/offramp/2010/05/08/13583/centenarian-norman-corwin-to-patt-morrison-first-d/.

30. Langguth, 2.

31. Bannerman, 36.

32. Norman Corwin MGM inter-office memo to John Houseman, April 7, 1955, Corwin Collection, Thousand Oaks Library.

33. Jeff Burbank, "Conversations at the Cinematheque."

34. "Norman Corwin: The Making of Lust for Life," *American Legends,* posted March 2006, http://www.americanlegends.com/Interviews/norman_corwin.html.

35. Corwin letter to Roney.

36. Norman Corwin MGM memo to John Houseman, March 4, 1955, Corwin Collection, Thousand Oaks Library.

37. Norman Corwin letter to John Houseman, July 28, 1955, Corwin Collection, Thousand Oaks Library.

38. Houseman, *Unfinished Business,* 343–44.

39. Bannerman, 224.

40. Gregory White Smith & Steven Naifeh, "Murder in Auvers? Forensic Expert Weighs in on Van Gogh's Cause of Death," VF Culture, *Vanity Fair,* November 7, 2014, http://www.vanityfair.com/culture/2014/12/vincent-van-gogh-murder-mystery#.

41. Norman Corwin, *Holes in a Stained Glass Window* (Secaucus, NJ: Lyle Stuart, 1978), 123–24.

42. *Lust for Life* film dialogue.

43. Corwin memo to Houseman, March 4, 1955.

44. James Naremore, *The Films of Vincente Minnelli,* (NY: Cambridge University Press, 1993), 139.

45. Norman Corwin MGM memo to John Houseman re: paintings, March 28, 1955, Corwin Collection, Thousand Oaks Library.

46. Norman Corwin letter to V. W. Van Gogh, August 2, 1955, Corwin Collection, Thousand Oaks Library.

47. Cyril Ressler, "Lust for Life," *The Harvard Crimson,* December 1, 1956.

48. Vincente Minnelli, *I Remember it Well* (Hollywood, CA: Samuel French Trade, 1974), 289.

49. Langguth, 159.

50. Bannerman, 314–15.

51. Mark Gabrish Conlan, "Lust for Life (MGM, 1956)," *Movie Magg* (blog), August 3, 2013, http://moviemagg.blogspot.ca/2013/08/lust-for-life-mgm-1956.html.

52. "Review: *Lust for Life,*" *Variety,* December 31, 1955.

53. Bosley Crowther, "Screen: Color-Full Life of Van Gogh; 'Lust for Life' Tells the Story Through Tints," *New York Times,* September 18, 1956.

54. "Norman Corwin: The Making of Lust for Life," *American Legends.*

55. Jeff Burbank, "Conversations at the Cinematheque: Norman Corwin for Lust for Life."

56. "Francisco de Goya," *Encyclopedia of Old Master Painters*, www.visual-arts-cork.com/oldmasters/goya.htm.
57. Ibid.
58. Diane Corwin Okarski telephone conversation with author, October 15, 2014.
59. Turner/MGM scripts, 2045.f-N-2; 2045.f-N-5, Margaret Herrick Library, Academy of Motion Picture Arts and Sciences.
60. "The Naked Maja" Brief Synopsis, Turner Classic Movies, http://www.tcm.com/this-month/article/345153|178904/The-Naked-Maja.
61. Bell, 38.
62. Ibid., 37.
63. Langguth, 167–70
64. Turner/MGM scripts, 2045.f-N-6.
65. "The Naked Maja," *Filmfacts 1959*, 107–9. In Manuscript Inventories, Fan Scrapbooks—Gardner, Ava, compiled by Lon Busich, Clipping file, #19 1954–1960, Margaret Herrick Library, Academy of Motion Picture Arts and Sciences, Beverly Hills, CA.
66. "Film Review: *The Naked Maja*," *Variety*, March 25, 1959, 6.
67. "Smudge," *New Yorker*, June 20, 1959.
68. Philip K. Scheuer, "*Naked Maja* Film Not So Revealing," *Los Angeles Times*, April 6, 1959.
69. "Lombardo-Koster Film Must Depend on Ballyhoo Angels," *Hollywood Reporter*, March 20, 1959, 31.
70. Richard W. Nason, "Screen: Canvas of Goya; *Naked Maja* on Bill with *Man in Net*," *New York Times*, June 11, 1959.
71. "Bad History Worse Than Obscenities," *Variety*, February 5, 1960.
72. Bell, 148–49.
73. "Vice Squad Drapes 'Naked' Billboard," *Hollywood Reporter*, April 15, 1959.
74. Milton Esterow, "22 Stories Above Times Square," *ARTnews*, November 2009, 107.
75. Scheuer.
76. Langguth, 177–78.
77. Ibid., 183.
78. Bell, 149.
79. Norman Corwin letter to James Fischer, October 31, 1960, Corwin Collection, Thousand Oaks Library.
80. Craig Butler, review, *Madison Avenue*, http://www.allmovie.com/movie/madison-avenue-v100882/review.
81. Bell, 150.
82. Langguth, 211.
83. Bell, 277.

PART TWO

SOUND

Corwin and Transmedia Authorship

4

NORMAN CORWIN'S RADIO REALISM

Jacob Smith

In the summer of 1948, radio writer and producer Norman Corwin was on a cross-country train trip. His boss, CBS president William Paley, happened to be on the same train, and the two had lunch together. As previous chapters in this volume have made clear, Corwin was one of the network's stars, the creator of broadcasts that were the jewels in the crown of CBS's nonsponsored programming. Over lunch, the two men discussed the future of the network, and Paley stressed the increased importance of programming with "mass appeal" in the competitive postwar broadcasting business. Corwin took Paley's comments as an indication of imminent changes in network policy, changes that would not be favorable to his approach. Sure enough, when CBS offered him his next contract, the conditions were so poor that he refused to sign it.

Historians of American broadcasting have tended to see this anecdote as a defining moment that signals the end of an era of progressive, experimental radio and the dawning of a more commercially driven paradigm of broadcast entertainment.[1] From this perspective, the 1948 meeting between Paley and Corwin was perhaps the last time that the networks and a cohort of modernist writer-producers were moving in tandem before the latter were unceremoniously left on the side of the tracks as the train of broadcasting sped into the future. This was not the end of Corwin's involvement in radio, however, and to continue the metaphor, we might say that Corwin hitched a ride on another train that carried him to one further station along the track of American radio history. The ride that Corwin hitched was with United Nations Radio, where he served as Chief of Special Projects from 1948 to 1952.

In chapter 1, Neil Verma described how Corwin came to be known as the poet laureate or bard of the golden age of American network radio due to the distinctive authorial signature of his acclaimed broadcasts.² As a writer, Corwin blended poetry and prose, narrative and documentary, all in the service of a vision of social justice that celebrated the common man. As a producer, he explored the expressive properties of radio as a sound art. Corwin has long held a privileged place in American radio history, but little has been written about his UN broadcasts. This is a shame, because they have much to offer readers interested in a range of topics: radio and sound culture to be sure, but also film theory, the history of media technology, and dynamics of mid-century globalization. The decade after the end of World War II was an important period in Corwin's career when his *media* authorship became decidedly *transmedia,* and this chapter is a companion to Mary Ann Watson's account of Corwin's move to Hollywood film production (chapter 3) and Shawn VanCour's discussion of his television work (chapter 5). Though still working in radio, Corwin's tenure at the United Nations was a time when he adapted his style to new sound recording technologies of the postwar era. Corwin's integration of recorded sound into his radio style is a notable example of what Verma calls the "mineralization" of live radio, or what Raymond Williams might have described as a merging of amplificatory and durative forms of media.³ In short, Corwin's work at United Nations Radio gives media scholars a rich case study in the interaction of technology and authorial style.

I approach the question of Corwin's style from a theoretical framework provided by the writing of M. M. Bakhtin. Bakhtin saw expressions of individual style on a continuum with other kinds of social utterances. For him, individual style in everyday social interaction was inseparably related to "speech genres" that grew out of the various spheres of social life: class-, race- and ethnic-based vernaculars; regional accents, subcultural slang, and professional jargon. Novels and dramas were "secondary speech genres" that "absorbed and digested" the primary ones. Bakhtin was not interested in distilling a text to locate the author's individual expression but instead aimed to amplify the heteroglossia of speech genres that could be heard in a text. After all, the artistic nuances of the author's unique voice could only sound when heard against the background of heteroglot voices and speech genres. By this understanding, style is the way in which authors orchestrate social languages to refract their own particular expressive intentions.⁴ Bakhtin's aural metaphors are well suited to Corwin's radio broadcasts, which often sought to depict the "voice of the people" at the same time that they established an unmistakably individual authorial style. As we shall see, postwar recording technologies had an influence on Corwin's approach to orchestrating voices.

In addition to Bakhtin's literary theory, Corwin's use of recording during the late 1940s and early 1950s should be placed in dialogue with theoretical writing on cinematic realism. In several classic essays, André Bazin broke with previous theorists by declaring that sound had come "to fulfill the Old Testament of the cinema" by pushing cinematic style towards realism.[5] Noel Carroll argues that Bazin offered a new type of theory, one "sensitive to the masterpieces of sound film," and invested in the notion that sound had "enhanced the recording capacity of the medium."[6] Film theorists tend to be interested in sound recording only as it relates to the cinema, but what if we took seriously Bazin's claim that the "primacy of the image" was accidental and explored postwar sonic realism on its own terms? Corwin's postwar "radio realism," created first at CBS and then for the United Nations, demonstrates how sound technologies influenced the recording capacity of media other than film during this era.

Corwin's radio work was, like the Italian neorealist films championed by Bazin, closely associated with World War II and its aftermath.[7] Bazin wrote that the war had deeply influenced both European cinema and American filmmakers, who had translated the horrors of the war into an "ethic of realism."[8] In Dudley Andrew's words, the war spurred a desire for cinematic approaches that were "responsive and responsible to a descriptive mission." "The world to be represented had become too vast, too rapid, too complex and violent for standard cinematic representation," Andrew writes. "Thrust outside the studio, cinema struggled to grasp a confusing reality."[9] Corwin struggled to grasp the war-torn world through sound and described it in broadcasts that utilized portable devices, location recording, and the mnemonic function of the indexical trace. In the process, he defined a style of radio realism that was intertwined with recording, and that calls for an approach that combines Film Studies and Sound Studies.[10]

The years between 1947 and 1952 were far more than the twilight of Corwin's network-era celebrity; they were the dawn of a new phase of sonic authorship when his populist message was given a truly global scope, and his poetic radio style was adapted to a new technological context. Corwin's vision of a "citizen of the world" was not without its shortcomings, but his UN broadcasts can still evoke powerful emotions and are stunning sonic texts that deserve to be heard again in our own era of global flows. The postwar evolution in his approach is best heard in relation to an earlier style of modernist radio, and so I begin with a brief consideration of Corwin's work before and during World War II.

ON A NOTE OF TRIUMPH

Corwin was hired to work as a writer, director, and producer at CBS in December 1938, where he created a poetry series entitled *Words without Music* (this era of Corwin's career is described in detail by Troy Cummings in chapter 6.)[11] The show was a critical success, and Corwin was soon writing and producing his own original scripts for the prestigious Columbia Workshop in two series that bore his name: *Thirteen by Corwin* and *26 by Corwin*. This was the first time that CBS had given a proprietary title to a series along these lines and, according to Corwin, it was "unheard of" in the case of the Columbia Workshop, which had a policy of guest directors.[12] Corwin thus attained a novel degree of authorship in the radio industry, and his work became associated with several distinctive themes and techniques, chief among them antifascism, anticommercialism, and the expressive use of realistic sound effects to dramatic ends.[13]

Hailed as a thoroughly modern hybrid of poet, dramatist, and technician, Corwin was well placed to become the nation's official radio bard during World War II. Corwin's work with the government began when the U.S. Office of Facts and Figures (OFF) invited him to write and produce a broadcast celebrating the 150th anniversary of the Bill of Rights.[14] The show, entitled "We Hold These Truths," reveals Corwin to be a Bakhtinian author extraordinaire, capable of orchestrating the heteroglot voices of farmers, clerks, and bricklayers of the early American colonies as played by a cast of Hollywood stars like James Stewart and Edward G. Robinson, with the voice of none less than President Franklin D. Roosevelt thrown in for good measure.[15] Planned as a patriotic media event, the show took on new meaning when it was aired on December 15, 1941, just a week after the Japanese attack on Pearl Harbor. "We Hold These Truths" garnered the largest radio audience for a dramatic performance up to that time and brought Corwin more national recognition than ever before.[16] It also made him an obvious choice to spearhead a radio propaganda campaign produced by the OFF (later the Office of War Information).[17] Corwin wrote and produced the wartime series *Passport for Adams* and was head of the production unit for the thirteen-part *This Is War!*[18]

Corwin's prominence on network radio during the war coincided with the medium's prominence in American cultural life. Judith Smith is among scholars who argue that radio was a critical site for creating national unity and public support for the war.[19] Corwin's attainment of a central position in radio's war effort lends credence to Smith's claim that the nation's wartime goals were nearly indistinguishable from the interests of socially progressive writers. She writes that "for a brief time the vision of a labor-led movement against fascism and Jim Crow segregation coincided with national goals, expanding the range of representative Americans as well as the meanings of community that flourished within the cultural mainstream."[20] Corwin paid tribute to the antifascism of the "common man in uniform" in his 1944 radio play "Untitled," which featured Hollywood star Frederic March. In his description of the show, Corwin wrote that "the citizen who hated Fascism before it was fashionable to do so, was and is the first patriot of our time."[21] The play is a modernist drama that presents the story of a soldier named Hank Peters told from multiple perspectives in a manner akin to Orson Welles's *Citizen Kane* (1941): we hear from Peters's mother, the doctor who delivered him, his teacher, a girlfriend, the local newspaper editor, the German soldier who killed him, and finally Peters himself.[22] Once again, Corwin's authorial voice sounds among heteroglot voices, and his style emerges as a particular tact in the handling of social speech genres.

Corwin's most acclaimed wartime broadcast was "On a Note of Triumph," which celebrated the Allies' victory in Europe. "On a Note of Triumph" was the capstone of a dizzying broadcast day in which the networks put on a show of truly global scope with live pickups from all major battlefronts.[23] Corwin had long been fascinated by the "space-annihilating properties of broadcasting," and his May 8 show wove itself into the sonic tapestry of the broadcast day through a style of modernist radio characterized by dramatic leaps across space and time in order to understand the interconnected present.[24]

Consider for example, a sequence from the show during which narrator Martin Gabel enacts an imaginary journey to speak with American soldiers still fighting in the war's two theatres of operation.[25] In the midst of a joyous musical celebration of Hitler's defeat provided by the Almanac Singers, Gabel asks listeners to "take your good ear out of low range: whisk it high, hoist it up to cirro-stratus country, up to where a B-29 has wing-room." Here is an example of what Gerd Horton calls the "you-technique," which was often used by radio writers to pull listeners "out of their armchairs and into the cockpit of a fighter plane, onto the deck of a destroyer, or into a ditch on the front line."[26] Listeners travel with the microphone across the Atlantic Ocean to meet American servicemen on the continent, who proceed to ask a series of probing questions about the war. In order to address one question, Corwin returns to the space-annihilating properties of broadcasting: "Hoist yourself fifty feet higher than Everest," Gabel instructs listeners, and "run westward in pursuit of the sun." We overtake an American airplane to speak with the pilot, and then we are told to look down to the surface of the sea where American warships are on patrol. We plummet to one of the ships, avoiding the updraft of its smokestacks, fall through a ventilator on the portside aft, and shout our greetings to a sailor in the engine room. In the next instant the listener is implored to go overboard, diving "into the sea and under it: five fathoms down," where we beat on the hull of a submarine on the ocean floor.

This sequence is a vivid example of Corwin's pre-1946 "kaleidosonic" style, which Neil Verma posits as one of the two dominant formulas used by radio directors of the 1930s to create a sense of auditory space. The "kaleidosonic" mode was often heard in news dramatizations like "The March of Time" and created the feeling of a "shifting sonic world" by aurally leaping from place to place. It contrasts with an "intimate" mode in which the listener is positioned alongside a "carefully selected character for the duration of the drama."[27] Corwin was a master of the kaleidosonic style, as can be heard in the globe-circling microphone of the "On a Note of Triumph" sequence described above. Corwin's individual style then, is the result of orchestrating diverse places as much as diverse voices; that is, it is kaleidosonic as well as heteroglossic.

Verma notes that both the intimate and kaleidosonic registers were tied to the affordances of live broadcasting: intimate dramas played on the ephemerality of radio sounds and the "impermanence of the spoken act"; the kaleidosonic aesthetic was a "specimen of the golden age of the point-to-mass mode of mediation, the aesthetic echo of the very concept of broadcast speech."[28] The kaleidosonic style of "On a Note of Triumph" made audible the vast global scale of the war, acknowledged the spatiotemporal dynamics of network broadcasting, and allowed the show to conform to the texture of the broadcast day.[29] Corwin's ability to toggle between intimate and kaleidosonic styles made him appear to be a master of the medium, and "On a Note of Triumph" certainly provoked a passionate response in listeners. CBS received over four thousand letters and thousands of telephone calls regarding the show.[30] A critic for the *Saturday Review of Literature* suggested that the broadcast had crucial significance for the entire medium of radio: "if you wish to realize how fully radio has matured in an incredibly short time, and to comprehend its special possibilities when it is operating at its distinguished best," the author stated, "you need only hear 'On a Note of Triumph.'"[31]

Like Orson Welles's "War of the Worlds," "On a Note of Triumph" is an iconic radio text of the golden age of American radio, but Corwin's professional triumph proved to be short-lived. His first major radio project after the war garnered neither the large audiences nor the critical accolades of "On a Note of Triumph" and indicated Corwin's movement from the center to the periphery of network radio. It also marked a new chapter in Corwin's exploration of the expressive possibilities of recording technology.

ONE WORLD FLIGHT

In February 1946, Corwin announced that his next radio project would document a trip around the world retracing a journey taken four years earlier by Indiana politician Wendell Willkie. Willkie had been chosen to be FDR's representative on a forty-nine day diplomatic trip around the world to visit the Allied nations in 1941 and 1942, and he documented his mission in the best-selling book *One World* (1943). When Willkie died in 1944, his supporters established a memorial foundation in his name to fund an annual trip retracing the historic mission. On February 18, 1946, Corwin became the first recipient of the Willkie Foundation's One World Award.

Corwin documented his flight around the world with a portable wire recorder, one of several new sound technologies that had been developed during the war. Armed Forces Radio Network reporters had taken wire recorders onto the battlefield during the war, but Corwin used this wartime technology to document the sounds of the world just after the conflict had ended.[32] Such a novel approach was not without its difficulties: Corwin's prototype wire recorder stopped working early in the trip, and it was difficult to find technicians with the skills to repair it.[33] Despite the technical problems posed by the wire recorder and the arduous task of editing one hundred hours of material into a coherent series, *One World Flight* was completed and made its CBS premiere on January 14, 1947. From its debut episode, *One World Flight* showcased the "authentic sounds" captured by Corwin's wire recorder.

The premiere episode of *One World Flight* opens with "you-technique" statements (you're standing in a metro station under the heart of Moscow; you're strolling along a street in London; you're in the library of a pleasant house in New Delhi, India), but each statement is followed by one of the "authentic sounds of foreign places and voices of foreign people" captured by Corwin's wire recorder. This opening sequence encapsulates the series' stylistic hybridity: *One World Flight* combines an intimate association with Corwin as narrator with a kaleidosonic sense of spatiotemporal movement, but adds the fascination of documentary recordings. Press coverage suggests that the documentary status of Corwin's recordings was the show's chief point of interest, with many critics referring to the nuances of particular voices. The "gravity" of the Danish premier's voice could not be "reproduced on the printed page," wrote one reviewer: "There are inflections in the sound of the human voice that cannot be duplicated in print."[34] *New York Times* critic Jack Gould declared that the voice of Indian prime minister Jawaharlal Nehru was "as full of infinitesimal currents as the Ganges, and as mysterious."[35] The recorded heteroglossia of the show consisted of the voices not just of politicians but of artists (like Soviet composer Sergei Prokofiev and film director Sergei Eisenstein) and of "common people," such as a Cockney street peddler in London and an Italian war widow.

Corwin's emphasis on documentary sounds in *One World Flight* was something new in his radio style and represented the emergence of a radio aesthetic based primarily on the compilation of location recordings. Francesco Casetti's discussion of cinematic "gazes" can help us to place this emergent style in relation to Verma's intimate and kaleidosonic modes. Casetti describes a "kaleidoscopic gaze" that resembles Verma's kaleidosonic mode of audioposition in 1930s radio: it provides a "partitive whole" in which fragments "make themselves known as such" while also forming "a comprehensive vision."[36] Casetti contrasts cinema's kaleidoscopic, or "partitive," gaze with an "intensive" gaze that focuses on the "salient element, instead of the total design," fixing on a "portion of reality" and finding in it "the keystone of the entire situation."[37] The intensive gaze recalls Verma's intimate mode in some respects, albeit with an emphasis on the significant photographic detail. The partitive and intensive gazes describe two cinematic protocols, the former exemplified by modes of editing that unite disparate shots into a coherent whole, and the latter exemplified by a close-up that allows the viewer to revel in a significant photographic detail. Following Casetti, we might say that *One World Flight* negotiates a new fault line in Corwin's radio aesthetic, with the operative tension not between the intimate and the kaleidosonic but between the partitive and the intensive; that is, between the spatiotemporal compression afforded by network broadcasting and the inexhaustible sonic richness of the documentary recording.[38]

It is appropriate that Casetti's film theory should make its entrance at this point in my argument since Corwin's postwar radio style bears a family resemblance to postwar cinematic realism. As stated in the introduction to this chapter, film theorists have argued that the turn to cinematic realism was encouraged by the recording capacity of sound and the traumatic experiences of World War II.[39] Recording and the memory of wartime trauma are combined in a striking sequence in the final episode of *One World Flight*. Corwin describes searching through documentary recordings for the show and coming across a disc of Nazi air attacks made by the BBC in 1940. Though it contained the "authentic soundtrack of a mere twenty seconds out of Britain's war" and so was "only a fragment of one of a thousand nights of terror," it became for Corwin a Proustian aide-mémoire. "What came from my loudspeaker jolted me back to those days," Corwin says, "and made me realize anew how much has been forgotten." Here, recordings are sonic resistors in the circuitry of radio modernism, indexical traces whose intensive appeal grounds the partitive tendency to leap across time zones and recalibrates radio's temporal register from the interconnected present to the just-receding past.[40]

This sequence is perhaps the most vivid demonstration of how the series wove together radio and recorded sound in order to acknowledge wartime trauma. That stylistic synthesis bears similarities to postwar cinematic realism, but there are more literal ways in which *One World Flight* moved in tandem with realist filmmaking. Consider that the episode of the program recorded in Italy features an interview with Sergio Amidei, the screenwriter of neorealist classics like *Shoeshine* (1946), *Paisan* (1946), and *Germany Year Zero* (1948). During the broadcast, Corwin describes attending a screening of the writer's recent film *Rome, Open City* (1945), which he refers to as a symbol of Italy's rebirth.[41] The Amidei sequence in *One World Flight* makes explicit a larger constellation of connections between Corwin and postwar cinematic realism.

André Bazin wrote that neorealist films were "first and foremost reconstituted reportage" and presented "a revolutionary humanism."[42] The same could be said of *One World Flight*'s location recording, interviews with "real people," and documentary style. In terms of depicting a "revolutionary humanism," consider that the American Communist newspaper the *Daily Worker* hailed *One World Flight* as "the voice of the people."[43] Notably, the same page of the *Daily Worker* containing this review also featured an ad for Rossellini and Amidei's *Rome, Open City*, which was enjoying a two-year run in New York City. *One World Flight* and Italian neorealist classics thus shared elements of style, an ideological sensibility, and an appeal to a similar progressive demographic.

Italian neorealist films are known for their unhappy endings, and *One World Flight* concluded on a similarly stark note. In the final episode of the series, Corwin observed that the reservoir of good will toward the United States that Willkie had found five years earlier had "drained to a dangerously low level." "We are suspected, disliked, resented and even hated in some of the very countries where Willkie found the greatest appreciation and friendship for us in 1942." Like Willkie before him, Corwin reminded listeners of the need to fight fascism at home and played an interview with an Austrian refugee who stated that the "lynching of Negroes gives me an uncomfortable feeling because I think of Nazi Germany and the persecution of the Jews and other peoples."[44] Perhaps the unvarnished message of the series was one reason that *One World Flight* did not attract the same large audiences that had heard his wartime broadcasts.

CBS's decision to schedule the show on Tuesday evenings certainly did not help. A writer in the *New Republic* described listening to *One World Flight* on a "little prewar set" in his kitchen, captivated by the voice of Prime Minister Nehru, whose words were "poetry of a high order." Nehru was being drowned out however, by another kind of poetry that was issuing from a more powerful radio set in the author's dining room. That poem went as follows: "My favorite brunette is only three; when she wants her daddy, she calls for me." That bit of doggerel was an entry in a jingle-writing contest to promote Bob Hope's latest film, *My Favorite Brunette* (1947), and was broadcast on Hope's Pepsodent radio show, which aired opposite Corwin on NBC.[45] The *New Republic* author concluded that *One World Flight* was destined to be heard by a miniscule portion of the radio audience because CBS had seen fit to put the program "in the death watch," opposite Hope. According to Michael C. Keith and Mary Ann Watson, many liberals saw that network decision as a sign that "socially conscious broadcasting was losing support at CBS, once the leader in that realm."[46] A critic at the *Daily Worker* urged readers to do everything in their power to support the "great and articulate voices" heard on *One World Flight:* "Send your letter to CBS" and ask for "a better broadcast hour for the best show CBS has on the air!"[47]

The fate of *One World Flight* was an indication of the way network winds were blowing, and not just at CBS. The conflation of national interests with antifascist radio writers like Corwin was coming to an end. Corwin's radio aesthetic had been central to many Americans' experience of World War II, but it soon became peripheral and even subversive after the war.[48] The *Daily Worker*'s enthusiasm for *One World Flight* was, by some accounts, the motivation behind a House Un-American Activities Committee (HUAC) request for scripts of the series, and Corwin was placed under government surveillance.[49] Corwin was targeted by anticommunist organizations of this era, with the result being that he was a high-profile victim of the postwar blacklist (see Thomas Doherty's analysis in chapter 2).[50] "The 1950s were an awful decade," Corwin stated, "it was a miserable time, a period when reaction crested and when life for a liberal became very strained and, to some, untenable. There were suicides." Furthermore, Corwin grieved what he saw as the death of his medium: "I had been riding a wonderful charger—a beautiful horse, the saddle and equipage of which was furnished by a great network—and that horse was shot out from under me. I suffered along with all of the other serious radio artists."[51]

Another factor in the collapse of the "wonderful charger" of radio was, of course, the emergence of television, a medium that Corwin did not see as a viable alternative for his work at this time (an opinion that would change, as Shawn VanCour will discuss in chapter 5). In 1948, Corwin wrote that television was still in its "economic and technical diapers," and he predicted that "the entrepreneurs" of the medium were going to be "absorbed with advertising techniques long before they get down to problems of creative writing."[52] By 1951, Corwin's disillusionment with broadcasting was such that he could offer a two-word prescription for success in radio: "be mediocre." Radio, he claimed, was interested only in "the safe, routine, unspectacular, competent, journeyman script . . . with maybe a fresh twist no bigger than what you give to a lemon peel in a Martini."[53] It was in this oppressive political climate that Corwin had his disheartening 1948 meeting with CBS president William Paley, and soon thereafter severed his ties with the network.

One wonders what might have developed had there been no blacklist or had Corwin been more open to moving into television. Exiled from network radio and loathe to work in television, Corwin took his style of Popular Front radio to the United Nations in 1948.[54] Though it came to be his swan song at CBS, *One World Flight* initiated an exploration of the possibilities of mineralized radio that continued throughout his next three years at the United Nations.

CITIZEN OF THE WORLD

UN Radio was primarily a vehicle for the dissemination of news, but Corwin was hired to head a subdivision that would create "special programs" dramatizing the work and purpose of the organization.[55] In March 1949, the United Nations issued a press release stating that Corwin was responsible for programs that would address "major themes of international concern" and present the "dramatic and human side of the United Nations' work."[56] Corwin saw the UN job as an alternative to the commercially driven media industries, as indicated by his comments to *Newsweek*: "as public-service radio sinks, the Columbia Workshop remains moribund, [and] the whole retrenchment for television forces public-service radio into a corner[,] . . . United Nations radio is sort of water seeking its own level. More and more, it represents the aesthetic phase of radio." The magazine added that most of the writers at the UN were "old hands at effective experimental radio writing" who had been "driven elsewhere by radio's 'retrenchment.'"[57] Besides writers, Corwin's

UN shows featured a cohort of blacklisted talent that included actors Lee J. Cobb, Edward G. Robinson, José Ferrer, and Martin Gabel and the composer Lyn Murray. UN Radio may have been an alternative to network radio in terms of content, style, and personnel, but we should note that Corwin's programs were made possible by a deal whereby the networks allowed him to use their production facilities at no cost.[58]

Corwin brought his heteroglossic and kaleidosonic style to the United Nations but gave it a cosmopolitan twist. Corwin's new position mandated that listeners be addressed as *global* citizens, and his first script experimented with a global address and was, in fact, broadcast around the world. "Citizen of the World" aired in the United States on CBS on July 10, 1949, and a recording of the show was made available to networks in England, Canada, Australia, New Zealand, South Africa, and Malta. The script was rebroadcast on Pakistan Radio in Urdu translation, on All-India Radio, and on the BBC Far East Service in Burmese and Siamese.[59] Whereas Corwin's earlier broadcasts had taken listeners hurtling over continents or from the stratosphere to the ocean floor, "Citizen of the World" demonstrated how the "typical" American home was interpenetrated by the rest of the world. At one point in the broadcast, an unnamed "citizen of the world" asks the listener, "You think the world has little to do with you? You're so mixed up with the world right this minute, inside and out, past and present, that you can't tell where you begin and the world leaves off." In order to dispel the misconception that Americans owed nothing to "foreign parts or people," listeners were asked to take "a typical American, 100% self-sufficient, relaxing at home after his dinner. He lives, let's say, in Memphis, Tennessee." A second voice interjects, "named after the capitol of ancient Egypt." The first voice continues, "and he's just finished drinking coffee," to which the second voice adds "from Venezuela." The sequence continues in this fashion: "he sits back and strikes a match (invented in France), lights up a cigar (invented in Cuba), and picks up the evening paper (invented in China), to read in bold print (invented in Germany), about the state of Florida (named by Spaniards)," and so forth.

The first thing to note about this sequence is that it manifests another similarity between Corwin's postwar work and Italian neorealism. In an 1953 interview, the neorealist scriptwriter Cesare Zavattini described his desire to "excavate and identify" an ordinary moment in everyday life and then "send its echo vibrating into other parts of the world" in order to dramatize a sense of interdependence in modern experience.[60] He gave the example of a hypothetical film that depicted a woman buying a pair of shoes and then expanded upon that action to pursue a series of questions: "What is her son doing at the same moment? What are people doing in India that could have some relation to this fact of the shoes? The shoes cost 7,000 lire. How did the woman happen to have 7,000 lire? How hard did she have to work for them, what do they represent for her?" In this manner, the apparently mundane subject of purchasing shoes could be the basis for a film that gave viewers access to "a vast and complex world."[61] The typical-American-home sequence in "Citizen of the World" works in a similar way to excavate everyday experience, sending an echo vibrating to foreign parts and people in the service of enacting global citizenship.

Before going further into Corwin's UN work, it is important to recognize that his vision of world citizenship is not without its problems. John Tomlinson points to ideological shortcomings with what he calls the cosmopolitan disposition, one of which is the male gender bias crystallized in the phrase "man of the world." As we can see in the typical-American-home sequence described above, the "citizen of the world" in Corwin's show is assumed to be male: *he* relaxes after his dinner; *he* sits back; *he* glances at a clock. This is certainly symptomatic of sexist norms of language from the era, but it also betrays the gender bias of the show. Some of Corwin's subsequent UN broadcasts feature significant sequences on women's rights, but the hour-long broadcast of "Citizen of the World" features only two very brief statements from women.[62]

"Citizen of the World" can also be criticized for sharing a Western bias typical of much cosmopolitan discourse. "It is primarily westerners," Tomlinson observes, "who get to be the globe-trotters."[63] Along with this Western bias comes the tendency to denigrate locally situated cultural experiences. The United Nations of Corwin's era was criticized for having such a Western bias, and Zoe Druick describes how the agency was characterized as "a handmaiden to American foreign policy, insinuating Western technology and capital into oil rich buffer zones around the Soviet Union's sphere of influence."[64] Given such criticisms, we should note that the movement of people, resources, and information in "Citizen of the World" is uniformly one-way: "specialists" from industrialized Western nations are sent to Siam, Venezuela, Bulgaria, and Haiti. One sequence in the show concerns the introduction of powdered milk to a Bulgarian village. The villagers, as represented by children, are coaxed to drink the strange beverage. Their hesitance is portrayed as a state of ignorance to be overcome, but given what we now know about the marketing of Nestlé products in Africa, for example, the villagers had good reason to be skeptical. In this show and others, Corwin champions UN goals of global modernization that are difficult to distinguish from the project of Western capitalist expansion.[65]

Despite these ideological blind spots, Corwin's show has much in common with Tomlinson's ideal "citizen of the world," who is able to grasp the pluralism of cultures and remain open to cultural difference such that they live simultaneously in global and local registers.[66] Tomlinson claims that such a cosmopolitan disposition can be fostered in part through access to a "globalizing media experience," and Corwin's "Citizen of the World" broadcast seems to agree, judging by a sequence that takes radio as its subject.[67] Narrator Lee J. Cobb explains that, though the typical American thinks that "he is alone in his little room, and out of touch with things," there is "passing through his room and his body, a hundred vibrations of light, sound and speech. A chow-chow of amateurs, aircraft, shortwave, TV, AM, FM, flowing right through him." Corwin broadens the radio spectrum beyond these broadcasts to describe the "conversations of ships at sea," the "pidgin English" spoken in "the backwoods of New Guinea," and shortwave broadcasts "from everywhere, all crowded into a little room that was just minding its own business."

The radio sequence in "Citizen of the World" presents a solution to the danger that, in applying the kaleidosonic mode to a global address, that style could implicitly reinforce a mode of Western-style modernization across the globe in a way that ignored indigenous forms of knowledge.⁶⁸ The unidirectional movement of knowledge in much of "Citizen of the World" could begin to sound like an authoritarian monologue, but the radio sequence opens up the possibility of a return to Corwin's heteroglossic style, only now on a global scale. The show's message about the coexistence of the global and local got through to at least one listener: *New York Times* critic Jack Gould wrote that "Citizen of the World" "drove home the point that the individual has no alternative to the acceptance of world citizenship because modern transportation and communications have knitted the globe together so tightly."⁶⁹

Corwin's next UN broadcast provided another variation on a global kaleidosonic address, this time by combining the partitive and intensive modes of listening in a manner similar to *One World Flight*. "Could Be" was broadcast over NBC in the United States in September 1949 and was rebroadcast in England, Australia, Hong Kong, the Philippines, Malaya, New Zealand, and South Africa.⁷⁰ The show's title indicates its rhetorical concern with the future, and narrator Martin Gabel introduces the broadcast as a celebration of "the undated, unscheduled, but entirely possible creation of an era of world progress that *could be*." Gabel describes the show as an audio portrait of "what could happen if nations of the world got together and attacked common problems with the same vigor, determination, and resources with which from time to time they have attacked each other." After this prelude, the voice of a radio operator calls, "Come in, Year X," and an audio dissolve brings us to the roof of the UN building in New York City, a location that recalls wartime reporting as well as the famous scene in Welles's "War of the Worlds" when a reporter describes a Martian invasion of New York City from a rooftop. Whereas Welles dramatized an apocalyptic collapse of civilization, Corwin enacts a utopian rebirth, a future in which the wartime sense of Allied unity and the power of industrial war machinery were put to peaceful and constructive ends. The radio announcer in "Could Be" describes the imminent launch of Task Force One, an international Blitz for Peace that puts sonar technology in the service of fishing operations, and fleets of military aircraft are used to exterminate vermin and open a dam. These task forces are described through simulated radio reports from around the world, punctuated by carefully staged glitches, static, and interruptions reminiscent of Welles's "Panic Broadcast."[71]

"Could Be" features a partitive unity of various places and times but adds an intensive approach when, halfway through the show's simulation of radio's worldwide reach, we hear a seven-minute "excursion into the past" composed of documentary radio broadcasts from the war years, including the wailing sounds of air-raid sirens in London. The excursion-into-the-past sequence of "Could Be" uses recordings as sonic resistors that pull the listener back to the recent past, and so recalls the moment in the final episode of *One World Flight* when recorded sound evoked the experience of war. "Could Be" thus emerges as a work of sound art that ties a complex knot of temporalities: Corwin recalls the past while speaking of the future, and a kaleidosonic aesthetic once tied to the interconnected present represents a possible future that is understood in relation to archival recordings of radio's past.[72]

"Could Be" attempts to rekindle a sense of wartime unity, a project that must have resonated with Corwin's personal sense of alienation from the ideological climate of the Cold War era. Corwin wrote in 1951 that "in the dark of this despised century, now half eroded, there are few aspects of the world community that can bring joy or even hope to its inhabitants."[73] Rejecting an incipient consumer and corporate culture invested in promoting "Better Living Through Chemistry," he argued that "turbo-jet engines, penicillin, deep-freezes, plastics, telescopes, and isotopes" had not significantly raised the level of human happiness. "Instead," he wrote, "the more techniques we acquire and the closer we press the secrets of the cosmos, the more clumsy seem to become our social relationships."[74] For a generation that had seen "two-and-a-half world wars, three major and a score of minor revolutions, all without any improvement to its state of mind," where was there to look for hope? Corwin's answer was the subject of his 1950 broadcast "Document A/777": the 1948 United Nations Declaration of Human Rights.

Historian Paul Kennedy writes that the Declaration of Human Rights enjoyed enormous renown at this time, with translated copies hung in schools and libraries around the world.[75] The declaration did not have the force of law, but for Corwin, it was a powerful reminder of "the principles of universal freedom for which so many ghastly wars have been fought." As he had done with the American Bill of Rights for the broadcast "We Hold These Truths," Corwin transformed the declaration into a historical narrative, describing it as a story about all the people who had struggled for human rights. The memorialization of the past was aligned to the future: Corwin wrote that the declaration gave its readers "renewed faith in the human spirit and the courage to plough ahead through discouragement after discouragement, setback after setback."[76] Like "Could Be," " Document A/777" looked to the past in order to imagine a more progressive future.

"Document A/777" aired on the Mutual network in March 1950 and on the BBC Light Programme in January 1951.[77] The show opens with the you-technique familiar from Corwin's wartime shows, but it is implemented here with a certain ironic distance. Over ominous music, narrator Van Heflin places the listener at the heart of an espionage thriller: "You have a rendezvous on an island twenty miles outside New York City," the listener is told, where you seek information about a "man-made force thousands of times greater than the hydrogen bomb" that is small enough to fit into a handbag. This second-person address continues as we make our rendezvous, enter a bookstore, and buy a copy of the Declaration of Human Rights. Heflin laughs and says, "Sure, that's the way it is on radio. Catch the listener on a fishhook dangled in air . . . an angle of urgency in the voice, a promise of bombs and spies and secret rendezvous." The intimate style of this prologue draws listeners in while simultaneously announcing that United Nations Radio is a self-aware alternative to network radio's conventional techniques. Here is an example of what Bakhtin calls "double-voiced" discourse whereby Corwin's individual style is revealed through a detached handling of the conventions of radio drama.[78]

The rest of the broadcast is structured around a dramatization of the December 1948 meeting of the Third General Assembly of the United Nations in Paris, where the vote was cast to ratify the Declaration of Human Rights. Corwin halts the proceedings when the names of certain national delegates are called, and then changes the scene to show how the history of that nation speaks to the document's various amendments. For example, when China is called to vote, the scene shifts to a vignette on the execution of poets and scholars in China, leading to a discussion of Article 19, which concerns the right to freedom of opinion and expression. The show is thus a textbook illustration of Corwin's mobilization of the heteroglossic and kaleidosonic, but note that, as was the case with *One World Flight* and "Could Be," "Document A/777" combines that approach with the intensive appeal of documentary recordings. In fact, the show was recorded and edited on the recording format that superseded the wire recorder—magnetic tape—in part to facilitate the participation of its all-star cast, which included not only Heflin as narrator, but Charles Boyer, Ronald Colman, Lena Horne, Lee J. Cobb, Charles Laughton, Joan Crawford, José Ferrer, Laurence Olivier, Vincent Price, and Edward G. Robinson.[79] Because it was impossible to schedule such an impressive roster of talent for a single session, the production was staggered over several days and recorded in both New York and Hollywood. The finished show was then edited together from over three hundred individual segments.[80] In other words, the partitive mode heard on "Document A/777" did not serve as an acknowledgment of the technological base of live broadcast radio as much as it represented the persistence of a residual technique that was now created through tape editing.

The show's most intricate braiding of the partitive and intensive modes of listening can be heard during its concluding sequence. Once the national roll call has ended, the documentary power of recorded sound takes center stage in the form of an actual recording of Herbert Evatt, president of the Third General Assembly, who announces the ratification of the declaration. Documentary recordings of President Evatt are followed by the sound of the bells of Notre Dame as the delegates leave the Assembly, which are transformed by music and narration into a metaphor for the Declaration itself. Heflin declares that, just as the peal of the bells radiates around the world, so do the "mighty overtones" of Document A/777 radiate the "first vibrations of world conscience." In the form of sound waves, the declaration penetrates all aspects of social life, "inundating the byways and back-alleys of every town, lapping around factories and schools[,] . . . running like quicksilver through homes, stores, offices[,] . . . flashing through the union hall, the courtroom, the polling booth[,] . . . dancing along the radio antenna on your roof, running like fire through the condensers and tubes of your receiver in your room as you sit and listen at leisure."

The use of the bell as aural metaphor is great radio writing to be sure, but there is more to be said about this concluding sequence. First, note how a partitive mode emerges from but is also grounded in the intensive appeal of documentary recordings. You might have noticed that recordings of bells and sirens are a consistent sonic motif of Corwin's work from this era: recall the central place held by the sound of air-raid sirens in the excursion-into-the-past sequence of "Could Be" as well as the final episode of *One World Flight*. R. Murray Schafer claims that sirens and bells belong to the same class of "community signals," and describes church bells as a centripetal sound that defines an "acoustic community" circumscribed by their audible range.[81] Bells and sirens were radiogenic "sound souvenirs" that viscerally brought back memories of the war against fascism and so were useful resources for Corwin as he sought to recreate a sense of wartime community.[82] In short, bells and sirens were "earcons" in Corwin's sonic repertoire: that is, they were sonic events that contained "special symbolic meaning not present in the sound wave."[83] "Document A/777" provides another example of how Corwin created a postwar radio style that combined a partitive unity of disparate times and places with the intensive power of documentary recordings. In some of the last broadcasts of his tenure at the United Nations, Corwin's radio realism consisted almost entirely of documentary recordings.

FEAR ITSELF

The use of documentary recordings became a common trope of UN Radio productions during Corwin's time there, judging by a number of programs that took the form of what Bazin called, with reference to the *Why We Fight* series, an "edited ideological documentary."[84] Consider "Fear Itself" (1950), which was the third program in a six-part UN series produced by Corwin. "Fear Itself" begins with the sounds of London's Westminster Abbey bells ringing on V-E Day, which narrator Martin Gabel describes as the "bells of yesterday." What follows is a history of the five years since the end of the war as constituted by archival recordings. We hear reporters discussing the destruction of Berlin, news coverage of the Japanese surrender, the explosions of a nuclear test in the Pacific, and the sounds of Cold War radio jamming to illustrate the disintegration of American-Soviet relations. Perhaps most affecting is a recording from the Belsen concentration camp, where "God Save the King" is played by newly liberated survivors on a "rickety, out of tune" piano in the SS canteen. Through its use of documentary recordings, "Fear Itself" is one of Corwin's most sustained explorations of the potential for an intensive mode of listening to bear sonic witness to recent events and might be understood in terms of Siegfried Kracauer's argument that durative media like film and sound recording have the redemptive power to allow audiences to face subjects that are "too dreadful to be beheld in reality."[85]

"Fear Itself" demonstrates that a culture of postwar media witness existed beyond film. In fact, a review of "Fear Itself" noted that the show's "authentic actuality recordings" included material that had become familiar to many listeners via phonograph records, in particular, Columbia Records' December 1948 long-playing record *I Can Hear It Now*. Corwin's CBS colleagues Edward R. Murrow and Fred Friendly were responsible for *I Can Hear It Now*, which was an anthology of documentary sounds of the war years. Murrow and Friendly's record shared some of Corwin's sonic vocabulary, including that most resonant of postwar earcons: the air-raid siren. On *I Can Hear It Now*, we hear an air-raid siren as Murrow narrates, "If you were in Manila[,] . . . Singapore or London, you know the terror of that sound. You know it can never be imitated. It is the shimmering wail of a hundred sirens bouncing off the echo chambers which are a bombed city's dead buildings and deserted docks."

I Can Hear It Now surprised the record industry by becoming a runaway best seller, with more than 125,000 units sold in the first two months after it was released. Critics were dazzled by it: *Billboard* referred to it as "one of the most arresting record albums ever to hit the retail market," and a writer for the *Saturday Review of Literature* said it was "the most exciting" record he had ever heard.[86] Like Corwin's edited ideological documentaries from this era, *I Can Hear It Now* was a stunning piece of sound assemblage. The result of months of work, it had involved gathering five hundred hours of recordings from radio stations and archives around the world, recording a hundred hours of material onto magnetic tape, and then editing that material down to forty-five minutes.[87] In fact, Friendly stated that Columbia probably wouldn't have bothered with the project if it hadn't been for the fact that the industry was besieged by a national recording strike by the American Federation of Musicians (AFM).[88] Without musicians in the studios, record companies were on the lookout for new formats, and studio engineers had the extra time needed to assemble piles of archival recordings. Friendly even said that they considered dedicating the album to AFM leader James Caesar Petrillo to thank him for spearheading the strike.[89]

The success of *I Can Hear It Now* set off a cycle of documentary and history albums. Among the "documentary" albums that followed it were two additional volumes of *I Can Hear It Now;* Victor's *The Quick and the Dead,* an LP about atomic energy featuring Bob Hope; Columbia's *You Are There,* a recorded version of the CBS radio series in which reporters re-created historical events; London Records' *Prelude to Pearl Harbor* (1950); *The Greatest Moments in Sports* (Columbia, 1955); and even several documentaries on the United Nations, including *This is the U.N.* (1950, Tribune Productions) and *Voices toward Peace: From the Official Archives of the United Nations* (Decca, 1960).[90] The trend continued into the next decade, most notably in the form of several John F. Kennedy memorial LPs.

If we combine the public appetite for these documentary records with Corwin's use of sound recording on his postwar broadcasts, we come up with a widespread culture of sound realism during the same years that Bazin theorized influential new forms of cinematic realism. Bazin's claim that the primacy of the image in cinema was historically and technically accidental might serve as a visa allowing sound culture entry into the discussion of postwar realism. We might go further, however, and say that the primacy of the *cinema* has been historically and technically accidental in the larger study of postwar realism across a range of durative media forms. Sound recording not only fulfilled a certain "Old Testament of the cinema" but also had its own history of central texts, preferred protocols, sonic iconography, and innovative creative workers—prominent among the latter being Norman Corwin.

Corwin's work reveals the limitations of relying solely upon a cinematic model for all forms of recorded realism. To illustrate, let's return to Corwin's "Fear Itself," which ends where it began, with the "bells of yesterday," only now they are slowed down and distorted. Gabel asks if the "bells of jubilation that sounded five years ago" will be "a mockery five years from now.... Or shall they find again their own true pitch and rhythm, and ring again for total victory ... of reason over fear itself." Under his narration, the speed of the bells slowly increases until they become recognizable as the Westminster Abbey chimes that began the show; a poetic parallelism of sound effects and narration as the bells find their own "true pitch and rhythm."

The bells of "Fear Itself" are documentary recordings meant to make listeners recall a wartime past that was experienced to a significant degree via radio, and as such they are part of a larger tendency in Corwin's postwar broadcasts both to invoke a lost sense of wartime unity and to mourn the loss of a previous era of radio. But also note how the bells at the end of "Fear Itself" are treated in a manner that Jean Epstein has called "slow-motion sound."[91] The malleability of recorded sound is put on display here in a way that refutes Bazin's claim that sound encouraged cinematic realism because it was "far less flexible than the visual image."[92] In fact, postwar recording technologies served at once to facilitate a documentary function and to amplify the flexibility of sound art, as heard in the work of Epstein, musique concrète composers, and musicians like Les Paul. Sound recording's relationship to realism is much more complex than the assertion of an all-determining medium ontology, a point that Bazin's many interpreters have been eager to make in regards to film. Radio has a decidedly open and ambiguous relationship to realism, as Rudolf Arnheim explains: in radio, he writes, real sounds and voices are not bound to the physical world but claim "relationship with the poetic word and the musical note," such that radio artists are given "the exciting possibility of making an amazing new unity out of pure form and physical reality."[93] Corwin's slow-motion bells of yesterday show him to be a radio artist who explored those new unities of sonic form and physical reality, and his UN broadcasts mobilized that aesthetic to acknowledge, represent, and remember the war and its aftermath.

WINDOWS ON THE WORLD

Corwin wrote that United Nations Radio represented "the high ground to which responsible radio drama retreated" in the immediate postwar years, providing an alternative to the American networks.[94] For a moment, it even looked as if Corwin's UN broadcasts might offer an alternative to Hollywood filmmaking. In 1950, Corwin published a letter in the *Hollywood Reporter* in which he suggested that the film community take up a "new ambassadorship" by working with the United Nations. He argued that Hollywood's service to the United Nations would help to "heighten the stature of the industry and secure its deserved position of respect throughout the world."[95] These overtures were tentatively reciprocated when Corwin signed a contract with MGM to write a film adaptation of "Document A/777." Kirk Douglas was said to be among the interested parties.[96] As Thomas Doherty shows in his chapter of this volume, Corwin's name came up during several anti-Communist hearings around this time, and the plans for a film version of "Document A/777" were suspended by MGM production chief Dore Schary.[97] Meanwhile, the American radio networks sought to distance themselves from the United Nations and cut off Corwin's free access to their studio facilities. Corwin stated that Americans who worked with the United Nations were "deeply suspected and that included me.... I was untouchable to patriotic Americans."[98]

"Windows on the World" (1951) was one of the last programs Corwin produced at the United Nations; notably, it was made without a cast of Hollywood stars or network studio facilities. Instead, Corwin and eight colleagues moved through the United Nation's new permanent headquarters in New York equipped with small tape recorders and recorded impromptu interviews with UN workers. The show used the Secretariat Building's vertical structure as the framework for a "floor-by-floor ascent," with candid glimpses of UN workers from many countries illustrating the scope of the organization's activities.[99] Corwin stipulated that interviews be unscripted and that business in each office go on as usual, allowing listeners to hear interviewees interrupted by the telephone, helicopters buzzing overhead, and an employee who provides what Corwin called a "stream-of-consciousness with typewriter-obligato."[100] The use of nine different tape recorders resulted in a huge amount of material, and *Variety* reported that the show had set "some sort of record for taping facilities," requiring six days, six Ampex tape machines, three associate producers, and eighty-four reels of tape to complete.[101]

The distinctive production method for "Windows on the World" was a way of making do without top stars or the network's studios, but it also marks the culmination of the shift to recording in Corwin's approach to sound. Here is a radio realism consisting of location recording, the use of nonprofessional performers, and reliance upon the capture of happy accidents and extensive tape editing. "Windows on the World" is an update on *One World Flight* with a more reliable recording technology and an artistic orchestration of voices from around the world that is constructed without leaving New York City.

"Windows on the World" should also be heard as a bookend with Corwin's first UN show, "Citizen of the World." In the two years between those broadcasts, Corwin found ways to adjust his kaleidosonic and heteroglossic style to a global context and, to my ears, defuse some of the ideological shortfalls of the earlier show. We hear more female voices in "Windows on the World" than on previous broadcasts and the voices of workers in a greater variety of professional roles.[102] Corwin's portable microphones encountered a multinational UN staff and captured the voices of workers from nations such as West Africa, Argentina, and China. Their voices work to bring a more inclusive sound to Corwin's kaleidosonic mix, and the topic of Western colonialism is even addressed head-on when we hear UN diplomat Ralph Bunche assert that "Colonialism is one of the prime factors in generating wars. There can be no secure foundations for peace or for freedom in the world so long as a substantial part of the world's population is not free and is subject to attack by aggressor-minded people or nations."

"Windows on the World" marks the end of a trajectory in Corwin's career as a sound auteur in which he fostered new unities of partitive and intensive listening and orchestrated a mineralized heteroglossia with the aid of recording technologies. The show concludes on the top floor, where Secretary-General Trygve Lie describes the Secretariat Building as a "great living switchboard" that brings "the world together as it has never been brought together in the past." Lie might have been talking about Corwin's radio work, which is something like a great living switchboard as well, with Corwin as the switchboard operator, nimbly weaving voices into a larger conversation. The UN building may have been a great living switchboard, but it was also an archive of documents, images, and recorded sounds. At one point in the 1951 show, Corwin even listens to a recording of "Document A/777" during his visit to the UN radio department. Corwin was a switchboard operator in some regards, but by the time that he made "Windows on the World," he was also a documentarian, exploring the expressive possibilities of a rapidly expanding archive of recorded sound.

NOTES

1. Keith, Michael C., and Watson, Mary Ann, eds., *Norman Corwin's One World Flight* (New York: Continuum, 2009), 202; Barnouw, Erik, *The Golden Web* (New York: Oxford University Press, 1968), 241–42; and Verma, Neil, *Theater of the Mind* (Chicago: University of Chicago Press, 2012), 81.
2. Studs Terkel writes that Corwin was "the bard of radio's Golden Age" Terkel, Studs, "To the Bard," in *13 for Corwin* (Fort Lee, NJ: Barricade Books, 1985), 9.
3. Verma, 228; and Williams, Raymond, *Problems of Materialism and Culture* (London: Verso, 1980), 55.
4. Bakhtin, M. M., *Speech Genres and Other Late Essays* (Austin: University of Texas Press, 1986), 60, 62.
5. Bazin, André, "The Evolution of the Language of Cinema," in *What Is Cinema?* (Berkeley: University of California Press, 1967), 23, 33.
6. Carroll, Noel, *Philosophical Problems of Classical Film Theory* (Princeton, NJ: Princeton University Press, 1988), 96.
7. Bazin, André, "William Wyler, or the Jansenist of Directing," in *Bazin at Work* (New York: Routledge, 1997), x. See also Bazin, André, "On *Why We Fight*: History, Documentation, and the Newsreel," in *Bazin at Work*, 188; and Watts, Philip, "The Eloquent Image: The Postwar Mission of Film and Criticism," in Andrew, Dudley, with Joubert-Laurencin, Hervé, eds., *Opening Bazin* (Oxford: Oxford University Press, 2011), 221.
8. Bazin, "William Wyler," x.
9. Andrew, Dudley, *What Cinema Is!* (Oxford: Wiley-Blackwell, 2010), 38.
10. On Bazinian realism, see Morgan, Daniel, "Rethinking Bazin: Ontology and Realist Aesthetics," in *Critical Inquiry* 32 (Spring 2006), 471; and Morgan, Daniel, "The Afterlife of Superimposition," in Andrew, Dudley, with Joubert-Laurencin, Hervé, eds., *Opening Bazin* (Oxford: Oxford University Press, 2011), 130.
11. Smith, Judith E., *Visions of Belonging* (New York: Columbia University Press, 2004), 16; and Williams, Albert N., "The Radio Artistry of Norman Corwin," *Saturday Review of Literature* 25 (7), 5.
12. Corwin, Norman, interview with author, March 30, 2011.
13. *Time* characterized his use of sound effects as being "exaggerated like a Hearst headline." "Radio: Prizes for Corwin," *Time* 47 (9) (March 4, 1946), 64.
14. See Blue, Howard, *Words at War: World War II Era Radio Drama and the Postwar Broadcasting Industry Blacklist* (Lanham, MD: Scarecrow Press, 2002), 11, 124. On "We Hold These Truths," see Verma, 77–81.
15. Verma, 79.
16. See Bannerman, R. LeRoy, *Norman Corwin and Radio: The Golden Years* (Tuscaloosa: University of Alabama Press, 1986), 74. On ratings for "We Hold These Truths," see Smith, 21.

17. Horton, Gerd, *Radio Goes to War* (Berkeley: University of California Press, 2003), 45.

18. Blue, 131; and McClinton, H. L., "This is War," *New York Times* (February 15, 1942), X10.

19. Smith, 21. See also Horton, 2. On World War II as a "radio war," see Douglas, Susan, *Listening In* (Minneapolis: University of Minnesota Press, 2004), 161–62, 179, 188–89; and Lingeman, Richard, *Don't You Know there's a War On?* (New York: Thunder's Press, 2003), 272.

20. Smith, 22, 2. As an example, Smith refers to the 1944 broadcast "Dorie Got a Medal," a collaboration between Corwin, the poet and author Langston Hughes, and folksinger Josh White. Smith, 26.

21. Corwin, Norman, *Untitled and Other Radio Dramas* (New York: Henry Holt, 1945), 64.

22. "Untitled" became "one of the first major undertakings in televised drama" when it was adapted for WCBW-CBS in 1945. The script became "the most widely performed of any of Corwin's work, especially by military and naval personnel." Corwin, *Untitled and Other Radio Dramas*, 522–23. See also review of WCBW-CBS, New York, broadcast of televised "Untitled," May 1945, in Norman Corwin Papers, Thousand Oaks Library, Box 145, COR02421.

23. One reporter exclaimed that "space and time" meant nothing to those who arranged "the big broadcast" on V-E Day. "Truman Sets Mark in Radio Coverage," *New York Times* (May 9, 1945), 6.

24. Lenthall, Bruce, *Radio's America* (Chicago: University of Chicago Press, 2007), 194.

25. Corwin quote in Bell, Douglas, *Years of the Electric Ear* (Metuchen, NJ: Scarecrow Press, 1994), 71.

26. Horton, 53.

27. Verma, 63, 68. See also Arnheim, 120. For other discussions of radio and an intimate address, see Loviglio, Jason, *Radio's Intimate Public* (Minneapolis: University of Minnesota Press, 2005); and McCracken, Allison, "Real Men Don't Sing Ballads," in Wojcik, Pamela, and Knight, Arthur, eds., *Soundtrack Available* (Durham, NC: Duke University Press, 2001).

28. Verma, 70–71, 75.

29. On the radio networks and liveness, see Russo, Alexander, *Points of the Dial* (Durham, NC: Duke University Press, 2010), 86.

30. Corwin, *Untitled and Other Radio Dramas*, 535. For a negative review, see De Voto, Bernard, "The Easy Chair," *Harper's* 191 (July 1945), 33–36. Also see "Corwin for Everyone," *Billboard* (May 19, 1945), 4.

31. Brown, John Mason, "On a Note of Triumph," *Saturday Review of Literature* 28 (21) (May 26, 1945), 22.

32. See Lingeman, 223–24; Morton, David, *Off the Record* (New Brunswick, NJ: Rutgers University Press, 2000), 61–62.

33. Corwin stated that the wire recorder was "a big flop: "It was cranky and developed a big hum, you had to fuse the broken ends of a wire with a lit cigarette, it was a terrible nuisance. It was a terrible clumsy machine which was immediately supplanted by tape." Corwin interview with author, March 30, 2011.

34. Crosby, John, "Norman Corwin Travels Far Seeking One World," *Oakland Tribune* (January 23, 1947), 22C.

35. Gould, Jack, "One World Flight," *New York Times* (February 2, 1947), X11.

36. Casetti, Francesco, *Eye of the Century* (New York: Columbia University Press, 2008), 51, 35.

37. Casetti, 41, 43.

38. Tom Gunning emphasizes "the sense of a nearly inexhaustible visual richness to the photograph.... The photograph appears to share the complexity of its subject, to capture all its details, even those we might not ordinarily notice." Gunning, Tom, "What's the Point of an Index? Or, Faking Photographs," in Beckman, Karen, and Ma, Jean, eds., *Still Moving* (Durham: Duke University Press, 2008), 37.

39. Carroll, 96.

40. "On a Note of Triumph" was even made mandatory listening for German prisoners of war via translated OWI discs (Corwin, *Untitled and Other Radio Dramas*, 543–44, 439). See also "Corwin for Everyone," *Billboard* (May 19, 1945), 4.

41. In an interview, Corwin stated that he felt Amidei to be a kindred spirit. Corwin advised the writer not to go to Hollywood: "He went despite of my caution, and found out I was correct. . . . he was chewed up and spat out." Corwin interview with author, March 30, 2011.

42. Bazin, André, "An Aesthetic of Reality," *What Is Cinema?* vol. 2 (Berkeley: University of California Press, 1971), 20–21, 33.

43. Dial-ethics, "Norman Corwin's 'One World' Series Off to a Brilliant Start," *Daily Worker* (January 17, 1947), 11.

44. One critic claimed that Corwin's "momentous" message was that "many of the same forces—ignorance, intolerance and bigotry—which led to World War II are just as strong today as they were when Fascism first went on the prowl in Spain and Germany." Franken, Jerry, "Superb Corwin Preem Reveals Bigotry, Ignorance Rampant," *Billboard* (January 25, 1947), 8.

45. Carson, Saul, "Whose World Flight?" *New Republic* 116 (April 7, 1947), 41–42. This account is a nice indication of Alexander Russo's discussion of a shift beginning in the late 1930s towards multiple radios in the home, which served to divide the domestic space into "individualized zones of reception." Russo, 175.

46. Keith and Watson, 200. See also Franken, 8.

47. G. R., "Corwin Scores with Tense 'Warsaw Ghetto' Closeup," *Daily Worker* (February 11, 1947), 11.

48. Gerd Horton notes "the huge divergence" between the era before the war, when "the state's influence and alternative cultural and political visions were on the rise," and a postwar era during which "visions other than corporate ones were increasingly relegated to the niches of culture and politics." Horton, 4. On business leaders' systematic attempts to develop a "new vocabulary" to fight against the New Deal, see Bird, William L., Jr. *Better Living: Advertising, Media and the New Vocabulary of Business Leadership, 1935–1955* (Evanston, IL: Northwestern University Press, 1999).

49. Keith and Watson, 202–3.

50. Everitt, David, *A Shadow of Red* (Chicago: Ivan R. Dee, 2007), 18, 71, 172, 44–5; also Ceplair, Larry, and Englund, Steven, *The Inquisition in Hollywood* (Garden City, NJ: Anchor Press, 1980), 386; Blue, 349; Keith and Watson, 203–4; and Lewis, Jon, *Hollywood v. Hard Core* (New York: New York University Press, 2000), 14.

51. Bell, 136, 131.

52. Corwin, Norman, "I Can Be Had," *Theatre Arts* 32 (June 1948), 33.

53. "Radio: It's a Living," *Time* (January 29, 195. See also Bannerman, 188, 232; and Verma, 171.

54. On the influence of blacklist in film and radio, see Anderson, Thom, "Red Hollywood," in Ferguson, Suzanne, and Groseclose, Barbara, eds., *Literature and The Visual Arts in Contemporary Society* (Columbus: Ohio State University Press, 1985), 183–84. See also Schwartz, Nancy Lynn, *The Hollywood Writers' Wars* (Lincoln, NE: iUniverse, Inc., 2001).

55. Kennedy, Paul, *The Parliament of Man* (New York: Allen Lane, 2006), 31–32. See also Luard, Evan, *A History of the United Nations* (New York: St. Martin's Press, 1982), 17; "Corwin—1949," *Newsweek* 34 (September 26, 1949), 57. The long-term objective of the Radio Broadcasting Division was to operate its own radio stations, but in the meantime its aim was to service existing networks with broadcasts that illustrated the work of the United Nations. Cohen, Benjamin, "The U.N.'s Department of Public Information," in *Public Opinion Quarterly* 10 (2; Summer 1946), 146–48.

56. Press release, United Nations Department of Public Information, March 8, 1949, Norman Corwin Papers, Thousand Oaks Library, Box 51, COR00534. Corwin's role at UN Radio might be compared to film documentarian John Grierson, who was hired as head of the film division of UNESCO's Mass

Communications Department in 1947. See Druick, Zoe, "Reaching the Multimillions: Liberal Internationalism and the Establishment of Documentary Film," in Grieveson, Lee, and Wasson, Haidee, eds., *Inventing Film Studies* (Durham, NC: Duke University Press, 2008), 81; and Druick, Zoe, "UNESCO, Film, and Education," in Acland, Charles R., and Wasson, Haidee, eds., *Useful Cinema* (Durham, NC: Duke University Press, 2011), 94.

57. "Corwin—1949," 57.

58. Corwin stated that the networks paid for the studio costs of the UN shows for a time, but in the wake of this new round of political repression in the early 1950s, all of the radio networks turned against the UN, and began to charge for the use of their studio facilities. Corwin interview with author, March 30, 2011. See also Bigman, Stanley K., "The 'New Internationalism' Under Attack," in *Public Opinion Quarterly* 14 (2) (Summer 1950).

59. News clippings, Corwin Papers, Box 167, COR03235 and Box 143, COR02377. For a discussion of postwar citizenship, see McCarthy, Anna, *The Citizen Machine: Governing by Television in 1950s America* (New York: New Press, 2010), 10–14.

60. Zavattini, Cesare, "Some Ideas on the Cinema," in Dyer MacCann, Richard, ed., *Film: A Montage of Theories* (New York: E. P. Dutton, 1994), 221.

61. Zavattini, 221, 225.

62. These women are Mildred Fairchild of Chicago, who talks about conditions for working women, and an unnamed aid worker in Haiti.

63. Tomlinson, John, *Globalization and Culture* (Chicago: University of Chicago Press, 1999), 187–89.

64. Druick, "UNESCO, Film, and Education," 82.

65. Lisa Parks writes about discourses of "global presence," noting that the meanings of liveness "were indistinguishable from Western discourses of modernization, which classified societies as traditional or modern, called for urbanization and literacy in the developing world, and envisioned mass media as agents of social control and economic liberalization." Parks, Lisa, *Cultures in Orbit* (Durham, NC: Duke University Press, 2005), 23. See also Curtin, Michael, "Connections and Differences: Spatial Dimensions of Television History," *Film & History* 30 (1) (March 2000), 51.

66. Tomlinson, 194–95.

67. Ibid., 189.

68. I am paraphrasing Druick, Zoe, "UNESCO, Film, and Education," 90.

69. Gould, Jack, "Programs in Review," *New York Times* (July 17, 1949), X7.

70. "A Report to the National Broadcasting Company on the NBC–United Nations Project, 1949 from the Public Affairs and Education Department," submitted by Jane Tiffany Wagner, Director of Education, October 1949, in Norman Corwin Papers, Thousand Oaks Library, Box 77, COR00964.

71. Verma, 71.

72. Thanks to Neil Verma for his insights on the temporal dynamics of "Could Be."

73. Corwin, Norman, "This Is Document A/777," *Radio Times* (January 19, 1951), 5. In Corwin Papers, Box 51, COR00533.

74. Corwin, "This Is Document A/777."

75. Kennedy, 179–81.

76. Corwin, "This Is Document A/777," 5.

77. On reception of Corwin's UN shows in the United Kingdom, see BBC "listener research report" on "Document A/777" dated March 5, 1951, in Corwin Papers, Box 86, COR01129.

78. On double-voiced discourse, see Bakhtin, M. M., *Problems of Dostoevsky's Poetics* (Minneapolis: University of Minnesota Press, 1984), x.

79. Corwin interview, March 30, 2011.

80. Corwin, "This is Document A/777," 5.

81. Schafer, R. Murray, *The Soundscape: Our Sonic Environment and the Tuning of the World* (Rochester, VT: Destiny Books, 1994 [1977]), 178, 53–54. See also Corbin, Alain, *Village Bells: Sound and Meaning in the 19th-Century French Countryside* (New York: Columbia University Press, 1998), 95, 110; and Blesser, Barry, and Salter, Linda-Ruth, *Spaces Speak: Are You Listening?* (Cambridge, MA: MIT Press, 2007), 21.

82. "Sound souvenirs" are sounds that could be captured by recording technologies and stored in archives. See Birdsall, Carolyn, "Earwitnessing: Sound Memories of the Nazi Period," in Bijsterveld, Karin, and van Dijck, Jose, eds., *Sound Souvenirs* (Amsterdam: Amsterdam University Press, 2009), 169–70, 176–77. On the sonic experience of the air raid, see Connor, Steven, "The Modern Auditory I," in Porter, Roy, ed., *Rewriting the Self* (London: Routledge, 1996), 210. Corwin directed prospective radio directors to use a very specific BBC recording of the air-raid siren for "On a Note of Triumph": BBC sound effect disc Master No. 4193 (Library No. 19-B-12), to be precise. That sound could not be faked, Corwin wrote, "because too many Americans among those likely to hear your production are familiar with the real thing. A great many soldiers and civilians from this side spent time in England during the war, and they will accept no substitutes when it comes to the signal of an air raid over Britain." Corwin, *Untitled and Other Radio Dramas*, 494.

83. Blesser and Salter, 82.

84. Bazin, Andre, "On *Why We Fight*: History, Documentation, and the Newsreel," in *Bazin at Work* (New York: Routledge, 1997), p. 189. Corwin was producer-director and worked with writer Allen Sloane on the show "Fear Itself." "Pursuit of Peace," *Variety*, May 10, 1950, 26. Norman Corwin Papers, Thousand Oaks Library, Box 143A, COR02392.

85. Kracauer, Siegfried, *Theory of Film* (Princeton, NJ: Princeton University Press, 1997 [1960]), 300, 304–6. See also Rodowick, D. N., *The Virtual Life of Film* (Cambridge, MA: Harvard University Press, 2007), 61.

86. Ackerman, Paul, "Col. Album Captures Tensions of 1932–'45," *Billboard* (December 4, 1948), 17. "Runaway," *New Yorker* 24 (January 15, 1949), 22. See Taubman, Howard, "Records: History, Drama, and Poetry," *New York Times* (November 19, 1950), X9; and "Tribune Productions Preps 'This Is the UN' Package in 2 Speeds," *Billboard* (April 5, 1950,) 49. Also see Barnouw, 237.

87. "Runaway," 23.

88. On the AFM strikes, see Anderson, Tim J., *Making Easy Listening: Material Culture and Postwar American Recording* (Minneapolis: University of Minnesota Press, 2006), 8, 18, 38.

89. "Runaway," 23.

90. Taubman, X9; "Tribune Productions Preps 'This Is the UN,'" 49.

91. Epstein, Jean, "Slow-Motion Sound," in Weis, Elisabeth, and Belton, John, eds., *Film Sound: Theory and Practice* (New York: Columbia University Press, 1985). On "sound objects," see also Schafer, 192.

92. Bazin, "Evolution of the Language of Cinema," 33.

93. Arnheim, Rudolf, *Radio: An Art of Sound* (New York: Da Capo, 1972; 1936), 15.

94. Langguth, A. J., ed., *Norman Corwin's Letters* (New York: Barricade Books, 1994), 272.

95. "On the Air," *Hollywood Reporter* (April 10, 1950), page unknown, Corwin Papers, Box 51, COR00533.

96. Corwin Papers, Box 51, COR00537.

97. Everitt, 143. "U.N. Hiring Subversives, Senator Says," *Washington Post*. August 9, 1949, 3; Blue, 359; and Bannerman, 219.

98. Corwin interview, March 30, 2011.

99. "Windows on the World" was broadcast on the Mutual network in November 1951, and later rebroadcast in Canada, the United Kingdom, Australia, New Zealand, and South Africa. Corwin Papers, Box 88, COR01191; Box 86, COR01129.

100. Corwin, Norman, "Windows on the World," *Radio Times* (December 28, 1951), 5.

101. "Inside Stuff—Radio," *Variety* (November 7, 1951), page unknown, Corwin Papers, Box 88, COR01191. Also Corwin, Norman, Windows on the World, Interoffice memos, Norman Corwin Papers, Special Collections Research Center, Syracuse University Library, Box 16.

102. There are statements from female UN workers on global women's rights, the UN's Social Welfare Services, UNICEF, and the UN's Food and Agriculture Organization.

5

CORWIN ON TELEVISION

A Transmedia Approach to Style Historiography

Shawn Vancour

Assessments of Norman Corwin's legacy and impact since his death in 2011 have focused primarily on his period of greatest fame as a radio dramatist during the 1940s and 1950s. This chapter, by contrast, turns to a later and less discussed period in the career of America's celebrated "poet laureate of radio," exploring his work in the medium of television from the 1960s to the 1970s. CBS's fledgling television division, under the direction of Gilbert Seldes and Worthington Miner, had attempted adaptations of Corwin's radio plays as early as 1945.[1] However, Corwin's own involvement with the medium did not come until 1962, with his engagement as a commissioned screenwriter for ABC's prestige documentary series *FDR*, produced by the Sextant company and first broadcast in 1965. After scripting an additional ninety-minute documentary on the global film industry in 1964 (*Inside the Movie Kingdom*, NBC), Corwin's next work came as writer, director, and host of the syndicated Westinghouse series and Canadian coproduction *Norman Corwin Presents* (*NCP*), broadcast in the United States from 1971 to 1972 and on the CBC from 1972 to 1973. While this Westinghouse series was his most extensive and sustained involvement with the medium, Corwin's television work continued throughout the remainder of the decade, including screenwriting credits for at least five additional series, and concluded with a term as host of the short-film showcase *Academy Leaders* (PBS, 1979).[2]

Illuminating this important but little-studied period in Corwin's long and multifaceted career, this chapter explores the celebrated media auteur's efforts to adapt his well-honed radio technique for the comparatively new and evolving field of visual broadcasting. As Neil Verma has noted, by the 1940s, Corwin's radio work was already associated with a clear and distinctive style that was singled out for commentary in trade literature and alternately praised or parodied in popular magazines. This "Corwinesque" style, Verma contends, was defined by (1) a tendency to embrace and actively foreground creative risks (seen, for instance, in Corwin's self-consciously "poetic" or "literary" writing style), and (2) Corwin's seamless blending of what Verma calls a "kaleidosonic" style of narration (which rapidly "segues from place to place" and from one character to another) and "intimate style" (attached to a particular character's perspective of exploring his or her psychology and environment in depth).[3] While scholarship on these stylistic dimensions of Corwin's radio work is itself in a nascent state, this chapter argues that tracing the transfigurations of the Corwinesque across adjacent media platforms constitutes an equally pressing task. This emergent field of transmedia style historiography, it shows, can make important contributions to the study of media authorship, while moving beyond the artificial compartmentalization of "visual" or "sound" media to illuminate complex interplays and equivalencies between different sensory channels and modalities of media representation.

Applying the concept of "authorship" to mass media industries is a famously fraught task. Early critics such as Dwight MacDonald and Max Horkheimer and Theodor W. Adorno saw the assembly-line modes of production in film and broadcast media as inherently inimical to traditional forms of authorship, while scholars from Andrew Sarris to Horace Newcomb and Robert Alley in turn sought to redeem these media by showing their capacity to accommodate personal styles and individual expression despite their larger systemic constraints.[4] Subsequent poststructuralist critiques in the wake of work by Roland Barthes and Michel Foucault shifted the emphasis from forms of authorial expression to social constructions of authorship, and more recent work in production studies has interrogated both the economic functions of authorship (the author as brand) and previously neglected forms of group authorship operating at the levels of both above-the-line and below-the-line labor.[5]

Corwin's work for CBS at the height of his radio career offers a particularly strong case for traditional forms of authorship, benefiting from the network's investment in prestige, sustaining series that encouraged stylistic experimentation, operated free from the constraints of commercial sponsorship, and aggregated the normally distinct positions of writer, director, and producer to give budding auteurs such as Corwin an unusually strong degree of authorial control.[6] Despite the noncommercial nature of his radio series, Corwin's "authorship" also served an important economic function for the network, offering signs of programming distinction in an industrial climate defined by intense inter-network rivalry and simultaneous scrutiny from FCC regulators eager to curb tendencies toward excessive commercialism.[7] As Thomas Doherty notes elsewhere in this volume, the Corwin brand was significantly devalued in the decade following the Second World War, with Corwin placed under FBI investigation and "graylisted" by the film and broadcasting industries for his support of groups suspected of "un-American" political activities.[8] While the Corwin name gained renewed currency within the U.S. television industry in the 1960s and 1970s, this new industrial context would disaggregate the combined authorship functions that had distinguished Corwin's radio work and demand adaptation of his celebrated radio style to suit the prevailing aesthetic norms and expressive resources of the TV medium. Understanding these historical vicissitudes of the Corwinesque, I argue, requires a transmedia approach capable of tracking its shifting forms and meanings across the wide range of media platforms and industrial contexts in which it has been variably produced and inscribed.

Focusing first on Corwin's efforts to adapt his radio techniques in his initial *FDR* scripts, then on remakes of celebrated radio properties for *NCP*, at the pinnacle of Corwin's television career, this chapter opens pathways for further exploration of his larger television oeuvre through a method with equal relevance for understanding his contributions to related "visual" media of film and theater. The Corwinesque as a style, I argue, was not simply extended from radio to television, but rather strategically adapted and transformed, with defining techniques from its radio manifestations being alternately embraced or rejected in new televisual iterations. Understanding the Corwinesque as a transmedia phenomenon demands a theory of style that can accommodate these shifting techniques and a conception of authorship that permits an explanatory (vs. purely descriptive) account of them. The critical value of transmedia style historiography, I contend, rests not simply in mapping a style and its transposition from one set of media texts to another but also in explaining *why* particular sets of techniques are preserved, substituted, or discarded—a task that requires moving beyond reductive accounts of the artist's personal "intent" to a consideration of the larger institutional forces that structure acts of creative production. A critically effective analysis of the Corwinesque thus demands close consideration of aesthetic strategies pursued at the textual level, as well as the production contexts that gave those strategies their historical exigency and viability and invested them with economic value. In an effort to theorize these twin aesthetic and industrial dimensions of transmedia style historiography, I first turn to Rudolf Arnheim's important but neglected "gestalt theory of style" for methodological grounding, followed by an analysis of the aesthetic strategies and industrial exigencies informing Corwin's work, respectively, for *FDR* and *NCP*.

DEFINING STYLE HISTORIOGRAPHY

While better known to media scholars for his earlier work on the medium-specific properties of film and radio, medium theorist Rudolf Arnheim by the 1980s had turned his attention to a series of broader art historical debates on preferred methods and goals of stylistic analysis. Arnheim's most concerted engagement with this subject came in a paper for the American Society for Aesthetics in 1980, in which he argued for a "gestalt theory of style" that divorced the idea of "style" from any necessary ties to a fixed set of aesthetic techniques, while highlighting the role that contextual pressures play in shaping acts of artistic creation. Style as a gestalt, Arnheim argues, is not synonymous with the "aesthetic qualities" of an individual work or set of works but is instead an "intellectual concept" and "mental construct" of the historian.[9] Moreover, while works placed within a particular style class might appear as "unitary entities" when viewed "at low magnification," this remains only a gestalt unity, with these works revealing greater heterogeneity at higher levels of magnification and over longer spans of time.[10] The presence of particular aesthetic techniques, in other words, no more guarantees the applicability of a given style-concept than the application of a particular style-concept guarantees the presence of particular aesthetic techniques. Style-concepts are instead formed, in Arnheim's view, on the basis of structural unities that signify not the mere presence of techniques but a perceived "way of making, defined by a particular use of the medium, the subject matter, etc."[11] Rather than an inventory of devices, style historiography is an analysis of regularities in their patterns of use—a concern not simply with aesthetic techniques but with the effects at which they are aimed. As Arnheim explains, "gestalt theory can study the conditions that make a structure remain constant although its vehicle undergoes changes," enabling historians to recognize the continued applicability of a style-concept despite shifts in the particular techniques associated with its "way of making."[12]

Arnheim's method has important ramifications for analyzing the aesthetic dimensions of the Corwinesque. To begin, Arnheim's principle of the non-identity of style-concepts and aesthetic qualities permits recognition of the Corwinesque's applicability as a style-concept for works created at different times and in different media, using different techniques. Televisual manifestations of the Corwinesque may be expected to assume a different form than their radio counterparts, but without sacrificing the coherence of the larger style-concept. Second, Arnheim's functionalist approach to style demands a consideration not simply of the repetition of techniques from one medium to the next but of what film theorist David Bordwell describes as "functional equivalencies," where new technologies and techniques are deployed to familiar ends.[13] Televisual manifestations of the Corwinesque were frequently adjusted to the perceived demands and possibilities of television presentation, using different techniques than their radio counterparts, while remaining oriented toward similar sets of aesthetic effects. Finally, Arnheim's principle of heterogeneous unity enables recognition, at higher levels of magnification, of instances where specific elements of the Corwinesque are refused in favor of devices aimed at wholly different sets of effects. Both *FDR* and *NCP* frequently substituted visually equivalent techniques for earlier radio devices but at other times pursued competing stylistic tendencies whose presence by no means invalidates the Corwinesque's continued applicability as a style-concept.

Arnheim's account of style, however, is not restricted to aesthetic analysis, moving also into contextual considerations that raise larger questions about the nature of authorship.[14] Approaching style as a gestalt unity for Arnheim demands we consider the complex "field of forces" within which that style is configured.[15] Although the artist's personal intent is not irrelevant for such considerations, "the way an artist views his own work" may differ from the "style his work displays when considered in the context of the whole period" or "as part of an artist's entire oeuvre."[16] Moreover, since "the individual derives entirely from its genetic tributaries and environmental influences," it is necessary to consider the larger contextual factors that delimit an artist's choices and structure possible ways of making.[17] Corwin's work on *FDR*, for instance, was enabled by a brief demand for "quality" documentary series in the early 1960s, and *NCP* was created in response to new openings for independent prime-time series and incentives for coproductions on Canadian soil during the early 1970s. Within these contexts, the Corwinesque served as a sign of product quality that could be mobilized in product pitches to networks and foreign distributors, as well as in marketing discourses for television viewers.

However, these production contexts also necessitated the strategic adjustment of this style to new sets of industrial norms, while occasioning frequent clashes over creative control. As Troy Cummings shows in his essay for this volume, Corwin's work in radio prior to his employment with CBS served as a "formative period" that gave him the freedom to experiment with innovative techniques that he would further refine in his work for CBS, where the budding radio auteur continued to enjoy an unusually high degree of creative control.[18] Corwin's first experiences in media beyond radio presented considerable challenges, as Mary Ann Watson shows in her essay on his brief and ill-fated work for MGM during the 1950s; his role now limited to that of writer, Corwin frequently clashed with his higher-ups over perceived assaults on his creative freedom and artistic vision.[19] Corwin's early television career continued to be defined by various degrees of both "soft" and "hard" control—for *FDR*, demanding ongoing negotiations between Corwin and production executives at Sextant and ABC, and for *NCP,* with both Westinghouse executives and Canadian coproducers. Studying the Corwinesque from a transmedia perspective demands careful attention not only to aesthetic techniques, effects, and equivalencies but also to the industrial contexts in which this style could achieve positive valuation and the struggles to control its uses and manifestations. Applying Arnheim's insights on the role that larger extra-aesthetic "fields of forces" play in shaping acts of artistic production and style determinations lets us recognize these struggles for control as not compromises or corruptions of the Corwinesque but rather as its very conditions of possibility. The Corwinesque as a style-concept has no pure or originary state, existing only in and through its particular instantiations, mobilizations, and negotiations within the different media platforms, institutions, and contexts that define its historical shapes and meanings.

FDR: ADVENTURES IN AUDIOVISUAL NARRATION

As Corwin's initial point of entry into the television medium, *FDR* is a series particularly deserving of attention, offering opportunities for analysis of the production contexts in which televisual manifestations of the Corwinesque became possible and desirable, as well as the sets of aesthetic strategies associated with this style. As a means of marketing leverage, the Corwinesque aided producers in efforts at content branding, summoning signs of "quality" and distinction in promotional discourses aimed both at other industry members and members of the viewing public. Aesthetically speaking, the Corwinesque also promised solutions to a specific set of stylistic challenges, with Corwin's skill in kaleidosonic modes of narration offering producers an expedient means of moving rapidly through a series of competing narrative settings and perspectives. However, in keeping with Arnheim's principles of the nonidentity of styles and devices and aesthetic functionalism, new televisual iterations of the kaleidosonic employed visual devices absent from their earlier radio counterparts. Upholding Arnheim's principles of heterogeneous unity and extratextual influence, familiar elements of the Corwinesque were in other cases actively refused in response to larger institutional pressures—most notably, Corwin's penchant for long passages of poetic voice-over narration, which series producers deemed inappropriate for television and eliminated from the final program.

Created by newly formed Sextant Productions for ABC as a follow-up to its 1960–61 Emmy-winning series on Winston Churchill, *FDR* formed part of a larger documentary boom that, as Michael Curtin writes, "culminated more than a decade of discussion regarding the appropriate uses of television" and an effort to make good on broadcasters' failed promises to fulfill their dual mission of "enlightenment as well as entertainment."[20] As one of a growing number of series aimed at redeeming what FCC chair Newton Minow in his 1961 address to the National Association of Broadcasters had excoriatingly labeled the "vast wasteland" of popular television programming, pains were taken from the start to position *FDR* as a "quality" production that was innovative in its content and approach.[21] In the lead-up to its originally scheduled fall 1962 premiere, executive producer and Sextant founder Robert Graff explained to *Variety* readers that "Sextant must do something of another quality of range," and although series on controversial public figures were formerly unacceptable in an industry that traditionally "avoided anything that isn't absolutely safe," such productions were now embraced by ABC and had already "landed a winner" with Sextant's *Churchill*.[22] Advertisements for Sextant's fall 1962 lineup similarly stressed its commitment to "creat[ing] productions of imagination, quality and impact," and to reinforce this image, viewers were reminded of the top-shelf talent roster that Graff had assembled: from production credits by *Churchill* producer Ben Feiner to consulting and voice work by Eleanor Roosevelt, acting roles by screen greats Charlton Heston and Arthur Kennedy (as FDR), and scripts by noteworthy playwrights such as Corwin, who received single-author writing credits for both the double-episode premiere and the climactic series finale.[23] Nonetheless, the focus on a divisive presidential figure proved a harder sell to advertisers in the context of growing political divisions of the 1960s than the company's earlier *Churchill* production, delaying *FDR*'s network debut until spring 1965.[24]

As noted by scholars from Jane Feuer to Michael Newman and Elana Levine, although authorship is a critical factor in legitimating quality television, it is also a particularly contested category in media defined by collective modes of production.[25] In Corwin's case, this authorship was a matter of considerable negotiation. Corwin himself insisted on a contract clause guaranteeing him sole authorship over his scripts and protection from any subsequent rewrites by ABC staff, then later demanded (without success) that the network remove his name after plans were announced to split his special one-hour premiere into two half-hour episodes without his consent.[26] While Corwin fiercely protected his artistic vision, his authorial control was in fact questionable from the start, with producers Graff and Feiner providing him in advance with rough sketches of each episode and furnishing him with preselected photographs, recorded interviews, stock footage, and supplementary dramatizations shot without his creative input weeks and months in advance of his scripts. In a letter to Graff and Feiner, Corwin likened his role in this process to an "open-field run" in which he was charged with winding the ball past different players whom his producers had placed on the field, toward a fixed goal line, except in this case he was also responsible for positioning those players, making the task one of both running and "open-field arranging." This effort was not helped, he warned, by Graff and Feiner's insistence that players Corwin had already pulled from the game "[come] off the bench" and get back on the field. "There are so many players with numbers on their backs who just *had* to get in the game," Corwin complained, that even for a double episode, his producers' expectations might prove unrealistic.[27] However, despite bristling at some of the restrictions placed upon him, Corwin also assumed a much more active role in the production process than originally anticipated, requesting many additional audio and visual materials beyond what Graff and Feiner had supplied and including in his scripts a level of detail that often exceeded the bounds of standard screenwriting to cross over into the realm of the directorial—thus providing opportunities for reimagining the Corwinesque in a new, specifically televisual register.[28]

Given the paucity of film footage prior to FDR's entry into politics, Corwin's script relied heavily on still photographs for its visuals, prescribing a series of quick cuts and dissolves that, backed with the dialogue he had scripted, would at times translate to shot lengths of two seconds or less. When Graff and Feiner expressed concerns as to "whether or not such a prolonged sequence of still imagery will give us the necessary punch and excitement," Corwin offered the twofold reply that "there is nothing you can do about it [anyway], since there was no film" and that they were "mistakenly worried," since with "proper camera movement and editing, even greater interest can be generated than in motion picture footage."[29] Here, as an aesthetic model, Corwin referred them to Arthur Lipsett's 1961 *Very Nice, Very Nice*, which in under seven minutes explored a wide array of competing perspectives on global politics, nuclear war, urban crowding, consumerism, and the space race, using hundreds of juxtaposed still images (some flashed on-screen for only a few frames) and an equally elaborate system of audio montage.[30] While Graff and Feiner were not quite as bold and experimental as Lipsett, they nonetheless took Corwin's direction to heart, hiring acclaimed visual effects artist Fred Martell to apply his celebrated "stills-in-motion" technique pioneered on the "Young Mr. Lincoln" episode of NBC's *Project XX* and described by *Variety* as "the technique of subjecting still photos to panning, zooming and dissolving to create a feeling of movement" (a method revived more recently by documentarian Ken Burns).[31]

A particular variant of this technique that Corwin claimed "to my knowledge ... has not been used before" was what he called the "index motif," consisting of panning and tilting shots in extreme close-up across index entries from published works on FDR that highlighted key themes explored by Corwin's opening episode and the series as whole. For instance, following a clip on Roosevelt's "ruthlessness" by noted psychologist Carl Jung that launched a segment on FDR's personality, close-ups of an index entry from Secretary of the Interior Harold Ickes's autobiography were shown listing FDR's various personality traits, while accompanying voice-over narration echoed, "Ruthless is Dr. Jung's word. Others use other words: Deceptive, shy, affectionate, angry, affable, snobbish, compassionate, bewildering, sadistic, and so on."[32] A rapid montage of scenes from FDR's youth followed, backed with voice-overs of family members explaining how his capacity to inspire was accompanied by an "arrogance" that made him many enemies. Such moments garnered effusive praise from *New York Times* critic Jack Gould, who saw Corwin's technique as "result[ing] in a profile of magnificent dimension, warm and human, yet also recognizing the qualities of overbearance that helped make [FDR] a controversial figure."[33]

Placed in the service of a multiperspectival mode of narration, such techniques suggest an updated version of Verma's "kaleidosonic" style that distinguished much of Corwin's earlier radio work. This style, as Verma explains, rapidly "switch[es] through a series of static fixed positions across its playing space," as "listeners hear dozens of settings depicted or discussed" from a variety of narrative perspective: "No voice speaks in all scenes ... and no person frames the horizon of the fiction."[34] If the kaleidsonic's preferred technique was montage, then through its corresponding shifts in narrative perspective, it constituted what we might here call a specifically *polyvocal* montage—a technique that, as Jacob Smith notes, Corwin further refined in his later UN work using postwar tape recording and editing technologies.[35] For his television scripts, Corwin's producers in fact insisted on this need for varied perspectives, explaining in a "Statement of Purpose" for their series that *FDR* would not be a panegyric to the great man but rather offer "conflicting interpretations of events" by both "family companions" and FDR's "political opponents."[36] In notes on Corwin's first script, Feiner emphasized this point, warning him against excessive "adulation" and insisting, "We need conflict. We feel we need to hear people who are strongly opposed to FDR, in the first show."[37] To this end Corwin's earlier broadcasting experience served him well, with swift cuts between opposing audio commentary paralleling techniques he had refined through decades of radio work, here supplemented by new visual techniques, such as his index motif, that allowed for a visual survey of competing perspectives echoed in the accompanying audio track.

If the Corwinesque was in these cases actively preserved through a series of functionally equivalent visual techniques, in other cases Corwin's radio style proved not an asset but a distinct liability—most notably in his penchant for prolonged passages of poetic voice-over narration. In his initial script for *FDR*'s half-hour series finale, for instance, voice-over narration accounted for nearly fourteen of his nineteen pages, in some cases running more than four pages without interruption. In his notes for revision, Feiner politely suggested to Corwin that not each on-screen moment need be accompanied by narrative commentary, explaining that, "if we can so understate the story through the use of the most terse and most poignant comments we will achieve a feeling that the emotions of the writer and narrator are too strained to permit volubility."[38] As Corwin explained in a subsequent letter to program coordinator Peter Davis concerning a reenactment of Roosevelt's death being shot for this episode, he was very much "in agreement with [Feiner's] point of view about keeping the narration down to a ruthless minimum and letting the emotional power of the pictorial matter take over," and to this end had substantially pruned his original script.[39] Indeed, Corwin's revised version not only honored Feiner's request for "terser" language but also cut all dialogue completely during several moments of heightened emotional impact. In a critical scene depicting the shock that swept the nation and world upon news of FDR's death, for instance, Corwin's original script accompanied a montage of news tickers falling silent, storefronts closing, subways stopping, and English and Canadian assemblies suspending their sessions with corresponding narration describing each shot: "The tireless tickers that had hammered out the news of his triumphs . . . now fall silent"; "Throughout the country, stores close"; "In New York subways, trains stop running," and so on. The revised version, by contrast, included narration only to distinguish the

Canadian and British assemblies, relying otherwise wholly on the minimal diegetic sound supplied by the accompanying footage.[40]

Thus, while Corwin had developed with relative ease new audiovisual variations on his familiar kaleidosonic style, television also presented America's poet laureate of radio with the more difficult lesson of knowing when to lay one's words to rest—when, in other words, to suspend speech in favor of silence and allow the image itself to rise to fore. These adaptations and refusals emerged through a series of complex institutional negotiations that sought on one hand to preserve and capitalize on the Corwinesque as a sign of program quality and source of aesthetic innovation, while on the other hand adjusting it to established sets of industry norms and preferred modes of television representation.

NORMAN CORWIN PRESENTS: REIMAGINING CORWIN FOR THE TELEVISION GENERATION

After an additional screenwriting credit in 1964 for his work on Sextant's ninety-minute special *Inside the Movie Kingdom,* Corwin's next and most famous foray into television came with the launch of Westinghouse's syndicated prime-time series *Norman Corwin Presents.*[41] As with *FDR* before it (and in keeping with Arnheim's principle of extratextual influence), institutional exigencies created an environment in which the Corwinesque could achieve renewed economic viability—from a demand for independently produced prime-time programming content and a shift in target demographics within the U.S. television industry to changes in the Canadian regulatory context that created favorable conditions for international coproductions. As with *FDR,* although authorship of *NCP* was split, Corwin's role in program production was heavily promoted and the Corwinesque was again positioned as a sign of product quality and programming distinction. Featuring several prominent adaptations of familiar Corwin radio properties, the series also offers ripe material for exploring the aesthetic dimensions of the Corwinesque, revealing like *FDR* both a strategic adaptation and selective refusal of familiar stylistic elements. Some of these episodes actively rejected the kaleidosonic, upholding Arnheim's principle of heterogeneous unity by eliminating a signature element of Corwin's style in favor of more conventional modes of television narration. At the same time, many of these episodes actively embraced the poetic modes of speech expurgated from Corwin's *FDR* scripts, as part of a larger tendency toward self-conscious displays of style and theatricality that extended to the visual register as well as the sonic. Reflecting Arnheim's principles of aesthetic functionalism and separation of style and technique, these episodes preserved elements of Corwin's earlier radio style while employing new visual techniques to achieve familiar aesthetic goals.

Shot on tape as part of a six-program Westinghouse lineup sold to network affiliates and owned-and-operated stations for the 1971–72 season, *NCP* was developed in response to the FCC's newly implemented 1970 Prime Time Access Rule (PTAR), which sought to break network control over prime-time schedules by requiring eight half-hour slots be filled each week by local and nonnetwork productions. While most stations had opposed the unwelcome costs of producing or purchasing additional programming, Westinghouse chief executive Donald McGannon had been particularly vocal in championing the new rule, embracing it as an opportunity to expand the activities of his company's production unit, Group W. While Westinghouse's sixth intended series fell through due to contract disputes and was replaced by the 1969–70 BBC comedy *Doctor in the House*, *Norman Corwin Presents* joined four additional Group W series that were each structured around a single personality who served as host and defining authorial presence. These included a new Tom Smothers vehicle (to replace the brothers' canceled 1967–69 CBS series), an American iteration of David Frost's *Frost Report* (based on his 1966–67 BBC series), Mal Sharpe's *Street People* (a *Candid Camera*-style program that had enjoyed a successful radio run on San Francisco station KGO several years earlier), and San Francisco personality Ron Magers's *Electric Impressions* (a program of popular youth music pulled up for national distribution from Westinghouse's own San Francisco station, KPIX).[42]

In a September 1971 *New York Times* interview promoting this new lineup, McGannon claimed that it would offer a corrective to lackluster network programming, which "had become cautious, less innovative and less pioneering ... [and] had lost its compelling quality," particularly for the "youth audience" that sought programming "relevant to our times."[43] This message had been pushed by Westinghouse in the preceding month as well, in a traveling trade show that promoted its lineup by stressing the innovative approach, irreverent humor, and antiestablishment sensibilities of each host, in what *Variety* described as a "rock 'n' roll, five-screen, World's Fair-style extravaganza" with "precisely timed graphics, animations and film samples of five up-for-sale series," all backed with go-go music and popular Beatles tracks. Promos for Corwin's series included excerpts from the premier episode, "One Man Group," billed as offering send-ups of cultural heroes from Niccolò Paganini to Sigmund Freud, and "Two Gods in Primetime," whose talk show–style interviews with the gods Venus and Mars culminate in the latter ceding his title as God of War to the far worthier and infinitely more brutal human race.[44]

Even when not directly articulated to the youth demographic with which prime-time programmers of the late 1960s and early 1970s were increasingly preoccupied, Corwin's authorship was consistently foregrounded in series promotions, with Westinghouse offering regular assurances to prospective buyers that "Mr. Corwin will write many of the shows and will be directly involved in all of them."[45] Adding his personal audiovisual stamp of approval to each production, Corwin also appeared on camera at the start of each episode, introducing the evening's feature with some brief notes on the circumstances behinds its production and content, reprising a role that Cummings notes he had regularly played in his earliest, pre-CBS radio productions.[46] In this role as program host, Corwin lent his authorizing presence even to those productions in which he had minimal involvement, symbolically reclaiming a level of authorial control repeatedly denied him in his relegation to more limited writing roles in his prior Sextant productions. However, as with *FDR*, the real extent of this authorship may be questioned. Although Corwin claimed in his official biography that he had written or selected all scripts for the show himself and "had veto power over all decisions," Westinghouse executive George Moynihan also maintained an active presence on the set, along with producer Arthur Joel Katz of Arjo Productions, to which Group W had farmed out immediate production responsibilities.[47] Further complicating matters, Westinghouse had availed itself of CTV president Murray Chercover's efforts to lure producers of U.S. syndicated series into coproduction deals with his commercial network in Canada, whose Toronto and Vancouver studios boasted production costs less than half those incurred for comparable stateside productions. Pursuing American coproductions permitted the CTV to skirt its import quotas and sell the series as domestic content to advertisers or other distributors (in the case of Corwin's program, to the competing CBC network for its Canadian debut).[48] However, in addition to shooting on Canadian soil, qualifying as a domestic production also demanded incorporation of Canadian labor, including not only below-the-line studio workers but also domestic writing, acting, and directing staff. As such, entire episodes of the "Corwin" series were devoted to showcasing prominent Canadian writers like M. Charles Cohen or celebrated directors such as George McCowan.[49] Nonetheless, enjoying top billing as a writer, director, producer, and program host, Corwin had a far more direct hand in shaping this series than his previous work for Sextant, offering valuable opportunities for analyzing the Corwinesque in its fully developed televisual register.

Several episodes of *Norman Corwin Presents* offer straightforward adaptations of plays developed by Corwin for the *Columbia Workshop* at the height of his radio fame in the 1940s. However, not all of these embrace Corwin's earlier radio style or seek functional equivalents for its associated techniques. Corwin's adaptation of his 1945 play "The Gumpert Affair" (retitled "One-Man Group" and starring Canadian actor Don Harron) stages some of the most radical departures from his earlier radio work.[50] A tale of everyman Charles Gumpert, who channels the spirit of famed violinist Niccolò Paganini, the television iteration employs the framing device of Gumpert's wife, Elsa, seated on a plane discussing his personality changes with a psychiatrist she has just met, who suggests Charles see him for an appointment. Arriving in the psychiatrist's office later that week, Charles, who has no prior knowledge of psychoanalysis, is suddenly overtaken by the spirit of Sigmund Freud, mystifying the psychiatrist with his thorough grasp of Freud's work, before storming out to never be seen again.

The radio version, by contrast, includes straight voice-over narration by Elsa without the framing device of the plane conversation and inserts a montage of Charles assuming several additional personalities at the end of the episode. As biographer Douglas Bell observed in a 1994 interview with Corwin, in its original radio version the play "contained much more movement [and] flights from scene to scene," whereas several scenes conveyed via direct narration in the radio script were in the televised version communicated indirectly through Elsa's dialogue.[51] As an example, when the spirit of Paganini suddenly departs him in mid-concert, Gumpert is publicly humiliated and endures verbal abuse from residents of his hometown in Passaic, New Jersey. In the radio version, this is rendered through initial voice-over narration by Elsa, followed by quick alternations between diegetic dialogue and further voice-over:

> *Elsa.* Poor Charles. The report of his concert in the newspapers was treated so humorously that, as you can well imagine, he became the victim of coarse jokes and the cause of much laughter, and even back in Passaic. I should say, especially in Passaic! He was hooted at by ruffians on street corners –
> *Ruffian.* Why doncha try the trumpet, Gumpert!
> *Gumpert.* That, as I see it, is none of your concern.
> *(Ruffians laughing)*
> *Elsa.* And rude children on our street corners made up rhymes about him –
> *Little Girl.* Little piddle piddle, answer me a riddle, who plays the fiddle and stops in the middle? Dumpy gumpy Gumpert, that is who! B-O plenty stinks, and so do you!
> *Elsa.* Poor Charles! He took it hard.
> *Charles.* Elsa –
> *Elsa.* Yes, Charles?
> *Charles.* I tell you, it's getting to be more than I can bear!

In the televised version, by contrast, all dialogue in this scene is rendered by Elsa, on whom the camera remains fixed while she relates these incidents to her interlocutor on the plane, mimicking the voices of the ruffians and little girl as she repeats their insults, then in place of the final exchange between Charles and her, simply exclaiming:

> Poor Charles! We were terribly hurt every time we picked up a newspaper. Time magazine referred to him as a "Paganincompoop!"

Beyond the level of the script itself, however, differences in audiovisual style also contribute to the sense of abrupt shifts in scene in the radio version, as transitions to scenes with Charles are not only far fewer in the TV version but more explicitly marked. In addition to fading out the ambient engine noise at the end of each plane scene as the image dissolves to a corresponding flashback sequence with Charles, changes in background scenery signal clear shifts in setting that are reinforced by establishing shots that either open each flashback or answer an initial close-up to reveal the characters' new surroundings. Once each setting is established, the resulting flashbacks run anywhere from one to four minutes before returning to Elsa and the psychiatrist on the plane. In the radio version, by contrast, dialogue not only alternates more rapidly between Elsa's voice-over narration and her diegetic conversations with Charles, but scenes are also free of ambient sound that might aid in establishing setting, while microphone distance and reverberation levels that might otherwise provide spatial positioning cues (what Verma describes as "audioposition") remain constant throughout the entire episode.[52] Changes in setting and narrative frame are thus not only more frequent but also lacking in sonic markers, resulting in a series of abrupt shifts that throw the listener continually off balance. If the radio version thus exults in the kaleidosonic, its small screen counterpart actively refuses televisual analogues in favor of a more conventional style, deliberately signposting and reinforcing scene changes through multiple layers of audiovisual redundancy, then exploring each new space in depth before returning to the frame story of Elsa on the plane.

In contrast with "One-Man Group," Corwin's next adaptation, "A Soliloquy for Television" (based loosely on his 1941 "Soliloquy to Balance the Budget") discards the conventional, unmarked style of television narration for a regime of self-conscious stylistic display, while pursuing direct televisual equivalents for techniques employed in its radio forebear.[53] Opening with soliloquist House Jameson cursing the adding machine of the commercial broadcaster that "Throws honest Greeks like Euclid out of work" and "usurps the pen" with an "efficiency [that] can be disgusting," the radio play proceeds to offer a series of poetic ruminations in loose verse on such weighty topics as war, death, God, progress, and human happiness. While written in the same style and taking up nearly identical themes as its radio counterpart, the televised version features almost entirely new settings and dialogue, adding race relations to the agenda and taking advantage of its video origins to stage elaborate visual gags such as a fencing duel between soliloquist Brock Peters (of *To Kill a Mockingbird* fame) and his chroma-keyed double.[54] From an opening tour of the studio set and its associated video equipment to a demonstration of the laugh machine, this episode like its radio counterpart interweaves existential contemplations with a seeming effort to lay bare its own production apparatus. However, this apparent transparency proves deceptive, as both soliloquies ultimately revel in their capacity to summon fantastic objects and spaces seemingly out of thin air.[55]

In the radio version, for instance, the Soliloquist's monologue leads the listener on an itinerary through a surreal concatenation of increasingly strange spaces:

Well, time is getting on; let's push [. . .] through doorless doors—

(Footsteps on wood)

And down the ramp—
> *(Footsteps cross to stone)*

And past the eyeball of the Asiatic dragon [. . .] then through the iron gate—
> *(Open and close an iron gate)*

A few steps west—
> *(Steps)*

Then turn the corner, kick the carpet up, and open the trap door.
> *(Sound of heavy door creaking)*

Below, among an organ loft of stalactites and stalagmites, worn smooth by sweeping airs, is kept a captive wind. We'll pay it our respects.
> *(Wind enters and builds)*

There, do you hear it sighing? That is it. Let's take the spiral staircase down.
> *(Descending steps)*

"Soliloquy for Television" pursues this same aesthetic agenda, with the Soliloquist entering and exiting a series of spaces and settings that seem to materialize or vanish at will. Opening with establishing shots that follow Peters riding into the studio on a bicycle and circling its perimeter, the episode immediately reveals the props and playing space for the acts that follow. Much of acts 1 and 2 describe a seemingly logical movement across this space—from an initial position stage right toward the opposite edge of the studio's main cyc curtain (stage left) and back again—with staging that seems as though it could be played in real time, in the style of a live anthology drama. The majority of Peters's shifts in stage position are likewise shot in continuous takes that give the sense of a fluid, live performance similar to that found in the earlier radio play, while the Soliloquist's itinerary across the otherwise well-defined space of the studio set and back again are punctuated by corresponding encounters with objects and set pieces that seem to materialize out of thin air. The conclusion of the first movement across the length of the cyc (stage left) at the start of act 2, for instance, comes with Peters's arrival at a the mock-up of a chapel interior that was absent from this position in earlier shots. Completion of the return movement to the starting end of the cyc at the beginning of act 3 is likewise marked by Peters's discovery of a large row of bleachers in an area of the set that remained vacant up to this point, while a camera change immediately following this shot reveals the laugh machine standing in the space through which Peters has just passed on his way to the bleachers. The chroma-keyed fight sequence follows, at the conclusion of which a high-angle crane shot of Peters dragging his slain double across the floor lowers to eye level to reveal a third seemingly instantaneous shift in setting, with the space behind him that was empty throughout the preceding fight sequence now filled with dark outlines of oversized tombstones. This new setting provides the occasion for a closing rumination on the afterlife and a reminder:

> For twenty-three-odd minutes I've been playing live, whereas you know and I know that I'm in a cathode tube, on tape: reversible, repeatable, erasable.

While the radio soliloquy summoned its objects and places into existence on the fly, in the course of a seamless live performance, this final remark makes clear that the techniques of the video drama have instead relied on careful editing. Lest there be any confusion on this point, Peters then retrieves his bicycle and rides off the set in a final long shot that reveals the studio restored to its original position, minus the chapel, bleachers, and tombstones that stood there only moments before. While not kaleidosonic, properly speaking, the stylistic logic dominating both the radio and television iterations of "Soliloquy" evinces a similar predilection for abrupt and unexpected spatiotemporal shifts, a game of "fort-da" that summons new objects and worlds into existence and banishes them just as swiftly into oblivion. Different devices are used to achieve these goals in the video medium than in its live radio counterpart, as Peters makes clear in his closing monologue, but the aesthetic objective is the same and the two dramas remain, from a functionalist standpoint, stylistically of a piece.

The self-conscious displays of style that distinguish the Corwinesque in "Soliloquy," as well as other episodes, foreground a presentational attitude or stance of what may be called "theatricality."[56] While invited to revel in its surreal spatial transformations, viewers of the play are also continually reminded of the artifice behind them and the fact that the play remains but a play. Although "One-Man Group" minimizes its theatricality, other Corwin adaptations in the series accentuate it. An examination of a third adaptation, "The Undecided Molecule," reveals several larger tendencies in this regard.

Based on the eponymous 1945 radio play about a molecule placed on trial for refusing to assume any established elemental form, the televised version stars Milton Berle as the trial judge and is written like its radio forebear entirely in rhyming verse.[57] Like "Soliloquy," it employs a single-set design, with the judge's bench on a raised platform in the rear, flanked on either side by platforms for the prosecution and defense, and a witness box in the center occupied by the defendant. Backdrops are minimalist in design, consisting of a colored cyc behind pillars of white scaffolding, and the playing space remains evenly illuminated with high-key lighting for the duration of the drama. The obvious problem of how to visualize the undefined molecule itself is resolved through the admirable nonsolution of hiding it from view, within a shielded metal box from which issue periodic beeps and squeals that are translated by a court interpreter. This minimalist set design on one hand stemmed from economic motivations. As Corwin later remarked in an interview about the program, "Bear in mind . . . that these were remarkably low-budget shows. It was for budgetary reasons that we went to Canada in the first place."[58] At the stylistic level, however, this stripped-down visual aesthetic plays a distinctly functional role, as in "Soliloquy," by accentuating the play as a performance—thus excusing both the absurdity of its premise and the potentially off-putting use of poetic verse (sufficiently controversial in golden-age radio drama and all but unheard of in 1970s television).

Like "Soliloquy," "Undecided Molecule" includes numerous moments of direct audience address, here by Berle. The first of these occurs when Berle's defense attorney objects to his decision to dismiss the court early for lunch, calling Berle a "fascist." Rising from his seat and turning toward a nearby camera as it moves in for a jib shot framing him in close-up, Berle stares into the lens, then grins and breaks frame to deliver his line directly to the viewing audience:

> How could I be a fascist?
>
> Why I'm so benign I hardly even beat my wife,
> My children bow before me.
> I'm much admired by rattlesnakes,
> And birds of prey adore me.
>
> I'm tender and I'm sensitive,
> And anti-insurrectionist.
> I wouldn't hurt a cobra,
> And I'm anti-vivisectionist!

This theatricality is further foregrounded by a three-camera setup that, despite the added mobility of the dolly-mounted jib, largely adheres to rules of proscenium staging. Beyond its celebration of its video origins in effects sequences such as the Peters duel, "Soliloquy" also consistently penetrates the space of the performance along the z-axis to catch other cameras, the edges of the cyc, or miscellaneous studio equipment in frame, while incorporating multiple high-angle shots that expose various wires, rails, and boom lines. Cameras in "Undecided Molecule," by contrast, though partially penetrating the performance area, never cross an imaginary line along the x-axis at the foot of the judge's bench and (except for a high-angle reestablishing shot at the start of act 3 and symmetrical shot to close the act) remain at eye level, while never hinting at any space beyond the edges of the set. Far from offering a more illusionistic viewing frame, however, this strategy merely foregrounds the artifice of the set design, while preserving the sanctity of the judge's bench that forms the proscenium from which Berle, smiling at the camera, delivers the bulk of his star turns. In both cases, as with the live radio productions before them, the performance is framed just as such—a strategy further accentuated by Corwin's appearance at the beginning and end of each episode to comment on his latest play, in the style of anthology drama hosts from preceding decades.

Although not equally strong in all episodes, this tendency toward theatricality is frequently foregrounded in the series, as both a strategic response to the economic realities of independent syndicated programming and an important stylistic carryover from Corwin's earlier radio work. In conjunction with visual gags such as the magical appearances and disappearances of objects in "Soliloquy," these self-conscious displays of style signal the Corwinesque's persistence despite the rejection of other key stylistic elements such as the kaleidosonic in episodes like "One-Man Group." As with *FDR*, these examples show the value of Arnheim's insistence on style as heterogeneous unity, as well as his efforts to separate style-concepts from fixed sets of aesthetic techniques and instead shift consideration to the aesthetic ends to which those techniques are deployed. These strategies were pursued, finally, within the industrial contexts of 1970s U.S. and Canadian television, which gave the Corwinesque new value but also delimited its possible forms of expression. An Arnheimian mode of analysis can help us reckon with such complex sets of institutional negotiations and understand their impact on practices of transmedia authorship.

FATE OF THE CORWINESQUE: DIRECTIONS FOR FURTHER STUDY

Despite Westinghouse's promotional efforts, few of its prime-time access shows succeeded—a fact that Westinghouse blamed on a combination of PTAR waivers issued by the FCC and audience predilections for syndicated favorites from the 1950–60s that had been pulled from the vaults to fill the new prime-time void.[59] *Variety*, for its part, speculated that Westinghouse's marketing struggles were more a reflection of the "anger and frustration of station managements" at McGannon's role in the passage of PTAR than an indication of "whether or not the product looked promising."[60] Whatever the reason, of Westinghouse's six shows, only *The Frost Report* and its BBC import, *Doctor in the House,* were successfully sold to stations outside of Westinghouse's own chain and renewed for a second season. In Trendex studies of viewership for the nation's top twenty-one prime-time access shows, *Norman Corwin Presents* placed particularly poorly, ranking in the bottom three (albeit scoring slightly better in viewer satisfaction among those who watched than did many of its competitors).[61] Thus, just as the presence of Corwin's name on the credits of *FDR* had done little to aid ABC in its bid to secure sponsorship, Corwin's authorship did no better in securing financial success for Westinghouse; while accruing symbolic capital for their producers, Corwin's shows at an economic level remained staunch failures.

Despite these difficulties, Corwin made several further ventures into television in the years that followed, completing a one-off script for a documentary special on Japanese Army general Tomoyuki Yamashita (ABC, 1974), a television adaptation of his popular *Plot to Overthrow Christmas* (PBS, 1974), a *Hallmark Hall of Fame* adaptation of his stage play *The Rivalry* (NBC, 1975), contributions to scripts for the seven-part fiftieth anniversary retrospective *CBS: On the Air* (1978), and even a brief run as host of the public television program *Academy Leaders* (PBS, 1979). However, these assignments were limited mainly to writing roles, with NCP representing by far his most active and extensive involvement with the medium over the course of these two decades.[62]

In discussing Corwin's televisual authorship, I have observed Arnheim's four principles of style historiography, stressing the need to (1) divorce the concept of a style from any necessary ties to a particular set of aesthetic techniques, (2) determine the larger sets of aesthetic effects at which any given techniques associated with a style are aimed, (3) recognize styles as heterogeneous unities that demonstrate competing tendencies when viewed both synchronically and diachronically, and (4) consider the larger contextual forces that shape particular instantiations of a style within particular media at particular historical moments. Although limited to writing credits for his initial entry into television with Sextant's *FDR* series, Corwin played a significant role in shaping the resulting audiovisual style of the episodes to which he contributed. However, while his experience with a kaleidosonic style of narration served him well in his task of "open-field arranging" as he strove to order an otherwise baffling array of source materials and competing perspectives on FDR, his traditional reliance on voice-over narration proved an aesthetic liability whose excesses producers sought to curb. For NCP, I have highlighted instances where styles similar to those of Corwin's earlier radio work are pursued (the series of fantastic spatial transformations in "Soliloquy," for instance, and tendencies toward self-consciously poetic speech and theatrical style of presentation in both "Soliloquy" and "Undecided Molecule"), as well as cases where televisual iterations of the kaleidosonic are actively refused (e.g., "One-Man Group"). Although the preceding analyses by no means exhaust these two series, they do suggest the continued applicability of the Corwinesque as a style-concept for Corwin's television productions—though such continuities are by no means guaranteed (not all of Corwin productions or all aspects of them being equally Corwinesque), and in its televisual manifestations the Corwinesque may assume a significantly different form than in its earlier manifestations in Corwin's radio productions.

More specifically, following the principles of transmedia style historiography outlined above, I have argued that the Corwinesque as a style (1) remains distinct from the particular set of radio techniques with which it has been commonly associated, (2) where present, is often linked to alternative techniques in television that may be regarded as functional equivalents of earlier radio devices (aimed at similar aesthetic goals and effects), (3) may persist despite countertendencies toward selective refusal of individual techniques or goals, and (4) in its televisual manifestation was both enabled and limited by particular configurations of economic and regulatory forces within the 1960s–70s U.S. and Canadian television industries. A more thorough study of the Corwinesque in Corwin's television productions from this period may reveal further stylistic elements of importance, while Corwin's largely neglected literary, stage, and film work suggests many additional avenues of study. Finally, while Corwin himself had exited the television field by the end of the decade, the approach to style historiography adopted here (divorcing a "style" as such from the given techniques used within a particular work or medium) enables recognition of the Corwinesque in works authored not by Corwin himself but by those whom he directly inspired or by others who, faced with similar contextual circumstances, pursued similar aesthetic strategies and goals. In an era that is now irrevocably post-Corwin, the Corwinesque may in this sense still prove very much alive and well.

NOTES

1. "Corwin's 'Untitled' Makes Tele Debut," *Televiser: Journal of Video Production, Advertising, and Operation* 1, no. 4 (Summer 1945), 24, 28, 58–62. The first documented adaptation was a live production of Corwin's *Columbia Workshop* play, "Untitled," broadcast on May 24, 1945, for a special program promoting the Treasury Department's final war bond drive.

2. For an overview of Corwin's television work, see Douglas Bell, *Norman Corwin: Years of the Electric Ear* (Metuchen, NJ: Scarecrow Press, 1994), 287–88.

3. Neil Verma, "Radio's 'Oblong Blur': Notes on the Corwinesque," chapter 1 in this volume.

4. Dwight MacDonald, "A Theory of Mass Culture," in *Mass Culture: The Popular Arts in America*, ed. Bernard Rosenberg and David Manning (Glencoe, IL: Free Press, 1957), 59–73; Max Horkheimer and Theodor W. Adorno, *Dialectic of Enlightenment: Philosophical Fragments*, trans. Edmund Jephcott (Stanford, CA: Stanford University Press, 2002); Andrew Sarris, *The American Cinema: Directors and Directions, 1929–1968* (New York: E. P. Dutton, 1968); Horace Newcomb and Robert Alley, *The Producer's Medium: Conversations with Creators of American TV* (New York: Oxford University Press, 1983).

5. Roland Barthes, "Death of the Author," in *Image-Music-Text*, trans. Stephen Heath (London: Fontana Press, 1977), 142–48; and Michel Foucault, "What Is an Author?" in *The Foucault Reader*, ed. Paul Rabinow (New York: Pantheon Books, 1984), 101–20. For examples of efforts to grapple with the industrial dimensions of media authorship from production studies perspectives, see Vicki Mayer et al., eds., *Production Studies: Cultural Studies of Media Industries* (New York: Routledge, 2009); and Jonathan Gray and Derek Johnson, eds., *A Companion to Media Authorship* (Malden, MA: Wiley-Blackwell, 2013).

6. On CBS's investment in sustaining programming during this period, see Erik Barnouw, *The Golden Web: A History of Broadcasting in the United States*, vol. 2, *1933–1953* (New York: Oxford University Press, 1968), 55–89.

7. For more on the economic value of Corwin's authorship for CBS, see Shawn VanCour, "Norman Corwin: Radio at the Intersection of Art and Commerce," *Sounding Out: The Sound Studies Blog*, July 30, 2012, http://soundstudiesblog.com.

8. See Thomas Doherty, "Norman Corwin and the Blacklist," chapter 2 in this volume.

9. Rudolf Arnheim, "Style as a Gestalt Problem," *Journal of Aesthetics and Art Criticism* 39, no. 3 (Spring 1981), 282–83.

10. Ibid., 284–85.

11. Ibid., 285.

12. Ibid. For a lucid discussion of Arnheim's ideas of "structure" and "way of making," see Colin Burnett, "Arnheim on Style History," in *Arnheim for Film and Media Studies*, ed. Scott Higgins (New York: Routledge, 2011), 229–47.

13. For a summary of the functionalist approach, see David Bordwell, *On the History of Film Style* (Cambridge, MA: Harvard University Press, 1997), 149–57. On "functional equivalents," see David Bordwell, Janet Staiger, and Kristin Thompson, *The Classical Hollywood Cinema: Film Style and Mode of Production to 1960* (New York: Columbia University Press, 1985).

14. As I have discussed elsewhere, this contextualist strain is an important but neglected component of Arnheim's larger research agenda, extending back as far as his earliest writings on film and radio. See Shawn VanCour, "Arnheim on Radio: *Materialtheorie* and Beyond," *Arnheim for Film and Media Studies*, ed. Scott Higgins (New York: Routledge AFI Film Readers Series, 2010), 177–94.

15. Arnheim, 284.

16. Ibid., 285.

17. Ibid., 286.

18. Troy Cummings, "Media Primer: The Formation of Style in Norman Corwin's Early Radio Projects," chapter 6 in this volume.

19. Mary Ann Watson, "Norman Corwin and the Big Screen: Artistic Differences," chapter 3 in this volume.

20. For the Emmy award (to composer Richard Rodgers), see "ABC-Paramount Records Offers Heartiest Felicitations to Mr. Richard Rodgers . . . " *Billboard*, June 2, 1962, 13. For Curtin quote, see Michael Curtin, *Redeeming the Wasteland: Television Documentary and Cold War Politics* (New Brunswick, NJ: Rutgers, 1995), 19.

21. For the full text of Minow's speech, see Newton N. Minow, "Television and the Public Interest," available at "Top 100 Speeches," American Rhetoric, http://www.americanrhetoric.com/.

22. Murray Horowitz, "Graff Sees 'Noah' Opening Floodgates Toward 'Pushing Out Perimeters of TV,'" *Variety Weekly*, June 13, 1962, 25, 38. Although Sextant productions did not run exclusively on ABC, the network held a $1.5 million stake in the company and, in the case of *FDR*, maintained 50 percent ownership of the series; see Gene Arneel, "Sextant, of Video Antecedents, Sets One for Theatres: Sean O'Casey's Biopic," *Variety Weekly*, March 20, 1963, 7.

23. For advertisement, see "Sextant," *Variety Weekly*, March 28, 1962, 28.

24. Sextant and ABC had at one point even contemplated a series launch in fall 1961, garnering praise from the National Parent Teacher Association in its otherwise grim annual assessment of fall programming lineups; see "Parent-Teachers Org Takes a Dim View of '61-'62 TV," *Variety Weekly*, August 30, 1961, 1, 61. While the premier episode was completed in time for a fall 1962 launch, the series was postponed, then back on ABC's schedule again for the 1963–64 season before again being cut because, according to *Variety*, "a Presidential election is coming up next year and sponsors were scared of potential Democratic Party propaganda angles in the show;" see "'FDR' Scratched from ABC-TV Sked," *Variety Weekly*, June 12, 1963, 40. ABC did not air the program at the start of the fall 1964 season, instead launching it in spring 1965 to fill a half-hour gap created by an expansion of its prime-time programming feed; see "After 3-Year Wait, ABC-TV Slots 'FDR,'" *Variety Weekly*, December 23, 1964, 19. As of January 3 (only five days before its premiere), the show still had no sponsors, but by January 13 ABC had succeeded in lining up two short-term buyers to save the show from immediate cancellation; see Val Adams, "Prime Time Talk," *New York Times*, January 3, 1965, sec. X, 15, and "ABC's 'FDR' Coin," *Variety Weekly*, January 13, 1965, 32.

25. Jane Feuer et al., *MTM: Quality Television* (London: BFI, 1985); Elana Levine and Michael Newman, *Legitimizing Television: Media Convergence and Cultural Status* (New York: Routledge, 2012).

26. For contract negotiations, see Letter from Norman Corwin to Ben Feiner, November 10, 1961, FDR Series Correspondence, Box 21, Norman Corwin Papers, Special Collections Research Center (SCRC), Syracuse University Library, Syracuse, NY. Follow-up correspondence from his agent offered assurances that "Under no circumstances will you be collaborating with any [other] writer.... This is your assignment and is not a collaboration." See Letter from William Cooper to Norman Corwin, November 13, 1961, ibid. For reports of Corwin's later request that his name be removed from the credits, see Val Adams, "Prime Time Talk," *New York Times,* January 3, 1965, sec. X, 15.

27. Letter from Norman Corwin to Ben Feiner, February 19, 1962, FDR Series Correspondence, Box 21, Corwin Papers, SCRC, Syracuse University Library. This was not Corwin's first excursion into screenwriting nor his first conflict as a screenwriter with producers who questioned or subverted his creative decisions; see Watson, "Norman Corwin and the Big Screen," chapter 3 in this volume.

28. For requests for additional materials, see Letter from Norman Corwin to Ben Feiner, December 12, 1961, FDR Series Correspondence, Box 21, Corwin Papers, SCRC, Syracuse University Library. As Corwin explained in this letter, "I am persuaded that [this episode] has to be an extraordinary mural.... As you may gather from the number of items in the accompanying pages, I am working toward a mosaic on a scale proper to our particular heldenleben [hero's life]"—a work that, he stressed, would require "fast-cutting text and image" and a "complexity of architecture" unlike that seen in any other television presentation to date.

29. For Graff and Feiner's feedback on Corwin's initial draft, see "Notes for Mr. Corwin, Episode #1," February 2, 1962, FDR Series Research Materials and Notes, Box 21, Corwin Papers, SCRC, Syracuse University Library. For Corwin's reply, see Letter from Norman Corwin to Ben Feiner, February 19, 1962.

30. Letter from Corwin to Feiner, February 19, 1962. For a copy of Lipsett's film, see Arthur Lipsett, *Very Nice, Very Nice* (National Film Board, 1961), available at National Film Board of Canada website, http://www.nfb.ca/film/very_nice_very_nice/.

31. "Stills-In-Motion as TV Technique A Martell Click," *Variety Weekly,* August 12, 1964, 29, 34.

32. The "index motif" was first introduced as such in the second draft of Corwin's script and continues to be identified by this name in his third, and final, draft. See "Incomplete Drafts, Program #1," Second Draft, Versions 1 + 2, FDR Series Typescripts, Box 21, Corwin Papers, SCRC, Syracuse University Library. For Corwin's explanation of this device and comments on its use on specific pages in his second draft, see Letter from Corwin to Feiner, February 19, 1962.

33. John Gould, "TV: Distinguished Documentary Series on 'F.D.R.': President's Biography Bows on A.B.C.," *New York Times,* January 9, 1965, 51.

34. Neil Verma, *Theater of the Mind: Imagination, Aesthetics, and American Radio Drama* (Chicago: University of Chicago Press, 2012), 66; see also 70.

35. For discussion of the stylistic dimensions of Corwin's use of tape recording technology, see Jacob Smith, "Norman Corwin's Radio Realism," chapter 4 in this volume.

36. "The FDR Series: A Statement of Purpose," October 10, 1961, FDR Series Correspondence, Corwin Papers, SCRC, Syracuse University Library.

37. For warning against excessive adulation, see "Episode #1, First Draft, Notes," February 1, 1962, FDR Series Research Materials and Notes, Box 21, Corwin Papers, SCRC, Syracuse University Library. On need for conflict, see "Notes for Mr. Corwin, Episode #1," February 2, 1962, ibid. Graff and Feiner pushed Corwin even further in this direction in comments on his second draft, noting that, "If possible, we'd still like to inject more adverse comments and criticism into the script"—see Letter from Ben Feiner to Norman Corwin, February 26, 1962, FDR Series Correspondence, Box 21, Corwin Papers, SCRC, Syracuse Library.

38. Letter from Ben Feiner to Norman Corwin, June 1, 1962, FDR Series Correspondence, Box 21, Corwin Papers, SCRC, Syracuse University Library.

39. Letter from Norman Corwin to Peter Davis, June 7, 1962, FDR Series Correspondence, Box 21, Corwin Papers, SCRC, Syracuse University Library.

40. See "Early Drafts, Program #26," First Draft (13–14) + Second Draft (6–7), FDR Series Typescripts, Box 21, Corwin Papers, SCRC, Syracuse University Library.

41. For *Inside the Movie Kingdom*, see Val Adams, "TV to Offer an Informal Look at Moviemaking in Many Lands" *New York Times*, January 7, 1964, 67.

42. Initially slotted as Westinghouse's sixth show was a program titled *Flavors*, which was to feature a series of "social comment singers" anchored by the personality of songwriter and comedian Mason Williams; see "Group W's $5-Mil Show Role with No Exceptions to the (McGannon) Rule," *Variety Weekly*, March 31, 1971, 40. One month after announcing their intended development of this series, however, Westinghouse had dropped it from its lineup, picking up *Doctor in the House* as a replacement; see "Syndies in Focus as Group W Slots 5 Primetimers" *Variety Weekly*, April 28, 1971, 34.

43. John J. O'Connor, "Will It Pay To Be Different?" *New York Times*, September 12, 1971, D27–28.

44. Harry Harris, "Group W Puts Psychediller-Thriller On the Road in Boffo Barnum Style," *Variety Weekly*, August 18, 1971, 32.

45. Westinghouse Corporation, "Starting This Fall, These Five New Shows Will Get What They Deserve: An Audience," *Variety Weekly*, June 9, 1971, 39. On the rise of the youth market as a valued demographic, see Todd Gitlin, *Inside Prime Time* (Berkeley: California, 2000), 203–20; and Aniko Bodroghkozy, *Groove Tube: Sixties Television and the Youth Rebellion* (Durham, NC: Duke, 2001).

46. See Cummings, "Media Primer," chapter 6 in this volume.

47. For Arjo, see "Joel Katz's Deals with U-TV & SG, Plus Gr. W Series," *Variety Weekly*, June 2, 1971, 37. For Moynihan's involvement, see "TV-Radio Production Centres in the U.S. and Abroad," *Variety Weekly*, September 15, 1971, 54.

48. Les Brown, "U.S. Video's 'Go North, Young Man' Puts Focus on CTV's Chercover," *Variety Weekly*, September 1, 1971, 34, 43. As Brown explains, relying on imports actually meant a cost deficit for CTV programmers, as the network was required to pay its members station compensation fees for any time filled by them and could not sell the corresponding ad time. Domestically produced content, by contrast, did not require payment of compensation fees, and the CTV was permitted to sell ad time for these programs. On sale of distribution rights to the CBC, see "CBC-TV Buys 'Corwin,'" *Variety Weekly*, December 15, 1971, 30. For further discussion of the increased emphasis on domestic content in Canadian broadcasting policy of the late 1960s–early 1970s, see Robert Armstrong, *Canadian Broadcasting Policy* (Toronto: University of Toronto Press, 2010), 43–44. For a summary of Toronto's expansion as a major North American production center during this period and the resulting boom in runaway productions by U.S. film and television producers, see Marsha Ann Tate, *Canadian Television Programming Made for the United States Market* (Jefferson, NC: McFarland, 2007), 38–44.

49. For a longer list of Canadian names associated with this series, see Canadian broadcaster John Corcelli's entry on the program for the Canadian Communication Foundation's website, "Norman Corwin Presents," September 2005, http://www.broadcasting-history.ca/.

50. "L'Affaire Gumpert," *Columbia Radio Workshop* (CBS, August 21, 1945); and "One-Man Group," *Norman Corwin Presents* (Group W, 1971).

51. Bell, 245–46.

52. For a discussion of audioposition, see Verma, *Theater of the Mind*, 35–38.

53. "Soliloquy to Balance the Budget," *Columbia Radio Workshop* (CBS, June 15, 1941); and "Soliloquy for Television," *Norman Corwin Presents* (Group W, 1972).

54. As Corwin recalled in his interviews with Bell, one of the few direct demands made by Westinghouse producer George Moynihan, was his insistence "to have more programs of black interest" (a demand that Corwin surmised "was largely conditioned by the fact that their stations in Baltimore, Philadelphia, and Pittsburgh were watched by blacks more than any other group"). Producer Joel Katz

actively pushed to have an African American lead for "Soliloquy" and brought Peters to Corwin's attention as a potential fit for the part. See Bell, 252, 249.

55. For a discussion of speech's capacity to call objects and events into being in radio drama and the role sound effects played in reinforcing these linguistic effects, see Tim Crook, *Radio Drama: Theory and Practice* (New York: Routledge, 1999), 70. For discussion of the importance of speech, in particular, see Andrew Crisell, *Understanding Radio,* 2nd ed. (New York: Routledge, 1996), 143–63.

56. For discussions of theatricality in television programming, see David Barker, "Production Techniques as Communication," *Critical Studies in Mass Communication* 2, no. 3, (September 1985), 234–46; Robert Vianello, "The Power Politics of 'Live' Television," *Journal of Film and Video* 38 (Summer 1985), 26–40; Lynn Spigel, "Installing the Television Set: Popular Discourses on Television and Domestic Space," *Private Screenings: Television and the Female Consumer,* ed. Lynn Spigel and Denise Mann (Minneapolis: University of Minnesota Press, 1992), 2–39.

57. "The Undecided Molecule," *Columbia Radio Workshop,* (CBS, July 17, 1945); and "The Undecided Molecule," *Norman Corwin Presents* (Group W, 1971).

58. Bell, 242.

59. Donald M. McGannon, "Group W Topper Weighs 'Phase 1,'" *Variety Weekly,* February 9, 1972, 39, 44.

60. Bill Greeley, "Welk and 'Heehaw' the Pacesetters," *Variety Weekly,* April 5, 1972, 49, 88.

61. As prime-time access shows did not receive adequate ratings for inclusion in national ratings, other metrics were used, such as the Trendex survey. In Trendex's initial survey of the period from September premieres to November sweeps, *Norman Corwin Presents* ranked 19th out of the 21 programs for which viewing numbers were calculated and dead last among Westinghouse's series. However, when asked to rank their favorite prime-time access shows, Corwin's fared slightly better, coming in 15th out of 21 and beating out *Street People, Smothers,* and *Electric Impressions* for viewer satisfaction with the quality of the programs viewed; see "Trendex Pilots Study on How Prime-Access Shows Stack Up," *Variety Weekly,* December 1, 1971, 30.

62. Writing credits for Corwin's episode of *The Hallmark Hall of Fame* are attributed to his pseudonym, Donald Cormorant.

6

MEDIA PRIMER

Norman Corwin's Radio Juvenilia

Troy Cummings

I had capacity for anger, and still have. And my anger became my best friend then because it compelled me to write that piece. . . . I don't want to give you the impression of the long haired poet who is seized with the divine afflatus and goes off to his attic and writes an immortal poem. No, I was angered; but in a controlled way, and I thought, "those sons of bitches." And what you do then is sit down and do something about it. And all I could do was write a piece.[1]

So Norman Corwin wrote "They Fly through the Air with the Greatest of Ease" (1939). He aimed his anger squarely at contemporary civilian air raids in Spain and Northern Africa and dedicated the radio play with biting irony: "Mr. Corwin dedicates this program to all aviators who have bombed defenseless civilian populations and machine gunned helpless refugees."[2] The result, armed with free-verse narration and the music of airplane engines, was a timely work that brought him into national consciousness, but in his controlled anger something also clicked in his development as a radio artist. He took the final step toward a basic yet definitive template in his radio art: a balance of poetry, music, and scenic realism that he had been working toward for years. In February 1939, when "They Fly through the Air" first aired, Corwin was still a fresh hire at CBS, having worked there less than a year. John Dunning wrote, "so swift was his rise, once it began, that he seemed to burst upon the scene a complete, polished, and original talent."[3] But there is little mystery to Corwin's exceptionality in 1939. Before he stood in the director's box, he faced the microphone, spending nearly a decade in local radio newscasting, writing radio publicity, and independently producing two experimental series. This early period was when he honed the basics of his signature style, radio writing voice, and public mission. Like juvenilia of most artists, it is a time full of humble starts and abandoned paths but key to understanding later success. The goal of this essay is to form a stronger narrative of Norman Corwin's progress as a young radio artist in order to unearth the roots of his mature style. His early radio projects, *Rhymes and Cadences* (1934–1935), *Poetic License* (1937–1938), and the first episode of *Words without Music* (1938–1939), form a juvenile body of radio work. These experiments in poetry and music tell the story of Corwin's quest for his own dynamic radiogenic style, his mission to create original art in word, music, and sound that tapped into "intellectual and sensorial experiences unique to radio."[4]

RHYMES AND CADENCES

At seventeen, straight out of high school, Corwin started a job as a reporter at the Greenfield, Massachusetts, *Recorder*.[5] Two years later, in 1929, he became the newscaster and the radio editor for the *Springfield Republican* in Springfield, Massachusetts. As a newscaster, his job was to rewrite news dispatches into radio bulletins and read them over the air on WBZA and its Boston simulcast WBZ. This process "had a great deal to do with the evolution of my theories of writing for the ear instead of the eye," he later said, and during this time he began "developing a definite sense of cadence" on the radio.[6] As the *Springfield Republican*'s radio editor, he also wrote daily guides and schedules to help listeners navigate the airwaves and ran a weekly column about radio. As a critic, he developed strong opinions about broadcast poetry, a "radio staple" of the early 1930s.[7] In a *Springfield Republican* article, he wrote:

> For years now certain poets, writing for the daily press or for periodicals, have been pumping up verse no more esthetic than chewing gum. For years too, radio bards have been twittering undistinguished poetry full of silver linings and hearty smacks-on-the-back, (the species of poem which argues that if you've broken a leg you should be very grateful you didn't break two, and that if you've got plenty of nothing, why nothing's plenty for you). Some of these radio minnesingers have served elaborate specimens of the banana royal category of verse—poems performed in a velvety baritone, andante cantabile, and assisted by muted strings of an organ, playing the mellowest of Chopin or Debussy.[8]

Corwin scathed this style of poetry presentation in "Radio Primer" (1941), when a poet buries himself in a time capsule along with the poem "Wings over Everything." The message to the future begins:

> If you broke a leg this morning, do not mind;
> You could have broken two or gone stone blind.
> If your skull was badly fractured, do not fret—[. . .][9]

This reoccurring mockery, well into his network career, betrays how deeply formative this particular annoyance was. Later "Radio Primer" ribs, "the best soporifics have voices deeper even than narrators, mainly because they feel the world more keenly."[10] A sober voice then reads a lexically littered parody backed by "Auld Lang Syne" on electric organ:

> *Soporific.* When Phoebe doth her grummons gather up
> And in the trancid night forsoonly sup
> Of myrrh and the smerds of Arcady,
> When chumblers in the dim-lit aspenade
> Bestrew the glamorantine of the glade,
> Then come, love, cast thy wampts and cherybdibs
> And frolls and fulsome friptures on the air,
> For hearts that beat in wambledon garoome
> Can ne'er the druid fluid frume the flume.[11]

Respected at WBZA as the chief news correspondent, in 1934 Corwin asked management for his own show.[12] His pitch stated that he would "avoid the homely philosophical type of poetry currently popular."[13] His fifteen-minute program, *Rhymes and Cadences,* was simple. Corwin would read poems, each followed with music by pianist Benjamin Kalman. For around a year, starting in the spring of 1934, Corwin and Kalman intermittently broadcast episodes of *Rhymes and Cadences.*

The poems in the first episode of *Rhymes and Cadences* reveal social and artistic sensibilities that would define Corwin's career. This episode featured two poems by the longtime New York columnist Franklin P. Adams, "The Rich Man" and "Xanthiam Follied," which address romantic tropes and social inequality with swift colloquial wit. "Epitaph on a Commonplace Person Who Died in Bed," by Amy Levy, is a somber look at poverty and death, and it couples well with "Aftermath" by Siegfried Sassoon. "Aftermath" intimates the cost of war, a main theme throughout Corwin's career. Robert Carlton Brown's "I Am Aladdin," the longest poem, is in five sections that dart around unified only by their pomposity and proximity. One of the sections is a lament for unrequited mermaid love, which builds a bridge to the last poem of the episode. Originally, Corwin intended to end with David Morton's sonnet "Old Ships." But gathering courage before the show went on the air, he substituted his own poem, "Ocean Symphony"—at once positioning himself next to successful poets and tenaciously using the radio program as a vehicle for his own poetry.

Simple lists of the poems and piano selections functioned as scripts for much of *Rhymes and Cadences.* Corwin had a penchant for improvised announcing as his short-lived WMAS interview program, *Journals* (1934), suggests. The show featured unscripted casual conversations with noteworthy guests, a rarity in the day.[14] He provided titles and authors in between the poem and piano selections of *Rhymes and Cadences* but may have dabbled with improvisation. During this time he was interested in the "informality of scriptless discussions" on air that created "the illusion of eavesdropping for the listener."[15] Innovative announcing was a goal; "the idea was old, the technique new," he wrote.[16] Although he did not continue in this scriptless vein, his special attention to form reveals two distinct purposes: attention to content (poem and music choice, ordering, and performance) and attention to how this content was framed, what was called continuity in the argot of the day.

The transition from casual announcing to poem reading was left to Corwin's natural skill, although from time to time he arranged for local poets to read on *Rhymes and Cadences*, giving him the opportunity to hear how authors interpreted their own works out loud. "If all the poets who are only so-so readers could be made into good or even fair readers, we'd be doing something," he wrote in 1938.[17] According to Corwin, David Morton and Carl Sandburg were poets whose speaking measured up to their writing, but he wondered if he would be wrong to suggest that Robert Frost "be coached on the interpretation of his own poems."[18]

True to its name, *Rhymes and Cadences* had a conscious musical aim as well. Corwin and Kalman experimented in comparative moods by purposefully alternating poetry and music without overlapping the two. "I thought the listener has work enough cut out to appreciate the words and music separately," Corwin said.[19] Contemporary music recitals often included poems to complement musical pieces, but in this series this relationship is reversed, making the music incidental to the "mood of the poem."[20] In the first episode Corwin penciled in the generic suggestion of blues to follow the lighthearted poems by Adams and twice the music of Brahms to resonate to the somber poems of Levy and Sassoon. He also specified Nikolai Rimsky-Korsakov's *Scheherazade*, the tone poem of "One Thousand and One Nights," to follow Brown's "I Am Aladdin." Humble first steps in a long career of imaginative music cueing.

Rhymes and Cadences was a simple series, but it already contained kernels of his mature style. There is the contrast of colloquial and poetic syntaxes, early incarnations of the alternating scenic realism–poetic narration template of his most memorable radio plays. Corwin exhibits musical forethought in terms of pairing, performance, mood balance, and variation within a playlist, which grew into his later boldness in musical cue writing and successful cooperation with composers. But the most important and perhaps the most ethereal aspect of *Rhymes and Cadences* was his simple choice to fill time with a selection of complementary poems. This created a simple radio art template of poetically charged moments in tandem, which allowed him liberty to improvise in choice, order, elocution, and framing continuity while keeping poetic affect central.

There is a ratio between artistic freedom and artistic quality in Corwin's oeuvre. *Rhymes and Cadences* paid nothing; it was a side project for Corwin that put him in an artistic place of free creation. He would battle to protect this kind of freedom the rest of his career. As Shawn VanCour notes in his chapter in this volume, "Corwin on Television," Corwin would rather his name be scrubbed from the credits than present a compromised version of his work. An album of the radio play "Between Americans" was produced by MGM in 1948. Corwin was not involved in the production, and his first impressions upon hearing the "slovenly botch" sum up his views on artistic compromise nicely:

> I wouldn't have it in the house. I burned my copy. Did you ever burn records in a fireplace? It's good sport. Seems there is a sort of shellac between the laminations of compressed soot, or whatever it is, that goes into the discs, and this burns with a fat, oily, carboniferous flame. Jolly.[21]

Finally, the threat of dictated content and restrictive pressure for commercial viability are why he walked away from CBS in 1948.

POETIC LICENSE

In 1936, Corwin moved to New York City and began work at Twentieth Century-Fox as a radio publicist. As at the *Springfield Republican,* converting print to radio copy—"radioese"—was part of his job.[22] He also wrote blurbs about current Fox films for radio stations throughout the country to read on air. Now in New York City, Corwin pitched a poetry program at WQXR on Long Island, a station with a fine-art milieu.[23] The station manager, Elliot Sanger (1897–1989), considered his pitch, first asking Corwin to tone down his regional accent for a second audition. Corwin returned with a reformed palate and soon began to produce *Poetic License,* which ran from June 1937 to April 1938 for over forty episodes.[24]

For the most part *Poetic License* abandoned the musical aspect of *Rhymes and Cadences.* However, for two episodes of *Poetic License,* Corwin invited pianists to perform short pieces he had composed. As a child Corwin had a spurt of violin lessons and "thanks to this little aborted career as a violinist" learned to read music.[25] And at the age of twenty-two he was quarantined in a room with a piano when it was feared he had tuberculosis. During his recovery, he began to compose short piano pieces and continued to compose off and on throughout his twenties. One *Poetic License* episode featured two of these compositions, a musical response to Arturo Giovannitti's "'The Walker" and a tone poem of James Weldon Johnson's, "Go Down Death." These pieces were positioned in the same way as music in his earlier series, yet went beyond by being original programmatic music. He was much more invested in the few original compositions of *Poetic License* than in the music of *Rhymes and Cadences,* yet it took too much energy and time to compose regularly.

Instead, Corwin used the extra space as an opportunity to expand his portfolio of thematic techniques. In one episode, Corwin played disc jockey and featured recordings of Carl Sandburg and Robert Frost. He built other shows around themes like inebriation, war, biblical poetry, and poets killed. Two episodes explored the art of poetic portraiture from several different angles. He also dedicated shows to single authors, such as Walt Whitman, Sandburg, Sarah Teasdale, David H. Lawrence, and himself. By using a theme, he was able to craft shows with internal synthesis, and so it becomes easier and easier to think of these episodes as individual radio plays. One episode, "Variations on Mary Had a Little Lamb," is a miniature radio play. An entirely original work, "Mary," as he called it in his letters, satirized the very thematic format of *Poetic License* and was groundbreaking in Corwin's career for a few reasons. Although short, it contains inaugural snippets of radio drama and early examples of his comic wit applied to radio. Also, a later NBC broadcast of "Mary" may be the earliest extant audio recording of Norman Corwin's radio art.

"Variations on Mary Had a Little Lamb" is, as the musical genre implies, in sections and in each section Corwin and actress Peggy Burt voiced a different duo of characters. The NBC version of "Mary" had an introductory announcer, sound effects, and orchestra. The first of the six variations mocks the *March of Time*, a popular radio series that dramatized news events. The lamb's persistent pursuit becomes a featured news story: "news-hawks, quick to gather at the scene, question the pretty, pert, petulant lass."[26] Next a policeman: "Calling all cars, be on the lookout for Mary, M-A-R-Y.... She is being followed by a lamb, L-A-M-B."[27] A subdued newspaper article by a "super-cautious, ultra-conservative daily newspaper" follows:

> It was learned from usually reliable sources at a late hour last night that the girl, alleged to be receiving the attentions of what impartial observers were reportedly unanimous in believing was an ordinary lamb, is known by the name of Mary.[28]

Then in a little dramatic scene, Gertrude Lawrence talks on the phone to Noel Coward. Lawrence flamboyantly presents "Mary Had a Little Lamb" as the possible plot of a new play. Then two scriptwriters discuss turning the nursery rhyme into a full length film with Busby Berkeley–like dance numbers.

The final scene, true in its virtuosity to the typical climax of variations on a theme, is a duet featuring Corwin and Burt as surrealist poets. The poem for two voices displays Corwin's daring as a radio artist—he had even referred to himself in the introduction to "Mary" as "one of our better known young poets."[29] There is a breathless pace in this final variation allowing the listeners little time to digest the barrage of nonsense and humor until the final short punch line:

> Corwin. Is there any any is there nonesuch no one on some boa brooch a bray a brace lace so catch a key to keep back Mary's lamb keep back Mary's lamb from following all the way following all the way; so the Gertrude Stein
>
> Burt. Yes, Gatsby coming, and lots of which it is not as soon as it.
>
> Corwin. Worse, eighteen point six.

> *Burt.* No speaks thee thirteen.
> *Corwin.* How brought now?
> *Burt.* Thunder head cow folly.
> *Corwin.* Slangin' gnat slapper.
> *Burt.* Ruby pig widgeon
> *Corwin.* However whereas and withal
> *Burt.* As herein before provided
> *Corwin.* If, but, and be it resolved that one, Mary
> *Burt.* Two, the lamb, but you are still evading the issue: When is the next train to New Zealand?
> *Corwin.* This I cannot tell you, for that your name is Mary, and for that you are lamb-followed!
> *Burt.* Oh ho, ah ha, I begin to understand.
> *Corwin.* You must grasp the overtones and the undertones and the side tones and the bottom tones and the inside out tones and never-the-which-however tones
> *Burt.* Are you following the script, Iago?
> *Corwin.* Are you following your lamb, Mary?
> *Burt.* So, where is the nearest exit?
> *Corwin.* Around and about, above and below, thick and fast.
> *Burt*: They will never guess the meaning, it is later than they think ha-ho!
> *Corwin.* Hank Greenburg lives in the Bronx but plays for Detroit.
> *Burt.* Don't evade the issue.
> *Corwin.* What have you to say before you die?
> *Burt.* Baaaaah.[30]

During a radio interview with Corwin, John T. McManus noted, "Yeah you told me one time that it didn't matter to you how your stuff looked in print as long as it was listenable."[31] Corwin's lyric virtuosity in this final variation had immediate sonorous and semantic effects. The phrases, some nearly sung, demarcate rhythms of 2/4, 3/4, or 4/4, and these fluidly shifting meters together with the alternating male and female timbres achieve a primitive musical construction.

In the original version for *Poetic License,* one "Mary" variation was in the style of an epitaph from Edgar Lee Masters's *Spoon River Anthology.* This variation was removed from the NBC broadcast, but it shows that Corwin admired Masters's masterpiece. He would set selections of this work twice more in his career, first in another episode of *Poetic License.*[32] This episode had various guest voices including Corwin's brother Emil, and Corwin's tailor, a Russian immigrant.[33] In a work like *Spoon River Anthology,* as well as *The People, Yes* or *Leaves of Grass,* other influential anthologies he adapted multiple times, there is a model from another medium for Corwin's radio works during this period; he conceived of himself "as a kind of anthologist" building a single larger work from a collection of poems.[34] He also used the analogy of the artist creating a "mosaic" varying color through individual pieces to describe his own style.[35]

Another notable *Poetic License* episode, November 17, 1937, like "Mary" went beyond simple recitation. Here Corwin arranged poems by various poets, including "Killers" by Sandburg, for a group of performers with basic sound effects. He wrote:

> In arranging (or orchestrating) these poems, I have taken certain liberties with the original texts, adding or cutting words and phrases wherever I felt that such scoring would benefit the radio version of the poem.[36]

This statement is a basic description of the majority of works in his first series at CBS, *Words without Music*.

But before moving on to *Words without Music*, it is important to examine how the structural continuity of *Poetic License* changed from that of *Rhymes and Cadences*. In *Poetic License*, Corwin began to carefully compose his announcements and integrate himself as a central character in the dramaturgy of the episodes. The August 23, 1937, *Poetic License* episode, which he referred to as "War Program," is a good example of this shift to involved, scripted announcing, opening with "On my way here tonight I passed no barricades, I was challenged by no sentries, and I walked the sidewalks of New York."[37]

"War Program" begins with self-examination, pointing out how absurd a poetry radio program might be to citizens of war-torn nations. "In fact, I don't think an audience of Shanghaians or Madrilenos [referring to the contemporary Second Sino-Japanese War and Spanish Civil War] would be particularly interested in anything anybody had to say about poetry right now."[38] However, he made an exception for poetry on the radio that abhorred war and worked for peace, prophesying nearly his entire wartime radio career. First he pointed out the levels of anti-war sentiment in the arts:

> Music is generally so abstract that it can't be bothered; painting (until lately) has glorified rather than condemned the institution; the cinema, bless its celluloid soul, has occasionally struck out at the enemy; and prose writers have with some glory done well by the keepers of the peace.[39]

Poetry was a different case:

> But poetry alone among the arts—and poets, among the artists, have been consistently at odds with the makers of war . . . poets, because they have a way of wielding the sharpest words, because they fuse and compress into the briefest forms the widest philosophy, the tallest wisdom, the deepest emotion . . . because in their dealings with beauty they have come to love peace and order and brotherhood, and to hate war and disorder and inhumanity and exploitation.[40]

After a substantial introduction for a twelve-minute program, Corwin provided only one or two sentences to introduce each poem in the program. But this introduction makes Corwin a character in the episode, unabashedly highlighting his own views. The style of writing also leaned toward poetics. One of the eight poems he chose was his own "Claire De Lune," later adapted for *Words without Music*. In an early draft of the "War Program," this poem ended the episode, introduced by "But there will be more aftermaths . . . tomorrow and tomorrow and tomorrow . . . And here is a piece of my own, written some time ago, but (I'm afraid) applicable this very night."[41] The repetition of *tomorrow* three times framed by ellipses, a reference to *Macbeth*, was a brief moment of expressive performance repurposing continuity as a vehicle for poetics. The step from what may have been improvised, casual announcing in *Rhymes and Cadences* to scripted, eloquent continuity in *Poetic License* shows how Corwin was not willing to let announcing be an objective role with set parameters. It was a direct line to the listener to be tapped for artistic expression.

Corwin was not in the habit of working in preexisting radio genres and preferred customization. In *Poetic License* (also an unpaid job), he broke his own mold repeatedly, searching for an artistic vantage that would allow him more freedom, more originality, more opportunity to match his gifts with those of radio. Now his struggle would be to fuse originality and technical innovativeness, exemplified in "Mary," with the poetic voice that was blossoming in the continuity of *Poetic License*.

WORDS WITHOUT MUSIC

In May of 1938, Corwin was hired at CBS and began training as a director and producer.[42] Before he was given his own show, which was the plan, he directed and codirected radio programs.[43] He worked on a handful of shows, including episodes of the educational series *American School of the Air*, the soap opera *County Seat*, and the documentary series *Americans at Work* and *Living History*. This period was Corwin's first real experience with the mixing console and organizing a large staff.[44] He continued adapting poetry, including selections from Sandburg's *The People, Yes* for *American School of the Air*. And apparently, Corwin freely experimented while directing. Gilbert Seldes (1893–1970), who produced *Americans at Work* at the same time that Corwin was directing the show, had some criticisms. Corwin recounts, "there were some earnest but always friendly arguments . . . mainly about what he considered my too free use of sound."[45] Many radio writers cautioned against experimenting with sounds and sound effects. Arch Oboler (1909–1987), Corwin's contemporary, wrote with picturesque harshness that radio drama had been wearing "undersized three-cornered pants" too long, slowing development because writers focused on techniques such as montages, "symbolic musical effects," and "sensational sound effects," instead of on good story writing.[46] Luckily, Corwin ignored criticisms like those of Seldes and Oboler, for his technical boldness went hand in hand with his idealistic boldness.

After directing at CBS for six months, Corwin went to see William B. Lewis with the idea for his third poetry program.[47] Lewis agreed to fund a pilot episode. It was a resounding success, and the program *Norman Corwin's Words without Music,* as Lewis titled it, was created. This new series entirely abandoned the simple poetry reading used in *Rhymes and Cadences* and *Poetic License*. Instead, he would apply a variety of methods toward poem adaptation, including sound effects, multivoice arrangements, dramatizations, and musical accompaniments, and he wrote original works specifically for the series. *Words without Music* was Corwin's first program with a budget and access to professional radio personnel, and this half-hour show allowed him more freedom than ever to let his imagination take flight. His audience also increased from a potential hundreds of thousands on WQXR to millions that could hear any national CBS program.

In addition to imaginative adaptations, *Words without Music* included original short radio poems and the half-hour radio plays "The Plot to Overthrow Christmas" and "They Fly through the Air" by Corwin. He was still a "frank propagandist for poetry," but his method of presenting poetry was so extreme that it needed explaining:[48]

> The Workshop offers a new treatment of the old art of poetry, a technique of orchestration and augmentation created expressly for radio. This technique adapts for the enjoyment of the ear poems written originally for the eye, and in doing so full use is made of the freedom implicit in the title *Poetic License*.[49]

Corwin took poetry adaptation to a new level, shifting his focus to innovative interpretation. A second broadcast of the pilot episode aired on December 4, 1938, this time as the first episode of *Words without Music*. This second version had many changes, and Corwin was put in the position of defending the musicality of his program because of its awkward title—a title that he did not choose. Instead he resolved to frame this series as radio art that existed simultaneously as music and poetry. The new introduction replaces the word *poetry* with *song*:

> Columbia offers a different treatment of the very old art of song—*Words without Music*. This experimental program is based on the theory that words, when arranged in the right way, are music in themselves; and to support this theory Norman Corwin has taken a number of poems and applied them to the special uses of radio through the combined techniques of orchestration and augmentation.[50]

The phrase *orchestration and augmentation* in both introductions refers to pseudomusical techniques that manipulated timbre, rhythm, tempo, dynamics, and general pitch range. Corwin orchestrated poems by assigning multiple voices where characters or narrative streams were present, by specifying gender and tonal range for effect, or by layering voices. For example, consider Corwin's setting of Walt Whitman's "When I Heard the Learn'd Astronomer," which begins with the voice of an astronomer speaking in dense technical terminology. This jargon fades to a low volume and underpins Whitman's short poem. The differing syntaxes make the counterpoint poetic as well as musical in timbre and rhythm.

Augmentation refers to the lengthening of a poem for effect whether through the repetition of a word or words, through tempo alterations, or through the addition of sound effects and other extrapoetical material. Corwin's adaptation of a fragment of Sandburg's *The People, Yes* uses augmentation through repetition and slowing of tempo. Note Corwin's typography, how he uses capital letters for increased volume in the word *ALL* and spaces between letters to lengthen the ending words:

ALL

a machine needs
is a little regular attention
and plenty of grease
and plenty of grease
and plenty of grease
    a n d p l e n t y o o g r e a s e[51]

He pairs this text with a clacking, mechanical sound effect that "SLOWS DOWN AND STOPS" with the line "p l e n t y o o g r e a s e."[52] This sound sequence goes beyond the proverbial horse hooves and trains used elsewhere in the episode.

The slowing of the text and other purely vocal techniques Corwin employed in *Words without Music* were inspired by a contemporary movement of poetry performance art called verse choir. The movement originated as an educational method in the United Kingdom in the 1920s but soon became popular in the United States and was practiced throughout the country in grade schools, high schools, and colleges. At its simplest, verse choir was a group recitation of a poem in unison, but more complex forms abounded. Techniques included multiple choir antiphony, grouping by gender and vocal range, soloists, duos, and other pairings. Varying dynamics and timbre contrasts were used for dramatics.

Corwin became familiar with verse choir at Amherst College in Amherst, Massachusetts, during the mid-1930s. His relationship with David Morton and John Theobald, both professors at Amherst and former guests on *Rhymes and Cadences*, exposed him to the thriving spoken poetry movement at the college, which included verse choirs formed by students. Amherst was the town of many successful poets, most notably at that time Robert Frost, and Corwin submitted an article to his old newspaper, the *Springfield Republican*, about poetry in the college and town:

> Poetry hangs from the branches of Amherst's trees. It follows you down the streets. The hills surrounding the town have poetic ore in them. The grass grows greener in Amherst because it figures some poet will come along any moment and write about it.[53]

There was a definite connection between Corwin's experiences at Amherst and his decision to arrange poetry for multiple voices. In fact, this lengthy, thorough newspaper article was published August 1, 1937, the day before the first performance of "Mary" on WBZA.

Carl Sandburg's "Killers," featured in *Words without Music* and earlier in the series *Poetic License* is an example of an adaptation with verse choir technique. Corwin was attracted to the euphony as well as the sentiment of "Killers," its strong ethical questioning as well as its sharp consonants. Sandburg's poem described the psychological strain on a state appointed executioner, and the word *kill* in various forms is a structural element of the poem. The last line of the poem includes four forms of the word: "I am the killer who kills today for five million killers who want a killing."[54] Corwin created an overture and coda of sorts out of this percussive word, a "PYRAMIDING" effect of six voices joining in one at a time, repeating "Kill, Kill, Kill, Kill."[55] These disquieting verse choir constructs frame Corwin's adaptation.

For the body of the new radio poem, Corwin turned Sandburg's evocative lines into an inner-poetic continuity. First consider the announcer's introduction to "Killers," a typical use of continuity: "Jesse James was one type of killer; but in a poem by Carl Sandburg we have a psychological portrait of another kind of killer."[56] This sentence easily guides the listener from one poem to the next. But within "Killers" a new level of continuity/content or frame/feature relationship is signaled by two distinct voices or streams of sound: (1) the poet's voice and (2) extrapoetical sound effects, realistic scenes, and verse choir techniques. Corwin turns the poet into the narrator of a radio drama.

The sonic suggestions within the lines of "Killers" then become invitations for extrapoetical material. When the shooter "pumped the bullets," three jarring gunshots sound out. The poem describes a trial, and a floating voice declares "Guilty."[57] Extrapoetic courtroom testimonies appear as islands of radio drama realism in the poem's midst:[58] "And when I got there I found the body of the victim lying on the sidewalk"; "and I'm on my way to the movies, to see a gangster pitcher, and all of the sudden . . ."[59] Finally, when the executioner is haunted by a rhyme from his childhood, female voices distorted through a stock filter effect speak twice: "I'm to be queen of the May, Mother, I'm to be queen of the May."[60] The internal cues in the original text of "Killers" trigger all of these voices and sounds. "Killers" is a miniature radio drama with an uninhibited poet as narrator—a microcosm of Corwin's mature style. This is why "They Fly through the Air," produced months later in *Words without Music,* is such an key step in understanding Corwin's artistic development. In both "Killers" and "They Fly through the Air" the narrator is a blatant poet; the narration is a free verse poem; moments of scenic realism, including voices, music, and sound effects, are extrapoetical material cued by continuity, rising in and fading out as a radio poet directs them to. The radio drama, "They Fly through the Air," is an expansion of the template of the experimental radio poem, "Killers." Corwin became a radio dramatist through years of experimenting with the relationship between music and poetry on the radio, not a direct attempt at conventional radio drama.

Words without Music had a budget for an announcer, and apparently Corwin felt obliged to use one, preventing him from easily interjecting himself directly into the dramaturgy of an episode as he had done in *Rhymes and Cadences* and *Poetic License*. This simple fact may have been why he stopped developing himself as an on-air radio personality. He had aspirations to act in film and even starred in his own radio plays from time to time, but other than in *One World Flight* (1947), he remained a writer, director, and producer, not finding a consistent podium for his physical voice and character on radio. Instead, the role of radio poet, most often anonymous, became the least inhibited outlet for his voice. He was not a fan of the conventional announcer or MC; in the variety show he directed, *The Pursuit of Happiness* (1939–1940), it would become his bane. In *Words without Music* Corwin seems most excited when the announcer is fictionalized as in "The Plot to Overthrow Christmas," or locked outside as in "They Fly through the Air," leaving us alone with the narrator as guide.

Although starting with another's poem gave him an easily repeatable way to create new radio art, he also began to compose original radio poems. In the first episode of *Words without Music* there are two, and they are the highlights of the episode. "Claire de Lune" and "Interview with Signs of the Times" are important points in Corwin's evolution of style. "Claire de Lune" may be his first use of simplistic background music in an original dramatic situation, and "Interview" the farthest he ever went with verse choir techniques. They each represent a separate extreme of music and poetry synthesis.

The technical effects for "Claire de Lune" are minimal but effective, as are its words. The beating of a solitary animal skin drum begins and continues throughout the radio poem:

Effect. MOURNFUL DRUMBEATS.. COMING AS THOUGH FROM A GREAT DISTANCE: HOLD MONOTONOUSLY UNDER THE FOLLOWING:

Listener. Far off in the night, drums,
No masque, no bergamasque, no lute, no caroling—
Just drums,
Drums,
Drums,

> Drums,
> Drums,
> > Say it again, drums,
> > Again,
> > Again,
> > > Men are marching tonight
> > > to kill men
> > > Men are marching tonight
> > > to kill men
> > > Men are marching tonight
> > > to kill me—
> ...... in the moonlight.[61]

Every line of this simple counterpoint brings attention to and adds connotations to the drumbeats, while the drum adds a nontextual yet material suggestion of reality to the scene. Both sound streams are transformed semantically in the second to last line with the word *me*. This personal pronoun changes the conceptual scene from poetic to dramatic. And the drum exists no longer as a metaphysical embodiment of the text, but becomes a second character of a drama—the war drum of the infringing horde.

Apposed to the simplicity of "Claire de Lune," the condensed complexity of "Interview with Signs of the Times" is unprecedented in Corwin's entire oeuvre. This one-minute-and-twenty-second radio poem pushed the limits of radio script typography with ten separate voices, seventy voice cues, contrapuntal textures, and five separate choir groupings. Directing the performance was nothing less than conducting a choir. Its themes cover electric signage, barrages of commercials, and trance-inducing advertisements.

"Interview" was a hit. There was a repeat performance on "Crosstown Manhattan" (1938) in the prestigious *Columbia Workshop* series directed at the time by William Robson. Richard Kostelanetz (b. 1940) later praised "Interview" as "an affectionate avant-garde sound poem about New York City."[62] Yet "Interview" was a hybrid, and while combining music and poetry, Corwin had, in a way, betrayed both. This may be why he later harshly criticized the radio poem as "slight, almost trivial, and altogether unmemorable."[63] Although he eventually abandoned most of his overt verse choir techniques, the genre allowed him to cross limits he had placed on himself. Verse choir needed no justification for word play, unexplained voices, interruptions, and passing parts of a line from voice to voice. Verse choir helped Corwin see that a poem was something to be chopped up, interrupted, and messed with. He cracked open the poem, and radio leaked out.

"Interview," although light and pleasurable, does not leave room for much involvement from the imagination. It gives the listener one unified language to decipher. While strict verse choir has an artistic potential that is no way tapped in

"Interview," for a musical technique Corwin needed something that left less chance of the imagination wandering, or rather, incited the imagination to wander in a guided direction. The finely crafted music cue was a straighter route to synergy between music and words. "Claire de Lune" kept words and music in separate streams. There is a slight imitation of rhythm in the speakers phrasing and the drumbeats, but the voice remains separate, firmly focused on delivering its message. The music of the drum remains separate from the voice except conceptually as it shifts from symbolic music to a dramatic sound effect. This wound up Corwin's five-year long aesthetic struggle to pair music and poetry while preventing them from detracting from one another. "Claire de Lune" is the child of this persistence, a grave 4/4 beat pulsing through its veins. His old fear of music and poetry overlapping is left mute because this is not a poem arranged for radio anymore but a *radio poem,* a category of artistic composition where sound and music can be as poetic as text. The clash of the music and words, the sonics and semantics, is where the magic happens, compelling the listener's imagination. Years later Corwin dissected and defined this process in "Anatomy of Sound" (1941), the namesake of this volume, laying out his theory of the radio sound effect's ethereal potential.[64]

CONCLUSIONS

From his first poetry program to the first episode of *Words without Music,* Corwin's voice went through many transformations. From conventional announcer to reader of poetry to invested character in a larger dramaturgy to virtuosic vocalist, and, when we all but cease to hear his actual voice, he became an unnamed narrator, a radio poet. During this productive period, he built a singular style of music accompaniment and musicality, poetic continuity, and what he called "mosaic structure," a thematic collage template fueled by eclectic variation.[65] These are fresh, small-scale practices in his early projects but became pillars of his style from 1939 on. These techniques, inaugurated on a large-scale in "They Fly through the Air" and epitomized in radio plays such as *On a Note of Triumph* and *We Hold These Truths,* touch nearly all of Corwin's radio art, from his straightforward radio dramas to his experimental features.

Corwin had explicit goals in early radio projects: to combine music and poetry in better ways than the current practice and to fill an intellectual void in broadcasting with substantive, contemporary poetry. He combined these explicit goals with dreams of perhaps becoming a successful poet, writer, and even composer. LeRoy Bannerman's *Norman Corwin and Radio* documents his early efforts at writing and poetry but leaves out Corwin's musical aspirations. Bannerman states, "Corwin, who never had a music lesson in his life, knew [music's] emotional power," clearly presenting Corwin as a nonmusician.[66] This may have been conscious on

Bannerman's part as Corwin purposefully hid his musical endeavors later in life. "I carefully hide that. . . . I'll bury it in the earth, but there it is. I wrote it."[67] But in his twenties, before and as he began to work at CBS, he had not buried his dream to compose yet. Late in life, when directly asked he replied:

> Oh yes, I pursued it with every intention of being a more than occasional composer. But I quickly gave that up when I realized how much creative effort went into the writing and production of radio. There were people who had the right to compose and I didn't.[68]

This musical current was an indispensable part of his development as a radio artist. His first series had a dual poetic and musical aim because of it. He thoughtfully composed music for episodes of *Poetic License*, which no doubt prepared him to communicate and appreciate the composers he later worked with. One of his piano pieces, "Go Down Death," was transcribed for choir and performed by Corwin and the Golden Gate Quartet in the January 15, 1939, episode of *Words without Music*. In his radio play "Double Concerto" (1941), he composed an electroacoustic work by recording a live choir and manipulating playback speeds. He also conceived of a typewriter concerto in "You Can Dream, Inc." (1944), which Alexander Semmler (1900–1977) composed following Corwin's programmatic directions and hands-on demonstrations. And he collaborated on radio operas—"The People, Yes" (1941), "Esther" (1941), "The Lonesome Train" (1944), and "Dorie got a Medal" (1944). He was particularly proud of the musicality of "Wolfeiana" (1941). "Psalm for a Dark Year" (1941) is a scored thirty-minute prayer service employing instrumentation and musical motifs cued by Corwin. Although his early dream of "composing symphonies" never happened, Corwin left his musical legacy.[69] He funneled this desire into his radio art and, with the help of many excellent composers, continued in his musical activity. However, he was much more comfortable behind a typewriter than a piano. His poetry efforts came easier than music yet were also molded into a media-specific practice.

Poems began as objects to be positioned by Corwin. In *Rhymes and Cadences* Corwin composed words to frame these poems, and in *Poetic License* his continuity began to resemble poetry. Then verse choir burst the poems into pieces, changing them from objects to outlines as in his adaptation of "Killers." Corwin still wanted to showcase his own poetry, but he had collected a diverse set of techniques in poetry presentation. He had intimately discovered the difference between poetry on the radio and radio poetry. This was not the traditional poetry he may have dreamed of writing in his younger days but a different kind altogether. His first thirty-minute original radio plays are long radio poems. In "The Plot to Overthrow Christmas" (1938), Corwin is "an Ogden Nashian tune-spinner" writing his announcer and narrator directly into the rhyming verse.[70] The next radio play, "They Fly through the Air," "had teeth in it. It had bite and had irony. It had anger."[71]

The tone and technique of Sandburg's "Killers" echoes through; there are not niceties, just killers and the killed. "They Fly through the Air" was still a rough beginner's work compared to his later mastery. It still had "heavy, awkward alliteration" and other "gosheries" according to Corwin, but its basic template—free verse narration with eclectic sectional variation—was a monumental stylistic step.[72]

On a Note of Triumph is the paramount example of this style in maturity. It featured simple colloquialisms, a constant ebb and flow of background music, snippets of radio drama scenes, musical interludes both sung and instrumental, and sound effects on demand for any of these other elements. Given this cornucopia of techniques and its weighty themes—world peace, universal human rights, and the cost of war—*On a Note of Triumph* leaves the listener with the impression that a mixture of story, symphony, newscast, sermon, essay, conversation, ballad, and documentary have all just occurred in the midst of a grand free verse poem. Yet this theme-and-variation model is not the only one Corwin used. There are many examples in his oeuvre without poetic narration.

Works such as "El Capitan and the Corporal" (1944) are story driven, employ realistic dialogue as a main technique, and are narrated by characters. But these radio plays can be heard as parts of larger works. Take *26 by Corwin* (1941). This was not merely a collection of radio plays but a specific radio series identified in the opening of each episode, a large eclectic collage that took months to hear originally, unified by its contrasts into a statement of the versatility of radio art. The first three episodes of *26 by Corwin* are wildly non sequitur: "Radio Primer," a comical instructional A to Z of radio backed by a chipper choir; "Log of the R-77," a listen-in to the last minutes of a doomed submarine crew; and "The People, Yes," a radio opera adapted from Carl Sandburg's book of the same title. This blatant contrast for affect was in Corwin's artistic DNA. The atomic level of Corwin's poetry relies heavily on friction between two word lists—"crickets and dynamite," "test tube and blue print," *Overkill and Megalove, God and Uranium* . . ."[73] In *Rhymes and Cadences,* Corwin made short lists of poems to create this friction. Years later in *One World Flight,* he made a list of cities, countries, and regions of the world to build an epic radio series. Larger series were built as large themes and variations, whereas when he had a single important show to make, such as *We Hold These Truths* or *Could Be,* he most often would use the condensed collage style with poetic narration. The complexity, size, and range of his skill and budget grew, but this basic model was key throughout his radio career in the micro and macro.

Norman Corwin cleared an impressive path. He started with a notion about the potential of poetry and music on radio and eventually developed his own particular radiogenic style on live radio, affecting millions and ensuring his legacy in American radio history. Aggrandizing statements are vital for popular narratives, like the title

Poet Laureate of Radio or Ray Bradbury's suggestion that Corwin was taught to write by Walt Whitman and William Shakespeare.[74] But the more Corwin is shown as having been a work in progress, the better we can know and appreciate his work. For instance, Carl Sandburg was a decisive influence on Corwin. Certainly the work-in-progress-Corwin looked up to and imitated this poet. Like the haberdasher Gumpert in "L'Affaire Gumpert" (1945), who channels the spirits of famous departed, often it seems that Corwin channeled the style, message, and spirit of his friend. Noting the intimacy of these men, perhaps it is not too far a leap to presume that one of the most eloquent odes to Corwin's life work in radio be repurposed from Sandburg.

The introduction of *The People, Yes*—a book that Corwin adapted portions of five times for radio and once for stage—fuses a staggering range of genres into a short statement, pent up with potential. Picture the twenty-six-year-old Corwin opening the book for the first time, excited by the grand breadth of the following overture. It could just as easily introduce a future publication of the complete radio plays of Norman Corwin:

> Being several stories and psalms nobody would want to laugh at
> Interspersed with memoranda variations worth a second look
> Along with sayings and yarns traveling on grief and laughter
> Running sometimes as a fugitive air in the classic manner
> Breaking into jig time and tap dancing nohow classical
> And further broken by plain and irregular sounds and echoes from
> The roar and whirl of street crowds, work gangs, sidewalk clamor,
> With interludes of midnight cool blue and inviolable stars
> Over the phantom frames of skyscrapers.[75]

NOTES

1. Norman Corwin, Bannerman-Corwin Interviews, tape 5A, Norman Corwin Collection, American Radio Archives, Thousand Oaks Public Library, Thousand Oaks, CA.

2. Norman Corwin, "They Fly through the Air with the Greatest of Ease," 19 February 1939, Goldin 46247, J. David Goldin Collection, Marr Sound Archives, University of Missouri Kansas City Miller Nichols Library, Kansas City, MO.

3. John Dunning, *On the Air: The Encyclopedia of Old-Time Radio* (New York: Oxford University Press, 1998), 165.

4. Margaret Fisher, "Futurism and Radio," in *Futurism and the Technological Imagination*, ed. Gunter Berghaus (Amsterdam: Rodopi, 2009), 241.

5. R. LeRoy Bannerman, *Norman Corwin and Radio: The Golden Years* (Tuscaloosa: University of Alabama Press, 1986), 9.

6. Norman Corwin, *CBS Radio Spotlight*, 12 May 1940, tape C-2, Norman Corwin Collection, American Radio Archives, Thousand Oaks Public Library, Thousand Oaks, CA.

7. Bannerman, *Norman Corwin and Radio*, 20.

8. Norman Corwin, "Amherst Carves New Slice of Fame as She Creates a Poetry-Speaking Town," *Springfield Sunday Union and Republican*, 1 August 1937, 3E.

9. Norman Corwin, *Thirteen by Corwin* (New York: Henry Holt, 1942), 36.
10. Ibid., 42.
11. Ibid., 43.
12. Norman Corwin, "Early Works," Bannerman-Corwin Interviews, tape 2, Norman Corwin Collection, American Radio Archives, Thousand Oaks Public Library, Thousand Oaks, CA.
13. Norman Corwin, "Original Manuscripts, 1934–5," typescript, p. 55, Norman Corwin Collection, American Radio Archives, Thousand Oaks Public Library, Thousand Oaks, CA.
14. Norman Corwin, *Norman Corwin's Letters*, ed. Arthur J. Langguth (New York: Barricade Books, 1994), 24.
15. Ibid.
16. Ibid.
17. Ibid., 36.
18. Ibid.
19. Norman Corwin, interview by author, 12 November 2007, Los Angeles.
20. *Microphone*, 26 May 1934, 3.
21. Norman Corwin, *Norman Corwin's Letters*, 115.
22. Norman Corwin, "Early Works," Bannerman-Corwin Interviews.
23. "Norman Corwin with Peggy Burt: Poetic License," *Variety*, 26 January 1938.
24. Elliot Sanger, Bannerman-Corwin Interviews, tape 20b, Norman Corwin Collection, American Radio Archives, Thousand Oaks Public Library, Thousand Oaks, CA.
25. Norman Corwin, interview by author, 12 November 2007, Los Angeles.
26. Norman Corwin and Peggy Burt, *Magic Key of RCA*, 13 March 1938, tape C-2, Norman Corwin Collection, American Radio Archives, Thousand Oaks Public Library, Thousand Oaks, CA.
27. Ibid.
28. Ibid.
29. Ibid.
30. Ibid.
31. John T. McManus, *CBS Radio Spotlight*, 12 May 1940, tape C-2, Norman Corwin Collection, American Radio Archives, Thousand Oaks Public Library, Thousand Oaks, CA.
32. "Spoon River Anthology" episode of *Words without Music*, 5–14–1939 log, in *Radio Series Scripts, 1930–2001: A Catalog of the American Radio Archives Collection*, compiled by Jeanette M. Berard and Klaudia Englund (Thousand Oaks, CA: Thousand Oaks Library Foundation, 2006), 372.
33. "Bob Edwards Show," 26 July 2005.
34. Norman Corwin, *Years of the Electric Ear: Norman Corwin Interviewed by Douglas Bell* (Metuchen, NJ, and London: Directors Guild of America & Scarecrow Press, 1994), 13.
35. Ibid., 75.
36. Norman Corwin, "Poetic License 17 November 1937," typescript, p. 1, Norman Corwin Collection, American Radio Archives, Thousand Oaks Public Library, Thousand Oaks, CA.
37. Norman Corwin, "Poetic License August 23rd, 1937," typescript, p. 1, Norman Corwin Collection, American Radio Archives, Thousand Oaks Public Library, Thousand Oaks, CA.
38. Ibid.
39. Ibid., 1–2.
40. Ibid. 2.
41. Ibid. 4.
42. Norman Corwin, "Notes to Poetic License Series," typescript, p. 1, Norman Corwin Collection, American Radio Archives, Thousand Oaks Public Library, Thousand Oaks, CA.
43. *Current Biography* (New York: H. W. Wilson Company, 1940), 197.
44. Norman Corwin, *Years of the Electric Ear*, 21.

45. Michael G. Kammen, *The Lively Arts; Gilbert Seldes and the Transformation of Cultural Criticism in the United States* (New York: Oxford University Press, 1996), 258.
46. Arch Oboler, *Fourteen Radio Plays* (New York: Random House, 1940), xvi.
47. Norman Corwin, *Years of the Electric Ear*, 30.
48. Norman Corwin, *Norman Corwin's Letters*, 33.
49. Norman Corwin, *Poetic License*, 3 November 1938, Haendiges 89730A, cassette.
50. Norman Corwin, "Words without Music 4 December 1938," typescript, p. 1, Norman Corwin Collection, American Radio Archives, Thousand Oaks Public Library, Thousand Oaks, CA.
51. Norman Corwin, "Words without Music 4 December 1938," p. 28.
52. Ibid.
53. Norman Corwin, "Amherst Carves New Slice," 3E.
54. Carl Sandburg, *Smoke and Steel* (New York: Harcourt, Brace and Howe, 1920), 99.
55. Norman Corwin, "Words without Music 4 December 1938," pp. 18 and 20.
56. Ibid., 18.
57. Ibid., 19.
58. Ibid.
59. Ibid.
60. Ibid., 20.
61. Ibid., 9. Line spacing reflects original script.
62. Richard Kostelanetz, "The Radio Dramatist Norman Corwin," *American Drama* (1992), 50.
63. Ibid., 52.
64. Troy Cummings, "Radiogenic Radiophonics: Dissecting the Sound Effect," in "Mood-Stuff and Metaphoric Utterance: Norman Corwin's Radio Art" (master's thesis, University of Missouri Kansas City, 2013), 95.
65. Norman Corwin, *Years of the Electric Ear*, 75.
66. Bannerman, *Norman Corwin and Radio*, 9.
67. Norman Corwin, Bannerman-Corwin Interviews, tape 6A.
68. Norman Corwin, interview by Troy Cummings, 12 November 2007, Los Angeles.
69. Norman Corwin, *Norman Corwin's Letters*, 378.
70. Norman Corwin, Bannerman-Corwin Interviews, tape 5A.
71. Ibid.
72. Norman Corwin, Bannerman-Corwin Interviews, tape 4A.
73. Norman Corwin, *More by Corwin* (New York: Henry Holt, 1944), 343. Norman Corwin, *Untitled and Other Radio Dramas* (New York: Henry Holt, 1945), 484.
74. Les Guthman, *Corwin*, videocassette (80 min.), University of Southern California, School of Journalism, 1996.
75. Carl Sandburg, *The People, Yes* (New York: Harcourt, Brace, 1936), v.

7

FIX YOUR EYES ON THE HORIZON
AND SWING YOUR EARS ABOUT

Corwin's Theatre of Sound

Ross Brown

My brief here is to listen and respond to Norman Corwin's 1940s radio drama as *theatre*. This chapter therefore takes its view of Corwin from the auditorium, understanding *theatre* to be both a spatial and conventional *architecture* within which performance and live audience take place and are configured one with one another, and a construction of the histories and qualities of *theatricality*. It examines Corwin and the familiar epithet *theatre of the mind* in relation to the phenomenology of audience and an expanded concept of *auditorium* as a dramaturgically constructed aural apparatus. Rather than screening a "movie" for the mind's eye, it proposes that through dramaturgy and studio technique, Corwin builds a hearing space of his audience's situation and imagination, and that this auditorium becomes an instrument of his agency as a radio artist. The "heteroglossic" and "kaleidosonic" radio tapestries that Jacob Smith describes earlier in this section, are therefore not observed flatly, from a distance, but immerse the listener within their fragmentary diegesis. A spatial relationship between the aural body of the listener and the performance is imagined, which changes at the command of dramaturgy. This suggests that Corwin's authorial control was not confined to the script and studio production process, but that it extended to the authorship of *listening*—even of *the listener* as a participative audience member.

There follows a subjective account (mine) of an audition of Corwin's *On a Note of Triumph* (1945). I describe a sequence of spatial configurations and transformations—a narrative scenography contingent on my aural technique and participation. My dynamic "picturing" of Corwin's theatre space (which is more than a visualization) is coached by the setting and the content of the spoken text, by instructions on how I must listen, and by subtly shifting ratios between a number of different acoustic and performative registers. I plot such "cues" against a matrix comprising, on one axis an acoustic spectrum that ranges from the closely microphonic voice through to more ambient sound and spatially reverberant speech, and on the other, a spectrum of performative registers that ranges from the radio presenter through studio-actorliness to theatrical projection. However, equally as insistent as Corwin's aural manipulations of my spatial imagination are the interjections he makes to estrange me from it, to bring me back to earth and the material actuality that I am simply listening to a radio program. After my account I will reflect on Corwin in relation to a history of theatrical aurality from the eighteenth-century Picturesque to Brecht.

. . .

A radio on a fridge: an overture and then a voice, in the rhetorical register of an orator; around it, the reverberation of a hall or theatre. "So they've given up. They're finally done in and the rat is dead . . . Seems like free men have done it again!" The voice is addressing the "common men of this afternoon" who defeated the supermen of tomorrow. There isn't any surround sound (of course), just a voice and some music coming from the mono radio set, and I don't exactly visualize it, but in some other way behind my eyes, I *picture* myself in an auditorium. The overture is reprised and then . . . a different voice? Well, certainly a different register and phonic persona.[1] "By popular request the Columbia Broadcasting system presents a repeat performance of *On a Note of Triumph*." A studio announcer's voice in friendly radio space. The auditorium evaporates. I am simply a radio listener, here and now, and the radio is just another object in my personal world of sound. As it happens, I am doing the dishes but according to Norman Corwin, I might equally well be playing bridge, reading, conversing, or smoking.[2] There is suddenly no more hall to the announcer's voice. The only space indexed by this new sound is the vacuum in the warmly distorting amplification tubes of its radiophonic signal chain seventy years ago, into which my kitchen with its Wi-Fi and transistor amplification now opens. The voice introduces Martin Gable as narrator and Bernard Hermann as composer. Hermann's music picks up and leads us, with V-E Day bells ringing, back to Gable's voice, closer to the microphone, blocking most of the ambient reverberation of the room and consequently sounding radiophonic rather than theatrical, but actorly, not the radio announcer persona. Then a new performative register: that of a patriotic newsreel narrator. I know where I am now and what kind of program I am going to be listening to: a documentary propaganda drama.

The narration continues, the music dies away and the narrator's voice begins to acquire an oratorical cadence. As he gets into his stride, Gable becomes yet more actorly, moving back from the microphone. More of the reverberation of the performance space is revealed. The signal-to-ambience ratio decreases. Within this acoustic ratio but also between the rhetoric and resonance, a theatre space forms again. I am hazily imagining the sound coming from the forestage of a proscenium arch theatre. However, as before, it deflates the instant the scene switches to a folk song about dancing on Hitler's grave.[3] I am now looking into a scenic vignette—of a barn dance. If Gable had previously sounded as though he were projecting from the forestage, this scene is upstage of that, in the softer, smaller, and more contained acoustic of a furnished set (this is how I imagine it; it was most likely a separate studio). The barn dance fades as Gable's more acoustically live narrator voice returns, the space of the auditorium forming a halo around it. This voice steers the listener through a sequence of folk songs in different languages. These have a livelier acoustic than the American one, as though set further downstage of the set. The cadence of Gable's narration begins to ease up. I sense he is nearing the end of his introduction: "but fix your eyes on the horizon, swing your ears about, size up the day and date."

Up to this point the spatial configuration has matched a fairly standard format of American radio theatre from this period. An announcer—a radio voice—introduces a diegesis presented in a theatre voice. A musical framework, like a movie or a pit orchestra, interpolates interludes of extra-diegetic spacelessness. The voice of the narrator, its acoustic reverberation implying an actor performing in front of the curtain line, between the lively acoustic of the auditorium and the smaller acoustic of the stage scene, introduces a series of sketched scenes. It is a vaudeville format.

But from this point onwards, my seat in the auditorium becomes unfixed. I am going on a ride.

"Listen. Listen closely," Corwin instructs, through his narrator's persona, as though he is about to perform some close magic. He is. The voice remains constant on the forestage as the auditory scene changes behind it, like the sonic projection of a microphone that has grown wings and taken flight. The theatre ceases to be statically end-on and becomes a wonderland of mercurial reconfigurations and transformations of scale. I am guided from the personal intimacy of the whispering of my own internal monologue, to a bird's-ear view of the *theatrum mundi* heard from the clouds . . . no: through the headphones of the navigator of a B-29 bomber. Swinging about from scene to scene, my ear is paraded, under Corwin's instruction, through voices, sound effects, and music, across a map of Europe and beyond. And then:

> . . . so listen closely. In just a moment now. Don't expect to hear metallic speech from the rosette of amplifying horns on the high poles of the public address system. But listen for a modest voice as sensible and intimate to you as the quiet turning of your own considered judgment. Now we are ready, the next voice you hear will be that of the conqueror.

The "next" voice reprises Hank Peters, the everyman soldier of Corwin's *Untitled* (1944): "this boy, that boy, any boy at all with war still thumping in his ears" who asks, "Who did we beat and what did it cost to beat him. Is it all going to happen again?" We are back in a hall again. "Can it be," the rhetorical narrator hits the back of the auditorium again, "that our soldiers are footnoting the surrender?" No sooner have I been returned to the auditorium than I am switched back to the radiophonic vacuum-valve space of the microphone, only this time Corwin instructs me to *be* the microphone, on a stand, in front of which a prisoner of war is hauled.

"I'm a soldier, a little man, I merely obeyed orders." The narrator becomes interrogator and the microphone is now on the dock of a war-crimes hearing. Back in the auditorium of oratorical rhetoric, suddenly a new voice: an *acousmêtre*, an unseen omnipresence: "Observe him, note him well! " BIG REVERBERATION. And so it continues: the "reversible" microphone that embodies me flipping back and forth, the music, the dynamic registers of performance and their acoustic signatures and the instruction "listen, listen, listen"—all weaving together and adding up to an aural counterpoint, a cubist, radiophonic picture of multiple aural viewpoints. But all the while, and finally, the present-day noises and hums of a London kitchen, 2015, and a radio on a fridge.

. . .

The *theatre of the mind* that I picture when listening to Corwin is thus far from a flat projection of images on an intracranial movie screen behind my eyes but rather a spatially immersive, impossibly mutating configuration of stage and auditorium. We might also call this, in the contemporary use of the term, a *scenography of the mind,* an authorship of the performance of imagined space. Although the situations in which I "pictured" myself while listening to *On a Note of Triumph* were spatial and vivid, they were only fleetingly and vaguely visual. Let us think about this.

AURAL PERSPECTIVE: THE CROSS-MODALITY OF THEATRE AND THE IMAGINATION

Theatre Aurality

It is not a contradiction to say that one hears from a viewpoint. The physical placement of the ears in relation to the eyes centers the stereophonic, omnidirectional perception of acoustic space on the point of binocular convergence. This is seemingly just in front of the location of the internal monologue, at the seat of consciousness—the "thinkpoint" behind the eyes and between the ears. The eyes look outwards from, and thoughts are heard at, the center of a sphere of sound. I describe in *Sound* how theatre has, since its historical inceptions, configured itself around this sensory arrangement and played to what might be termed, perhaps oxymoronically, the *aural perspective* of its audiences, in spaces constructed or adapted to emphasize the energizing sensation of resonance.[4] Since the turn of the twentieth-century, theatre has also resonated in an *expanded architecture* of electroacoustic, intermedial, and virtual space. Theatres have been equipped with stereo, then surround-sound reinforcement. Recently the trend, in experimental theatre, has been for the sphere of sound to close in on the personal space of individual audience members, even into the "intracranial" sonic space between the ears. *Headphone theatre* and *theatre in the total dark* have become subgenres of "immersive theatre." So too has the intimacy of *one-to-one* or *many-to-one theatre*. There have been several experiments with binaural technology.[5] *Binaural theatre* immerses listeners not merely in a stereophonic left-right panorama but in an apparently omnidirectional aural space introduced directly to the ears, through headphones, from microphones also worn *in the ears* of a "dummy head," or those of an actor. The audience is thus able to hear from the viewpoint of someone else—an aural agent, representative or avatar, and the sound designer is able to manipulate and subvert this perception, switching to other points of view in other spaces or from other heads. These immersive theatre forms explore the relativities of scale, sensory fragmentations, and dislocated intimacies of contemporary, headphone-wearing semivirtual subjectivity. Their expanded auditoria envelope the body, as well as the monophonic "thinkpoint" the body encases, in a conditioned and controlled aurality that thus becomes a kind of immersive text. Alongside these new immersive theatre forms, the podcast has led to a revival of interest in and developed new forms of radio drama.

A flurry of publication has responded to this "aural turn" in experimental theatre, critiquing the ocular-centric bias of earlier discourses and building an aural paradigm for theorizing theatre.[6] Theatre is conceived not as a composition of the visual, the verbal, and the musical (with the occasional sound effect) but as a phenomenology, bound together by what the director Peter Sellars calls a "total program of sound" centered on the *au*-ral body (the prefix *au*- meaning air, or vapor, thus implying an atmospherically immersed subjectivity). A performance may be observed *over there,* on the stage, but it is also staged and performed *over here,* in the physical and imaginative space *around* the acoustically immersed, corporeal subjectivity of its audience.

The Theatrical Imagination

The monophonic thinkpoint sits behind the viewpoint at the center of an aural sphere of sound, but it also sits at the center of an auratically projected metaspace: the imagination. In the imagination, hearing and vision are less clearly demarcated. In theatre, where the imagination plays a heightened role in observation, it should not, then, be assumed that vision sits outside the immersive experience of this combination of acoustic and imaginative space. I describe the phrase "aural perspective" as seeming oxymoronic, but in fact the sublation of the supposed opposition between the ocular and aural it encapsulates is key to understanding not only the aurality of theatre but also its peculiarly immersive visuality, as well as mystical qualities such as "presence" that are often piously assigned to the live theatrical experience. It is also helpful in understanding the *imagined* visuality of radio and the reputed *vividness* of the mental images that are produced despite, or perhaps on account of, the "blindness" of radio's medium and the invisibility of its scenes.[7] They may be pictured, but I question that such radio images are vividly visual. Some vague visualization is involved in my imagining of Corwin's theatre, but in a way that cannot easily be disaggregated from my *general sense* of its space. Corwin's is a diegetic drama[8] but even when a radio play uses sound more mimetically to convey scenery and atmosphere, I only hazily glimpse visual details. If I try to focus on them, they are already gone, and when I try to recall them, I cannot categorize them for sure as visual or sonic phenomena. They have spatial perspective but a fugitive ephemerality, a continual dying. In other words, the visions I glimpse in my listening imagination have an acoustic quality.

The whole-body phenomenology of live theatre has been extensively theorized, but until recently only Clive Cazeaux, in his brief phenomenology of radio drama, has approached the subject in relation to radio theatre. Using Merleau-Ponty, he describes how, even when attending to a "sound-only" medium, other senses are potentially active in "invitational" relationships with one another. Accordingly, the sound of radio drama might be understood not as "a series of inadequate clues from an unlit world" but as "a medium that opens onto and generates a world and, as part of this world-generation, enjoys interaction and conjunction with the other senses."[9]

Don Ihde's phenomenology of listening and voice specifically addresses the multimodal space of the imagination, confirming that visualized scenes can have aural characteristics.[10] For example, whereas in the perceptual world one may hear but not see what is behind one's head (without turning around), in the imagination this need not be the case. Sounds of creaking, rustling, or twigs snapping behind you generate a mental image of their potential sources. A visible rear world has no basis in perceptual experience and yet we are able to imagine it. Ihde uses a mind game to illustrate this. He imagines a small red horse galloping on the floor behind him:

> I seem to be able to place [this] visually imagined object in any position in relation to the surrounding imagined space. And if this is possible—let each try for himself—then the space of visual imagery parallels in at least one aspect the space of the auditory field and not its visual counterpart.[11]

Such sensory cross talk suggests *synesthesia*, a condition somewhat romanticized by art history and famously experienced by Kandinsky, Messiaen, Nabokov, and others. But as O'Callaghan points out, synesthesia is "rare, isolated, quirky, and robustly illusory."[12] Cross-modality, on the other hand, is continually at work within processes of perception, as an organizing principle "to resolve conflicting information across different sensory systems, and commonly correct for noise and errors."[13] Bregman's *auditory scene analysis*, the psychoacoustic process of making sense of complex auditory environments, might be understood as a form of cross-modal picturing, cross-checking binaural auditory data with visual and other sensory "cues" in order to construct a scenography of sonic cause and effect.[14] With advanced scanning technology, neuroscientists are now able to observe "cross-wiring" of the senses at earlier, precognitive stages of perception. Electrical signals originating from auditory input can be observed converging with visual inputs on neurons in the optic tectum. Similarly, some neurons in the auditory cortex appear simultaneously sensitive to visual or tactile stimulation, with the effect of sharpening spatial sensitivity.[15] According to O'Callaghan,[16] cross-modality is apparently so "rampant" within the processes of perception that its objects should no longer be thought of as seen, heard, or smelled things but from the outset regarded as "mereologically complex individuals" with multimodality deep within their structures. Sound, in O'Callaghan's logic—even when heard in the total dark or delivered by a "sound-only" format such as radio—involves vision, because any sound has potential visibility within the structure of its event-object. This seems to confirm Cazeaux's phenomenological notion of the "beckoning" of vision by sound in radio dramas and his assertion that this "is not simply the point that the imagination is invited 'to fill in the gaps' left by the absence of imagery, but rather the more fundamental assertion that, from a phenomenological perspective, it is wrong to speak of an absence at all."[17] Regardless, therefore, of whether an artistic medium is sound-only, as radio, or silently visual, as painting, the phenomenology of its audience is an audiovisually spatial one. Such audiovisual spatiality is thus a shared characteristic both of aurality and visuality (if those are to remain separate categories). It also, I would argue, characterizes a mode of imaginative observation involved in watching or listening to any kind of theatre, or in enjoying other environments as theatre.

THE AUDITORIUM AS STAGE

Students who become too cozy in the studio or rehearsal room should always be reminded that drama may be composed on the page or the stage, but theatre *happens* in the auditorium, where performance becomes an audience experience. The spatial audiovisuality of audience, which I have just suggested *defines* theatre, is addressed in the architectures and terminologies of dramatic theatre. Whatever the *theatron* (in its Greek etymology "a place for seeing") shows to the eye on the stage, the attentive audience body experiences in the open, aural space of the *auditorium*. The expanded concept of *auditorium* that I expound here is, in fact, consistent with the word's derivation from the Latin *audire*, "to hear," as a noun whose grammatical form indicates an instrument or apparatus of agency for hearing. *Auditorium* began to appear in the English language in the mid-eighteenth century, usually (although not always) to describe a lecture hall or other room designed primarily for *audition*, or *audience*. The privileging of acoustic experience in such terms is implicit, although if we accept Ihde's or O'Callaghan's theories of cross-modality in perception and the imagination, then we should also consider that not only does the auditorium immerse the spectator's body in the resonance of the *sounds* of the performance, but it also aurally shapes and resonates the *whole* experience of the performance, including the visual. I and the eye watch the stage from the listening room, and the subjective character of our spectatorship is acoustic.

In a treatise on theatre acoustics that greatly influenced the Renaissance reconception of theatre, Vitruvius (c.75–25BC) states that auditoria should not be silent but should immerse the audience in a tuned resonance—excited by the sounds of the performance but with its own independent character and pleasures.[18] In terms of communication, one might consider this *system noise*—the material artifact of a technology of transmission—but as theatre, auditorium resonance is programmatic, fused to the signal and part of what constitutes a "live" sound. I have argued that other auditorium noise (the breathing, the constrained yet inevitable sounds of movement of a large body of people sitting silently together, the creaking and ticking of the building and its fittings, the noise leaking in) is also imbued into the program of modern theatre[19] and that the anxious tension between the effort of focusing on the performance and the palpable "aliveness" of the acoustically energized space of the auditorium is part of its thrill. The risk of circumstantial noise, as well as the halo of resonance, shapes and textures the spectator's engagement with the performance, and there is always potential for an acoustically alive auditorium to *distract* where the modern convention of silent listening confronts drama also played in the modern way, against a backdrop of silence.[20] In modern theatre's acoustically hybrid, intermedial auditoria (with loudspeakers everywhere), sound designers have learned to play to this anxiety by creating spacious surround-soundscapes with a palette of effects resembling those of a large creaky room (quietly, so that the audience is not entirely certain whether they are part of the production or part of the theatre's native soundscape).

Noise may be, by one definition, the opposite of signal and therefore outside the semiotics of drama, but within the phenomenology of the expanded auditorium it can thus be meaningful, even textual. This is the case in live, spoken theatre (if not so much in musical theatre) because even where the auditorium is extended by loudspeaker systems, the production is calibrated to the acoustically spoken voice and the sounds of actors moving about the stage. These are of the same scale and materiality as the noises of the auditorium and of the audience's own bodies and there is potential for uncertainty as to what is meant and what is accidental. In movie theatres, on the other hand, there is a clear divide between the materiality of the auditorium and the sound world of the film, which is entirely heard from loudspeakers and is usually recognizable, even in the surround-sound field, as being of a different register than the noises of one's neighbor breathing or a latecomer arriving. Surely though, the divide between the world of a radio play and the acoustic world of its reception, since its program is wholly mediatized and connected to its remote auditoria only by a one-way transmission of radio waves, is the starkest and most inviolable of all forms of theatre? Surely, the noisy conditions of the audience's audition—the noises of their living rooms or cars—can never be considered the author's work?

This may be the case, but Norman Corwin nevertheless deliberately *activates* and, in effect, amplifies the listener's auditorium rather than trying to silence it. It is characteristic of his style to address his audience directly *as listeners,* in *"far-flung"* domestic situations. As we have seen, *On a Note of Triumph* makes a leitmotif of an instruction to "listen" in different imaginative ways, which encourages an auditory self-consciousness. It is also characteristic of Corwin's style to declare, through his narrators, what he is doing as author: music and sound effects are announced or commented upon and their artificiality and dramatic function described. This is often done comically (as in *The Plot to Overthrow Christmas*), to create a relaxed, unpretentious theatricality. But while encouraging listeners to picture themselves, reflexively, as audience members in *his* theatre, he also coaches listeners (most explicitly in *Anatomy of Sound*) to think about the meanings of sound, of radio as its medium, and of everyday noise in modern life. By encouraging them to be reflexively aware of, and perhaps distracted by, their own aurality and the circumstances of their audition, he builds into his expanded auditorium an apparatus, or what Schultze calls an *auditory dispositive*,[21] that further conditions and controls what is heard. This may be an apparatus of dialectical estrangement,[22] to whose Brechtian connotations I shall return, or perhaps he simply hopes to introduce some of the presence and theatrical thrill of the noisy, live auditorium. Either way, this dispositive requires the audience to *picture* itself as attentive listeners in a noisily distracting world.

RADIO, THEATRE, AND THE EIGHTEENTH-CENTURY PICTURESQUE OF SOUND

The Mise-En-Scène

It has been suggested that throughout theatre's history, at times of "modernization," the production process becomes a laboratory for modelling and exploring new conditions of everyday life. Thus, the sounds theatre stages, the noises it bans, the auditoriums it constructs and so forth, can be taken as indicators of changing aural culture.[23] This production work is informed by a framework of practices and references that form a working knowledge of how meaning is made and communicated in theatre's acoustic dimension—a framework becoming known as the *dramaturgy of sound*. The Shakespearian scholar Bruce R. Smith describes an iterative loop between the voice, the early-modern urban environment, and the ear, which, he contends, transformed orality and aurality and set the conditions for the verbal craft produced in the "wooden O" theatres of London's Southbank.[24] In a similar way, Mladen Ovadija has recently argued that the sonic theatres, artworks and manifestos of Futurism, Dada, and other avant-garde movements of the twentieth century, in responding viscerally to the aural ferment of the age of the combustion engine, reproduction, amplification, radio, and mechanized warfare, relate to the emergence of a "postdramatic dramaturgy of sound" in experimental theatre in the latter part of that century.[25] Much of Corwin's radio theatre might be described as postdramatic (in its disinterest in character, fragmentary space-time, exposed theatricality, and declared technique), and in *Anatomy of Sound* he describes how the strangeness and the noise of modern aurality resonates in his radio theatre and its auditorium. However, rather than fetishize this, his dramaturgy often harks back to the discourses and theatre of an earlier stage of modernity, which by contrast might seem old-fashioned.

Twentieth-century critical distaste for what it perceived as the excesses and crassness of Victorian theatre led to the tendency to blame melodrama and spectacular for theatrical cliché and crassness. What this overlooked was their origins in the experimental theatre of the late eighteenth-century age of reason and revolution. Indeed, Shepherd has claimed that early English melodrama might be considered a kind of avant-garde.[26] Aside from the radicalism of the "new subjectivity" of this period, the material environment took on a new aurality. Across Europe, proto-melodramatic forms adopted a new approach to the nonverbal semantics of gesture and sound (including new ways of relating music to theatrical meaning). Corwin's is a theatre mainly of words, but he nevertheless frequently points to this aurality, the eighteenth century being never far from the frame of reference of his late 1930s and '40s radio work. It is there in his literary allusions, in the formal references to English pantomime in rhyming fantasies like *The Undecided Molecule* and *The Plot to Overthrow Christmas*, in the illustrated picturesque travelogue form of *An American in England: Cromer*, the taxonomic conceit and Paine-like trope of commonality in *Anatomy of Sound*, and in the riffs on Jeffersonian language and the historical vignettes of *We Hold These Truths*. However, it is also there more subtly in how he presents sound effects and the ways in which he frames a way of listening that is not only reflexive but also pictorial.

I am not the first to identify the echoes of the eighteenth-century in golden age radiophonic dramaturgy. A short 1947 article in *American Notes and Queries* entitled "Notes on the Early Progress of the Picturesque of Sound" by "Le Bruit"[27] links 1940s popular fascination with radio sound effects to a lesser-known English aesthetic movement, and specifically to the sensation caused by one of its key practitioners, the artist Philippe de Loutherbourg. De Loutherbourg was employed by David Garrick in 1771 as scenic artist, as part of his ongoing project to make legitimate[28] spoken theatre more sensorially engaging in response to the fashion for pictorial, melo-based[29] theatre forms from the continent. Garrick had been incrementally doing away with the apron, or thrust playing area, at the Theatre Royal Drury Lane since the 1760s, clearing the audience seating from the stage, and moving all the acting upstage of the curtain line into the "scene" (the upstage area pictorially framed by the proscenium arch). Drama was henceforth not merely played, but also scenically 'placed' (in French, *mise en scène*).

De Loutherbourg, a scene-painting prodigy from the Parisian salon and Opéra Comique, also took control of movement, dance, costume, lighting, and sound, and he did so from the aural point of view of the auditorium (not from onstage, as an actor). He did as much as anyone, until the Meininger's Ludwig Chronegk a century later, to make the audiovisual composition of the *scene* a part of authorial staging of a play, and for this he became a star attraction at Drury Lane, presenting his own harlequinades in support of the main "legitimate" feature.[30] Upon leaving theatre, De Loutherbourg created the Eidophusikon, an exhibit of moving, sounding pictures constructed in a fully equipped miniature stage, complete with automated, finely made and painted scenery, projection and lighting effects. The "stage," however, was set behind a frame on a false wall and made to look like a picture hanging in a gallery. There was music from a harpsichord (hidden from view between the wall and the picture space) and meticulously crafted sound effects. Often cited as a proto-cinematic novelty, the Eidophusikon was intended as a new art form that combined theatre with painting. De Loutherbourg, who also made paintings and aquatints of industrial landscapes, saw this as the obvious next step for the Picturesque, an aesthetic movement that projected a time-based and theatrically aural gaze on the natural world and scenes of everyday life.

The word *picturesque* needs glossing for contemporary readers. First proposed in the 1770s *picturesque* was considered a third aesthetic category (alongside *beauty* and *sublime*), and for almost a century, became a buzzword so overused, that it soon became vague and ultimately banal as a critical term (much like the term *postmodern* in the twentieth century). As a noun, it could be used in the same way as *mise en scène* (for example, a melodrama could be given an appropriately gothic *picturesque*). Not so much a movement as a "turn" in cultural discourse, the Picturesque (capital *P*) is traditionally regarded as a footnote to Romanticism. However the extent and reach of its praxis has recently been revised.[31] In its theatrically reflexive take on individual subjectivity in the sensational world, I see an important shift from the urbanization of the "public ear" that characterized Smith's early-modern aurality. Key to the picturesque dramaturgy of sound were scenic associations between sound, setting, atmosphere, and mood of the kind that we now take for granted, but which were not standard theatre effects before the end of the eighteenth century. To an extent, such picturesque uses of sound were theatrical realizations (or projections) of what Erlmann describes as a Romantic aurality.[32] However, where Romantic sonic tropes usually describe an ontotheological resonance (at times expressive, at times submissive or erotic) between the inner poetic self and the Aeolian or ethereally energetic fields of the natural environment (Coleridge's notion of "light in sound/sound-like power in light"), the Picturesque is more concerned with the sensational affect produced by the composition of environmental effects on the touristic aesthete. Beginning with guides to observing or sketching the landscape, it was concerned with finding the right compositional formulae to match a particular picturesque (in the first instance, domestically arable, maritime, or industrial, then, increasingly "metropolitan") to the right mood. Other picturesque products followed: aquatint travelogues and taxonomies of regional costume, dramaturgically designed country walks, and scenic theatre shows such as De Loutherbourg's.

In England, combined with the influence of French music-drama (or *mélodrame*), which had a storyboard-like template, the Picturesque influenced a new style of drama.[33] The play becomes less an uninterrupted flow, carried forward by a continuous momentum of action and consequence towards final resolution (the classical model), and more of a framework of sequential but self-contained pictorial units—a structure of scenic situations. Meisel, in his study of the interactions between the narrative, pictorial, and theatrical arts of the nineteenth century,[34] identifies this as an intransitive dramaturgy of serial-discontinuity: each scene builds to a situation where forward motion is halted in a frozen moment of stasis or suspense from which the next scene begins afresh. Curtain music from pit orchestras not only formed a part of the diegetic framework but also formed a commentary on the stage picture, underscoring the gestural emotions of the acting and building scenic energy towards climactic or suspenseful situational tableaux, which it froze in time with suspended chords. Rather than the disruption and resolution of cosmic order *being performed,* as had been done in classical drama, noises-off (or practical sound effects from the wings) now *enacted* the atmosphere and life of the stage picture. *Atmosphere*—the notion that scenic space might be infused with mood and that the air itself, when given a turbid materiality with smoke, light, and the noises of wind, rain, thunder, insects, and so on, might become a pictorially scenic element—pictorialized the Romantic connection between the corporeally imprisoned soul and the external elements. This became the salient feature of the mise-en-scène of nineteenth-century gothic melodrama and Shakespearian revival.

Frames, Technique, and the Radiophonic Mise-En-Scène

The term *Picturesque of Sound*, which Le Bruit references in 1947 in relation to the sonic craft of radio drama,[35] was coined in the early nineteenth century by William Pyne in his serialized book *Wine and Walnuts*.[36] In these stories, semifictionalized versions of Garrick, Reynolds, Gainsborough, and others tour 1770s London, in search of the essence of the Picturesque. The book gives a detailed account of the Eidophusikon, which Pyne knew from his youth, with particular attention to the role sound effects played in creating a synchronous, spatially kinetic picture show in the space behind its framed hole in the wall.[37] As Baugh describes,[38] de Loutherbourg's full-scale stage productions were living pictures that unapologetically showcased technical feats, which the Eidophusikon then distilled. This is often noted, along with later dioramic motion picture shows, as part of the prehistory of the movie, but the framed hole in the wall to a fictive "world beyond," although visible, might also be seen as proto-radiophonic. Aurally, as with his full-scale shows, the pleasure, perhaps the meaning, was in the acousmatic technique and ingenuity, not the believability, of the illusions. For example, in the unseen space beyond the frame, a whalebone spring was bounced off the skin of a muted drum to make the double sound of a cannon blast from a distant warship, seen within the frame floating on moving water under rolling clouds: first the initial thud and then its echo. The effect followed an initial visual flash and puff of smoke, mimicking the time delay of the sound crossing the bay.

Le Bruit likens contemporary fascination with these acousmatic effects to the 1940s public fascination with the use of cabbages and the like to make sound effects in radio theatre. He recounts a story from Pyne (also in Whitely's biography of Gainsborough[39]) in which Gainsborough compares an Eidophusikon thunderstorm to one raging outside the gallery, and declares the fake thunder to be the better. Where Romanticism valorized truth to nature, the Picturesque had no qualms about rearranging nature to better effect. It regarded qualities such as roughness, irregularity, and decay, noise, or atmospheric turbidity, or gloom as a palette of effects from which a "better" (or at least a more dramatic) version of nature might be composed (Ruskin famously derided this theatricality as a "parasitic sublime"). Unsurprisingly then, in his early guides to observing picturesque beauty, Gilpin frequently refers to the composition of the landscape in terms of stage design, even advising viewers to listen for noises that lend an appropriate atmosphere to the picturesque, or as he puts it, provide the correct "circumstances" of the picturesque "cast,"[40] according to the genre of the situation. Picturesque aesthetic tourists were not only observing the theatre of nature or the city, they were also observing themselves as actors in that theatre (sometimes carrying with them Claude Glasses, framed smoked mirrors that enabled them to take the eighteenth-century version of a dramatically moody "selfie").

From its Picturesque roots, therefore, nineteenth-century melodramatic and spectacular theatre had no need for Coleridge's famous "willing suspension of disbelief" because it wanted its audience to disbelieve and to be self-consciously involved in the theatricality, not the mimesis. Like Gainsborough, it preferred artificial thunder. Where Brecht later used acknowledged artifice to build a dialectical relationship between the audience and the diegesis, Picturesque theatricality simply delighted in it. It made a show of technical contrivance as techne, but in this it was not necessarily crass. The new techniques it explored, for observing, representing and reflecting, in their small way addressed bigger questions of their time about leisure, subjectivity, aesthetics, revolution, and war (when the route to the old, classical Grand Tour was both literally and symbolically blocked and with it many of the old certainties about world order).

Le Bruit's article compares 1940s radio drama to the Picturesque of Sound in its use of sound effects, but 1940s radiophonic innovation might be seen as part of a new dramaturgy of sound that spanned the time-based arts and that, like the Picturesque, was part of a broader change in auditory culture. Le Bruit claimed that the progress of the Picturesque of Sound had stalled in theatre, and that radio was making the running, but this was not entirely true. Harold Burris-Meyer's innovative use of amplified sound in the 1930s *Living Newspaper* format had drawn on newsreel sound and developed an intermedial and hybrid electro/acoustic auditorium in theatre as, in Europe, had Brecht, Piscator, and George Devine (who had used amplified auditorium surround-sound at the Old Vic in 1940). In 1930s cinema, after the initial assumption that the camera and the microphone must remain wedded, Rouben Mamoulian, who had learned his sonic craft in theatre in Moscow and London, developed an aural perspective that was independent of the viewpoint. This allowed the camera to roam free of the soundtrack, which consequently anchored itself more to the spatial imagination of the viewer than to the screened picture. In radio, Neil Verma describes the ways in which techniques of microphone selection and placement were developed in the 1940s to produce perspective in radio theatre space.[41] As described above, Corwin takes this further, using words and their sound to create a roving diegetic perspective that is the radio drama equivalent of Mamoulian's roving viewpoint. In all of this, concerns that listeners would not be able to make sense of new sonic techniques proved unfounded. Only a decade or so earlier, there had been concern in the radio industry as to whether listeners would be able to orient themselves to any unseen acoustic space relayed into their living rooms by the radio set, particularly if that space were to change. In his two-part article on *The Electric Ear,* Ian Macpherson (2011) relates the story of P. G. A. H. Voigt,[42] which employs an analogy of the radio set as a framed window, much like a proscenium arch or the aperture of the Eidophusikon. It illustrates how the spatial and pictorial imagination is instrumental to the adaptability of aural technique.

Voigt had, since the early days of the BBC urged radio engineers to take more account of the conditions of audition and the listening technique of the audience in their homes. He suggested a pictorial mind-model:

> Before going on to the question as to how sounds should be reproduced it is necessary to have some conclusion as to how they should sound, and to have some mental picture of ideal reproduction. And this "picture" to be useful, should fit all conditions of listening.[43]

The "mental picture" that Voigt proposes and upon which he continued to elaborate in professional broadcast circles after he relocated to North America in the 1940s,[44] became known as his "hole in the wall" model.

Early engineers were worried about the potentially disorienting effect (in terms of establishing a consistent sense of auditorium and stage space) of changes in scale of reverberation between different microphone placements. Alternatively, if the microphone were to offer a *fixed* point of audition, there was disagreement as to what the standard position should be. If close to the performer, it would capture minimal ambient reflections and the performance would appear to make its sound directly *in* the listener's room rather than in another space first (which would aesthetically not suit concert music unless the listener happened to live in a concert hall). If set back, the microphone would capture the reverberation of the studio or theatre, which would be too echoey for clear speech. Drama, moreover, benefited from intermediate positions and varying degrees of ambience according to scene. Voigt's hole-in-the-wall theory suggested that varying microphone positions need not be disorienting if one pictured radio sets as open windows through which the acoustic world of the studio or theatre could be heard and performed.

> Let us assume now that some lucky citizen is by some magic carried, complete with his listening room, into the Concert Hall and can listen direct through his open window to what is coming in from the stage. If he is suitably placed, he can see the Artist and receive the direct sound wave without any alterations. The first echo reaching him from behind will be a short time echo of the type which belongs to his room. There will be the other usual room echoes, and in addition, there will be long time echoes belonging to the Concert Hall, but they will enter his room by the open window, that is from the same direction as the initial direct sound.[45]

If less ambience is required, the more closely miked sound would be consistent, on the listener's side of the window, with the sound simply being made closer to the outside of the window. Voigt's model also makes provision for the completely radiophonic voice whose space of origin appears to be only the anechoic vacuum tubes and circuitry of the radio apparatus itself:

> There is the special case when the Announcer or the Artist is close up to the microphone. The particular non-electric arrangement corresponding most nearly to that

special case, I visualize as occurring when the Announcer or the solo Artist steps up close to the opening in the room above-mentioned and makes his announcement, or plays his instrument for the special benefit of the listener inside the room. If the distance in the Concert studio between the microphone and the Artist is increased, the effect, to the listener, should be that of the Artist receding further and further from the opening and consequently his voice as heard direct should be accompanied by a bigger and bigger proportion of the reverberation which belongs to the Concert Hall. The reverberation which belongs to the listening room is, however, fixed and ordinarily the listener is so accustomed to it that he is not conscious of its independent existence.[46]

Remarkably, by 1945 Corwin is sufficiently confident in his audience's spatially imaginative listening technique that he can hinge his narrative on the instruction to "fix your eyes on the horizon and swing your ears around."

CORWIN'S MODERNIST PICTURESQUE

Corwin's command of his radio auditorium is such, through subtle shifts within an indexical matrix of signal-to-ambience ratio and performative registers, he can mobilize his audience's points of audition, embody them in imaginary props and then in an instant, return them to a theatre auditorium. I think my imagined sense of Corwin's radio space being centered on or upstage of the curtain line of a fluidly plastic theatre/auditorium configuration is consistent both with Voigt's paradigm of radio aurality and with Corwin's frequent allusions to a theatrical paradigm of late eighteenth-century modernity. Far from being old-fashioned, this reference supports his political championing of "commonality."[47] In *Anatomy of Sound*, which uses a conceit similar to a Picturesque taxonomy, Corwin brings this all together in one clear exposition: a "lecture" on microphonics, intermedial acousmatics, noise, and effects (with, it should be noted, a section directly addressing scenic energy in melodrama):

> We are living, my good and far flung friends in the age of amplification. Practically everything today is amplified. The man who calls out numbers in the bingo concession, the auctioneer giving away the beautiful, unbreakable fountain pen at less than cost. The keynoter at the political convention. The president at his inaugural. The sound truck on main street advertising the circus has come to town. The counter man relaying orders to the kitchen. All sounds can be amplified. A heart beat can be made to sound like far off drums in Africa. Here is another specimen—a man bites some celery. It makes a little noise, but unless he is an exceptional biter or the celery is unusually crisp, you can't hear his chewing more than two feet away. Take an ordinary microphone like the one I'm speaking through and place it at this man's jaw and you won't hear much if anything, but put a little contact microphone against his teeth and you'll get this. Now, if celery can sound like thunder, what can thunder sound like?[48]

At the end of the section on melodrama, he addresses the role of silence and dares to broadcast dead air. The effect is momentarily to move his stage *through* Voigt's window, into the listeners' domain and the noises of their remote auditoria. It is a silence reminiscent of the modernist dramaturgy of Maeterlinck, Chekhov, Galsworthy and others,[49] who, following the decline of "melo" underscoring and overstated atmosphere in legitimate theatre, introduced silence as a loaded, almost tactile, material.

> You have just heard silence, racing around the world at the incredible speed of light. The silence cutting through the tangled ethers of the globe, straight into your living room. I hold my tongue a moment in studio B, station KMX on seventh hour, Hollywood California and little whirlpools of eddies of silence play on every rooftop in America.[50]

Silence reveals local noise. It reveals place. It shines a light on the auditorium and the listener and is arguably the signature sound effect of modernist theatre. Corwin uses dead air to create a networked silence that unites all the local living rooms of its reception into one big auditorium. This becomes another trope of his address to "common" men and women and the commonality that binds them across the vast and acousmatic separations of the big American broadcast. Given circumstances produced this rhetoric within a propaganda frame, but Corwin's remains a theatre of contemporarily aural "everymen." His valorization of commonality recalls Thomas Paine, the radicalism of melodrama's origins, and the epic theatre of Brecht and Piscator, but it also speaks to—or creates a picturesque of—the contemporary modern moment.

When compared to the more mimetic British style, Corwin's radio drama is characteristically American in its narrated diegesis, although his is especially "knowing" and "declared". He uses the cross-modal stage space of his listeners' imaginations not to suggest an *alternate* world but to make a theatre of *this* one. He demands a dialectic rather than empathetic form of audience. Brief scenes or vignettes are set up and performed but do not invite the listener into their world. Characters are not intended to be believable, only the actors (Gable, Stewart, Welles, Sondergaard). What is important is the *storytelling apparatus,* which is so strong that it can show us the unbelievable: the subjectivity of a microphone, eddies of silence on every rooftop. More than the *story*, the methods, languages, and conventions of Corwin's *storytelling,* along with the references inscribed in the fascia of its diegetic framework (idiomatic music, announcements, and so on), are the instruments with which he engages his audience in his propaganda or political message. Birdsong, ticking clocks, or city traffic are rarely used to set scenes, and music provides genre and framing rather than mood. Sound effects are often announced as such or have the feeling of being kept in audible quotation marks or italics. Little attempt is made to disguise—indeed every attempt is made to remind the listener that while it might at times sound like a theatre, this isn't a theatre at all, but a concoction of the radio studio, pictured through a time/space window by a network of listeners in their own rooms doing their own things. And yet between the studio and these listeners, a theatre space is agreed.

Corwin creates a picturesque that estranges his audience from the modern, wartime conditions of their listening, and therefore enables it to reflect on them in a sober dialectical relationship to his text, rather than through empathetic listening. Brecht regarded such listening as theatrical "intoxication" and points out that "what [radio drama] finds in front of the set is the individual—and of all alcoholic excesses none is more dangerous than solitary drinking."[51] Corwin, like Brecht, wanted his audiences relaxed but intellectually alert, and rather than solitary, part of the community of a big broadcast. It was John Reith who perhaps first observed that too much theatricality on the radio prevented the listener from being drawn into the world of the play, and this is precisely why Corwin emphasizes the theatre of his drama. "Too much striving for theatre effect and too little attempt at discovering the actual radio effect when the play is received in distant homes," Reith had warned, using "arts and tricks in the same way as for the stage" would be "fundamentally wrong" for radio. "The quickest way to alienate sympathy for and interest in radio plays," he went on, "is for any 'staginess' to be suggested, either in characters or method of treatment."[52]

Corwin's direct addresses and his expositions on technique work as *verfremdungseffekt*,[53] Brecht's term for the deliberately alienating effect of undisguised artificiality. Corwin is likely to have been influenced by Brecht and Piscator's epic theatre —it had certainly directly influenced 1930s Federal Theatre Project productions such as *It Can't Happen Here* and the *Living Newspaper* whose documentary-drama form and use of radiophonic and cinematic sound relates to Corwin's dramaturgy. Epic theatre thought seriously about sound. In *Sound in the Theatre*, Harold Burris-Meyer, responsible for the *Living Newspaper*'s groundbreaking use of intermedial sonic montage, describes a "scope" of theatre sound[54] similar to Corwin's treatise *Anatomy of Sound*. The spatial voice of Corwin's oratorical wartime narrator persona is much how one imagines the "voice of the living newspaper."[55] Corwin admired Brecht and was keen to work with him. This almost happened in 1946–47, when the exiled communist was struggling, under HUAC scrutiny, to find a producer for the American version of *Galileo*. FBI notes on a bugged phone call between Charles Laughton and Brecht's wife describe how Laughton stated that he had just read two scenes of the play to Mr. Norman Corwin, who immediately stated he would like to direct it. Laughton went on to point out that this was a good thing. Corwin "is a tremendous personality in the country and is a number one patriotic American". He inferred that it would be advantageous for such a man to produce this play of Brecht's, who might be called a "Communist."[56]

CONCLUSION

After all was said and done, the program coming out of radio sets on a million fridges or in a million cars across America was just sound, and this was often Corwin's point. His sound was part of a bigger sonic picture resonating in a bigger auditorium of "your sound and my sound and everybody's sound, because sound is common and let's not forget that."[57] Contrasting the Romantic materialism of Wordsworth's 1806 sonnet "The World Is Too Much with Us" with this contemporary picturesque of a community soundscape, he presents life as an aural journey:

> Sound is always with us late and soon
> And all our days can easily be traced by ear.
> There is such a thing as average sound in people's lives and it's a very simple matter to log a day's career in decibels. For example now, the average American day might sound like this: First reverie [sound effect]. Then having drilled a tunnel through your sleep, you rise and break your fast [sound effect], and while you read your paper [sound effect], observing that the fires of the world are spreading quietly, quickly towards your feet and number, the coffee smugly percolates [sound effect]. The toaster jumps [sound effect] up with the news that a slice of bread has just been toasted.[58]

Brecht, speaking in 1932, saw radio as the potential apparatus of a new theatre of mass communication:

> Were there a theatre of epic drama, of didactic documentary performance, then radio could carry out an entirely new kind of propaganda [...] namely genuine information, indispensable information.[59]

Corwin's theatre is not quite that, or perhaps it is more than that. In this chapter I have described a theatre "of the mind" in two ways: a theatre of the spatial imagination and of dialectical engagement. But I have also argued that it is a theatre not only of the mind but of the body in an extended auditorium of the 1940s soundscape and a 150-year-old theatre tradition.

I finish this chapter with the opening of *Anatomy of Sound,* which illustrates several of my key points. Firstly, the narrator speaks directly to the audience. A relaxed auditory dispositive is established by the permission she grants for the audience to be only half-listening as they drive, play cards, smoke or read. Having made them aware of their auditoria, she makes it clear that she is an actor in a studio. There are then two diegetic framing devices: an announced "token" sound effect *(verfremdungseffekt)* and then a similarly announced "formal introduction." The "play" then begins, but by now we know that the theatre will happen in our auditorium, not an imagined *other* world.

> How would you like to get up before an audience of four million people and introduce yourself? Would you rap on the edge of a glass with a spoon to get attention like

this? Do you think that would quiet such an audience? Would you clear your throat like this? [Clears throat.] Or would you try to ride over their various noises by shouting through a public address system the traditional salutation: "Ladies and gentlemen." Suppose some of your audience were playing bridge and others were arguing and others were lying down reading newspapers—would that terrify you? It would me, I know. Except at this moment when I am addressing four million people and thousands of them are playing bridge and talking across my voice and riding in automobiles and reading things—I'm not at all terrified. That's because there are four bare walls of a radio studio around me and I cannot see your faces. I cannot see 100,000 cigarettes light up in the dark across 8 million square miles of curving continent. So it becomes relatively easy to introduce myself to perfect strangers, [but] seclusion has an etiquette of its own. Therefore, I will now do so after a token sound to separate this informal prologue from a formal introduction.

Thank you. From Hollywood, the Columbia Workshop presents me, Gale Sondergaard, in the treatise for solo voice entitled the "Anatomy of Sound," written and directed by Norman Corwin and program number 18 in the series *26 by Corwin*.

Now, how shall we anatomize sound for you—with formulas and scientific talk? Well, hardly.

NOTES

1. Peter Sellars describes the microphone as analogous to the mask or persona of Greek theatre. Peter Sellars, Introduction, *Sound and Music for Theatre*, D. Kaye and K. Lebrecht (New York: Back Stage Books, 1994).

2. Norman Corwin, "Anatomy of Sound," CBS radio broadcast, *Columbia Workshop Presents 26 by Corwin*, 1941.

3. "Rally 'round Hitler's Grave," performed by Pete Seeger and the Almanac Singers.

4. Ross Brown, *Sound* (Basingstoke: Palgrave Macmillan, 2010).

5. In dark and lit productions, such as David Rosenberg's *Ring*, 2013, and Complicite's *The Encounter*, 2015.

6. Ross Brown, *Sound*; Ross Brown, "Sound Design: the Scenography of Engagement and Distraction," in *Theatre and Performance Design: A Reader in Scenography*, edited by J. Collins and A. Nisbet (Abingdon: Routledge, 2010), 340–348; Ross Brown, "The Eleventh of the Eleventh of the Eleventh: The Theatre of Memorial Silence," in *Soundscapes of the Urban Past: Staged Sound as Mediated Cultural Heritage*, vol. 5, edited by Karin Bijsterveld (Bielefeld: transcript-Verlag, 2014), 209–221; *Theatre Noise*, edited by Lynne Kendrick and David Roesner, (Newcastle-Upon-Tyne: Cambridge Scholars, 2011); Mladen Ovadija, *Dramaturgy of Sound in the Avant-Garde and Postdramatic Theatre* (Montreal: McGill's University Press, 2013); George Home Cook, *Theatre and Aural Attention* (Basingstoke: Palgrave Macmillan, 2015).

7. For example, Martin Esslin, "The Mind as a Stage," *Theatre Quarterly* 1, no. 3 (1971): 5–11; R. Arnheim, *Radio*, translated by M. Ludwig and H. Read (London: Faber & Faber, 1936); A. Crisell, *Understanding Radio*, 2nd ed. (London: Routledge, 1994); and M. Shingler and C. Wieringa, *On Air: Methods and Meanings of Radio* (London: Arnold, 1998). I am indebted here to Farokh Soltani's forthcoming PhD thesis on the ocular-centrism of radio drama.

8. As in Plato's distinction with "mimetic" drama, in *Republic*, Book III.

9. C. Cazeaux, "Phenomenology and Radio Drama," *British Journal of Aesthetics* 45, no. 2 (2005): 157–174.

10. D. Ihde, *Listening and Voice: Phenomenologies of Sound*, 2nd ed. (Albany, NY: State University of New York Press, 2007).
11. Ibid., 209.
12. Casey O'Callaghan, "Lessons from beyond Vision (Sounds and Audition)," *Philosophical Studies* 153, no. 1 (2011): 158.
13. Ibid.
14. See Albert S. Bregman, *Auditory Scene Analysis*, 2nd ed. (Cambridge, MA: MIT Press, 1999).
15. See J. Schnupp, I. Nelken, and A. King, *Auditory Neuroscience: Making Sense of Sound* (Cambridge, MA: MIT Press, 2011), 207, 221.
16. O'Callaghan, "Lessons from beyond Vision."
17. Cazeaux, "Phenomenology and Radio Drama," 158.
18. Vitruvius, Book V, *On Architecture*; see Brown, *Sound*, 154–163.
19. Since the "new drama" of the turn of the twentieth century, when silence and pause became dramaturgical elements, and by which time silent listening had become conventional.
20. See Brown, *Sound*, 96–104.
21. Holger Schulze, "On the Corporeality of Listening," in *Soundscapes of the Urban Past: Staged Sound as Mediated Cultural Heritage*, vol. 5, edited by Karin Bijsterveld (Bielefeld: transcript-Verlag, 2014), 195–209.
22. W. Benjamin, *Understanding Brecht*, translated by Anna Bostock (London: NLB, 1973), 15.
23. For example, M. Wallis, "Thinking through Technē," *Performance Research* 10, no. 4 (2005): 1–8.
24. Bruce R. Smith, *The Acoustic World of Early Modern England: Attending to the O-Factor* (Chicago: University of Chicago Press, 1999).
25. Mladen Ovadija, *Dramaturgy of Sound*.
26. Simon Shepherd, "Melodrama as Avant-Garde: Enacting a New Subjectivity," *Textual Practice* 10 (3), 1996: 507–522.
27. Or "the Noise"—no doubt a play on the pseudonyms used in eighteenth-century pamphleteering.
28. That is, licensed by Royal Patent to produce spoken plays.
29. That is, involving music within its scenes, as underscoring or framing.
30. For example, the pivotal *The Wonders of Derbyshire* (1779), which not only transformed scenic art but turned the Peak District into a national tourist attraction.
31. Stephen Copley and Peter Garside, eds., *The Politics of the Picturesque: Literature, Landscape and Aesthetics since 1770* (Cambridge, UK: Cambridge University Press, 1994).
32. Veit Erlmann, *Reason and Resonance: A History of Modern Aurality* (Cambridge, MA: Zone Books, 2010).
33. J. Swindells and D. F. Taylor, eds., *The Oxford Handbook of the Georgian Theatre 1737–1832* (Oxford, UK: Oxford University Press, 2014).
34. Martin Meisel, *Realizations: Narrative, Pictorial, and Theatrical Arts in Nineteenth-Century England* (Princeton, NJ: Princeton University Press, 1983), 38–42, 97.
35. Le Bruit (pseud.), "Notes on the Early Progress of the Picturesque of Sound," *American Notes & Queries* 5, no. 8 (1947): 115–119.
36. William Henry Pyne, *Wine and Walnuts: Or, After Dinner Chit-chat*, vol. 1 (London: Longman, Hurst, Rees, Orme, Brown, and Green, 1824), 296.
37. See Brown, "Sound Design," 340–348; Christopher Baugh, "Philippe de Loutherbourg: Technology-Driven Entertainments and Spectacle in the Late Eighteenth Century," *Huntington Library Quarterly* 70, no. 2 (2007): 251–268; and Pyne, *Wine and Walnuts*, 281–305.
38. Baugh, "Philippe de Loutherbourg."
39. William T. Whitely, *Thomas Gainsborough*. (London: John Murray, 1915), 370.

40. William Gilpin, *Observations Related Chiefly to Picturesque Beauty, Made in the Year 1776, On Several Parts of Great Britain*, vol. 2 (Cambridge, UK: Cambridge University Press, digitally printed edition, 2014), 133.

41. Neil Verma, *Theatre of the Mind: Imagination, Aesthetics, and American Radio Drama* (Chicago: University of Chicago Press, 2012), 33–57.

42. Ian Macpherson, "The Electric Ear, Part Two: The Sound Film 1926–9," *New Soundtrack* 1, no. 2 (2011): 113–132.

43. P. G. A. H. Voigt, "Sound Reproduction" (lecture demonstration), *Proceedings of the British Kinematograph Society*, no. 7, 1932. (My emphasis.)

44. In lectures and demonstrations from as early as 1924; see Bruce C. Edgar, "An Interview with P. G. A. H. Voigt, Part One," *Speaker Builder* 3 (1981): 12–16, https://community.klipsch.com/forums/storage/3/714028/An%20Interview%20with%20PGAH%20Voight%20Part%201.pdf; and P. G. A. H. Voigt, "A Controversial Idea from England," *Audio Engineering* 34, no. 10 (1950): 40–66.

45. Voigt, "A Controversial Idea," 40.

46. Ibid., 40.

47. Thomas Holcroft, whose *Tale of Mystery* (1802) is acknowledged as the first melodrama, was a radical involved in publishing Thomas Paine's *Rights of Man* in England.

48. Corwin, "Anatomy of Sound," 0:23:43–0:25:57.

49. Brown, *Sound,* 73–81.

50. Corwin, "Anatomy of Sound," 0:16:20–0:16:30.

51. Bertolt Brecht, "Radio as a Means of Communication: A Talk on the Function of Radio," *Screen* 20, no. 3–4 (1979): 24–28.

52. See Alan Beck, *The Invisible Play: B.B.C. Radio Drama 1922–1928*, Savoy Hill, http://www.savoyhill.co.uk/invisibleplay/mainindex.html.

53. For a summary of relaxed, dialectic audience and estrangement in epic theatre, see Benjamin, *Understanding Brecht*.

54. H. Burris-Meyer and V. Mallory, *Sound in the Theatre* (Mineola, NY: Radio Magazines, 1959).

55. J. Woodruff, "A Voice in the Dark: Subversive Sounds of the Living Newspapers and the Flint Sit-Down Strike of 1936–37," *Interference Journal* (2013), http://www.interferencejournal.com/articles/noise/a-voice-in-the-dark.

56. James K. Lyon, "The FBI as Literary Historian: The File of Bertolt Brecht," in *The Brecht Yearbook*, vol. 11, edited by John Fuegi, Gisela Bahr, and John Willett (Detroit, MI: Wayne State University Press, 1983), 225, http://digital.library.wisc.edu/1711.dl/German.BrechtYearbook011.

57. "Anatomy of Sound," 0:02:45.

58. Ibid., 0:03:30.

59. Berthold Brecht, *Radio as Means*.

PART THREE

EAR

On Corwin's Influence

8

TRANSATLANTIC OR ANGLO-AMERICAN CORWIN?

Tim Crook

For a few months in the middle of the Second World War, Norman Corwin was dispatched to Britain to create a series of sole-authored features on the theme of *An American in England*. It was a joint venture between CBS and the BBC and represented phase 2, after *This Is War!*, of Corwin's contribution to the cultural propaganda arm of words at war. This chapter investigates how the auteur sound-feature-maker sought to avoid Allied government interference and "tell Americans exactly what I saw in England" in 1942.

While focusing on these productions, the analysis seeks to explore whether Corwin was on a straightforward transatlantic adventure or experiencing a process of Anglo-American solidarity that was culturally, politically, and ideologically transformative. For Corwin was, from a British perspective, an American liberal with Jewish heritage opposed to the British Empire. What did they think of him? The answer has been explored in an examination of his files in the BBC Written Archives and evidence of the reception of his work in Britain.

The evidence is that he was celebrated as a powerful and creative influence in dramatizing the theatre of the mind. He was adopted enthusiastically as an effective deployer of the munitions of the mind through the aesthetic of his radio-program-making in the Allied struggle against Germany, Italy, Japan, and its Axis allies.

But the archives are not dominated by the propagandist imperative. The BBC's programming elite realized he was not only a kindred creative spirit but also a radiogenic auteur and trailblazer. He had the admiration and support of the BBC's director of productions Val Gielgud, head of features Lawrence Gilliam, and an effective British alter ego, D. G. Bridson—who would resonate and mirror an equally powerful exchange in Anglo-American program-making from Britain to America and America to Britain.

The BBC carried out a cultural intelligence gathering exercise on Corwin's potential in 1942, and a surviving file discloses the beginning of an Anglo-American dynamic that made Corwin one of the most regularly produced living American radio dramatists of the Second World War period and the fifteen years that followed.

The relationship extended beyond the *convivencia* of joint CBS and BBC broadcasting projects. In the process of recognizing his intrinsic qualities as a poetic and dramatic radio storyteller, the BBC would commission original productions of his plays with English casts for broadcast to the British audience. The BBC realized his verse plays and exploration of the human condition entertained and were relevant to the sensibility of the popular British radio audience. Corwin would not be ghettoized into a minority high cultural backwater. He was a writer suitable for the Forces program (the precursor to the Light Programme) as much as the Home Service.

POLITICAL AND POETIC SYMPATHIES

Milton Allen Kaplan emphasized that after Corwin flew to England in 1942 to write and direct the seven-part series *An American in England*, he returned to manage the American dimension in 1943 of *Transatlantic Call: People to People*.[1] This was a prose series to be heard "simultaneously by listeners in Great Britain and the United States." The British dimension was directed by Corwin's kindred spirit D. G. Bridson—described by Kaplan as "the English radio poet."[2]

The association of Bridson and Corwin in BBC Written Archives correspondence and files is a recurrent theme. They were mutual admirers and collaborators. They were both published poets and dramatists in the radio and sound context. Indeed Corwin's reputation and enthusiastic reception owed much to the distribution, reading, and analysis of his volume *Thirteen By Corwin* (1942). Bridson's work had been published in T. S. Eliot's periodical *Criterion*, and his reputation would soar with the publication of his Second World War verse play *Aeron's Field* in 1943, described by the *Listener*'s radio critic Grace Wyndham Goldie as both radiogenic and in verse and breaking "into the week's programmes like an explosion. So slightly deafened but delighted, we sit back to consider its thunderous reverberations."[3] In his published memoirs *Prospero and Ariel: The Rise and Fall of Radio: A Personal Recollection*, Bridson described Corwin as one of radio's most accomplished craftsmen. He said "An American in England" was

> a sheer delight to everyone who believed in radio writing as a creative art. Unlike "Britain to America," which had gone out on the Overseas Service, the series was broadcast in both countries. The ironic humour of the writing, and the keen observa-

tion behind it, were particularly appreciated over here. They made the American viewpoint infinitely more sympathetic to those who had known it previously only at second hand. All who were lucky enough to work along with him on the programmes had the highest admiration for Corwin's gifts.[4]

Corwin shared many of Bridson's aesthetic and political dramatic interests. When in Britain, although Corwin eschewed the emotional cant of "hate media"—all too feasible in the psychologically febrile sound medium of a global war—he attenuated his negotiation of representing British society by choosing to investigate from the bottom up. This makes his program-making communitarian journalism—certainly in terms of research. He was therefore mirroring what can be described as the doctrine of radio theatre workshop—the dramaturgical expression of documentary performance by investigating and witnessing the grassroots of social experience. This would then be transformed into an expression of the radio dramatic arts by realistic script and performance, verse drama, and characterization by music and sound design.

This dynamic and aesthetic made Corwin an ally of the BBC post-Marxist school of radio documentary makers from the Manchester-based Northern Region of the 1930s that included D. G. Bridson, Archie Harding, Olive Shapley, and Joan Littlewood. His feature or dramatized documentary technique would parallel the theatre workshop culture that would evolve from 1945 in Joan Littlewood and Ewan McColl's touring Theatre Workshop. Closely monitored and shadowed by the Security Service MI5, it would eventually locate to the East London Theatre Royal Stratford East in 1953.

The most radical and progressive "radio feature" making at the BBC during the 1930s was produced by the Manchester "left wing" school of documentary sound, with D. G. Bridson pioneering political verse drama, such as *March of '45* in 1936. This was a multiple-studio-produced epic dramatizing Bonnie Prince Charlie's invasion with the Scottish clans of England in 1745 and can be interpreted as symbolizing social rebellion against oppression and injustice. A trace of concern about the impact on English-Scottish relations was recorded in the BBC written archives during a remake in the 1940s.

Bridson's career as a freelance and staff producer in the BBC would be characterized by negotiating the forces of institutional censorship by producing socially questioning creative writing and production. Sometimes it would result in direct censorship and withdrawal of productions after they had been listed in the *Radio Times* and were in mid-rehearsal.[5]

Bridson's approach to censorship was practical and evolutionary. He would be assertive but never nihilistic in reaction to the consequences. He would try to find a solution by persuasion or alternative outlet or try again at a later time. His first application for a staff job in 1934 was rejected largely because of his politics and the mischief that resulted in his freelance scripts *Prometheus* and *Scourge* being pulled from the schedules for alleged political subversion and indecency. But he would apply a second time and get in. His overtly political script *Builders*, which debated the aspiration for a more equal and welfare-based state after the war, would be blocked from broadcast. He could still find a welcoming place for transmission in Australia.[6] One memo survives in the Norman Corwin files of Bridson intervening to prevent censorship of the rebroadcast of one of the episodes of *An American in England*:

> I am afraid I cannot agree to the cutting of the above script for use in the Overseas Service. . . . I think that it would be most unfortunate if a cut version were put out on short wave, in view of the fact that a large number of people might have heard the original, and to take a poor view of our censoring American material. For that matter, I am sure that Corwin himself would be most unwilling.[7]

We do not know which part of the program faced excision, but we do know from the handwritten annotation on the memo that the Overseas Service agreed with Bridson's point of view.

Bridson's mentor and sponsor in his early years at the BBC was the head of features in Manchester, Archie Harding, who went on to have a major influence on the culture of feature production in the BBC and beyond by taking on the role of chief instructor. This meant he devised all the induction training courses for new producers joining the BBC—a post he held during Corwin's sojourn in England in 1942. While in Manchester, Bridson and Harding had developed the radio feature form into more challenging "social documentaries."[8]

Scannell and Cardiff would observe: "In the second half of the thirties most of the interesting and innovative work in features and documentaries was being done in Manchester."[9] Bridson himself recognized how Harding's enthusiasm for his work meant that *March of '45*

> was his favourite demonstration piece, and as his students included radio producers from all over the world, news of the programme naturally got around. Archibald MacLeish referred to it as a prototype (unheard by him) in his preface to *The Fall of the City*. Milton Allen Kaplan quoted from it copiously in his *Radio and Poetry*. Louis MacNeice paid handsome tribute to it in his foreword to *Christopher Columbus*.[10]

The BBC written archives have specific documentary traces of Corwin being welcomed into the Harding and Bridson bosom. Harding attended the playback of Corwin's first *An American in England* episode at Broadcasting House, and BBC head of features Laurence Gilliam specifically wrote to Corwin at the Savoy Hotel, where he was staying, that he would be arranging a follow-up meeting as soon as possible:

Will you name a date for dinner soon? Archie Harding, whom you met this morning, would very much like to meet and talk. He is really the granddaddy of features, having done some of the earliest radio experiments in this country and is now in charge of staff training. I am sure you would be interested to meet him.[11]

Corwin and Bridson also shared the accolade of being pioneers of the "radio ballad." Many of the *An American in England* series episodes were scored and conducted by Benjamin Britten and the RAF symphony orchestra. This was a creative engagement between a social and verse documentarist with a modernist music composer. In the result, music became a powerful dramatic characterization. Corwin himself recognized that in "London by Clipper" Britten's "music for this series must rank with the best of Herrman and Murray, at the very top of radio's serious work. The cues that Britten composed for the takeoff and blackout passages were so powerful and graphic that I urged him to develop what he had written to make a suite of it."[12] One of the most exquisite expressions of evocative dramatic scoring is achieved in the episode "Women of Britain" (24 August 1942) when Joseph Julian goes into the London underground for the first time and his descent by steep staircase and escalator is symbolized by increasingly menacing orchestral plunges of bass and low note instrumentation; Julian has every reason to say "half way to hell now."

Corwin's appreciation of the power and potential of folk music led to his direction of Earl Robinson's *Ballad for Americans,* starring Paul Robeson (CBS 1939), and the ballad opera *Magna Carta* by Maxwell Anderson and Kurt Weill (CBS 1940), both being included in the *Pursuit of Happiness* program series. This was followed by his direction and production of Robinson and Lampell's *The Lonesome Train* in 1944.[13]

The creative fusion of classical, folkloric, and modernist musical expression with realistic social writing and verse drama powers the concept of the radio opera or ballad. Such chronology, therefore, would suggest that Corwin was probably the influence on Bridson when he fashioned the radio ballad *The Man Who Went to War* with Harlem poet Langston Hughes in 1944. This was a joint NBC-BBC project.

Bridson argues in his autobiography that he had broken "entirely new ground: in the event I came up with radio's first ballad-opera."[14] He said he wanted to produce "a Negro musical, written around a war theme, which would give lively expression to the Negro character, his humour and his supreme artistry."[15] The language used here now seems patronizingly naïve, but it is a fact his project was rooted in an original Langston Hughes script with Paul Robeson, Canada Lee, and Ethel Waters performing. Bridson says in his autobiography that the limited budget meant it was not carried by an American network but was heard by ten million listeners in Britain. Bridson argues: "As a gesture of friendship from one people to another, *The Man Who Went to War* was probably unique. As a prophetic echo of the Negro's post-war struggle for Civil Rights, it might have been a timely warning. Either way, it was quite one of the most popular broadcasts I ever had on air."[16]

The Man Who Went to War was broadcast from the United States to the BBC Home Service on 6 March with a repeat on 29 May 1944 and was listed in the *Radio Times* as starring Paul Robeson and being in the form of a "Ballad opera by Langston Hughes, arranged and directed by D. G. Bridson. This modern folk tale, performed by an all-Negro cast, presents the story of the ordinary people of all the United Nations under the stress of war." Corwin's landmark transmission on CBS of the radio opera/ballad *The Lonesome Train* was on 21 March 1944. It is not clear if Corwin and Bridson were competing to claim the credit for being the first to develop and produce the radio ballad. However, it is certainly the case that they shared the same interest and contribution in pioneering the creative form. Furthermore, this could be said to have been accelerated by, or at the very least benefited from, their direct involvement in the Anglo-American cultural interchange of radio cultures at this time.

The fact that *The Lonesome Train* has endured as the totemic radio ballad of March 1944 compared to *The Man Who Went to War* can also be explained by the fact it had American radio network exposure and multiple archiving, including a separate gramophone version recorded and distributed by Decca. The BBC sound masters for the Bridson/Langston Hughes radio ballad were destroyed through bureaucratic indifference and incompetent airmail dispatch. However, a significant discovery by the media historian Michele Hilmes in 2010 that a transcription disc of the broadcast was preserved in the U.S. Library of Congress means that the sound textual dimension of this significant radio feature has been retrieved for academic and cultural appreciation.[17] The BBC does not have any archived copies of its productions of Corwin's work during the 1940s and '50s. It is hoped that resourceful researchers of the future may be able to find them hidden in public and private archives.

CORWIN AND THE BBC

The output of Norman Corwin on BBC Radio extends from 1942 to 2005. He was last heard in interview form at the age of 95 in an hour-long documentary. The program was produced by a BBC radio drama director who attended a radio drama conference in London in 2000 that included the presentation of a paper on the postmodernist dimensions of Corwin's 1945 play *The Undecided Molecule.*

Until 1942 Bridson argued that American radio "had little to teach us" apart from the days of the Columbia Workshop productions that inspired the BBC to broadcast Archibald MacLeish's *Fall of the City* and Pare Lorentz's *Job to Be Done* in the late 1930s.[18]

Corwin's reputation as a pioneer and creative auteur of radio storytelling was based on the reception of his volume *Thirteen by Corwin*. There is no evidence in the BBC Archives that the BBC investigated later publications of his scripts, such as in *More by Corwin* (1944) and *Untitled and Other Radio Dramas* (1945).

Corwin's British project was a collaborative agreement between Ed Murrow, the CBS European director in London, BBC head of drama Val Gielgud, and head of features Laurence Gilliam. On 26 June 1942 Murrow made clear the political and propagandist objectives:

> to promote understanding between the peoples of Great Britain and the United States, toward the closest collaboration in the prosecution of the war; to create through such understanding, a fuller appreciation of the indivisibility of the fight; to countervail anti-British sentiment and the Propaganda of Division, within the United States.[19]

Each thirty-minute program was "designed to show the common man of Britain to the common man of the United States."[20] Murrow described the Corwin CBS/BBC collaboration "the most ambitious effort in the field of Anglo-American information and understanding ever undertaken by an American Network."[21]

BBC head of drama Val Gielgud issued the corporation's battle plan for Corwin's arrival on 1 July 1942. Gielgud described Corwin as "the distinguished producer of the Columbia Broadcasting Corporation."[22] There were only twenty-seven days to go for the first of seven half-hour weekly broadcasts. Gielgud said the responsibility of his department to give Corwin what he wanted and needed was "a priority owing to the great importance of the programmes."[23] The live transmissions would go out Mondays and Tuesdays at 4 A.M. British time, with each program having an acting company of sixteen, a twenty-six-piece orchestra with conductor and last-minute copying facilities, possibly two studios, and rehearsal time from 3 P.M. each Sunday. In the end Corwin had at his disposal the sixty-piece symphony orchestra of the Royal Air Force—which in peacetime had been the London Philharmonic—and the BBC's largest and best-equipped studios at Maida Vale.

Gielgud assigned the BBC drama producer Dallas Bower, who had previously carried out an enthusiastic and favorable cultural intelligence report on Corwin's canon of radio play scripts published in *Thirteen by Corwin*. Bower declared: "I think some of the plays in this volume are the best writing specifically for radio that I have yet come across."[24] Bower said of *The Odyssey of Runyon Jones*, "one of the best pieces of radio light fantasy I have read."[25] He said of *They Fly through the Air with the Greatest of Ease*, "The narration is in verse of a quality whose imagery is clear and rhythm sustained."[26] He said of *The Plot to Overthrow Christmas*, "The whole play is in verse. It is extremely well done, very amusing, and has an excellent shape." Of *Ann Rutledge* Bower recommended acquiring the rights for early production because it was "a piece of first class dramatic writing. [. . .] It is very topical."²⁷ *Seems Radio Is Here to Stay* was described as a "brilliant script." *Appointment*, set in a German concentration camp, was "a fine play" and merited acquiring for production. In total Bower recommended that the BBC secure the UK broadcasting rights for eight out of the thirteen plays contained in the volume.

Corwin's arrival in Britain to work at the BBC was a source of inspiration beyond the genres of radio drama and documentary. The editor of BBC *Radio Newsreel*, John Irwin, was hoping for an "audience" with the American radio guru:

> We would be very happy to have him come and see us at any time convenient to him. I would add in fairness that we are naturally very interested in his reactions to our methods, and would no doubt tax him with many questions, for we are eager to learn a great many things that we feel he would be able to teach us.²⁸

Corwin had a punishing schedule of writing, direction, and production while in England, and shortly before his first direction and production for the BBC of his own script *Appointment*, the welcoming hagiography reached the public via C. Gordon Glover in the *Radio Times* on 17 July 1942:

> Corwin thinks, dreams, lives radio. He writes it with a sense of sound and a command of rhythm that distinguish his approach from all others. His plays could be performed *through no other medium whatsoever*, and that, surely, is the final criterion by which broadcasting should be judged.²⁹

The BBC archives hold the clearest evidence that "Mission Corwin" as outlined by Ed Murrow was an unqualified success. The BBC's director general Robert Foot sent a cable to CBS boss William Paley:

> BBC Governors ask me to send you heartiest congratulations in which we all share on Corwin's splendid series "An American in England" Please convey our appreciation these outstanding programmes to Corwin and Julian and all staff concerned.³⁰

The series was also a resounding success in the United States. The BBC retained a Western Union telegram revealing that by 3 November 1942 the series was carried by 88 stations out of 117 CBS affiliates.³¹

The BBC commitment to producing and broadcasting Corwin's playwriting continued through the late 1940s and 1950s for set-piece United Nations Radio projects such as *Could Be* (1949), *Document A/777* (1951), and *The Charter in the Saucer* (1955). The gramophone version of *The Lonesome Train* would be broadcast in 1956 and 1960.

The BBC Corwin files also reveal that the longer he remained out of radio, having gone to write for Hollywood, and out of contact with BBC radio-program-making, there would be a more critical and questioning attitude to suggestions that his work should be rebroadcast or produced.

By 1953 an assistant in the Drama Script Unit, Anthony Brown, appeared to adopt the default attitude that he needed to find reasons not to produce Corwin plays: "they are all too dated or else too firmly rooted in American culture, to be useful to us."[32] Those previously produced "do not seem to me to be worth reviving."[33] *Old Salt* "does not seem to me to quite come off."[34] Only *My Client Curley* and *The Odyssey of Runyon Jones* may have been worth repeating.

BBC drama producer Raymond Raikes seemed to be determined that *My Client Curley* would be exterminated and never heard again:

> I don't care for this at all. *Not* Norman Corwin at his best—indeed not true Norman Corwin at all—but an adaptation of someone else's idea. And what an idea! The buildup of a performing caterpillar—for nearly 30 minutes—and then, when it is about to be in the big money, it is lost—only to discover on the last page it has "turned into a butterfly!"
> As if one couldn't see this coming for at least 25 minutes.
> It is pretty low level listening—packed full of adverts for every sort of American article—and the level of humour?
>
> DOCTOR 2. We are lepidopterists!
> AGENT. Lepidopterists? But Curley's a caterpillar, not a leopard.
>
> Not for me![35]

This withering and patronizing denunciation of Corwin's work presumes to know the real Norman Corwin, is suffused with anti-American prejudice, and is physically stabbed with an aggressive scoring of the final exclamation mark in longhand blue pencil.

It would appear that Corwin's agent was not promoting the rich range of his radio playwriting, and the BBC had only one copy of one of his published volumes, with interest and curiosity being revived every decade. It is astonishing that nobody at the BBC had either read or listened to "The Undecided Molecule" (1945), which has been successfully workshopped with British and international students at Goldsmiths every year since 2005. It is consistently appreciated as a universally understood and intertextually entertaining and poetic masterpiece on the dangers of science and nuclear power.[36]

The BBC from the late fifties through the counterculture decade of the 1960s was focusing its inspiration for international innovation in form and ideas from the continent via Samuel Beckett, the Theatre of the Absurd, and "kitchen sink" working-class writers from the North. It can be argued that despite transmitting the Decca recording of *The Lonesome Train,* the BBC missed an opportunity of fashioning a new chapter in Corwin's original radio playwriting output by not commissioning new work from him.

However, it can also be said that Corwin's political imperative was focused on finding solutions to the madness of nuclear war and the nightmares of the 20th century. Perhaps Corwin's significance as a radio writer should be recognized in terms of his political and didactic qualities. Through the United Nations he was channeling his creative radio talent to make the world a better place and save humanity.

Such proselytizing and earnest liberal evangelizing was noted by BBC audience survey and meticulous press-cutting compilation. Corwin's BBC files contain an excoriating review by Robert Robinson in the *Sunday Times* for the BBC United Nations 1955 set-piece production of *The Charter in the Saucer*:

> The surest way of turning the dramatic form into a cemetery is to bury propaganda in it. For confirmation of this thesis, I choose as an example "The Charter in the Saucer" (Home). This represented itself to be a playlet, and turned out to be a sales counter: that the article on sale happened to be that admirable institution the United Nations diminished my irritation not a wit. *Did* we require this "fantasy" about a visiting Martian—flying saucer, B.B.C. Rep., Sir Laurence Olivier and all—before we could swallow the "commercial" it embodied? If that principle is conceded it will not be long before they are dramatizing the nine o'clock news.[37]

The BBC was fully prepared to support Corwin's audio-dramatic politicking. When celebrating the UN Charter's declaration on human rights in the 1951 production of *Document A/777*, Corwin was able to write a full-page article in the *Radio Times* to stress "the importance of the Universal Declaration of Human Rights as a focus of hope and encouragement."[38]

The article also explained how the one-hour program was a mosaic of three hundred separate sound sequences recorded in New York City and Hollywood, staggered over a period of many days with none of the international "personalities" taking a fee for their participation.

In 1945 BBC head of features Laurence Gilliam wrote an article for the *Radio Times* as a kind of cultural prologue for British listeners to prepare them for the Corwin phenomenon. In the country whose broadcasting doctrine did not easily mix creative storytelling with political controversy, Gilliam cleverly hailed him as "the O. Henry of Radio" rather than the Leon Trotsky or New England bolshevist of broadcasting: "He has something of the O. Henry in his make-up—and what a writer for radio O. Henry would have made?"[39]

Gilliam addressed the political activism in Corwin's work: "a still unexhausted source of intriguing fantasy or vehement liberalism. Personally, I would settle for the fantasy, but I shall always be interested in whatever he does."[40]

CORWIN AND THE BRITISH

The *American in England* series can be evaluated as a fascinating political intervention by a liberal American into the politics of representing British society. Corwin survives control and censorship because his ideological imperative is framed and shielded by his propagandist mission to win the war by fostering Anglo-American friendship and solidarity.

Joseph Julian as a reporter is not a loud Yank popping bubble gum into the faces of British people who have been alone in being the free world's lightning conductor for Nazi and Fascist aggression. He is on a quiet, respectful listening and learning journey of discovery. This is evident in any close textual consideration of the scripts and sound including "London by Clipper," "Home Is Where You Hang Your Helmet," "An Anglo-American Angle," "Cromer," and "Clipper Home." Corwin said he wanted the character Joe to be "young, thoughtful, friendly, impressionistic, curious, neither standing in awe of the British nor patronizing them."[41]

BBC director of features Laurence Gilliam had no doubt about Corwin's intentions when he observed in his 1945 *Radio Times* article on Corwin,

> his quick, observant eye and acute ear enabled him to catch the subtle half-tones in which the true British character is revealed. He had no mercy for the pompous official panjandrums who were sometimes misguided enough to take him on what they called a "conducted tour." They would suddenly realize they had lost him, only to find him in a fish queue or a four-ale bar or at the bottom of a bomb crater talking to the "real guys," as he called them. A lot of those "real guys" remember him as a friend at a time when they were very glad to have friends from overseas.[42]

Norman Corwin's *American in England* programs were not true socialistic ensembles with actors ventriloquizing their observation of lives in the community, but Corwin was chronicling through his own creative eyes and ears, and he scored the words of those he wished to represent in the language of the new literature of dramaturgical radio feature, musical, and drama-documentary. He was selective and biased in favor of what became the postwar Labour social democratic culture. This was certainly the case of the most popular episode of the series, "Cromer."[43] Debunking the Tories, privilege, injustice, and winning the war for the promise of a better tomorrow is how Britain is imagined for the Americans, and, of course, what would have pleased D. G. Bridson so much was how British society was imagined for listeners in Britain:

> *Mitchell.* After they'd burnt my hat I used to bring it around, every election, and display it under a sign which said, "Tory Argument." (*Laughs*)
> *Joe.* Personally, I think the Tories have burnt all their hats behind them. (*More laughter.*)
> *Mitchell.* I don't know. They've learned some manners. Why, there was a man tried seven times to get on the council here, and he was defeated each time. Finally he was *invited* to become a member.[44]

Corwin created a wide span of representation of the British people and their culture and politics before and after in other features such as "To Tim at Twenty"

(1940), about the RAF gunner who will not return from his mission, and "Welcome to Glory" (1941), in which a London fishmonger who was blitzed in Westminster Abbey dialogues with the ghost of good Queen Bess, who blew away the Spanish Armada hundreds of years before.

"To Tim at Twenty" could have been the inspiration for iconic Humphrey Jennings film *Diary for Timothy*, which in the documentary form turns the birth of a baby boy in that last year of the wearying Second World War into a moving anthem of hope for humanity. It is fascinating that Corwin himself was so inspired by a scene in Humphrey Jennings's montage film documentary *Listen to Britain* (1942) that he replicated it in "Home Is Where You Hang Your Helmet": "I did not myself attend the concert by Myra Hess in the National Gallery, but saw an excellent film of the event, in which the whole setting, and much of the music, was reproduced."[45]

"This Above All" (1945) appears to criticize British colonial policy and its class system, and "Untitled" (1944) even connotes a subtle and more-than-subtextual call to give up the Palestine Mandate for a Jewish state and homeland: "Will someone give my best to Marian the day that Palestine is taken up?"[46] Corwin, to use his own words, had never been an "an admirer of the way British diplomacy has fumbled, ducked, and double-talked its way around the problems of Palestine and India."[47] He well knew that Palestine was "one of those subjects His Majesty's government would rather you didn't bring up."[48]

The success of Corwin's Anglo-American affair could have been derived from his essential democratic instinct as a humanitarian committed to fairness, decency, social justice, and equality. When he first arrived in battle-scarred London, he was a privileged American star and cultural celebrity. But that would not blunt his ability and determination to identify with the street level of everyday life of wartime Britain. He shared overcrowded third-class railway carriages on all-night journeys to Liverpool and King's Lynn where there was standing room only. Rather than type up his scripts in the comfort of his Savoy Hotel room, he would scribble them on his knee in Hyde Park—bench-level with the Londoners welcoming more than a million GIs to roll back the Axis dictators from occupied Europe.

He was thus more than a transatlantic tourist or program executive fulfilling a foreign jolly or assignment. He was part of a truly Anglo-American interpenetration of radio aesthetics in the midst of historical military, political, social, and cultural hurricane storm waves.

In one of the final programs of *An American in England*, Corwin found the words to say that he had been part of a transformation in which Britons and Americans were both proud and asking only for the time and place to meet the enemy:

And whether it's to be the funeral pyre of all freedom or the forge in which is shaped the hopeful new world of the common man, was what common men were dying for that night. The train sped on. England slipped past me in the dark. I was leaving a strong and valiant people to return to one.[49]

NOTES

Documents quoted from the BBC Written Radio Archives at Caversham (WRAC) are listed under the BBC's cataloguing of their files.

1. Milton Allen Kaplan, *Radio and Poetry* (New York: Columbia University Press, 1949), 11.
2. Ibid.
3. Douglas Geoffrey Bridson, *Prospero and Ariel: The Rise and Fall of Radio: A Personal Recollection* (London: Victor Gollancz, 1971), 74.
4. Ibid., 94.
5. Ibid., 39–40, 46–47.
6. Ibid., 94–96.
7. D G Bridson memo to Overseas Service, 13th February 1943, BBC WRAC.
8. David Cardiff and Paddy Scannell, *A Social History of Broadcasting*, vol. 1, *1922–1939* (London: Basil Blackwell, 1991)134–52.
9. Ibid., 151–52.
10. Bridson, *Prospero and Ariel*, 60.
11. Laurence Gilliam to Norman Corwin letter, 29th July 1942, BBC WRAC.
12. Norman Corwin, *Untitled and Other Radio Dramas*, (New York: Henry Holt, 1945), 169.
13. Tim Crook, "Norman Corwin's *The Lonesome Train* (Live Broadcast) CBS 1944," *RadioDoc Review*, 1(1), 2014. http://ro.uow.edu.au/rdr/vol1/iss1/6.
14. Bridson, *Prospero and Ariel*, 109.
15. Ibid.
16. Ibid., 111.
17. Michele Hilmes, "Missing from History: Langston Hughes' *The Man Who Went to War*," 2015, http://blog.commarts.wisc.edu/2015/06/12/missing-from-history-langston-hughes-the-man-who-went-to-war-2/.
18. Bridson, *Prospero and Ariel*, 93.
19. Letter from Ed Murrow to Roger H. Eckersley, 26th June 1942, BBC WRAC.
20. Ibid.
21. Ibid.
22. Memo from Val Gielgud, 1 July 1942, BBC WRAC.
23. Ibid.
24. Dallas Bower Internal Circulating Memo for "DFD," 2nd May 1942, BBC WRAC.
25. Ibid.
26. Ibid.
27. Ibid.
28. Memo from John Irwin, *BBC Radio Newsreel* to R. H. Eckersley, American Liaison Unit, 29 July 1942, BBC WRAC.
29. C. Gordon Glover, "Introducing—," *Radio Times*, 17 July 1942.
30. Cable Robert Foot to William Paley, 5 February 1943, BBC WRAC.
31. To A. D. F. from Elmer Davies CBS, 3 November 1942, BBC WRAC.
32. "Plays by Norman Corwin," from Anthony Brown to Play Library, 31 March 1953, BBC WRAC.

33. Ibid.
34. Ibid.
35. Raymond Raikes to Anthony Brown, Script Unit, Drama, 17 November 1953, BBC WRAC.
36. Tim Crook, *The Sound Handbook*, (London and New York: Routledge, 2011), 58–62.
37. "Press Cuttings," review, *Sunday Times*, October 30, 1955, BBC WRAC.
38. Norman Corwin, "This Is Document A/777," *Radio Times*, January 19, 1951.
39. Laurence Gilliam, "The O. Henry of Radio," *Radio Times*, August 24, 1945.
40. Ibid.
41. Corwin, *Untitled*, 52.
42. Gilliam, "The O. Henry of Radio."
43. Corwin, *Untitled*, 528.
44. Norman Corwin, *More by Corwin: 16 Radio Dramas by Norman Corwin*, (New York: Henry Holt, 1944), 41.
45. Corwin, *Untitled*, 193.
46. Ibid., 62.
47. Ibid., 75.
48. Ibid.
49. Ibid., 218.

BIBLIOGRAPHY

Bannerman, R. Leroy, *Norman Corwin and Radio: The Golden Years*, Tuscaloosa: University of Alabama Press, 1986.

Barnouw, Erik, *Radio Drama in Action: 25 Plays of a Changing World*, New York & Toronto: Farrar & Rinehart, 1945.

Barnouw, Erik, *The Golden Web: A History of Broadcasting in the United States*, vol. 2, 1933 to 1953, New York: Oxford University Press, 1968.

Bell, Douglas, and Corwin, Norman, *Years of the Electric Ear: Norman Corwin*, Lanham, MD, and Oxford: Scarecrow Press, 1994.

Blue, Howard, *Words at War: World War II Era Radio Drama and the Postwar Broadcasting Industry Blacklist*, Lanham, MD, and Oxford: Scarecrow Press, 2002.

Bradbury, Ray, *13 for Corwin: Estimates of Norman Corwin, the #1 Writer-Producer-Director during Radio's Golden Age*, Fort Lee, NJ: Barricade Books, 1985.

Bridson, Douglas Geoffrey, *Prospero and Ariel: The Rise and Fall of Radio: A Personal Recollection*, London: Victor Gollancz, 1971.

Cardiff, David, and Scannell, Paddy, *A Social History of Broadcasting*, vol. 1, *1922–1939*, London: Basil Blackwell, 1991.

Corwin, Norman, *Thirteen by Corwin: Radio Dramas by Norman Corwin*, New York: Henry Holt, 1942.

———, *This Is War! A Collection of Plays about America on the March*, New York: Dodd, Mead, 1942.

———, *More by Corwin: 16 Radio Dramas by Norman Corwin*, New York: Henry Holt, 1944.

———, *Untitled and Other Radio Dramas*, New York: Henry Holt, 1945.

———, "Foreword," *Journal of Radio Studies*, 5, no.1, 1998, pp. 2–5.

Coulter, Douglas ed., *Columbia Workshop Plays: 14 Radio Dramas*, London: McGraw-Hill, 1939.

Crook, Tim, *International Radio Journalism: History, Theory and Practice*, London and New York: Routledge, 1997.
——, *Radio Drama: Theory and Practice*, London and New York: Routledge, 1999.
——, *The Sound Handbook*, London & New York: Routledge, 2011.
——, "Norman Corwin's The Lonesome Train (Live Broadcast) CBS 1944," *RadioDoc Review*, 1, no. 1, 2014. http://ro.uow.edu.au/rdr/vol1/iss1/6.
Denning, Michael, *The Cultural Front: The Laboring of American Culture in the Twentieth Century*, New York: Verso, 1998.
Hilmes, Michele, "Missing from History: Langston Hughes' *The Man Who Went to War*," http://blog.commarts.wisc.edu/2015/06/12/missing-from-history-langston-hughes-the-man-who-went-to-war-2/.
Kaplan, Milton Allen, *Radio and Poetry*, New York: Columbia University Press, 1949.
Keith, Michael C., "Norman Corwin: Words in Flight—An Interview and Comments, *Journal of Radio Studies*, 5, no.2, 1998, pp. 55–65.
Keith, Michael, C., and Watson, Mary Ann, eds., *One World Flight: The Lost Journal of Radio's Greatest Writer*, London and New York: Continuum, 2009.
Langguth, Arthur John, (ed.) *Norman Corwin's Letters*, New York: Barricade Books, 1994.
Long, Paul, "British Radio and the Politics of Culture in Post-War Britain: The Work of Charles Parker," *Radio Journal: International Studies in Broadcast and Audio Media*, 2, no.3, 2004, pp. 131–52.
Verma, Neil, "Norman Corwin's People's Radio," in *Theater of the Mind: Imagination, Aesthetics, and American Radio Drama*, Chicago: University of Chicago Press, 2013.

Documents quoted from the BBC Written Radio Archives at Caversham (WRAC) are listed under the BBC's cataloguing of their files.

Scriptwriter Norman Corwin
   File I 1942–1959 WRAC, RCONT1- Norman Corwin
      Dallas Bower 'Thirteen by Corwin' Internal Circulating Memo for 'DFD' 2 May 1942 BBC WRAC
      Letter from Ed Murrow to Roger H. Eckersley 26 June 1942 BBC WRAC
      Memo on Norman Corwin from Val Gielgud 1 July 1942 WRAC
      Memo from John Irwin, BBC *Radio Newsreel*, to R. H. Eckersley, American Liaison Unit, 29 July 1942 BBC WRAC
      Laurence Gilliam to Norman Corwin letter 29 July 1942 BBC WRAC
      To A. D. F. from Elmer Davies CBS 3 November 1942 BBC WRAC
      Cable Robert Foot to William Paley 5 February 1943 BBC WRAC
      D G Bridson to Overseas Service memo 13 February 1943 BBC WRAC
      Plays by Norman Corwin from Anthony Brown to Play Library 31 March 1953 BBC WRAC
      Raymond Raikes to Anthony Brown. Script Unit, Drama 17 November 1953 BBC WRAC
      Press cuttings Sunday Times 30 October 1955 BBC WRAC
   File II 1963–1967 WRAC, RCONT2- Norman Corwin

    WRAC R47/150/1
        Corwin, Norman 1942–1945
    WRAC R8/329/1
        Drama Repertory Company, CBS Features: Corwin, Norman 1942

Radio Times Archive, Goldsmiths, University of London

Glover, C. Gordon, 'Introducing—' *Radio Times* 17 July 1942
Gilliam, Laurence, 'The O. Henry of Radio' *Radio Times* August 24, 1945
Corwin, Norman, 'This is Document A/777' *Radio Times* January 19, 1951

    The archivists and librarians of BBC Written Archives at Caversham, Kate O'Brien and Samantha Blake, and at Goldsmiths, University of London, Alice Measom and Lesley Ruthven, provided invaluable assistance for the research of this chapter.

9
—

THE ODYSSEY OF ME AND NORMAN CORWIN

David Ossman

The Bill of Rights doesn't offer freedom from speech. To silence an idea because it might offend a minority doesn't protect that minority. It deprives it of the tool it needs most—the right to talk back. Exemptions are for tax laws, not the Bill of Rights. Sure, it's a high price. But if you want a bargain-basement bill of rights, I know a lot of places you can get one. They're very quiet places because no one makes noise. Correctness silences noise. I say the more noise the better.
—NORMAN CORWIN, DECEMBER 1991

The book probably came to me on my birthday. I was at John Adams Junior High School then, so it must have been in 1950. Those were the black, white, and *noir* days in Los Angeles. It even snowed that winter, on our urban playground, which was normally covered with blacktop. Kids got to gym class by taking a tunnel under a major downtown LA street. Schoolwork on the west side, sports on the east.

Me, I hated junior high gym class. I was willing to change into gray shorts, but I sat out the games. It was a matter of principle with me, I guess. I wore glasses and the idea of someone throwing a ball at my face—which, of course, boys often do—allowed me somehow to rule myself out.

I made a deal. I read instead. One warm spring afternoon, sitting alone on a bench, I dipped into a new book—a pretty fat one called *The Fireside Book of Dog Stories*.* I wasn't much of a dog lover, but when I discovered you could open up the dust jacket and it would unfold into a giant "Dog Map of the World," I got more interested.

Inside I found comic drawings by James Thurber, a Jack London call-of-the-wild story, and, not so far in, a radio script. It was the first script I'd ever seen, and I'd been a radio fan since the year that script, "The Odyssey of Runyon Jones," was first presented—1941:

---

* *The Fireside Book of Dog Stories,* edited by Jack Goodman, Introduction by James Thurber, Simon & Schuster, New York, 1943.

> *Music. Introductory cue; plenty of harp and strings for glitter.*
> Runyon. (*timidly*) Is this the department of lost dogs?
>   Clerk. Yes.
> Runyon. I'm looking for my dog.

Wow! The lead actor in this play was a kid my age! Baseball, kickball, basketball on asphalt faded back into the rest of the city as I started to read the script aloud:

> "I'm looking for my dog."
>   "Runyon Jones."
>   "It's a terrible name, but Mother says I will like it when I grow up because it's distinguished, she says. The other boys call me Onion."

Funny already! Who wrote this stuff? Norman Corwin. The sixth of *26 by Corwin*. I'd never heard Corwin's CBS broadcasts, none of them. Like *The War of the Worlds*, I had to wait for the records to come out—78 rpm albums at first.

A little later in the script:

> *Assorted tick-tocks, including bells and chimes which keep striking under the following scene at various perspectives in the studio, some quite far off.*

Sound effects! And in this simple direction, Corwin revealed "how it's done" and "why it sounds like that." Perspectives. A first lesson in radio writing and directing right from the Master's pen.

Runyon Jones is in search of his dog, Pootzy. First he must navigate a Celestial bureaucracy—but his lost pup isn't to be found in Dog Heaven. Perhaps Curgatory! But you can't get to Curgatory from Heaven unless you go through Father Time, Mother Nature, a Magic Harp, and a Fearsome Giant!

Of course, Runyon will be reunited with Pootzy, but I won't tell you how. Spoiler alert! The end of the script never fails to bring tears to my eyes. "Not a dry eye in the house" we predict when we plan a production. Here're the last few words:

> *More footsteps. At length:*
> Runyon. Do I look all right?
> Officer. (*chuckling*) Oh, yes, Mr. Jones.
> *Clear, clean sound of doorknob and the beginning of the door opening, whereat there is an immediate dissolve into:*
> *Music. Conclusion.*

Corwin would publish all his scripts with precise notes both personal and technical. He adds three pages after the script, in which he tells where "the impulse to write this dog story" came from, gives a detailed guide to casting the play, directing the actors, constructing effects, including microphone placement and use of "echo."

It was incredibly generous of this genius-of-the-medium to share with everyone—especially me, wanting to know how to make radio plays—his intimate knowledge of how the medium works.

Not long after reading "Runyon Jones," I volunteered to write a script to celebrate George Washington's birthday. Of course I began with "Runyon" as a model. Using the junior high's classroom intercom system, I voiced, with a pal, my own totally Corwin-influenced radio script to celebrate George Washington's birthday. It was "broadcast" throughout the school.

It wasn't until the 1960s, after Network Radio's demise, that I had the opportunity to hear records of the most famous of Corwin's own radio plays, *On a Note of Triumph*, and begin to gauge the power of his language. *Triumph*'s repeat airing, following the astonishing V-E Day broadcast on May 8, 1945, was released by Columbia Records, "believing that this program should live on in its original form and not be lost on the evaporating air waves," on six 12-inch 78 rpm records in a popular album with notes proclaiming Corwin "an authentic phenomenon of the present age . . . one of the most eloquent, vigorous and tireless exponents of the cause of liberation." There was also a star-quality photograph of Corwin himself. He must have been hard to miss in the 1940s.

I searched for and collected radio scripts and production books published from the 1920s through the 1950s—most of Corwin, works by Archibald MacLeish and Arch Oboler—but no young writers I knew cared much about these relics from the pre-TV age.

Corwin himself had moved on to Hollywood and film writing. He was literally out of sight for a generation growing up in the sixties. Listeners who might be attracted to the Spoken Word section of the record store could take home Allen Ginsberg and Dylan Thomas, Shakespeare and Samuel Beckett, Lenny Bruce and Phyllis Diller, but except for *Hear It Now*, Norman's Golden Age was not spinning on the hi-fi turntable.

Troy Cummings, in his essay in this book on Corwin's early radio projects, notes that Norman learned his craft producing programs of poetry. These programs became more and more thematic, and the "continuity" or narrative between the poems became more and more important. It was in the writing of continuity that Corwin soon excelled. Quickly, the connections between poems or quotations became the meat of the program.

My radio production career followed a parallel path. In the early days, 1960, on WBAI in New York, we broadcast a regular reader of poems. Just the sort of show Corwin found lacking in his time. I developed an interview-and-reading series with younger "New American" poets, called *The Sullen Art*. Like Corwin I learned to write for radio by writing program continuity and, later, adapting the work of authors like Thoreau and e. e. cummings for the ear. This Corwin-inspired writing led, inevitably, to The Firesign Theatre's first LPs.

The last three years of the sixties provided a rare opportunity for some artistic freedom to rise again in major media. Columbia Records and AM radio, now fertilized by a decade of "underground" FM, allowed the creation of The Firesign Theatre as a sort of spoken rock band.

My Firesign partners (Peter Bergman, Phil Austin, and Phil Proctor) and I spent a good deal of our "writing" time in 1968 discussing Corwin and the radio production styles of the 1940s and '50s that we were then engaged in turning into multitrack comedy albums.

My working notes for our new album *How Can You Be in Two Places at Once, When You're Not Anywhere at All?* begin with the unfinished statement "The trouble with Norman Corwin . . . "

Corwin we mainly understood through his wartime tributes to America, Democracy, and the Common Man. That felt too rah-rah-America for us as Viet Nam blazed on, but Corwin's scale of studio production was huge and the live performances were usually stunning and star-filled. His work, we agreed, reveled in both poetry and common speech, had a strong, emotional story line, and employed music as a rich texture throughout.

In the postwar years, Corwin's style of production had waned and most broadcasts were half hours of popular genre entertainment. They were easy to spoof.

The B side of *How Can You Be in Two Places at Once*, "Nick Danger, Third Eye," was based on comedy radio detective characters of the early 1950s on shows like *Sam Spade* and *Johnny Dollar*. "Nick" was originally meant to be a one-off half-hour radio comedy, in the manner of Norman Corwin's famous *Thirteen*, since we had recently performed a dozen weekly live-radio half hours in a cabaret setting.

In the spirit of anarchy, Firesign sent up all the common conventions of studio-based radio production and reminded old-timers of the countless gaffes, in-jokes, and hazing that were a well-known part of network radio history. My character Catherwood is particularly pesky in revealing that the sound of fire is really cellophane and, worse, that he's run out of script pages.

The A side however, bearing our lengthy philosophical question as its title, begins in a hallowed Los Angeles location—the Used Car Lot—and ends up with an extended "movie musical" USO-style production number, "Bringing the War Back Home." The atmosphere of wartime in 1968 brought Firesign back to the wartime of Corwin and his "voices of the people" style of both dramatic and documentary writing.

The Lonesome Train, a very popular play by Millard Lampell and Earl Robinson, which Corwin directed in 1944, was still being played on the radio from the Decca record release. The mixture of patriotism, sentimentality, and celebrity, so extraordinarily well-mixed in Corwin's day, seemed like an apt and more complex format to have fun with.

Compare Firesign's closing musical revue with these lines from Lampell:

> And you know who Lincoln's people were? / A Brooklyn blacksmith, a Pittsburgh preacher, / A small-town tailor, a back-woods teacher, / An old store-keeper shaking his head, / handing over a loaf of bread, / A buffalo-hunter telling a story / Out of the Oregon territory. / They were his people; he was their man.

Lonesome Train came out of the Almanac Singers, possibly the earliest performers in the mid-century revival of American folk music (the group included Lampell and Pete Seeger), and was an influence on Corwin as well:

> We can tell you, Hirohito
> Now that Hitler's down,
> Better buy a black kimono,
> Cause you're on your last go-round.
>
> Round and round Hitler's grave,
> Round and round we go.
> Gonna lay that fellow down,
> So he won't get up no mo'.

That from "On a Note of Triumph," and this from "Between Americans":

> America is all things to all her people—prairie to Nebraskans, coal to Scranton miners, cameras and raw celluloid to the picture boys in Hollywood, the stink of crude oil to the men who work the wells . . . Sure, sure. That's the way it goes. Or isn't it? What does this country mean to you?

And a bit later, voices chant, "Mill towns . . . steel towns . . . tobacco towns . . . mining towns . . . cotton towns . . . farmhouses . . . railroad sidings . . . " and so forth.

There was a tempo, a rhythm, a thrust to Corwin's language and also to his style as a director of talented actors that lent itself to impeccable performance.

Here's a bit of *How Can You Be*'s "The American Pageant" dialogue coming after a stirring parody of a sixties anthem:

> *Babe.* This land is made of mountains!
> This land is made of mud!
> This land has lots of everything
> For me and Elmer Fudd! . . .
>
> *Joe.* Stop!

Desk Clerk. It wasn't always like that!

Joe. No. First they had to come from towns with strange names like . . .

Eddie. Smegma!

DC. Spasmodic!

Eddie. Frog!

Joe. And the far-flung Isles of Langerhans.

Babe. But who were they?

Joe & Eddie. They were small, angry men, with hairy faces and burning feet . . . We was running away from Poverty, Intolerance, the Army and the Law . . . and the Army . . .

DC. And we took to them!

Eddie. And they took to us!

DC. And what do you think they took?

Chanting Chorus. Oil from Canada! Gold from Mexico! Geese from their neighbor's backyard! Boom, boom! Corn from the Indians! Tobacco from the Indians! Dakota from the Indians! New Jersey from the Indians! New Hampshire from the Indians! New England from the Indians! New Delhi from the Indians! . . .

Babe. Indonesia for the Indonesians!

Joe. Yes, and Veteranarian's Day . . .

DC. So how about that, Mr. Smarty-Pants Communist? Mr. College Professor? Mr. Beatnik? Mr. Hippie? What have you done for *me* lately?

Firesign was also drawn to Corwin's experience as a blacklisted writer during a decade that destroyed so many Hollywood careers. As Los Angeles–based writers ourselves, we worked in the same studios, both radio and film, that Corwin inhabited and in which the blight of the blacklist still could be felt.

Firesign's third album, *Don't Crush That Dwarf, Hand Me the Pliers,* released in 1970, features as the lead character a Hollywood radio and film writer-director who had been blacklisted; alone in his Hollywood Hills bungalow, he watches his life unfold via the Late Show. If not exactly based on Corwin, "George Tirebiter" was certainly suggested by what I knew of his experience.

I had been a friend of Ray Bradbury's since I was 16. We met at the Los Angeles Science Fantasy Society and at SF conventions; we corresponded. I wrote a radio adaptation of "Mars Is Heaven" for him. I occasionally visited with him at his home. He encouraged me (and thousands of others) and shared stories and told me how to write: "Everyday!!" He even called me one of his "sons!"

One day in 1971 I walked into a vast soundstage at the old Desilu/RKO studios in Hollywood, where Ray was mounting a production of *Leviathan '99*. It was a big show, Moby Dick in Space, with a lot of sound and lights. There, on stage, no doubt giving sage advice to Ray, was *his* lifelong friend and mentor, Norman Corwin. So it was that I finally embraced my "father" in the audio medium.

Reintroducing Norman to the new generation of radio producers, I directed a live broadcast production of "The Odyssey of Runyon Jones" in October 1989 at the tenth anniversary of the Midwest Radio Theater Workshop. The event had been created by community radio pals from Missouri who enlisted Peter Bergman and me to retrain actors, writers, and audio technicians in the art and craft of Live Radio Theater. Norman's art and craft.

Norman gave his blessing to the MRTW "Runyon Jones"; I found a perfect young man out of the middle of Missouri to play Runyon and, naturally, followed Norman's casting and directing advice. Norman himself introduced the play live.

The music and musical effects, vital to any production, came off almost as well as in the original and, as predicted, when the closing music ended, there was nary a dry eye in the house.

It was at that very Radio Theater Workshop in Columbia that the idea of a new radio production of Norman's 1941 presidentially commissioned, all-network, 150th anniversary celebration of the Bill of Rights, *We Hold These Truths*, arose. Richard Fish, a workshop participant and record producer from Bloomington, Indiana, remembers that he'd brought a copy of *More By Corwin* to the event, got to reading it, and noticed the impending anniversary. Anniversaries were the perfect excuse to produce big radio shows.

My wife and partner, Judith Walcutt, who was the Workshop's broadcast producer, and I had started our "radio movie studio" career with *The War of the Worlds 50th Anniversary Production,* which reached out to eager listeners on some thousand radio stations worldwide, and here was another 50th event for Otherworld Media!

It looked a little too big for the Missouri Workshop to handle, and Judith thought it might be fundable as a stand-alone program with the possibility of very wide broadcast carriage. After all, it was the 200th anniversary of the Bill of Rights.

Norman's original live broadcast had been heard by more than 60 million people. Jimmy Stewart narrated. Orson Welles, Walter Huston, Marjorie Main, and Edward G. Robinson were among the cast. FDR spoke from Washington. The Japanese had struck Pearl Harbor only eight days before the live broadcast on December 15, 1941.

We might have known better than to attempt the show if we'd read the Master's postscript notes. Corwin was burned out from writing and directing twenty-six relentless weeks of half-hour live shows. He was given twenty-six days to write and prepare the broadcast. With no research assistant (and no Google!), in order to even begin the writing, Norman spent twelve of those precious days learning as much as he could about the long and complicated struggle to get the Bill of Rights passed in 1791.

Norman had always been a last-minute kind of writer. He had trouble with the script. No doubt the one-hour format was a challenge after writing so many half-hours. Radio drama, at its simplest, is a narrative voice, and Corwin often used this voice (a poet, an announcer, an observer) and cast it with great skill.

He wrote and rewrote. His narrative line had a long way to go to create the important dramatic arc. With eleven days remaining before broadcast, Norman boarded the 20th Century Limited, where he was to start his fifth draft, secluded in his compartment. The script was still unfinished when Corwin arrived in LA on December 9 with six days to go before broadcast. The producers were worried.

Cross-fade as almost fifty years pass. Among the participants at the Midwest Workshop was a radio producer from Michigan, Michael Packer, who volunteered to raise some grant money for the venture. Judith and I contacted Norman, who remembered the original broadcast in detail (no surprise), said of course he'd be interested, and wished us luck in our quest for funding.

Almost a year passed. Judith and I had been living on Whidbey Island, Washington, since just before the birth of our son, Orson, featured as the "Crying Baby" in *WOW 50th*. Orson was now three and very popular "on the road" with his parents, so naturally he joined us on our trip to California to see Mr. Corwin in early October 1990. Norman lived near the UCLA campus and not far from Ray Bradbury's home in Cheviot Hills.

I remember Norman's bachelor apartment as being charged with his incredible lifetime. As a matter of fact, at eighty, he was going through his archives and the extra bedroom was filled with boxes and papers in mid-sort. I especially admired the large polished bookcase, shelves filled with leather-bound copies of his radio scripts. There were piles of books, beautiful rocks, crystals and geodes on flat surfaces everywhere and potted plants in the window, catching the California sun.

Norman, elegant and gracious as ever, welcomed us and our small, talkative son into his home. We adults, somewhat dazzled to be in the Master's lair, gushed on about this and that. Norman wondered who Michael Packer was and was irritated by an insinuation that any producers would sit in judgment on his "rewrites." Oops!

We explained Michael was looking for grant money for *We Hold These Truths 200* and it seemed he was beginning to get somewhere. "We will soon have the funds to cover your writer's fee," we said, hopefully, and in no shape or form would any of us rewrite Norman Corwin.

Little Orson, not in it for the business part, began to investigate his surroundings.

As it happened, among Norman's treasures was a cache of marbles. There were beautiful aggies and cat's-eyes and a child-size handful of translucent clear glass marbles. Their sheen reflected the sunny apartment windows like miniature soap bubbles. Orson came back and showed us. Beautiful.

"You can have those if you like them, Orson," said Mr. Corwin.

Orson looked curiously to his parents.

"You can have Mr. Corwin's marbles," said Judith.

We all looked at each other.

"That's quite something, to have Norman Corwin's marbles," I said, and we all laughed.

A few days later, after I had sent Norman a pitch about *Truths,* he wrote, "Great thanks. I am rushing off to the O.T.R. bash in Newark, but I just wanted to let you know that I appreciate your letter, and will give careful study to the B of R project in light of what you have written. More later."

It should be noted here that in 1941 Corwin was under contract to the Columbia Broadcasting System and also that his programs were unsponsored, or "sustaining" in the parlance of the day. His artistry was widely recognized. Both CBS and NBC underwrote "cultural" programming, and Corwin had become a star producer.

By the 1990s, public radio, in its various forms, was supported by underwriting in a variety of ways endemic to the nonprofit model. NPR and a few major stations might commission new programs, but radio theatre was not generally among them. An alliance with one of these production-oriented centers was necessary for distribution if you were an "independent" producer.

Some stations had seed money and offered their names to grant applications. The National Endowments for the Arts and Humanities and the Corporation for Public Broadcasting had been the principal sources for funds. The NEA was under perpetual Congressional attack, and its own funding diminished. Corporations might be found to underwrite radio productions. Foundations, even individuals could be approached.

Our budget for *WOW 50th* had come from an NEA grant and a much-later, much-needed major grant from McGavren Guild, a media representation corporation. Since doing a radio production in any way equal to the original *Truths* required an orchestral score, a huge star-filled cast, and perhaps even the president himself, not to mention commissioning Norman to do an updated script, we knew we'd have to round up our production funds from more than one underwriter. The broadcast date, December 15, 1991, loomed a doable year away. Judith began to cast around for grant money.

In the meantime we were asked by WETA, Washington DC's public radio station, to write and produce another epic, *The Empire of the Air,* embracing the history of radio in the first fifty years of the twentieth century through the lives of its creators, Howard Armstrong, Lee De Forest, and David Sarnoff. Our radio drama would be due for broadcast in February 1992, barely a couple of months after *We Hold These Truths*. Both needed a lot of production money.

As we went about funding these two large-scale productions, we naturally supposed the Corwin broadcast would be quickly underwritten by a major corporation and the standing committee funding the activities around the celebration of the Constitution. The U.S. government, however, was in hostile hands.

This is the sole entry on *Truths* from Judith's journal, post-uplink and broadcast, January 1992:

> We went through every possible emotion with the recent program, *We Hold These Truths*. I really felt that a huge spiritual war was being waged through us, for which we were puppets. It was difficult from the beginning and remained so to the end. Raising the money was nearly impossible. When at last the NEA saved us, I felt suddenly that the project had been lifted up out of the mire and made a vehicle for all of us to make a statement for the First Amendment—for true liberty and the right of Americans to keep speaking their minds. The struggle to get a major cast never ceased.
>
> Even in the end. Some people were there because they believed in Norman, some, I would say, were there for the Bill of Rights and some just for the money, pitiful as it sounds. But I will never forget working with Norman Corwin, who tested every fiber of my mind and patience and whom I will love as a rightful member of my family forever.

All of us will always love Norman, but it was, as Judith writes, "difficult from the beginning and remained so to the end." Even after a small grant had been obtained from the Ahmanson Foundation to cover the option on his old script, Norman resisted taking on the task of writing a new one. He wanted to be assured we had the entire budget covered before he started. "At my age I'm not going to write something that won't be produced," he declared.

We drew on our relationship with WETA, where Mary Beth Kirschner was national program director for radio. She and WETA's management were enthusiastic. WETA added some money to the pot, but nothing more was in sight. We were stalled. Pitches went out to the biggest supporters of public radio and, we hoped, the Bill of Rights, including the Pew Charitable Trusts.

On March 1, 1991, we seemed to have done it. WETA had a "go" from Philip Morris. The needed funds would arrive just in time. Norman, however, immediately refused to accept money from Philip Morris. Our main hope now was the Washington Commission on the Bicentennial, whose head was Chief Justice Warren Burger.

On March 30, I noted in my journal, "In spite of much enthusiasm and even $ from WETA, *We Hold These Truths* has run out of the money and today we found out the official Washington Bicentennial Commission had turned down funding."

We were devastated! Wait a minute! The august body that had been distributing pocket Constitution souvenirs since back in September 1987 and that was created to commemorate, besides the Constitution, "the formation of the three branches of government, and the Bill of Rights" had turned us down? The Commission's chairman was Ted Kennedy—how can this be?

Alas, our friend Michael had gone begging to Washington with no political influence behind him and, I wrote, "Natch, the commission was packed with rightwingers who took one look at Norman Corwin's name and trashed it out of hand. Now I'm not sure it can be saved, and it was a shoe-in, or seemed to be, a week before."

Not that we could let it go. *Truths* continued to take up a lot of our time, even though we had two or three proposals before the National Endowment for the Arts—pilots for *Radio Noir,* a mystery series meant to be produced on location; a series of audio plays by women writers, beginning with Ursula K. Le Guin; and Otherworld Air, a hugely ambitious project to create a multichannel spoken-word cable service. We were asking the NEH to fund a radio adaptation of *Gulliver's Travels.* We were trying to make progress on all fronts.

On May Day 1991, WETA signed an agreement with General Motors ("The Mark of Excellence") to underwrite *Empire of the Air.* With that piece in place, only six weeks remained before I had to have finished the first draft of a 90-minute *Empire* script. Right then, we hit on the idea of pursuing Garrison Keillor for The Citizen, the narrator of *Truths,* in hopes that his attachment would generate interest and revenue as soon as possible.

Truths dragged on. Things picked up with *Empire.* In June we traveled to Saratoga Springs to meet with Tom Lewis, who had himself just finished the nonfiction book our radio drama and a Ken Burns television documentary were to be based on: *Empire of the Air: The Men Who Made Radio.* Tom had been sending me chapters week by week and I was through with the first draft, influenced, of course, by Norman's lessons in craft.

No sooner had we arrived at the historic Adelphi Hotel than we had a call from the Pew Charitable Trusts. The Pew was interested in *Truths.* Judith immediately had to file a grant application. Of course, the only script we had was the 1941 original, which we knew had become politically dated.

Judith composed a lengthy fax assuring the Pew that "As Mr. Corwin proceeds with the contemporization of his script, we will provide him with all necessary resources to do a fair and accurate rewrite, including constitutional scholars and consultants to insure historical accuracy and a non-partisan approach to the current interpretation of the crucial issues."

Proceeding to jump through the next few hoops and protect Norman, Judith wrote, "He embraces the necessity for historical accuracy and a non-partisan viewpoint, but abhors any insinuation of censorship in the creative endeavor of bringing the crucial issues to light. For a man of his years and experience, this is an understandable concern."

A month later Judith was able to report to the Pew that *Truths* had received support from the American Booksellers Foundation for Free Expression and in August the Bicentennial Commission changed its august mind and came through with a $10,000 grant. Not nearly enough.

We thought perhaps if Norman spoke directly to the Commission's director of educational programs, one Dr. Herbert Atherton of Yale, he might be able to get that pecuniary amount increased.

On September 10, Norman responded with thanks to Dr. Atherton, who had sent him a package of publications. "As for next December," Norman wrote, "any hour-long presentation of the origins, history, and pertinence of the Bill of Rights on its 200th, must of necessity be a crowded canvas, especially since it has to accommodate not ten but seventeen amendments, the last two of which were not on the books at the time of the broadcast in 1941."

He continued with a tidy explanation of his well-practiced "simple" writing and production style:

> There will be need, more even than in that vintage production, for bold, simple, symbolic strokes to present the rights amendments as the spinal cord of the Constitution, and to indicate their significance in our lives today. Because of this it will be necessary to sacrifice academic inlays, footnoting, and exegesis. Elements of the approach I refer to are suggested in the original broadcast's treatment of minor characters and the Citizen narrator.
>
> By simple of course I don't mean ingenuous or unsophisticated, but clear, cogent, and assimilable. The material you sent me manages to be all that, and thus admirably serves its purpose. What the broadcast must convey in addition to information, is emotion that is not forced, but legitimate. Since issues of human rights more often than not engender powerful sentiments and passions, it would be remiss to shun that aspect.

Oh my, we thought, now is when we need Garrison Keillor! But the shy Minnesotan turned us down.

And then, unexpectedly, the Pew turned us down. They had problems with the proposal, not the least being the 1941 script, with few women in the cast, let alone in history, and virtually no representation of the diverse country America was rapidly becoming. Judith promised that Norman would correct that. She reminded them that Norman had been a blacklisted writer in Hollywood based on his liberal politics, no matter how well he had served his country during and after World War II with universally admired patriotic documentaries and dramas.

Maybe that was the key. (Norman claimed he was only "graylisted," but even that runs up against an Amendment or two.) In any case, the Pew did finally make the grant—on October 24—seven weeks to broadcast. We could finally ask Norman to start writing. Dr. Leonard Levy, a noted Constitutional scholar we'd contacted became Norman's historical advisor, but not until October 28, when we received funding from the Pew Trusts.

Whew! But with reservations.

Otherworld Media suddenly had a complicated portfolio of productions.

Two large casts had to be assembled for recording dates in Los Angeles. *Empire* was to be recorded in September at the Evergreen Studios in Burbank—a recording center well-known to every limo driver in LA. We would spend a week at the Oakwood Apartments in Van Nuys casting, then two more weeks recording twenty-four reels of voice-tracks, over 570 takes, which I would bring home and have edited in time for twelve days in the studio with master tech producer Fred Jones, scheduled for January 1992.

Of course, we didn't really know yet how many actors we would need for Norman's new script. We felt it wouldn't be that difficult, since Norman was a well-loved fixture in Hollywood and many of his friends would surely volunteer. How about Jimmy Stewart for The Citizen?

Norman wanted his old collaborator Bernard Herrmann, who wrote the original music for *Truths,* to compose a score for the new one. In the interests of equal opportunity, we asked a friend, NPR producer Deborah Jane Lamberton, then an announcer and programmer at WETA, to help produce this part of the production. She contacted her friend, Libby Larsen, a well-known Minnesota composer, who agreed to write and conduct the music for what could run over thirty "cues." A recording session was set for early December.

We also set Fred Jones as the technical producer and once again booked Evergreen Studios so that our stars would arrive on schedule. All of this seemed to give us a comfortable couple of weeks leading up to our satellite uplink on December 15.

In the meantime, back in July, Judith and I had accepted two irresistible jobs. Out of our familiar radio milieu, we took a commission to write a television mystery. *The Smoking Salmon* won a Regional Emmy for KCET in Seattle, but it wasn't our moment to jump media ships. At the same time, Judith was working with fantasy writer Ellen Kuschner on a Halloween special starring the great voice artist June Foray, scheduled to record in Boston in August. I had gigs in Chicago and LA before going to Missouri to produce a play for the Midwest Radio Theater Workshop in October.

Shades of Norman Corwin and CBS! Coast-to-coast, and not via the 20th Century Limited!

Judith and I were suddenly summoned to New York to present the American Public Radio board with our projected radio adaptation of *Empire,* of which only the opening couple of minutes and one short scene were actually playable. I had to leave Missouri in the midst of rehearsals for what was clearly going to be a high-pressure presentation.

To make it ultimately Corwinesque, someone had invited Frank Stanton—who had been president of CBS Radio from 1946 to 1971, was among the most formidable executives in the industry, and had been Norman's boss during the period when radio was becoming a jukebox instead of an art form—to "drop in." (Mr. Stanton had telegraphed Norman, "Grand job," after the original broadcast.) His unexpected presence was unexpectedly terrifying. It looked as if our *Empire* could crumble from the penthouse down.

Norman had begun faxing us a few pages starting in the late summer. By the middle of October, with me back at the MRTW, he had sent Judith "roughly two-thirds of the script." He explained, "since there is no transcript record of what was actually said at any of the big deliberations, I am entitled to extrapolations, and I have made them. This goes off in such haste that I have not been able to bind the pages. Back to grind."

After MRTW and a few days home, I was off to Cleveland. The "final" latest rewrite of *We Hold These Truths* arrived via fax while I was there. Judith wrote, "Crazy day. James Earl Jones confirmed. Jimmy Stewart is nibbling." My journal says it pretty clearly: "Came home to plunge into the anxiety of money, casting, music and production. How Judith did it I don't know, but she, and we, did."

On November 2 we received a fax from Norman: "As I bear down on the most demanding part of the script, I am troubled by a sense that the Rights project has never been very well glued together, and is now becoming unglued."

The problems were several, one taken care of quickly. Our erstwhile partner Michael Packer had sent a draft contract agreement to Norman without our knowledge. Responsibility for the entire project was now in the hands of WETA's legal department, and we told Michael he had confused Norman badly and that he had to go.

Norman's fax continued, "You assured me last week that the Sparks contract was null and void . . . But now I find myself toiling away, the prisoner of a deadline, without any agreement in hand. Nor have I received a penny in advance for weeks of work."

Overwhelmed by the relentless pressure to find money, to house and meet with the scholarly Dr. Levy, to respond to his suggestions, and to conduct the continuing casting calls for name actors, we had not responded immediately to Norman's first draft material. "If the delay is because you decided to first submit copies to Levy, the Pew Foundations, the Bicentennial Commission, WETA and Packer, for their opinions before forming your own, then you violate the understanding we reached early on, that the script is not subject to approval by APR or the Commission or the foundation or anybody else."

Ouch!

We prepared an agreement to cover Otherworld Media's relationship with Norman Corwin. Unfortunately, the wording suggested to Norman that now Judith and I would, in some way, continue to have "veto power" over the writing.

On November 7, he wrote, "I am suspending work on the script until certain things are straightened out."

By November 11 we had managed to straighten out the agreement, but a huge issue still separated us from Norman. "It saddens me," he wrote Judith, "that you and David see fit to make this a contest of wills." The script pages as they were arriving resembled the 1941 original in its exclusion of women and what we used to call "minorities." This was a crucial issue for our funders and for Judith personally. She and Dr. Levy had been sending suggestions to Norman and he hadn't integrated any of them into the material we'd seen so far.

On that same November 11, after a weekend meeting with Dr. Levy, I wrote Norman with several pages of "comments and factual suggestions." Nearly all were in the "first act" of the script. "Some are easy to fix," I wrote, heart in throat, "others present larger concerns. All this information is meant to help in what we recognize to be a complicated and difficult project. We're here to help. Please call us."

Dr. Levy wrote back, with a brief professorial critique of my comments ("good job, on the whole") and added some corrections to his own thoughts.

On November 14, Judith wrote to Mary Beth Kirschner at WETA, "We are totally up to our eyebrows and probably over our heads." Speaking of Dr. Atherton of the Bicentennial Commission,

> Why can't Atherton see that we can't cast without the $ to guarantee the offers???? Doesn't he see that this project will be doomed if we don't know the funding answer soon??? HOW can I call up Jimmy Stewart, Gregory Peck etc. without knowing the answer to the funding conundrum. Does he know that Norman wouldn't start writing until he felt assured that the production would move forward which wasn't until the Pew $ came in? ... A man 83 years of age doesn't want to spend his time writing something that will never see the light of day.

The rumor was that Ted Kennedy and Phyllis Schlafly had had a knock-down-drag-out over the Bill of Rights and that the Senator had prevailed. WETA was to receive a further grant to help with the educational piece of the production.

It wasn't until November 15 that Judith could contact our composer, Libby Larsen, about any progress. "I guess the script, such as it is, arrived," she wrote. "We are still waiting for the completion material, though we did just get a bunch more pages by fax which I am faxing on to you. The extant script will have to be recut and reshaped somewhat.

We are going to try and get some things in there that aren't there yet, so others will have to go, since, even before completion, we are over time (ain't it the way!)."

More questions went out from us to Levy on the 16th, who was testy about Norman's responses so far but provided a few more sources.

A new batch of pages arrived on November 17. Dr. Levy wrote:

> I think they are excellent—good history, good drama. . . . I just spoke to you and then called Norman. He seemed ecstatic in response to my praise. And, he was talking about a way to *end* the program by developing a thought from Jefferson that freedom is boisterous. . . . I kept stressing the material sent to him. I said I hadn't met him and did not know whether he had a problem reading. He said he had no problem, so I urged him to read what was sent, because sometimes the historical truths and facts are better than fiction and even better than literary license. He laughed and said he would read the stuff. . . . I'm glad I called Norman.

Both of us continued to do research and pass it along.

Norman's pages were being sent to and checked by Dr. Levy, who wondered why, by the end of November, he hadn't heard from anyone and there was no new script for him to look at.

What was happening in the three weeks remaining before our studio date was the actual writing and rewriting of what finally would become the script we used to record. If there was a "contest of wills" between Norman and Judith, Judith was on the side of history.

"I wanted you to know why," she faxed on November 19, "I have been leaning heavily on the inclusion of some of these materials in the script."

> I think it's because of what I have seen in my lifetime and believe to be right and true, that I am convinced of the importance of taking into account 50 years of scholarship since 1941, which has revealed the importance of the roles women, black people, and Native Americans in how we, the people of 1991, can interpret earlier American history and the Bill of Rights.
>
> Occasionally you have suggested that I am working on some sort of quota system for women and minorities in the program. The word "quota" seems to me to be one of those words which, like "liberal," has taken on derogatory meanings in the mouth of the current political regime. I am surprised to hear you use it, after what you've seen and experienced in your lifetime.
>
> I would never want to be thought of as "fulfilling a quota," when what I am doing is fulfilling a strong moral commitment to recognize the contributions which women and people of color have made in shaping our collective history.

Judith attached twenty-five pages of quotations and references, including Sojourner Truth, Frederick Douglass, Chief Seattle, and Chief Joseph. We spoke and argued at length with Norman, who resumed his work at last.

Corwin's original script was, like much of radio at the time, virtually female-free. The demands of the moment, and of the funding organizations, and of the producers pushed Norman into including many more voices, including Carrie Chapman Catt as a conarrator with The Citizen.

On November 22 he faxed,

> Here are 18 pages of revised script, accommodating all the historical and factual corrections made by Leonard and adding new scenes. I have also cut several scenes, and there is not a single page unaffected by changes.... Thanks to my cuts I am able to bring Carrie Catt in 15 or more pages earlier than in the first version. I am using Sojourner Truth in the House of Women's Rights at the Exposition, where she will be one of the effigies along with Aaron Burr and the editor of Puck. Douglass will be used also, and I have hopes for the Indian.

We now faced two weeks' time before our first studio day with actors, Saturday, December 7, the fiftieth anniversary of Pearl Harbor. We were running almost exactly on Norman's beleaguered 1941 schedule and remained in a continuous state of creative panic.

We called on Deborah Lamberton to join us in LA, where she produced the Libby Larsen music recording and mix on December 1 and 2. She would stay to log the studio takes on the coming weekend. We rang up Richard Fish in Bloomington and offered him "Associate Producer" if he'd come out and help. He arrived Friday, December 6, my fifty-fifth birthday, which we celebrated at Musso & Frank's, a Hollywood Boulevard fixture since the 1920s. Martini, lamb chops, creamed spinach. It was my last meal. I enjoyed it.

The doors opened at Evergreen Recording at 8:30 on Saturday morning. Our team was in place—Corwin, Kirschner, Jones, Lamberton, Fish, Walcutt, Ossman.

Ed Asner arrived. He was booked as The Editor and, not surprisingly, he looked the part. Asner stayed around most of the day and schmoozed. A *Wall Street Journal* reporter, John McDonough, who had been following the progress of *Truths* for a while, arrived and observed, taking notes. *Entertainment Tonight* sent a camera crew. Stars, personalities, and creatures of Hollywood arrived every few minutes, swooping in and out like air traffic at Newark. Norman greeted and embraced them all. Miraculously, there were scripts to give them.

We had reached widely for the putative "stars" of *Truths,* The Citizen and Carrie Chapman Catt. The hunt had not brought us any of the few remaining "names" of Old Hollywood. Where were the trusted voices of authority?

Close to our studio date, we gratefully received a gift from Steve Bochco, the writer and cocreator of NBC's hit *L.A. Law,* a large-cast law-office drama that ran from 1986 to 1994. Bochco had grown up "on Norman's knee," as he put it, and we now had two of his stars—Richard Dysart and Jill Eikenberry. Dysart was popular enough to win an Emmy in 1992 for his role as Leland McKenzie and had a well-mannered New England voice. He sounded the part and was solid and secure.

The *Truths* script had been parsed into about forty sequences, many of which featured completely different casts. There were also numerous solo readings, including all the Amendments and the Citizen's narration plus a couple of rousing tavern scenes with music and patriotic song.

We began with Asner, Dysart, and Brenda Vacarro as "Mercy Warren" and moved on through a long day that included being very nice to Norman Lear—a particular friend of Norman's. My Firesign partner Phil Proctor also stayed through the day, filling in bit parts when necessary and helping (with his Irish tenor) in the tavern scenes. We ended at 6:45 P.M., after 123 takes. Norman listened as we recorded them all and made his choices. Judith wrote checks.

The call for Sunday was 10:00 A.M. for James Earl Jones. Here was our biggest star name, complete with chauffeur and a secretary. As Richard Fish remembers, "He was an extremely nice guy, gentle and thoughtful." Jones was cast as "The Actor," a role played by Orson Welles in 1941. Welles was the actor to whom Corwin refers in his fascinating postscript essay as starting "an emotional passage at too high a pitch."

In 1991, the Actor's speech ran nearly three full pages. We spent an hour rehearsing the script. It is no secret that Jones is dyslexic. Once he has memorized a part, he has no problem delivering it at Academy Award level. Reading off a page is another matter. Recording began at 11:00 and continued for an hour. Jones took a break before the final piece, the First Amendment, and Ray Bradbury stepped in the studio to voice a short speech by John Adams.

When he returned, Jones nailed the reading: "Congress shall make no law respecting an establishment of religion, or prohibiting the free exercise thereof; or abridging the freedom of speech, or of the press; or the right of the people peacefully to assemble, and to petition the government for a redress of grievances." We looked at one another in the control room and noted the moment that Darth Vader, or was it Jack Jefferson or maybe King Lear, intoned the forty-five words that made us free.

Most of the rest of Sunday was devoted to scenes between The Citizen and Carrie Chapman Catt. Norman himself dropped in to voice Aaron Burr. George American Horse played Red Jacket, and Robert Hooks played Frederick Douglass. Rod McKuen stopped by to play Steven Vincent Benét. The last couple of hours (we broke at 8:00 P.M.) involved a number of actors still in the studio bringing their voices to a final montage of words from the Amendments.

Richard Dysart, tired as we all were, recorded the final paragraph of Norman's script: "All these rights Americans have. But none to be taken for granted . . . They are all ours. Enjoy them, honor them . . . Protect them."

Judith wrote more checks. We were five days from an all-network uplink—CBS, NBC, ABC, Unistar, and Mutual Radio, thanks to a collaborative promotional effort led by the National Association of Broadcasters and American Public Radio. It was the first such broadcast since the original in 1941.

There were several actors who were unavailable for the weekend recording sessions. Esther Rolle, who had played Lady Macbeth in the Haitianized Orson Welles Broadway production and was best known for her long-running role as Florida Evans in *Good Times,* did Sojourner Truth while we were in postproduction. Lamberton and Fish we sent to Santa Barbara to record Fess Parker as A Virginian. Fish, a coonskin-cap-wearing fan of Davy Crockett's was mighty impressed when Parker told him, "Well, remember what Davy Crockett always said: 'Be sure you're right, then go ahead!'"

Well, Davy, we weren't sure about anything. We had a total of 328 takes to sort through and edit. There were more than five-and-a-half hours of recorded voicetracks. Some of the editing was self-evident. In a very few cases there was only one good take of a scene or speech. In most cases, razor blades and splicing tape were in heavy use. Everyone on the crew set to work on editing blocks, hoping to reduce the total time to something anywhere near sixty minutes.

As in 1941, the production ultimately had to be timed to the second. Norman, as director of a studio cast, dealing with live broadcast conditions, had only a dress rehearsal to time out the show and make any cuts necessary. We had three days of editing and mixing ahead of us.

Sometime during the week Judith finally had time to calculate that she had written so many checks to so many actors that Otherworld's bank account was overdrawn to the point of atomic brinksmanship. Literally in the last possible seconds, on December 10, the National Endowment for the Arts came through with a final grant.

The Endowment, under John Frohnmayer, had been under continuous assault from the right, especially from Pat Buchanan. Our grant was so controversial that Frohnmayer signed the authorization just before he and his family left for Christmas vacation. He resigned shortly after.

On December 13, McDonough's article appeared in the *Wall Street Journal.* He began it in a blaze of truth:

> This weekend American Public Radio and writer/director Norman Corwin will tackle a very touchy subject. One that often divides America. A subject so fraught with potential controversy that when producers Judith Walcutt and David Ossman solicited 150 of America's largest corporations and foundations for funding, not a single one was willing to lend its name or money to the program. What is this too-hot-to-handle PR pariah that has frightened off many of our most distinguished philanthropic institutions? Take a deep breath, folks. It's the U.S. Bill of Rights.

We were all greatly cheered, but deep in editing.

Lamberton returned to Washington, where she recorded an "afterword" by Chief Justice Burger. Ironically, Burger had communicated with WETA on November 15, "I write you as Chief Justice to ask what you are doing on December 15th to take note of the 200th anniversary of the Bill of Rights? What can we do to be helpful?"

We had given Burger a short speech, identical to the one read by Corwin that opens the program: "200 years ago, on December 15th, the Bill of Rights became part of the Constitution of the United States. The most vital part."

Lamberton faxed back an urgent message. Burger wanted to rewrite the final sentence to read "a vital part of our system of justice." Corwin scrawled on the fax, "that's implicit—spoils the rhythm." He then sat down and wrote thirty seconds' worth of clichés, and we faxed them back. We tacked Burger on to the end of the show and had Norman read his own words. Yes, indeed, we agreed. The most vital part!

We had moved to Hollywood Recording Studios and had all the voices edited and music chosen by Tuesday night. By Wednesday afternoon we had laid up the final, edited takes (all on quarter-inch tape) in program order. Only then could we tell what we really had. Not surprisingly, but horribly, *We Hold These Truths* was running nearly a half-hour longer than our one-hour satellite window at noon on Friday.

Norman and Mary Beth left for dinner. Judith and I retired to Fred Jones's coffee room and began to edit the script. When Norman returned, he had settled at least on eliminating some weak performances. There were scenes and speeches he was willing to trim. Some hours were then spent with him doing more writing—connective material to be recorded to bridge the cuts. Some of the characters we had urged him to include had to go. Lines were steadily trimmed as we moved into the mix part of the production.

All the voice-tracks had to be placed on a 24-track master tape, along with the music, preselected sound effects, and background ambiences. We began at 5:20 P.M. on Tuesday evening. By 2:30 in the morning we had laid up the last lines.

Norman stayed with the production for many hours, finally deciding to leave at 9:30 P.M. on Thursday. I asked him for his parting words. Please, Norman, you're the Master, what's your advice?

"If there is a question of doubt, go for simplicity," he said. The Corwin Credo in a sentence.

We started the final mix-down at 3:30 on Friday morning. We finished at 9:30 A.M. The uplink was scheduled for noon. Only Pepsi and Hershey Bars from the office machines kept us awake, if not fully alive. It was too late to transfer the completed production from the large reel-to-reel tapes to the small DATs that were then commonly used for satellite uplinks. Worse, we didn't dare fight traffic on our way to USC's campus, where the public radio satellite uplink studio was. Now what?

Unknown to us, the rare and necessary equipment needed to tag onto the passing Telstar satellite at high noon was in an adjoining studio at Hollywood Recording. Tape machines were rolled into the uplink room and connected. Norman arrived, fresher than the rest of us, to listen, with us, for the first time, to the program we had been working on for so long. The phone rang.

It was Walter Cronkite: "Happy 200th, Norman!"

Norman sent us a package on Boxing Day. "I hope you had a good, restful Christmas after all the pressures of the show. The reaction on this end has been very good indeed. Lots of mail and calls."

It wasn't until next January 21 that I could find a moment to write another word in my journal: "The unbelievable pressure and anxiety of 1991 did not end until December 16, when we flew back to home for a family Christmas. *Empire* and the Corwin project took all our hours between early September and December and here I am back in LA to produce *Empire* in the next ten days."

And this is a fact: from the beginning Judith and I and Richard, Deborah Jane, Fred and Mary Beth, and those who joined us along the way were under Norman Corwin's personal and creative spell. He was charming, chivalrous, and a Hollywood star. He could also be stubborn and insensitive. He was ever a generous friend. I believe he had been that way in life and work throughout his career. Certainly *We Hold These Truths* was Norman's show, from beginning to end.

We and our funders had enabled one more unique Norman Corwin thumbprint on radio history by sharing every one of the overwhelming issues he faced in 1941—the writing, casting, studio protocol, and direction of a magnificent celebration. Norman shared most of the postproduction hours and choices with us. As with the original broadcast, there were glitches we had to live with. Happily, when the CD version was released later in 1992, six minutes cut from the broadcast were restored.

One last thing. The budget. Even with the NEA's penultimate-minute reprieve, we were short. And who stepped up to save us? Let me write it the way Norman might have. Cue Music Under . . .

Citizen. A Citizen. Yep, that's me. Just a regular Citizen from New Jersey who heard you folks came up still in the red. Well, I've written you a check. Here it is, friend. For the Bill of Rights. Use it or lose it.

Music. Up for final curtain.

SOURCES

LeRoy Bannerman, *Norman Corwin and Radio: The Golden Years*, University of Alabama Press, 1986.

Norman Corwin, *More by Corwin*, Henry Holt, 1944.

———, *On a Note of Triumph*, Columbia Records Set MM575, 1946.

———, *We Hold These Truths* (final script), WETA CD package, 1992.

Firesign Theatre, *Marching to Shibboleth (The Big Big Book of Plays)*, Not Insane, 2013.

John Frohnmayer, *Leaving Town Alive: Confessions of an Arts Warrior*, Houghton Mifflin, 1993

John McDonough, "The Bill of Rights at 200," *Wall Street Journal*, December 13, 1991.

Otherworld Media, archival script copies, correspondence, and document files relating to *We Hold These Truths* and *Empire of the Air*.

Personal journals of Judith Walcutt and of David Ossman.

10

WONDERING ABOUT *RADIOLAB*

The Contradictory Legacy of Corwin in Contemporary "Screen Radio"

Alexander Russo

In October 2011, when Norman Corwin passed away at the age of 101, more than a few obituaries noted that he had outlived his contemporaries. In doing so, they positioned him as the last survivor of a long-past era when radio mattered to the entire nation. Assumed in this description was that Corwin had no heirs because radio drama was equally extinct. Yet, a month earlier, another radio "boy wonder" was crowned when the MacArthur Foundation bestowed a "genius" grant on the then-thirty-eight-year-old Jad Abumrad. The foundation described its recipient as one "whose engaging audio explorations of scientific and philosophical questions captivate listeners and bring to broadcast journalism a distinctive new aesthetic." It added: "As a result of his meticulous editing and conversational approach to interviews with experts, the structure of *Radiolab* episodes often mimics the scientific process itself, complete with moments of ambiguity, digressions, reversals, and surprising conclusions that evoke in audiences a sense of adventure and recreate the thrill of discovery."[1] While the Foundation's description well captured the elements of *Radiolab*'s formal experimentation, it erred in describing this as a wholly new aesthetic. *Radiolab*'s production and distribution practices are representative of contemporary digital convergence culture, but its sonic aesthetics evoke the techniques of a much earlier era, specifically that of the radio documentary of post–World War II Norman Corwin. This chapter will explore how *Radiolab* represents both "screen radio" and a "theatre of the mind" through its use of digital production and distribution technologies that allow for an experimental use of sound.

Yoking recording technology and aesthetic practice illuminates parallels with an earlier moment of radio experimentation, Norman Corwin's postwar documentary projects, a topic explored in more depth in Jacob Smith's chapter in this volume. Then, the use of wire and tape recording allowed for innovative use of actualities that established many of the precepts of radio documentary that continue to govern industry practice. Yet, those practices were substantially different from prewar and wartime radio news and documentary modes of representation. That era of formal experimentation is echoed in the contemporary wave of what Virginia Madsen has called "reality fictions."[2] Finally, while there are many laudatory elements to *Radiolab*'s use of sound, its formal experimentation and thematic foci are not without dangers. Specifically, I discuss the controversial segment "Yellow Rain" as a product of a mismatch between different modes of sonic realism in radio documentary as a counterpart to the gendered and racial limits of Corwin's "cosmopolitan disposition."

RADIOLAB AS "SCREEN RADIO"

While Norman Corwin's work is regarded as the apotheosis of radio drama in a network age, in terms of production practices, it was unlike the era's typical broadcasts. Live and serialized radio drama in the 1930s and 1940s was known for its demanding production schedules for weekly, or even daily, broadcasts. In contrast, Corwin's reputation was built on one-off specials and limited-run anthologies. The former were unique productions that celebrated specific events, such as *We Hold These Truths* or *On a Note of Triumph*, which benefited from the singularity of their production. The latter, limited-run series such as *Thirteen by Corwin*, did not feature episode-to-episode continuity of more mainstream shows like *The Fred Allen Show* or daytime serials like *Guiding Light*. Their specialness allowed them to transcend the evaporation that accompanied live broadcasts. *We Hold These Truths* and *On a Note of Triumph* were deemed popular enough that they were recorded for rebroadcast and issued on phonograph for sale.

Although *Radiolab* is very much a product of the current digital age, it shares with Corwin an atypical production culture as compared to the norms of its era. Typical radio news and documentary is rigidly defined by its daily and weekly production demands. As Tim Crook notes, "the foundations of radio news journalism are to be found in the culture of national news agencies developed in the early part of the century to provide news services to the newspaper industry." Radio leveraged its ability to produce timely updates but left longer explanatory pieces to print journalism. Although there is some formal experimentation, radio journalism is tied to the explanation and actuality and to the tight deadlines of the daily broadcast.[3]

In contrast to that daily grind, *Radiolab* represents an example of "screen radio." As described by Michele Hilmes, screen radio is the combination of digital production, online distribution, and mobilized reception. Digital radio, she argues, gives radio a materiality and permanence that live, broadcast radio never possessed.[4] The possibility of archival availability, either online or on local devices via the pushed distribution of podcast apps, allows for extended and mobile reception parameters. Listeners are no longer required to tune into a station at a specific time to hear a fleeting broadcast, gone if missed. Rather, listeners can come to the program on their own terms and time frames. Although the program is syndicated nationally to over 505 stations, it has a larger audience (5.6 million monthly downloads) that listens via podcast than the 1.4 million listeners who hear it over-the-air.[5]

Radiolab's podcast orientation means it does not have to abide by traditional radio production and distribution rhythms. The show's production resembles that of quality cable television drama more than a traditional weekly radio show. Essentially, the producers make a certain number of episodes (five, but on occasion up to twelve), which they define as a season, and distribute them online and to local stations. They then take six months or a year to produce another season. In part, this production model reflects the difficulties the program had in gaining funding in its initial years. However, it also means that the show's producers are able to spend extended time and expend considerable effort in the editing process leading to *Radiolab*'s identifiable aural aesthetic.

The idiosyncratic production processes begets practices that resemble transmedia franchises more than traditional radio documentaries or weekly features. During its hiatuses, *Radiolab* releases shorter podcasts of individual segments or even segments of segments, although these are often less sonically complex than the hour-long shows. These resemble transmedia webisodes that are regularly featured in contemporary complex television franchises.[6] Other transmedia production practices are found on *Radiolab*'s extensive website. In addition to a complete archive of programs, each segment has an individual page with a narrative summary and links to visual images and written documents referenced in the segment or authored by persons heard in that segment. This aligns the show with public broadcasting's embrace of the digital screen to "enhance and extend the scope of their work."[7]

Additionally, the program's producers embrace the podcasting logic of amateur production. As elaborated by Jonathan Sterne and others, the designation and historical application of the term within a context of inexpensive digital sound production has shifted the terms of who can create and distribute sonic materials by allowing greater access.[8] *Radiolab* both conforms to and deviates from this amateur-centric model. On one hand, it is a product of a highly trained, institutionally based production staff. Yet at the same time within its own production processes, it is decidedly small-scale. A profile of Abumrad in *Wired* focuses on his home studio, where he develops many of the sound effects and musical beds for the program. Although this setup was fully built-out in part with the proceeds of Abumrad's $500,000 MacArthur grant, it nevertheless speaks to the decentralized possibilities of digital production.⁹ Second, *Radiolab* has partnered with PRX (Public Radio Exchange) and software designer 1 Trick Pony to produce an app that serves as both a gateway for traditional listening and a platform for remixing *Radiolab* programs.¹⁰ The show has thus embraced the logic of "participatory culture" by providing fans the raw material to remake the show as they wish. Yet even as *Radiolab*'s mode of production and distribution are of the digital era, its sonic aesthetics are more closely aligned with postwar radio documentary productions. It is here that the legacy of Corwin is most apparent.

SONIC AESTHETICS OF "REALITY FICTIONS"

Norman Corwin's postwar radio aesthetic was tied to possibilities and limits engendered by new wire and tape recording and editing technologies. The wire recorder allowed him to gather sound actualities from his trip and edit them into *One World Flight*. This was a departure from earlier radio documentary practice, where producers (including Corwin) often re-created events via in-studio sound effects, effectively blurring the distinction between actuality and reenactment.¹¹ *Radiolab*'s relationship to digital recording and editing technologies echoes those earlier moments. Digital recording, both audio and video, remove many of the financial restraints on recording. Without a need to pay for tape, producers can easily record larger quantities of material. Likewise, the flexibility of nonlinear digital editing allows editors to more easily access vast qualities of sound. This, in turn, allows sonically complex compositions to be more easily created than in the analog era. This is apparent in Figure 10.1, a screen shot the Pro Tools mix for the episode "Clever Bots," which is representative of a typical *Radiolab* segment. It demonstrates the digitally enabled complexity of the show's soundwork. Over a four-minute segment, there are thirty-six individual tracks and one hundred edits.¹²

Nonlinear digital editing programs like Pro Tools allow for complex sonic collages created by the deconstruction and reconstruction of individual sounds.¹³ Visually, we can see the juxtaposition of what may have been recorded as a single sonic element—a voice or a musical track—in spatial terms. Aurally, we hear these elements as they overlap in time. This represents the process by which the feeling of spontaneity and liveness is orchestrated in conjunction with intensive editing, which Virginia Madsen calls "reality fictions." This term encompasses a range of experimental editing choices and sonic juxtapositions that evoke emotion in audiences. While Madsen is uncertain to what extent radio producers were influenced by earlier network-era documentary, a review of *Radiolab*'s aesthetic strategies suggests that it is their roots.¹⁴

In *Theater of the Mind* Neil Verma devotes considerable space to mapping Norman Corwin's narrative style. Corwin, he argues, creates a "drama of space and place" through two modes of "audiopositioning," the "intimate" and the "kalei-

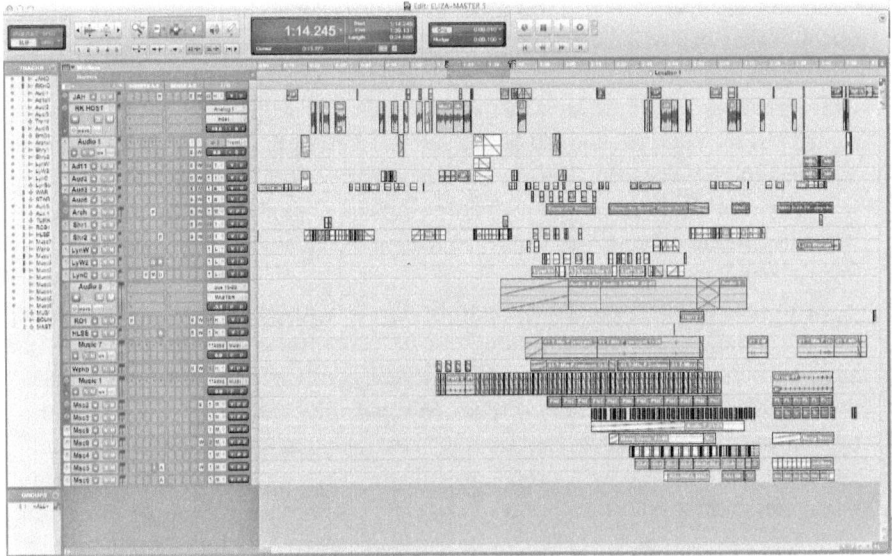

FIGURE 10.1. Screen shot of *Radiolab* episode "Clever Bots" in Pro Tools editing software.

dosonic." The intimate style positions the listener with one character for the length of the play, producing empathy with that individual. Listeners move with the character as he or she travels through a sonic world possessing "scenic and emotional depth." In contrast, the kaleidosonic style positions the listener at a remove from the events depicted. The listening position remains static while world shifts from one microphone position to another. In this mode, the world is "objectively" arrayed before us, creating a "shallow" and "highly public" feeling.[15] The intimate mode, continues Verma, is often composed of emplaced listening to the testimony of voices in succession. In contrast, the kaleidosonic mode observes large-scale events and converges disparate voices.[16] *Radiolab* shares with Corwin an ability to use both intimate and kaleidosonic audiopositioning of its listeners as well as a tendency to toggle between modes of "liveness" and the self-reflexively recorded and edited.

Like Corwin's work, *Radiolab* uses both "intimate" and "kaleidosonic" audiopositioning modes. Eleanor Patterson notes that show uses an "informal, conversational style" to engage listeners.[17] Andrew Bottomley argues that the show "mixes traditional elements of journalism with more artistic and dramatic elements" that are far more experimental than typical radio features.[18] As these accounts suggest, the prosody of the show is integral to its aesthetic operation. *Prosody* is a term from linguistics that describes the melody of language—how human expression is conveyed acoustically through durational, intensity, frequency, and linearity (abrupt vs. smooth changes) cues.[19] In this regard, *Radiolab* takes its inspiration from radiophonic aesthetics of previous eras. Robert Krulwich has described Corwin as "Homer in a modern form . . . a lyrical reporter who wrote and spoke like he was wearing a toga and sometimes was so spectacular you'd get dizzy listening, and sometimes seems a little too old fashioned and oratorical."[20] Krulwich appreciates the spellbinding wordplay. His objection is to the oratorical style—a style in line with Corwin's view that he was addressing a national public. Krulwich's appreciation and critique suggests ways in which *Radiolab* both engages with and alters the form of radio documentary.

Krulwich's comparison of Corwin to Homer demonstrates *Radiolab*'s attention to voice and dialogic narrative: it too is full of "dizzy oratory" but the presentation has a conversational tone, although it is no less constructed than Corwin's radio dramas. Abumrad and Krulwich speak in rapid-fire banter—far faster than the relaxed cadences of typical public radio fare. Frequently, this onslaught of language crowds and overlaps, producing a highly staged simulation of conversational flow. These vocal exchanges also play a structural role in defining the program's thematic object of study: the world of science. Abumrad and Krulwich alternately occupy roles as "voice of enthusiastic discovery" and skeptic, storyteller and inquisitor. Abumrad's voice is more nasal, higher pitched, and, notably, recognizably younger than that of grizzled veteran Krulwich, creating a contrapuntal effect. At the same time, the abrupt edits and quick transitions interrupt normal speech patterns (the aural equivalent to a cinematic jump cut) and create a highly stilted prosodic quality in the voices. So, while *Radiolab* seeks to use language and editing to re-create and convey the excitement of discovery, the clipped delivery produced by editing voices on top of one another also draws attention to the artificiality of the editing process. Abumrad claims the inclusion of asides and pauses leads to greater transparency.[21] This seemingly reflects a notion of radio realism described by John Biewen, whereby a regime of documentary sound grounded in the actuality is replaced by the search for an emotional truth.[22] Indeed, Abumrad describes the show's goal of using sound to "anchor and concretize ideas" and to provide "emphasis but not [delineate] emotion."[23] All of this is part of a stated desire to guide listeners but have them feel that they have reached the feeling on their own. Abumrad notes that "the difference between having something told to you and experiencing it yourself is an 'unbridgeable gulf.' It's that that gulf that separates good radio from bad, IMHO [in my humble opinion]."[24] What Abumrad is saying is that his narrative strategy is designed to collapse the distance between the narrator, the actuality, and the listeners to create a feeling of joint discovery.[25]

In addition to Corwin, the overlapping sounds of *Radiolab* reflect the influence of Walter Murch.[26] Abumrad has compared *Radiolab*'s use of sound to Murch's but seldom gives a full explanation of what that comparison is meant to evoke.[27] Murch, as Michel Chion argues, "uses sound and editing to create a new model of polyrhythm and polytonality, founded on the presence of multiple centers of attention." Not merely a counterpoint between sound and image, it represents a "profound shift, dispensing with the idea of a single rhythmic center to a film."[28] Murch creates "multiple layers of sound sliding over and under each other, without any one of them imposing a rhythm that dominated over all."[29] This sonic-layering aesthetic doesn't necessarily represent "the real" in the traditional sense of the recorded "actuality" that provides evidence or context.

Radiolab's sonic realism is grounded in the recorded re-creation of the experience of spontaneity and liveness. It juxtaposes sentence fragments from all the voices (analysis, counterargument, evidence) to create a conversation that proceeds dialectically, intersecting at a thematic resolution. In a typical radio documentary, reporters and narrator maintain separation from their subjects by explicitly signaling the movement from script to "tape." These techniques ranged from the explicit introduction of the "actualities" before running them to the prohibition of the use of the word *I* to avoid making the reporter part of the story.[30] In contrast, *Radiolab* does not separate "the real" from the narration's voice of authority. *Radiolab*, as NPR reporter Alix Spiegel notes, "renovates" those protocols toward "informality" by introducing most of the characters in a story at the beginning and then interweaving their voices without further identification of the speakers. Because all the voices are collaboratively telling the story, the distance between the reporter and the subjects is erased and made less formal. Citing *Radiolab* producer Lulu Miller, Spiegel describes a "flipped" process where "the tape erupts and interrupts the speech of the reporter. Poking through." Here, the reality fiction is created as sound and speech resonate with one another. This description explains why Radiolab violates typical news protocols by not removing mangled sentences, mismatched vocal levels, and cross-talk during the editing process. Rather they are precisely left in to create the feeling of spontaneity. Krulwich and Abumrad are quite conscious of this effect, with the latter noting in a *New York Times* profile, "It's a funny thing, when you find yourselves laboring for weeks to create what you felt at that first moment."[31] Describing *Radiolab*'s production process, Abumrad notes that the producers record a large amount of conversation between the hosts, saving only the few moments of "improvisational" spark. They then script the rest of the piece around those moments. So the prosodic qualities of Krulwich and Abumrad's conversation are edited to produce a dialectic of excitement, skepticism, and resolution that parallels the scientific method, the core problematic for the program.

Also like Corwin, Abumrad and Krulwich blend "intimate" and "kaleidosonic" styles. As their voices interact with a series of sounds—a third or fourth voice, out of studio "actualities," sound effects, and music—the listener toggles between multiple audio-positions. A representative example of this combination of styles on *Radiolab* can be heard at several points in season 2's episode "Detective Stories," an episode that the show's producers regard as the moment when the show hit its aesthetic stride.[32] The episode begins with a conversation between Abumrad and the manager of the Fresh Kills dump. This opening beat establishes an intimate style, with a central figure taking the listener to a specific location. The location is marked by background noise of the dump and by the "New Yawk" accent of the official. After the short segment, the action moves to the studio, where Abumrad and Krulwich establish the theme for the show, give some opening credit information, and move us to Egypt for the next narrative segment.

Typically, *Radiolab* narratives seek to pique the curiosity of the listener akin to the empathetic goals of the intimate style. However, the show will often undercut its attempts to hail the listener with self-reflexive effects. For example, this beat ends with a stylized looping of a New York Sanitation official describing the Fresh Kills dump as a "time capsule." As the phrase "time capsule" echoes eight times, Krulwich begins to chant "time capsule" in a lightly mocking tone that imitates accented phrase that concluded the actuality. Abumrad tells him, "You can stop that now." This opening is also notable because it alters and aestheticizes the actuality, something a pure documentary program would not do. The vocal repetition foregrounds the recording and editing process, self-reflexively exposing the show's construction. This is a frequent occurrence. The program often leaves in asides and other artifacts of the recording process. It frequently has the voices of the experts ask, "Should I just speak?" or "Is this on?" after they are introduced. These invoke a sense of transparency that puts the program's narration alongside the listen and, thus composed, we are going through the discovery and exploration process together.

The use of the intimate style to position the listener with the narrator is clear in another segment from that same episode entitled "Goat on a Cow." This segment follows Laura Starcheski across the country as she investigates the twelve-year story of a box of old letters found by the side of the road. This segment takes place at different locations, taking the listener on a trip through space and time, a hallmark of the intimate style. The voices mark these locations and moments. At the same time, it also uses elements of the kaleidosonic style because the narrative turns on particular events, moments where new evidence is found and new theories of the story of Ella Chase, the letters' recipient, are offered. In the start of this clip, Abumrad tells Starcheski to record Gordon's story and "make him tell it to you." She tells us she has no idea that she would get so involved. We then hear an actuality of her entering his apartment and greeting Erick Gordon, the man who found the letters. This transition echoes Corwin's technique of combining the intimacy of the narrating voice with the kaleidosonic experience of spatiotemporal shifts. As Gordon narrates, Starcheski's voice fades in and around those of the actuality, occupying both its space and that of the editing suite. When she interjects to provide context, Gordon's voice is not removed; it continues at reduced volume, telling its story under hers until at specific moment both voices say an identical phrase: "There was a goat standing on a cow's back standing on that field!" At this point Abumrad exclaims "What?!" causing Starcheski to repeat the phrase and remind us of the multiple layers of narration present. The techniques of juxtaposition with sporadic points of unification exemplify this segment's thematic thesis: that the letters hold different meanings for the individuals who come in contact with them. For Starcheski they are a reminder of her childhood desire to invent life stories of strangers; for Gordon, an English teacher who found the letters, they are a great mystery on which he can project his own imagined histories and build a teaching curriculum; finally, for Robert Chase, the owner of the letters, they represent a relief that he is no longer the archivist of his grandmother's life. Like Corwin's work, sound in "Goat on a Cow" combines intimate and kaleidosonic styles, creating pleasures that are linked not to narrative closure but to the process of sonically representing investigation and theorization. While not exactly the same as Corwin's signature "choral" vocal style, with voices chiming in from all directions, it performs a similar function, aurally representing a multiplicity of viewpoints that resolve in thematic conclusion.

DOCUDRAMA OF THE MIND

Radiolab is a "docudrama of the mind" where the intimate and kaleidosonic elements of movement through space include movement inside the body. This exemplifies a further connection to network-era radio drama, its concern with psychic processes. Radio dramas, Verma argues, contribute to an "enduring contemporary belief—the idea that questions of psychic life are always contiguous with questions about communication media, because radio stories present these topics as coupled and mutually complicit."[33] However, Corwin's network-era work and the contemporary approaches of *Radiolab* reflect the "structure of feelings" of their respective eras. The 1930s and 1940s were concerned with the psychology of nation and individual, with authority, persuasion, repression, and their impact on the psyche.[34] Our contemporary moment is also one where the workings of the mind are highly contested, largely through the burgeoning field of neuroscience. Neuroscientists and their popularizers (authors like Steven Johnson, Jonah Lehrer, Malcolm Gladwell, Barry Schwartz, and Oliver Sacks) make frequent appearances on *Radiolab*. A large proportion of *Radiolab* stories address the relationship between physiological and psychological processes and the degree to which our perceptions of free will and consciousness are biologically and chemically determined. Corwin was concerned about the collective consciousness of the body politic addressed by a mass medium; Krulwich and Abumrad thematically and sonically equate human consciousness with the individualized experience of the podcast.

One example of the conflation of radiophonic and psychological processes comes from a season 2 segment called "Out of Body, Roger."[35] The segment explores the phenomenon of pilots having out-of-body experiences while subject to high g-forces that drain blood from the brain. In this clip, there are three voices: Abumrad, Dr. James Whinnery, a scientist with the FAA who researched this phenomenon, and Tim Sestak, a pilot who was a research subject in Whinnery's study and was subjected to high g-forces in a centrifuge. However, as the clip progresses, Sestak's interview tape is edited to comment on his own recollection of the experience. The segment thus enacts three kinds of narration: scientific, retroactive first person, and a re-created in-moment first person. These layers slide into one another in a polyphonic manner. On certain phrases they speak in unison. At other times, they comment on one another. At the same time, a musical sound bed and sound effects provide rhythm and punctuation. These effects include stock sound (whoosh), re-creations (beeping of button), and actuality (centrifuge and inquiry from Dr. Bennett to Sestak). Unlike typical radio documentary, there is no audio signposting to register our position in relation to these sonic registers. Indeed, they freely intermingle with each other.

Another example of how *Radiolab* works as a docudrama of the mind comes from a segment in second season show "Musical Language." In this clip, Krulwich has (now-disgraced) science writer Jonah Lehrer expand upon a statement by Stanford professor Anne Fernald that "sound is more like touch at a distance."[36] As Lehrer explains the physical and neurological processes of hearing, sound effects provide what Walter Murch called "conceptual resonance," audibly enacting each stage of the "journey of sound into the ear."[37] The thing is that, with a few small exceptions (bones and water splash), every effect was created by digitally altered elements of Fernald's sentence. Abumrad extended the waveforms of the "ch" of *touch* with a "smeared" sound of her breath to sound like wind. The "ta" from *touch* was stuttered to into the sound of cilia bending. And the hard "s" in *distance* was transformed into a sound of electricity in neurons firing.[38] A linguistic description of hearing forms the raw material for sounds that symbolically represent the physiological process of hearing. In *Radiolab,* sounds of the mind are generated from sounds about the mind much like a fair amount of network radio drama (as described by Verma).

By demonstrating that radio is composed of nothing more than recognizable symbolic tokens, manipulated to convey meaning, and turned into story, *Radiolab*'s Corwin connection expands to conceptions of the imagination, autonomy, and consciousness. Like Corwin (and radio writers of the network era), Abumrad sees radio as both an act of "co-authorship" and "co-imagining" between the writer-performer and the listener. However, as he notes in an interview entitled "How Radio Creates Empathy," his job is to "put certain images and feelings in your head."[39] Abumrad is describing the concept of conceptual resonance, as discussed Walter Murch's introduction to Michel Chion's *Audio-Vision: Sound on Screen*. Murch argues that in the most successful sound editing, "sound makes an audience see an image differently, and then this new image makes us hear the sound differently, which in turn makes us see something else in the image, which makes us hear different things in the sound, and so on."[40] Murch is describing a reciprocal process that repeats without end, toggling between sound and image. However, it could apply just was well to multiple sound inputs in an audio production. The overlapping in studio dialogue, music, and actuality resonate with one another producing the experience of intellectual journey, but its manifest self-reflexivity masks a deeper attempt to guide the attention of the listener. Indeed, while Abumrad sees a connection to film editing, "conceptual resonance" resembles Norman Corwin's descriptions of his experience listening to recordings of Nazi air attacks for use in *One World Flight*. As Jacob Smith describes them, the recordings became a "Proustian *aide memoire*" that links past and present in order to "acknowledge trauma."[41] Significantly, Corwin views the experience as one of "revelation" that extends the meaning of the text and advances its goals of progressive humanism.

The linkage between discourses of the imagination and the ways that *Radiolab* is a docudrama of the mind is clear in the series' first episode, "Who Am I?"[42] One segment in this episode, "The Story of Me," suggests that what defines humanity is "introspective consciousness," the ability to abstract images or events into a story of self. Citing neuroscientist Vilayanur Ramachandran (a frequent contributor), Krulwich notes: "Only humans can take images from the real world, pull them into their heads, divide them into parts, and take those parts and turn them into abstractions." To demonstrate, Krulwich leads Abumrad through an example where the latter conjures the image "purple-striped red canary" in his head. Ramachandran follows, noting that only humans can rearrange and manipulate "tokens" of "bird," "striped," and "red" to "imagine" something that doesn't exist. The "peculiar human muscle" is that "ability to experience things and abstract them into a story. This definition is telling; while ostensibly it is about human consciousness, I would argue it could just as easily be seen as a description of the job of radio writer.

RADIOLAB'S WONDER AND A NEOLIBERAL STRUCTURE OF FEELING

While *Radiolab*'s aesthetic feats are to be lauded on their own terms, the question of their relationship to the larger culture in which they operate is more complicated and turns away from Corwin's ethos of liberal humanism. Corwin, as multiple commentators note, was an emphatic proponent of liberal humanism. For their part, Abumrad and Krulwich argue their program also has an overarching ethos, that of "wonder." The purpose of *Radiolab* is "to lead people to moments of wonder," which, in turn, is linked to its formal strategies and ideological address.[43]

This next section will argue that, counter to Corwin's outward looking humanism, wonder is a function of a neoliberal "structure of feeling" that focuses inward on individual enlightenment rather than outward toward social equality. Raymond Williams argues that it is possible to see common sets of values within the artistic forms of a given cultural moment.[44] The literature on neoliberalism is vast, but for the purposes of this argument, I will examine it as an orientation toward the world that retreats from an outward, public face toward an internally focused individual one.

Radiolab's sound is designed to produce an experience of wonder in the listener. Wonder, Philip Fisher argues, is the beginning of human experience. It is the instant where, unexpectedly, an answer is first seen, and what appeared to be chaotic or unconnected turns into order. Even if experienced before, wonder produces a feeling of pleasure in seeing again for the first time, of movement from "mystification to explanation."[45] Fisher sees wonder as a fundamentally visual phenomenon because sight allows for an all-at-once-ness to occur (his principal example is the rainbow). However, this overlooks one of the chief advantages of sound: its ability to seem natural and unforced. As argued above, although *Radiolab* operates as narrative (that is, over time) it is edited to create experiences of revelation where seemingly separated elements align into clarity. Indeed, Fisher notes that the aesthetics of wonder cannot be separated from a state of excitement and passion.[46] This aligns with *Radiolab*'s efforts to build the program around moments of spontaneity and revelation. Significantly, wonder is not "surprise," the goal of a program with which *Radiolab* is often compared, *This American Life*. The latter is self-centered, focused on personal experience, thus making it ripe for the kinds of retreat from the public to the private in an era of neoliberalism.[47] Wonder is somewhat less clear-cut. We can seek understanding but that drive is accompanied by a recognition that the forces we uncover are much more powerful than we are. It also focuses on individual revelation rather than society or community. It follows that one of the chief points of debate on *Radiolab* concerns the relative power of nature and culture where the two meet.

In some ways, the thematic of wonder echoes Corwin's commitment to liberal humanism. In *One World Flight*, Corwin sought to come to terms with the devastation wrought by World War II. Corwin finished his trip deeply concerned about the levels of international conflict and antipathy toward the United States, even as he remained convinced of the "powerful sense of fairness, as well as an overwhelming will and anxiety for peace, [that] pervades all of the peoples of the earth."[48] Elsewhere in this volume, Jacob Smith argues that Corwin's postwar works display "the operative tensions . . . between the partitive and the intensive; that is between spatiotemporal compression afforded by live network broadcasting and the inexhaustible sonic richness of documentary recording."[49] Within the formulation, itself drawn from Francesco Casetti's elaboration of cinematic gazes, the kaleidoscopic or partitive gaze draws attention to fragments, as such, that form an overall "comprehensive vision." In contrast, the intensive gaze focuses on one element as a "keystone" for the totality that is being examined.⁵⁰ The partitive, then, suggests the reach afforded by live broadcasts, whereas the intensive is rooted in the recorded actuality. While in Corwin's era the partitive and the intensive were tied to the technological properties of live, network broadcasting, today they are linked to the "reality fictions" engendered by digital recording and editing.

Although *One World Flight*'s modes of sonic realism were intended to illustrate the challenges and possibilities of the postwar period, Corwin found it difficult to adequately provide comprehensive scope without losing detail. As Smith notes, Corwin's philosophy of "world citizenship" in *One World Flight* reflects the gender and racial limits of the "cosmopolitan disposition." Echoing John Tomlinson, Smith notes that while global citizenship is in theory open to all, in practice it is white men that enjoy the fullest benefits of discursive participation and physical movement. In a similar fashion, *Radiolab* strives for a liberal pluralistic orientation and yet, at times, cannot help but replicate an ideological blind spot that places white men at the center of the narrative designed to produce listener "wonder" and that relegates people of color to an object status in that story.⁵¹

The tensions within liberal pluralism are readily apparent in the controversy over *Radiolab*'s program "The Fact of the Matter," specifically in the segment "Yellow Rain." As noted above, *Radiolab* is edited in a way to construct a sense of joint investigation or exploration and the production of a conclusion of wonder. In many ways, this episode is a departure for the series. To start, its central premise was to complicate the meaning of a truth. "Getting a firm hold on the truth is never as simple as nailing down the facts of a situation. This hour, we go after a series of seemingly simple facts—facts that offer surprising insight, facts that inspire deeply different stories, and facts that, in the end, might not matter at all."⁵² This theme represents something distinct from the sense of wonder discussed earlier. Indeed, as fans of the show noticed, the show had begun to divide its segments into ones that were more straightforward explorations of a scientific phenomenon and those that were more "philosophical" or "emotional."⁵³

"Yellow Rain" explores the claims that the Hmong people of Laos were exposed to chemical weapon attacks as they fled the Communist government in the early 1980s. The Reagan administration used this claim as a justification for restarting chemical weapon production. The first part of the segment features the voice of a former CIA official stationed in Laos, the testimony of Hmong refugee Eng Yang, who provides context of the persecution of the Hmong by the Laotian Communist government, and a series of actualities and news clips relating to the story and the decision to restart chemical weapons production. The narrative of a chemical attack was then juxtaposed with interviews several scientists who had tested samples of the yellow substance identified as the chemical agent. Although contemporaneous lab testing concluded that the substance was a chemical weapon and that the Russians were using pollen as a vector, the next section of the segment features two chemical weapons experts who were unable to replicate the initial lab's results. These scientists concluded that the lab had accidentally contaminated the sample with a microtoxin and that the yellow substance was, in fact, bee excrement. Government scientists ultimately confirmed their conclusions but no correction to the record, the U.S. Army field manual of chemical weapons, or apology for accusing the Russians was ever issued.

The controversial part of the segment came when Krulwich and *Radiolab* producer Pat Walters returned to Yang (as well as his niece, Kao Kalia Yang, who acted as a translator) to confront them with their findings. The producers made the choice to let the above conclusion stand, then cut to Kalia Yang, asking for a clarification before translating the statement that the evidence did not support his view that he was attacked by chemical weapons. When challenged by Yang and his niece to account for the illnesses suffered by the Hmong at the time, Walters's voice-over narration provides an alternative explanation, that the Hmong were on the run and under attack and that they misattributed deaths due to dysentery and cholera to chemical weapons dispersed by the bee poop. Yang rejects this explanation, citing his first-person experience. Krulwich then asks if Yang had seen anything, a plane, say, that would contradict the scientists' conclusions. Krulwich presses him on his explanation, noting there were other bombing attacks and he did not personally see the bee pollen fall or a plane dispersing chemicals. At this point, Kalia's voice takes over, emotional, nearing tears, translating her uncle's frustration that he granted the interview because he thought *Radiolab* was interested in the Hmong story, that the difference between regular bombs and chemical bombs is semantic because the Hmong were attacked and abandoned, and the Hmong people have suffered terribly. Then we hear her end the interview. This is followed by twenty seconds of silence. Abumrad speaks, noting that the interview did not in fact end; he then denies that *Radiolab* ambushed the Yangs but acknowledges that the staff was "troubled" by the interview.

Aside from the obvious fact that a podcast format allows for multiple codas created in dialogue with audience criticism, these additions to the text lay bare the ideological contradictions of "Yellow Rain." The final three minutes of the segment consists of Walters, Abumrad, and Krulwich debating the relative truths of the stories. Walters and Abumrad take the position that Yang had a point that their focus on one aspect of the Hmong story, the yellow rain, excludes a larger truth about the genocide of their people. Krulwich is less sympathetic, stating: "That is exactly what she's saying. And that is wrong. That is absolutely—to my mind, that is not fair to us. . . . It's not fair to ask us to not consider the other stories and the other frames of the story." He elaborates that because this story was used to justify chemical weapon production, if there had been a war and those weapons had been used, others would have died terrible deaths as a consequence. "I mean, that is not unimportant, it's hugely important. But it's not important to her. So should that not be important to us?" Walters replies that he had not appreciated the volume of pain they had experienced. Krulwich continues, "I thought her reaction was very balancing. But her desire was not for balance. Her desire was to monopolize the story. And that we can't allow." Walters and Abumrad recognize the important role of claims of being attacked by chemical weapons for the Hmong's advocacy to receive acknowledgment of the trauma they endured, but Krulwich is less empathetic. In a second coda, he acknowledges that many listeners were upset with him in particular for claiming Kalia Yang was trying to monopolize the conversation and apologizes for his tone. Yet he continues to defend the reporter's job of testing truth, but apologizes for not asking questions with more respect and gentleness in light of how much Yang had suffered.

In the controversy surrounding this episode, the criticism took several forms. The ways that the story was edited, Kalia Yang claimed, discredited her father and the Hmong's story.[54] They were not given titles. Other scientific evidence provided was supposedly not referenced. Other criticisms were linked to what seemed to fans to be a false apology by Krulwich. Listeners noted that Krulwich's claim that the Yangs were seeking to monopolize the conversation was preposterous, given that the producers have complete control over the final edit and get to choose what to include or exclude.[55]

In contrast to the explanations that *Radiolab* was racist or unrepentant, the controversy reflects the consequences of an epistemological blind spot created when the show attempted to shift from its inwardly focused orientation toward wonder to an outward focus on the public sphere. Walters notes that he "missed something" by failing to recognize the reaction that the interview would cause. While Abumrad does not specify what exactly was missed, one clue comes in the framing of the episode. As noted above, the episode was about conflicting definitions of truth. It contained two other segments. The first was an interview with documentarian Errol Morris in which Morris recounts his investigation of two photographs of the Crimean War. This story, serialized in the *New York Times,* ends with Morris establishing that a famous war photograph was staged, yet recognizing the ultimate irrelevance of that fact. The staged photograph was able to speak a truth about the experience of war more than an "accurate" one. The third segment was the story of a man whose friends recognized him as a habitual liar. They did not take it seriously until the man died and upon entering his house recognized he had been seriously mentally ill. The house was in squalor with no electricity or running water. They did not recognize this part of their friend and wondered which was the true identity: the personality when he was with them or the one when he was alone.

It seems clear that *Radiolab* expected a similar conclusion in their "Yellow Rain" segment, a wonder at complexity and ambiguity rather than a recognition of the loss that occurs when, as Abumrad states, "What do you do when three truths are right at the same time?" Their desire to have their narrative conform to one framework produced a blind spot of power that was reflected in the lack of consciousness about an alternative perspective. For many in the *Radiolab* audience, who, as Susan Douglas notes, turn to NPR with the expectations of hearing a progressive, pluralist worldview, "Yellow Rain" was as an affront.[56] This too parallels Corwin in certain ways. As Jennifer Stoever notes, despite his progressive political views, Corwin shared with many of his era a blind spot toward race. He advocated "color-blindness" in hiring, yet, as Stoever argues, this positions African Americans as "tools" like microphones that are "absolutely essential to broadcasting . . . [but are an] object with no inherent agency . . . [that] amplifies the voices of others, while speaking not a word of its own."[57] In the "Yellow Rain" segment the Hmong were not thought to have agency or an experience valued for its own right. Until the point of confrontation, they were merely objects in a larger narrative of "wonder."

"Yellow Rain" was part of a larger episode called "The Fact of the Matter" that represented a movement away from focusing nearly exclusively on exploring scientific phenomena and began including more stories that focused on emotional or philosophical issues. Starting with season 10 in 2011, the show vastly increased its output (doubling the number of episodes per season) and expanded its focus. Fans of the show criticized the shift during a 2013 Reddit AMA, especially after Abumrad and Krulwich denied that the program had changed.[58] Significantly, the point of contention was that the show was turning into *This American Life*. TAL, as Jason Loviglio has noted, uses sound and voice to produce a dramatic arc that conclude in what Ira Glass terms "delight" or "surprise."[59] Loviglio argues that the production of delight and surprise on public radio represents a structure of feeling of the neoliberal era that turns away from a shared public concern to issues of private interest. Thus, while nominally still "public radio," it reflects the sensibilities of an audience more interested in "social consciousness," a posture of multiculturalism and gender enlightenment that claims to seek "social change" but refuses to endorse any structural or systemic critique.[60]

CONCLUSION

In sum, *Radiolab* evokes and updates the radiosonic aesthetic techniques of Norman Corwin though, like him, it reflects some of the ideological contradictions of its era. Like Corwin's experiments with then-new wire recording technology that produced a new relationship to radio realism, *Radiolab*'s relationship with digital recording and editing push the formal boundaries of contemporary radio documentary. Still, there are certain kinds of techniques of audiopositioning that resemble those pioneered by Corwin, both individually intimate and multiply occupied kaleidosonic audiopositionings through sound effect and a rapid, overlapping, and contrapuntal prosody. Similarly, while Corwin and 1940s radio drama reflected a mid-century conception of the mind to the extent that programs became aural metaphors of the psychology of communication, *Radiolab*'s frequent focus on neuroscience and its use of sound to illustrate those concepts makes it a docudrama of and about the mind. However, following Raymond Williams, each of these sets of radio documentaries also represent the structure of feeling of the era of their creation. While Corwin's suggest hope and fear regarding large-scale international conflicts at the onset of the Cold War, *Radiolab*'s thematic of wonder represents a retreat from the public to the personal. Moreover, the show's most notable misstep came when it attempted to move beyond that orientation.

NOTES

1. "Jad Abumrad: Radio Host and Producer," MacArthur Fellows Program, 2011, http://www.macfound.org/fellows/1/#sthash.wwvILmvz.dpuf.

2. Virginia Madsen, "Your Ears Are a Portal to Another World," in Michele Hilmes and Jason Loviglio, eds., *Radio's New Wave: Global Sound in a Digital Era* (New York: Routledge, 2013), 137.

3. Tim Crook, *International Radio Journalism: History, Theory, and Practice* (New York: Routledge, 1998), 71.

4. Michele Hilmes, "The New Materiality of Radio: Sound on Screens," in Hilmes and Loviglio, *Radio's New Wave*, 50.

5. "New York Public Radio Media Kit," 2014, http://www.radiolab.org/static/resources/2014/Aug/07/New_York_Public_Radio_Media_Kit.pdf.

6. See for example, Jonathan Gray, *Show Sold Separately: Promos, Spoilers, and Other Media Paratexts* (New York: NYU Press, 2010).

7. Michele Hilmes, "The New Materiality of Radio: Sound on Screens," in Hilmes and Loviglio, *Radio's New Wave*, 50.

8. Jonathan Sterne, "The Politics of Podcasting," *Fiberculture* 12 (1), 2008. http://thirteen.fibreculturejournal.org/fcj-087-the-politics-of-podcasting/.

9. "Sound Scientist: Inside the Home Studio of *Radiolab*'s Jad Abumrad," *Wired*, February 2014, http://www.wired.com/2014/02/myspace_jad/.

10. "Download the Radiolab App," Radiolab, WNYC, http://www.radiolab.org/mobile/.

11. Jad Abumrad, "Terrors and Virtues," *Transom Review: A Showcase and Workshop for New Public Radio* 12 (4), July 2012. http://transom.org/wp-content/uploads/2012/07/jadabumrad_review1.pdf.

12. Matthew Ehrlich, *Radio Utopia: Postwar Audio Documentary in the Public Interest* (Champaign, IL: University of Illinois Press, 2011).

13. For comparison, John Thornton Caldwell argues that digital video editing allowed for a self-reflexive and excessive visual style on television in the 1980s, in *Televisuality: Style, Crisis, and Authority in American Television* (New Brunswick, NJ: Rutgers University Press, 1995).

14. Madsen, "Your Ears," 136–137.

15. Neil Verma, *Theater of the Mind: Imagination, Aesthetics and American Radio Drama* (Chicago: University of Chicago Press, 2012), 68.

16. Ibid., 73

17. Eleanor Patterson, "Mediating the Past: *Radiolab* Revisits the Crossroads," Antenna: Responses to Media and Culture (blog), July 25, 2012. http://blog.commarts.wisc.edu/2012/07/25/mediating-the-past-radiolab-revists-the-crossroads/.

18. Andrew Bottomley, "On Radio: *Radiolab* and the Art of the Modern Radio Feature, Antenna: Responses to Media and Culture (blog), January 11, 2012. http://blog.commarts.wisc.edu/2012/01/11/on-radio-radiolab/.

19. Frank Boutsen, "Prosody: The Music of Language and Speech," *ASHA Leader*, March 4, 2003.

20. Robert Krulwich, "Why I Love Radio," *Transom Review: A Showcase and Workshop for New Public Radio* 2 (9), November 2002, 6. http://transom.org/wp-content/uploads/2002/11/200211.review.krulwich.pdf.

21. Rob Walker, "On Radiolab: The Sound of Science," *New York Times Magazine*, April 7, 2011. http://www.nytimes.com/2011/04/10/magazine/mag-10Radiolab-t.html.

22. John Biewen, "Introduction," in John Biewen and Alexa Dilworth, eds., *Reality Radio: Telling True Stories in Sound* (Chapel Hill, NC: UNC Press, 2010), 6–7.

23. Walker, "On Radiolab."

24. Abumrad, "No Holes," 47–48.

25. Jad Abumrad, "Terrors and Virtues," *Transom Review: A Showcase and Workshop for New Public Radio* 12 (4), July 2012. http://transom.org/wp-content/uploads/2012/07/jadabumrad_review1.pdf.

26. Murch even contributed to *Radiolab* in the 2009 episode "Blink."

27. Abumrad, "No Holes," 45–46.

28. Michel Chion, *Audio Vision: Sound on Screen*, Claudia Gorbman, trans. (New York: Columbia University Press, 1994), 123.

29. Ibid., 122.

30. Alix Spiegel, "Ideas," *Transom Review: A Showcase and Workshop for New Public Radio* 14, November 2014. http://transom.org/2014/alix-spiegel/.

31. Walker, "On Radiolab."

32. *Radiolab*, "Detective Stories," Season 2, Episode, 1. http://www.radiolab.org/2007/sep/10/.

33. Verma, *Theater*, 6.

34. Ibid.

35. *Radiolab*, "Where Am I," Season 2, Episode 4. http://www.radiolab.org/story/91524-where-am-i/.

36. *Radiolab*, "Musical Language," Season 2, Episode 2. http://www.radiolab.org/2007/sep/24/.

37. Walter Murch, "Foreword," in Chion, *Audio Vision*, xxii.

38. Radiolab, "Making *Radiolab*," November 9, 2007. http://www.radiolab.org/blogs/radiolab-blog/2007/nov/09/making-radio-lab/.

39. Jad Abumrad, "How Radio Creates Empathy" (video). http://bigthink.com/videos/how-radio-creates-empathy

40. Murch in Chion, *Audio Vision*, xxii.

41. Jacob Smith, "Norman Corwin's Radio Realism," in Jacob Smith and Neil Verma, eds., *Anatomy of Sound: Norman Corwin and Media Authorship*. (Berkeley, CA: University of California Press, 2016), chapter 4, 12.

42. *Radiolab*, "Who Am I," Season 1, Episode 1. http://www.radiolab.org/2007/may/07/.

43. For "wonder," see Abumrad, "No Holes," 44.

44. Raymond Williams, *Marxism and Literature* (New York: Oxford University Press 1977), 129.

45. Philip Fisher, *Wonder, the Rainbow, and the Aesthetics of Rare Experiences* (Cambridge, MA: Harvard University Press, 2003) 21, 26.

46. Ibid., 120.

47. See Jason Loviglio, "Public Radio Storytelling and the Neoliberal Structure of Feeling," (unpublished draft); and Susan J. Douglas, "The Turn Within: The Irony of Technology in a Globalized World," *American Quarterly* 58 (3), 2006: 619–638.

48. Norman Corwin, "Postscripts to One World," in *One World Flight: The Lost Journal of Radio's Greatest Writer*, Mary Beth Watson and Michael Keith, eds. (New York: Continuum. 2009), 196.

49. Smith, "Norman Corwin's Radio Realism," 10–11.
50. Ibid., 11.
51. Susan Douglas, *Listening In: Radio and the American Imagination* (New York: Times Books, 1999), 319.
52. *Radiolab*, "The Fact of the Matter," Season 11, Episode 1. http://www.radiolab.org/story/239470-the-fact-of-the-matter/.
53. "We Are Jad Abumrad and Robert Krulwich, Together We Host Radiolab –AMA!" (Reddit post). http://www.reddit.com/comments/1go8ri.
54. See, for example, Olivia LaVecchia, "Behind Laos's Yellow Rain and Tears," *Minneapolis City Pages*, November 14, 2012. http://www.citypages.com/news/behind-laoss-yellow-rain-and-tears-6763660.
55. Jennifer Stoever, "On the Lower Frequencies: Norman Corwin, Colorblindness, and the 'Golden Age' of U.S. Radio," *Sounding Out! The Sound Studies Blog*, September 10, 2012. http://soundstudiesblog.com/2012/09/10/on-the-lower-frequencies_corwin_colorblindness_radio/.
56. Ibid.
57. Stoever, "On the Lower Frequencies"; and "We Are Jad Abumrad and Robert Krulwich."
58. Stoever, "On the Lower Frequencies."
59. Jason Loviglio, "Public Radio Storytelling," in *Electrified Voices: Media, Socio-Historical and Cultural Aspects of Voice Transfer*, Dmitri Zakharine and Nils Miese, eds., (Gottingen: V & R University Press, 2012), 4; and Jason Loviglio, "US Public Radio, Social Change, and the Gendered Voice," in Zakharine and Miese, *Electrified Voices*, 137.
60. Loviglio, "Public Radio Storytelling," 4; and Loviglio "US Public Radio," 137.

CONTRIBUTORS

JEANETTE BERARD is Librarian, Special Collections at Thousand Oaks Library, 2002–present. The collections at Thousand Oaks Library contain the American Radio Archives, which have collections including tape, acetates, transcription discs, and wire recordings related to American radio broadcasting. Berard has been librarian and archivist, Autry Museum of Western Heritage, 1998–2002; head of technical services, NASA Langley Technical Library, 1996–1998; photo archivist, NASA Langley, 1994–1996; library bid specialist, Data Research Associates, 1991–1994; librarian (intern), Los Angeles Public Library, 1989–1991; museum specialist, NPS, 1987–1989. Master of Library Science, UCLA; 1991; certified archivist, ACA, 2004.

ROSS BROWN is Professor of Theatre Sound at the University of London's Royal Central School of Speech and Drama. He has composed and designed for the Royal Court, RSC, and BBC Radio Drama and since 1994 has led the development of a new disciplinary approach to theatre sound, publishing on its dramaturgy and establishing discourse on theatre noise and aurality. Recent publications include *Sound* (Palgrave Readings in Theatre Practice) and "The Eleventh of the Eleventh of the Eleventh: The Theatre of Memorial Silence," in *Soundscapes of the Urban Past: Staged Sound as Mediated Cultural Heritage*, K. Bijsterveld (ed.).

TIM CROOK is Professor of Media and Communication at Goldsmiths, University of London, where he is head of Radio and Media Law and Ethics. He is also Visiting Professor of Broadcast Journalism at Birmingham City University. He has published many books on radio journalism, drama, sound, media law, and espionage literature. In a professional career in journalism, radio, and drama, he has won more than sixty awards and continues long-form investigative historical projects. His current research concentrates on George Orwell and radio, the origins of British audio drama, and the relationship between early political radio drama and modernism.

TROY CUMMINGS holds a Master's of Musicology from the University of Missouri–Kansas City. His 2013 thesis, "Mood-Stuff and Metaphoric Utterance: Norman Corwin's Radio Art," is a pilot study in musicology and radio art. He is particularly interested in exploring aesthetics and analysis in radio art across genres. He plans on continuing his research by pursuing his PhD and is currently working on a book about experimental radio art and artists from the late twentieth and early twenty-first century.

THOMAS DOHERTY is a cultural historian with a special interest in Hollywood cinema. Doherty is Professor of American Studies and Chair of the American Studies Program at Brandeis University. He is an associate editor for the film magazine *Cineaste* and a film review editor for the *Journal of American History*. His most recent book is *Hollywood and Hitler, 1933–1939*, published in 2013 by Columbia University Press.

MICHELE HILMES, Professor Emerita, taught media and cultural studies at the University of Wisconsin–Madison for twenty-two years. Her research areas include media history, television, radio, and sound studies. She is coeditor of *The Radio Journal* and a Standing Editorial Board member of *Oxford Bibliographies Online: Cinema and Media Studies*. Her books include *Radio Voices: American Broadcasting 1922–1952* (1997); *Network Nations: A Transnational History of British and American Broadcasting* (2011); *Only Connect: A Cultural History of Broadcasting in the United States* (4th edition, 2013), and most recently *Radio's New Wave: Global Sound in the Digital Era*, coedited with Jason Loviglio (2013).

DAVID OSSMAN is a founding member of the legendary comedy group The Firesign Theatre, as well as an actor and producer on many award-winning audio theater productions.

ALEXANDER RUSSO is Associate Professor in the Department of Media Studies at The Catholic University of America in Washington, DC. He is the author of *Points on the Dial: Golden Age Radio Beyond the Networks* (Durham, NC: Duke University Press, 2010), as well as articles and book chapters on the technology and cultural form of radio and television, sound studies, the history of music and society, and media infrastructures.

JACOB SMITH is Associate Professor in the Department of Radio-Television-Film and Director of the MA in Sound Arts and Industries at Northwestern University. He has written several books, including *Vocal Tracks: Performance and Sound Media*; *Spoken Word: Postwar American Phonograph Cultures*; and *Eco-Sonic Media* (all from UC Press), and has published articles on media history, sound, and performance.

SHAWN VANCOUR is Assistant Professor of Media Archival Studies in UCLA's Department of Information Studies. His research examines the development of dominant production practices and aesthetic norms for U.S. radio and television, their relationships with neighboring sound and screen media, and their transformations in the digital era. He is author of *Making Radio: Early Radio Production and the Rise of Modern Sound Culture* (Oxford University Press, forthcoming); articles in *Media, Culture & Society* and *Modernist Cultures*; and chapters in a series of edited volumes on media history, theory, and aesthetics.

NEIL VERMA writes about the history and aesthetics of sound in narrative-based art and media. He is the author of the award-winning book *Theater of the Mind: Imagination, Aesthetics, and American Radio Drama* (University of Chicago Press) as well as several historical and theoretical articles about sound in media. He has published in the *Journal of Amer-*

ican Studies, the *Journal of Sonic Studies, Velvet Light Trap, RadioDoc Review, Critical Quarterly,* and several edited volumes. Verma is Network Director for the Radio Preservation Task Force of the Library of Congress, and Special Editor at the sound studies site *Sounding Out.* He teaches at Northwestern University.

MARY ANN WATSON (PhD, University of Michigan, 1983) is Distinguished Professor of Electronic Media & Film Studies at Eastern Michigan University. She is the coeditor (with Michael Keith) of *Norman Corwin's* One World Flight: *The Lost Journal of Radio's Greatest Writer.* Watson is the author of *The Expanding Vista: American Television in the Kennedy Years* and *Defining Visions: Television and the American Experience in the 20th Century.* She has contributed chapters to many works, including *The Columbia History of American Television,* as well entries in the *Encyclopedia of Radio* and the *Encyclopedia of Popular Culture.*

www.ingramcontent.com/pod-product-compliance
Lightning Source LLC
Chambersburg PA
CBHW020328240426
43665CB00044B/888